MW00577539

The Clash FAQ

The Clash FAQ

All That's Left to Know About the Clash City Rockers

Gary J. Jucha

Backbeat Books
An Imprint of Hal Leonard LLC

Published in 2016 by Backbeat Books
An Imprint of Hal Leonard LLC
7777 West Bluemound Road
Milwaukee, WI 53213

Trade Book Division Editorial Offices
33 Plymouth St., Montclair, NJ 07042

The FAQ series was conceived by Robert Rodriguez and developed with Stuart Shea.

Printed in the United States of America

Book design by Snow Creative

Library of Congress Cataloging-in-Publication Data is available upon request.
ISBN 978-1-4803-6450-9

www.backbeatbooks.com

In memory of Miles and Bella

Miles was a sixteen-year-old tuxedo cat,
named for Miles Davis,
who loved Kim the best.

Bella was an eleven-year-old torti,
nicknamed "the punk,"
who often sat near me as I wrote *The Clash FAQ*.

They are tremendously missed.

Contents

Acknowledgments

When I wrote *Jimi Hendrix FAQ*—my previous contribution to Backbeat's FAQ Series—it was a somewhat lonely endeavor due to the lack of online resources. As much as Jimi is beloved, it is difficult hosting a website devoted to a musician who has been deceased for over four decades and whose image is closely guarded. It was an entirely different experience researching the Clash.

There are biographies, the best of which are by Chris Salewicz, Pat Gilbert, and Kris Needs; moving memoirs by Johnny Green and Ray Lowry; books of photography by Bob Gruen and Pennie Smith. You can find old newspaper articles, photo spreads, even interviews in foreign languages. There are obituaries, album and concert reviews, and blogs by former associates. More importantly, however, there are the websites devoted to the Clash containing a wealth of material. A few could almost be characterized as "Sandinistian." The ones I relied upon are all listed in the bibliography, but there is one I truly have to acknowledge because it was immeasurably helpful in the writing of *The Clash FAQ: All That's Left to Know About the Clash City Rockers.*

Black Market Clash has been around for over a decade but appears to only be accessible via Dropbox nowadays. Don't let this dissuade you from seeking out this site if you are a Clash fan. The site is invaluable. It lists every known Clash concert, links related articles and reviews, displays rare fan photos and memories, and provides info and reviews on all known bootleg recordings and film footage on a day-to-day basis. If you want to know what the Clash were all about, check out Black Market Clash. Hopefully rumors of a book will one day be more than mere rumors.

At Backbeat Books, I wish to thank Bernadette Malavarca, Senior Editor of Backbeat Books (and fellow cat lover), who has provided me indispensible assistance throughout the whole publishing process. If it weren't for Bernadette, you wouldn't be holding this book in your hands. Thanks to my copy editor, Tom Seabrook, for catching all the errors in my manuscript. Much thanks to the rest of the Hal Leonard Performing Arts Publishing Group team, including publisher John Cerullo and publicity and marketing manager Wes Seeley. Special thanks to Becky Terhune for designing the excellent cover.

This book would not exist if it weren't for Victor "HBV" Marinelli, a friend of mine who created the Hellbomb blog at the end of 2010 and asked if I wanted to be a contributor. Vic knew I was working on a novel set against a nonfictional backdrop of the Clash concerts during their extended residency at Bond International Casino (aka Bond's) in Times Square in May–June 1980. "Maybe you'll get a book deal out of it," he said. I thought that was unlikely, but I agreed to write for his blog anyway. Vic must've been clairvoyant, because shortly after we were up and running, then FAQ Series Editor Robert Rodriguez came across a Clash feature written for Hellbomb and asked if I'd like to contribute to the FAQ Series. Vic (and his wife Karen and their four children) have returned to the tri-state area, and Robert—a Beatles maven whose book *Revolver: How the Beatles Reimagined Rock 'n' Roll* I highly recommend—no longer serves as the FAQ Series Editor, but I owe both Vic and Robert an enormous debt of gratitude for being a published author.

Thanks to Terry Chimes, the Clash's original drummer, for making himself available for an interview.

Thanks to Rosemary Carroll for arranging permission to quote Patti Smith's ad-libbed comments on Joe Strummer during a performance of "Land" at the Stone Pony in Asbury Park, New Jersey, on December 28, 2002. Extra special thanks to Patti Smith who graciously edited those comments for inclusion in my book. Anyone who knows me, knows Patti is a true hero of mine—up there with Proust and Hendrix and FDR and Joe Strummer—and so Patti's fleeting involvement was a special experience for me.

Thanks to all my friends at Scientific Games for showing an interest in my books for Backbeat, especially my boss, Frank Candido, and Zack Zoeller, who photographed or scanned many graphics for me.

Thanks to Erik Wuttke for the many fruitful discussions we've had about the Clash and Joe Strummer.

Thanks also to Eilish and Megan Noone for asking me how my writing has been progressing. It's hard to believe that you are both close to finishing college and soon about to take on the world.

Thanks to Gerry and Kara Noone, my brother and sister-in-law. When I was growing up, Granny and Grandpa socialized on weekends with Granny's sister and her husband, just as my wife Kim and I do now. It's nice to see history repeating itself.

Thanks to my brother Brian for the Monday telephone calls, for keeping me up on what's happening in the family, and for turning me onto great television programs.

For my daughter Calla, let this be proof that it is never too late to accomplish something creative.

And, most of all, for my wife Kim, who makes so much in life possible. Joe Strummer once sang of "a rose" he wanted to live for. I found mine over twenty-five years ago.

Introduction

On November 12, 2015, at the Variety Playhouse in Atlanta, Georgia, I attended "a reading and conversation" that was part of Patti Smith's book tour for her curious memoir, *M Train*. The event was moderated by writer and music journalist Tony Paris.

After about an hour or so of insightful, often humorous conversation, Paris began asking Patti a series of questions in which he named two artists or objects and asked her to cite her preference and explain why. For example, when asked "Beatles or Stones?" Patti said, "Oh, the Stones. Let me clarify, I appreciated the Beatles more as I got older. But when I was skinny kid from Jersey, it was the Stones. I wanted to fuck the Stones."

Soon after, Paris asked Patti, "Sex Pistols or Ramones?"

"The Clash," Patti answered, without missing a beat, drawing hearty applause—mine included. I was pleased by this unexpected mention of the Clash because I was into my sixth month of researching and writing my latest contribution to Backbeat's FAQ series, the book you are holding in your hand. But it was another exchange that was more illuminating.

Patti had agreed to take audience questions, and the first was from a young woman who said Joe Strummer had inspired her and asked if Patti would share her thoughts on how Joe had been an inspiration. Patti paused, and then said, "When we got to London in—what was it?—1976, the Clash were just starting out. Their bassist, Paul Simonon, told me that when they didn't have the money to see me at the Roundhouse, they climbed up to the roof and found a hole and shimmied down to the floor. That's how they saw me. I was already formed so [Joe] didn't inspire me, but I admired him."

That answer reaffirmed the need for *All That's Left to Know About the Clash City Rockers*. The startling death of Joe Strummer on December 22, 2002, may have sparked a renewed interest in the Clash, but many aspects of their amazing journey from punk rockers to raga masters remained unexplored, especially from the American perspective of someone who had seen them twenty-five times in concert and on both sides of the Atlantic. With founding member/lead guitarist/occasional lead vocalist/arranger/*de facto* producer Mick Jones insisting 2013's *Sound System* is the last time he is remastering the Clash's master tapes, it is time for you to discover or rediscover why it is that, decades after disbanding, *the Clash still do matter.*

Because there's more to the Clash than just Joe and Mick. There's the contributions of original lead guitarist Keith Levene and original drummer Terry Chimes; there's Paul not only learning bass but creating a style that can only be characterized as one continuous line (his self-professed artistic ideal); there's "Topper" Headon, whose drumbeats launched a dozen or so hits and propelled unforgettable live performances. Over the course of eight tumultuous years, these six men showed thousands of young people they too could "do it yourself" and realize their potential.

Joe and Patti were both hippies at heart and fans of Jimi Hendrix. Patti crossed paths with Jimi in Manhattan and Joe saw him in concert at the 1970 Isle of Wight Festival; both recorded at Electric Lady Studios, Jimi's recording studio on 8th Street in Greenwich Village. It was as if they both gleaned something important from the guitarist who played it left hand. Jimi once said everything worth learning he'd picked up from records, implying that society had failed to properly school him. It was as if Joe, ever suspicious of who was operating society, and Patti, striving to be outside of society, were determined over the course of their recordings and concert performances to follow Jimi's lead and educate their fans and inspire futures where youth was not wasted in piss factories.

We still have Patti. Do not pass up the opportunity to spend a night with her, especially if she comes to your town with Her Band. As for Joe and the Clash, you need to reach for *Sound System* and their "old movie stills," but I have no doubt the sounds and visions of that west London band, the best UK punk band ever, can still teach you a thing or two.

1

You Must Start All Over Again

Assembling the Clash

In August 1976, with the aid of an odd, older man, Mick Jones founded the Clash. Though Mick was only a little over twenty-one years of age, the Clash was the fourth band he found himself playing a significant role in forming. One of the previous three bands had signed a recording contract with a major label, but only after Mick had been informed his considerable musical talents were not required. (Sadly, this foretold his eventual fate with the Clash in seven years' time.)

The band that would take five men from the Westway—a 3.5-mile elevated, divided highway overlooked by the tower-block flat Mick shared with his grandmother—all around the world began inauspiciously, at a concert for Liverpool's second most important band: Deaf School. It was in West Kensington's Nashville Rooms on August 2, 1975, that Mick struck up a conversation with Bernard (Bernie) Rhodes, a balding man in his thirties sized up by Mick as a piano player . . . and possibly a connection for the career in rock music Mick foresaw for himself. Bernie wasn't a piano player. But he was the man orchestrating Johnny Lydon's admission to the Sex Pistols.

Not that this meant anything to Mick. The Sex Pistols were still eighteen months away from their notoriety as Great Britain's Filth and Fury. It was possible, however, that Jones had brushed past future Pistols in SEX, the ballsy boutique on the King's Road in Chelsea, London, run by the dandyish Malcolm McLaren, a business partner of Bernie's who stocked clothing designed by Rhodes and others. The "Too Fast to Live, Too Young to Die" T-shirt Mick was wearing that evening in the Nashville Rooms was one of Bernie's designs, and Bernie—not a man to let his achievements (real or perceived) go unheralded—pointed this out to Mick.

Bernie also boasted of how his partnership with McLaren extended beyond the clothing store and into a venture that was music to the ears sticking out of Mick's long hair: band management.

London SS

The third band Mick formed existed only as an idea and never advanced beyond advertisements for musicians and auditions and rehearsals. London SS never played a single gig. And yet this phantom band was a phase in the genesis of the Clash through which passed a who's who of British rockers that repositioned the trajectory of rock 'n' roll history in the latter half of the 1970s. The list of London SS auditionees and members included co-founder and bassist Tony James (Generation X and Sigue Sigue Sputnik), bassist Brian James, drummer Rat Scabies (the Damned), bassist Paul Simonon, and drummers Nicky Headon and Terry Chimes (all future members of the Clash).

Kelvin Blacklock, lead singer of the Delinquents, a glam-rock band now signed to Warner Bros. Records and renamed Violent Luck, had introduced Mick to Tony James, perhaps to assuage Mick's hurt feelings over the missed opportunity with Warner Bros. If this is true, the match exceeded Blacklock's intentions. Tony was musically inept but in thrall to Mick, and his subservience was the ego-booster the latter needed.

Drawn together by a shared love of the New York Dolls' audacious clothing—hence the appearance of their hometown in the band's name—London SS was first bandied about as a possibility in March 1975 by Mick and Tony. They were looking to create not simply a rock band but *a rock band that would shock.* That is why they chose SS. The Waffen-SS was the elite corps of the Nazi Party known more to London's youth for its black uniforms than for its role in war crimes thirty years earlier. But with World War II still fresh in the minds of their elder countrymen, the young men were looking for a reaction like the ruckus Rolling Stone Brian Jones had caused in late 1966 when photos of him strikingly dressed in a Waffen-SS uniform—with and without girlfriend (and model) Anita Pallenberg—appeared in *Børge,* a Danish magazine.

The same month Mick met Bernie in the Nashville Rooms, Brian James answered an advertisement in the August 9 issue of *Melody Maker* for a lead guitarist (and drummer). Brian was more of a Stooges fan than Mick and Tony but he had the glam-rock look down pat, which is what Mick and Tony were really after, and Brian was invited to join London SS. He accepted, but since he was playing with Bastard, a Brussels-based band, he felt that informing his old bandmates first was the right thing to do.

Impatiently waiting for Brian's return, in September Mick and Tony rounded up drummer Geir Waade, who had been sacked from the Delinquents before Mick, as well as guitarist Matt Dangerfield, and the four began rehearsals while advertising for a singer. Geir knew the flat where two former Hollywood Brats—vocalist Andrew Matheson and pianist Casino Steel—were living, and the idea was kicked around of enlisting them in the London SS. (The Hollywood Brats were a London doppelgänger of the New York Dolls, but without the notoriety.) Mick Jones agreed to explore a merger.

Malcolm McLaren had managed the New York Dolls in their death throes. This is what gave him an interest in managing the teenage louts hanging out in his boutique who wanted to be rock stars. Mick also knew through Bernie that Malcolm had once expressed an interest in managing the Hollywood Brats; if that band no longer existed, reasoned Mick, then perhaps he'd want to manage the London SS with two former Brats in the line-up. This is why Mick, Tony, Andrew, and Casino paid a visit to the rehearsal room of the informally named Sex Pistols: Mick was hoping to impress Malcolm, whom he found there with three of the Pistols. Everyone present remembers the occasion, but no one was impressed. It was, however, Mick's first encounter with the Sex Pistols that he remembers.

One rehearsal with the London SS convinced the former Hollywood Brats that they were not a good fit. Certain that fame was still within reach, Andrew and Casino poached Geir and Matt. As far as the drummer and guitarist were concerned, this was the smarter bet. The Hollywood Brats may have signed a terrible contract and encountered problems getting their album released, but they were a known entity within the industry. A band fronted by Andrew and featuring Casino was far more likely to be offered a recording contract than London SS.

Mick was back to square one, but with a sidekick in Tony. And a mentor, Bernie Rhodes, who had attended some September London SS auditions. Although Bernie's find John Lydon was now rechristened Johnny Rotten and singing with the Sex Pistols, Bernie and Malcolm had parted ways over Malcolm's refusal to share management of the band. And so Bernie poured his energies into Mick's latest project. He even found Mick and Tony a rehearsal space. Though it was identified in early British press reports as a steakhouse, it was actually the Paddington Kitchen's basement on Praed Street.

Bernie Rhodes is a controversial figure, but what they say of Brian Jones—"No Jones, no Stones"—also describes Bernie's role in assembling the Clash. A shadowy, rarely photographed figure who was the antithesis of the narcissistic Malcolm, Bernie peppered auditioning musicians with offbeat questions that were provocative or combative—or sometimes both. He selected candidates based on attitude rather than talent. With Brian James finally back from Brussels, ads were placed in the music weeklies for

Mick Jones in 1976, the year he founded the Clash. *Julian Yewdall/Getty Images*

an Iggy Stooge clone as singer and a psychopathic drummer, the band perhaps thinking they wanted someone in Keith Moon's mold, in mental madness if not talent. Respondents were then telephoned by Bernie, who asked not of their musical influences but whether they'd read Jean-Paul Sartre.

More so than the vocalists, the drummers that came knocking later figured in some of British punk rock's best bands. Nicky Headon was asked to hit the skins harder and got the job but soon left to join the G.I.s, a soul group that toured army bases. (Not the Temptations, as Clash propaganda would have it, even as late as their 2008 coffee-table book *The Clash*.)

While Nicky was actually in the band for a week or so, Terry Chimes failed his audition. Terry was just as unimpressed with the London SS as they were with him. Recalling the audition in his e-book *The Strange Case of Dr. Terry and Mr. Chimes*, Terry remembers, "The band certainly wasn't ready to go and perform, it was more of an embryonic work in progress."

Chris Miller was one of the last to bash his drums in the Paddington Kitchen basement. His facial resemblance to a mouse sighted in the basement and the itchy skin disease he suffered with soon saw him dubbed with his eventual stage name: Rat Scabies. Rat and Brian hit it off musically, and when Brian became frustrated with Mick, Tony, and Bernie's predilections for picking musicians based on their appearance over ability, the two deserted London SS and formed the Damned, the first British punk band to make it onto vinyl.

Probably the last drummer to audition was Roland Hot, who could be heard on London SS tapes circulating in London's punk scene in 1977 and 1978, but that is not his most lasting contribution to the Clash. Accompanying the drummer to his rehearsal was a tall, gap-toothed boy with no interest in playing in a rock band but reeking of charisma: Paul Simonon. Seeing Paul as a possible vocalist, Mick and Bernie asked him to sing Jonathan Richman's "Roadrunner." "It was a bit of a disaster," Paul told *Passion Is a Fashion* author Pat Gilbert. There's a valid reason why Paul's wasn't heard on London SS's rehearsal tape: he couldn't sing.

The only permanent London SS members were Mick and the two James boys. They were known to rehearse MC5 numbers, the Flaming Groovies' "Slow Death," and Larry Willliams's "Bad Boy." The only songs of note to come from this phase of Mick's career were "Ooh Baby, Ooh" (the prototype for "Gates of the West") and "Protex Blue." London SS disbanded in January 1976.

"I think it was that Mick and Tony are such good friends they find it hard to be in a group together," Generation X's Billy Idol told *New York Rocker* journalist Richard Grabel in 1978. "Their ideas were too similar. You need some different ideas to make a complete group."

Different ideas would be one thing the Clash would never lack.

The Great Pretender

If Malcolm's genius was in retail, Bernie's was spotting talent. In addition to tapping the potential John Lydon didn't know he had, Bernie would also manage 2 Tone's premier band, the Specials (he's even name checked in their first single "Gangsters"), Dexy's Midnight Runners, and Subway Sect. London SS may have dissolved, but Bernie had spotted in Mick a talent that just needed the right accessories to flourish.

One such accessory might have been an American whose first stay in London is preserved in an infamous photo—often cropped—of two members of the SEX staff flanking fashion designer Vivienne Westwood. All three are pointing their posteriors at the camera, and each has one of the letters of the boutique's name written across their rump. The young brunette with her tongue stuck out and her right high-heeled leg raised high and bearing the letter "S" is Chrissie Hynde, future leader of the Pretenders.

Unable to stay in England because her work permit had expired and unable to persuade various Sex Pistols to marry her so she could stay in the country, Chrissie went to France, then returned to her hometown of Akron, Ohio, and afterward went back again to Paris, where she was a member of the Frenchies. Returning to London, she paired up with the equally bandless Mick Jones, who remembers in John Robb's *Punk Rock: An Oral History*, "Me and Chrissie . . . playing songs in my bedroom and we sang together: 'Something's Got a Hold on Me' and Aretha Franklin's 'Every Little Bit Hurts.' I was still a kid and she was quite exotic to me, being from America." And four years older.

Mick told Chrissie his manager saw the two of them being in a band named School Girl's Underwear—a name Chrissie objected to because it didn't suit the songs she was composing. Chrissie's songs rocked harder than Mick's, whose songs at this time were about sappy boy-girl relationships, one of which was "Deny," later to become a "Clash love song" (as Joe Strummer would introduce it in concert in De Montfort Hall in Leicester on May 28, 1977). Although she never received a songwriting credit, she is known to have supplied the song's coda, about the liar who is the object of the singer's affections. She is also credited with being the person who finally convinced

Mick his long hair was outdated. She even manned the scissors and did the deed herself.

Mick subsequently invited her on the Clash's White Riot tour in the spring of 1977—their first nationwide tour. "It was great," she told *Rolling Stone*'s Kurt Loder, "but my heart was breaking. I wanted to be in a band so bad. And to go to all the gigs, to see it so close up, to be living in it and not to have a band was devastating to me. When I left, I said, 'Thanks a lot for lettin' me come along,' and I went back and went weeping on the underground throughout London. All the people I knew in town, they were all in bands. And there I was, like the real loser, you know? Really the loser."

The Clash revisited "Every Little Bit Hurts" during the recording sessions for their second album, *Give 'Em Enough Rope*, in 1978. By then, Chrissie had been affiliated with Masters of the Backside (another phantom pre-punk band), Johnny Moped, and session work with recording artist Chris Spedding. Manager Tony Secunda was interested long enough for Chrissie to record a demo of "The Phone Call," which she played for Anchor Records' Dave Hill, who then paid off not only the back rent on her rehearsal room but two months' advance rent as well. Finally, someone saw Chrissie's talent for what it was; all she needed was a band to set this jewel in the middle of. Bassist Pete Farndon was asked to audition, the two clicked, and the Pretenders were born. She would have her first #1 hit single in Great Britain within a year—something the Clash would not achieve until 1991, long after they had disbanded.

The Young Colts

A chance meeting in late winter between Mick Jones and Paul Simonon on Portobello Road in the Notting Hill district that the Westway dissects was the impetus for the first Clash lineup. When Mick told Bernie about seeing the lanky Londoner again, Bernie advised Mick that Paul had what Mick's band needed: anybody could learn to play guitar, but not anyone had Paul's brooding good looks. When it turned out anyone but Paul could learn guitar, however, it was decided that Paul would have to be the bassist. Paul, however, was reluctant.

The Nashville Rooms, where Mick met Bernie, would play another role in the Clash's origin. It was in this venue that on April 3, 1976, Paul saw the Sex Pistols perform for the first time, and this is when he decided that yes, he wanted to play the bass and be in Mick's band. Mick borrowed a bass guitar from Tony James that Paul eventually purchased and painted the bass notes onto the neck of. He practiced endlessly to the Ramones' debut album, which was released that same month.

Paul was actually the third member of Mick's new group (referred to as the Young Colts in August 1978 in *NME*). It had already been decided that future Public Image Ltd. (PiL) guitarist Keith Levene would be the lead guitarist.

Still answering ads for drummers, Terry Chimes met with Mick again and was introduced to Paul ("who basically didn't seem to speak"), Keith, and vocalist Billy Watts, a Mick Jagger wannabe (which complemented Jones's desire to be the second coming of Keith Richards.) This audition was more musically satisfying to Terry than London SS's had been "because there seemed to be a stronger direction and a clearer vision of how we were trying to sound. Billy was interesting because he put an awful lot of energy into being the front man and made some weird-looking faces." And yet, when Bernie invited Terry back, the drummer "was rather shocked that Billy had been replaced by someone. . . ."

"I Met Some Yabbos"

The night Paul Simonon first saw the Sex Pistols, they were on the same bill as the 101'ers, local pub-rockers who had just recorded a single for Chiswick Records, "Keys to Your Heart." This should have been an optimistic period for the 101'ers' singer and rhythm guitarist: his band had been working toward this opportunity for two years. But watching the rambunctious opening band of kids setting up, he was stunned that they had a manager catering to the band's image and offering them clothing. The 101'ers' singer, by contrast, lived in a squat and owned one brown suit he washed after every performance. The singer witnessed the Pistols' performance and came away shaken. "They were on another planet in another century, it took my head off," he says in Jon Savage's *England's Dreaming*. The singer's name was Joe Strummer.

Unbeknown to Joe, his performance with the jackhammering left leg and Veg-o-Matic strum caught the attention of three youths who had come to the Nashville that same night to see the Sex Pistols: Mick, Paul, and Keith. They didn't like his band (even if the 101'ers were received well enough that the audience demanded three encores) but they liked him. Most importantly, Bernie Rhodes shared their opinion. This was the front man their band needed.

Shortly thereafter, while in the queue to collect his dole money at Lisson Grove's Employment Exchange during Easter week, Joe noticed three people eying him. It was Mick, Paul, and Viv Albertine, Mick's girlfriend (and future Slits guitarist). Certain he was about to be jumped outside for his money, Joe decided that he'd take out Mick—who's taller than people think but of slight build—and then make a run for it. It wasn't necessary. They were only staring at Joe because they knew he was the 101'ers' singer and the best front man in all of London. They never exchanged words.

With Joe a gigging musician who was getting written up in the British music weeklies, Mick and Paul thought there wasn't any chance of convincing him to throw in with their lot. Naturally they were unaware of the epiphanic effect the Sex Pistols had had on Joe, who was frustrated that his fellow 101'ers hadn't been similarly converted. Spotting Joe at one of the Sex Pistols' concerts at the 100 Club, where they had secured a Tuesday-night residency in May 1976, Bernie sensed something the others hadn't and asked Joe for his phone number: maybe, just maybe, the 101'ers' singer was looking for a way out of the pub-rock scene—a dead scene as far as Bernie was concerned. Mick and Paul were not informed of this.

Unable to reach Joe via phone, but with Keith in tow, Bernie attended the 101'ers' May 30 show at the Golden Pub on Fulham Road and afterward made an offer Joe was loath to refuse. Ironically for Joe Strummer, opportunity did come knocking but it came with considerable risk. Bernie's offer to front the band formed to challenge the Sex Pistols and prove Bernie's point to Malcolm that he had better instincts when it came to the music business meant that Joe had to chuck away not only the band he had spent two hard years getting heard by the British music press but his friends, too. Bernie gave him forty-eight hours to decide.

"When Bernie Rhodes said he was getting Joe Strummer in the Clash, I said, 'He's a bit old isn't he?'" original Sex Pistols bassist Glen Matlock recalled in a 2007 *Uncut* interview. "But Bernie said, 'No, I'll have ten years off him . . . ' And he kind of did."

While Joe agonized over his choice, Bernie contacted him again and told him he had only twenty-four hours to decide, not forty-eight. Joe attended a rehearsal, where he was introduced to the two blokes he thought planned to jump him outside the dole office, and was told one of them was going to be his new songwriting partner. They ran through two of Mick's songs ("1-2 Crush on You" and "Protex Blue") and Joe was energized by the fact that these three young men moved as much as he did when playing their instruments and much more than his 101'ers, which was one of his beefs with his pub-rock band.

Returning to his squat, Joe talked his choice over with anyone who'd listen, including 101'ers drummer Richard Dudanski, who was offered the open drum stool in Mick's band—an offer seconded by Bernie because Terry had not yet signed on.

Dudanski was wary of Bernie and declined the offer. "Joe went headlong into it, he made himself believe it," he told *Uncut* in 2007. (Dudanski is the drummer heard on the bulk of *Metal Box*, PiL's magnum opus.) "[It was] all based on the new punk ideology, which was against the hippies. There was a lot of Ministry of Truth stuff."

The 101'ers' soundman, Mickey Foote, cast his lot in with Joe too, accepting a role with a band that had never played live (and a band he probably hadn't even heard.) One of Joe's friends, Pablo LaBritain (later of the punk band 999), sat in behind the drums for the first rehearsals, until Bernie brought Terry back. Still reluctant to join, Terry was persuaded by the band's dedication and purpose in synthesizing their talents and realizing this fledgling group's sound. By mid-June, the first Clash lineup was complete, if nameless.

What's Our Name?

One of the most feverish debates for a new band is the one concerning their chosen name, and the five young men went through more than their share of them. Considering the band's eventual sense of positivism, it's hard to believe they entertained becoming the Psychotic Negatives. The Weak Heartdrops makes a little more sense, since it's from Jamaican DJ and recording artist Big Youth's song "Lightning Flash (Weak Heart Drop)," but the band's music was anything but weak, which soon led them to call themselves the Heartdrops—although this sounded too much like the title of one of Mick's early love songs. They had definitely decided on being the Outsiders until a record store proprietor they knew showed them a 1966 Capitol LP by a band with the same name.

Then one day, while reading the *Evening Standard*, Paul—a former art student perhaps most concerned about the budding band's image—kept seeing the word "clash" in political headlines. It tied in with the band's dynamics (in terms of both personalities and performance) and what Bernie was advising Joe and Mick to write about. A Who fan, Simonon liked the similarity to his favorite rock band's to-the-point (yet ambiguous) name. Perhaps it was an omen that everyone—except Keith—was willing to put their lives on the line for a band named the Clash.

2

He's in Love with Rock 'n' Roll Whoa!

The Clashical

The Rolling Stones. The Jimi Hendrix Experience. The Clash. More often than not, the rock bands that endure are a convergence of individual musical interests creating a unique blend; and rock music—being a mongrel music—is of all musical idioms the most adaptable. You'll hear that the Rolling Stones are just an R&B band, but Mick Jagger and Keith Richards's R&B preferences differed from Brian Jones's, while Bill Wyman was into American rock 'n' roll and Charlie Watts was a jazz purist. When speaking of the Experience's chemistry, Jimi Hendrix would talk of being "into the blues," while drummer Mitch Mitchell did his "jazz thing" and bassist Noel Redding was into "a rock bag."

This idea is verified in interviews with the Clash, with each member saying that it was the blending Mick's immense knowledge of rock 'n' roll, Joe's absorption of American rockabilly and Chicago rhythm and blues, Paul's reggae roots, and Topper's teenage years playing in jazz and soul bands that enabled them to prosper with a sound unlike any other. The effect of each of these musical idioms on the Clash will be addressed in due course, but gathered here are the band's rock 'n' roll forefathers, without whom the Clash are unimaginable.

The Beatles

Most people must've thought the Clash hated the Beatles; after all, wasn't Beatlemania phony? Joe said so in the first verse of "London Calling." But then why did the Beatles or Beatles imagery keep appearing in the Clash's songs? There's Lucy in the sky in "Julie's Been Working for the Drug Squad," or Joe injecting Rocky Raccoon into a live performance of "I'm So Bored with the USA" that's on the bootleg soundtrack for *Rude Boy*. Joe even considered for one night calling up John Lennon and asking if he'd consent to producing the Clash's second album.

No, the members of the Clash didn't hate the Beatles. Original drummer Terry Chimes remembers seeing them on television and being transfixed. Mick Jones, in *Westway to the World*, remembers, "I did my first concert playing a Beatles number with a tennis racket on the front lawn of the block of flats I lived at—I was about ten years old—for all the people walking by." The Beatles' version of "Rock and Roll Music" steered young Joe Strummer in the direction of Chuck Berry.

In fact, for all of his posturing, there's a lot in common between Joe Strummer and John Lennon. Both were art-school dropouts from middle-class backgrounds planted center stage in their respective rock bands, strumming electric guitars. Each had a unique stance. Both were volatile vocalists famous for being the wordsmith half of a popular songwriting duo. Both occasionally wrote patronizing political lyrics, but they could also be refreshingly poetic. Both were naïve romanticists who believed the world could be a better place. Both proved themselves capable of making rash decisions that led to failures the press made certain were not forgotten. Both died at a young age, just as they were making comebacks. Rock photographer Bob Gruen even photographed both John Lennon (in 1972) and Joe Strummer (in 1979) lying across the same Record Plant couch. It was evidence of God's sense of rhyme.

"I'd like to see somebody try and top the Beatles," Joe told *Punk*'s Judy McGuire in 1999, long after he stopped denying his hippie sensibilities. "Many people have tried."

The Rolling Stones

"No Elvis, Beatles, or the Rolling Stones!" Joe Strummer spat out in the chorus of "1977," the B-side of the Clash's debut single, "White Riot," released on March 18, 1977. Not only was it a punk manifesto summarized in one line, it was Joe taking up the gauntlet for his heroes "in 1977." Hearing the Stones' version of "Not Fade Away" had converted him into a rock 'n' roller—and one of the truest believers at that. "[It] sounded like the road to freedom! Seriously. It said, 'LIVE! ENJOY LIFE! FUCK CHARTERED ACCOUNTANCY!'" Joe explained to *NME*'s Sean O'Hagan in 1988. He was living at a boarding school when he heard the Decca single. "And that's the moment I think I fell for music. I think I made a subconscious decision to only follow music forever."

Joe wasn't the only member of the Clash inspired by the Rolling Stones. Mick's deliberately cultivated resemblance to Keith Richards was much noted by the music press and is on full display in the film *Rude Boy*. As a young teen, Mick had attended the Stones' free memorial concert for Brian Jones in Hyde Park on July 5, 1968, and was proud his presence was captured in some press photos. (Future Clash mentor Guy Stevens was also in attendance.) When teaching himself guitar, Mick often played Rolling Stones songs. The line in "Stay Free" about practicing "daily in my room" has been said by Mick to be a reference to time spent in his nan's flat learning Keith's solo for "You Can't Always Get What You Want."

Brian Jones's Rolling Stones were a major influence on Joe Strummer. *Author's collection*

So Mick was understandably hurt by Richards's put-down of punk rock, although it shouldn't have come as a surprise. Despite his rebel image, Richards is a bit of a musical traditionalist. He was strident in his complaints about glam rock—going so far as to attack a poster of Marc Bolan on one occasion—so punk rockers weren't going to fare any better. Mick defended Keith in "Jail Guitar Doors" when the latter was facing a drug trafficking sentence in Canada, but only a year later he told *New York Rocker*'s Ira Robbins: "I still love [Keith's] playing, but sometimes I think he seems like an ass."

Mick Jagger joined Richards in defensively putting down punk rock in the press and laying claim to the Stones having birthed punk rock, going so far as to say in 1976 that "Keith is the original punk rocker. You can't out-punk Keith." But as the forward-looking Stone (after Brian's death and bassist Bill Wyman's marginalization), it was Mick who could be found in New York City attending punk and new-wave concerts at Max's Kansas City and CBGB, checking out what his band was up against. The result was *Some Girls*. With six million units moved in the US, it is the bestselling album of all the Stones' best sellers. It is also an album where the Rolling Stones cop moves from Lou Reed, Patti Smith, the Ramones, and the Clash.

"Respectable" is the album's shortest track and an opportunity for the Stones to poke fun at themselves while ironically addressing punk statements on their diminishing relevancy—something Joe Strummer would do later in the year on "Cheapskates." Here, as in Strummer's best lyrics, such as "(White Man) In Hammersmith Palais," Jagger is talking of his own experiences.

Another Strummer comparison can be found in the way Jagger sets the song rolling with a very energetic rhythm track. It sounds very much like Strummer's rhythm guitar kicking off "English Civil War," the Clash's seventh single, although "Respectable" hit the streets before "English Civil War" did.

On September 25, 1982, Mick Jagger crossed paths with the Clash at JFK Stadium. The Clash were opening for the Who, but Jagger was not there to see his old friends from London. Rather, he attended because his daughter Jade's favorite band at the time was the Clash. Meeting the punk band backstage, Jagger noticed they were a bit nervous about performing in front of over 90,000 people. As Terry Chimes remembered in a *TRAPS* interview with Ian Croft, Jagger gave the band a bit of professional advice gleaned from often performing in front of large crowds: "[The Stones have] done lots of these and it is scary, but once you've done one, they're all the same."

By 1983, the Clash were imploding. Drummer Nicky "Topper" Headon had been fired because he was a heroin addict; guitarist/vocalist/songwriter/producer Mick Jones was about to be booted in a foolish act of punk purification. The rock world did not know this. The Clash were at the height of their popularity, and their influence could be heard on "Undercover of the Night," the opening track on the Stones' *Undercover.* Mick was a fan. "I quite like the Clash," Mick Jagger said as far back as 1980. "But they sound old-fashioned. It's fine. I'm very old-fashioned, too. The Clash remind me a bit of the early Stones albums." *Undercover* reminds one of the latter Clash albums, especially *Sandinista!,* with its blend of Latin rhythms, funky NYC hip hop, reggae, and social content. But it is still very much a rock 'n' roll album.

Recorded in 1983, "Undercover of the Night" is perhaps the best Rolling Stones song from the 1980s. ("Star Me Up" actually dates from 1978.) With its political message it can be seen not only as an attempt to keep up with the Clash but also as a successful attempt to keep up with the times. It's one of the Stones' better club numbers, especially the 6:21 "Dub Version."

Ironically, over time punks and the British music press would vilify the Clash by lumping the two bands together. "To be just like the Rolling Stones?" Joe wondered to Paolo Hewitt in a December 1980 *Melody Maker* interview, when he was asked about this comparison. "I mean, a thousand groups would give their right arms to be called that, although I don't particularly find it wonderful. But if we were, wouldn't we have a 24-track studio? For a start we haven't got our own houses. I'm talking about the old rock 'n' roll thing. You get a big house, you build your own 24-track in the basement, and when it's all done you can't think of a damn thing to record on it, right?"

Here, Joe was still resorting to mid-'70s criticism of the Stones, but years later, after some time spent out of the punk spotlight, he would admit to always admiring the Rolling Stones, even telling a story of the Clash's first lineup attending one of the Stones' concerts at Earl's Court in May 1976. These are the concerts the British music press often cited as evidence that the Rolling Stones were dinosaurs and passé, and yet here were the leaders of what would be the new guard, standing close enough to the stage to try and get the attention of Bill Wyman. Bill was known for being impassive and immobile onstage. In this he was a great visual foil to Mick's antic movements. Joe, however, was determined to get a reaction, and after every song in the Stones' twenty-nine-song set he would yell out Bill's name frantically.

Finally he got the Rolling Stone known to fans as Stone Face to look in his direction and crack a smile.

The Who

The earliest Clash rehearsals included Who covers, and the band's influence on their fellow Londoners can be seen and heard in many ways. Paul Simonon's swinging of his bass guitar was his attempt at emulating guitarist Pete Townshend's stage movement. And when the unreleased track "Deadly Serious" morphed into "Capital Radio," it retained the Who's "I Can't Explain" riff—a riff the Clash used again for "Guns on the Roof" and to best effect in "Clash City Rockers." If you listen closely, you can also catch strains of "Baba O'Riley" in "White Riot."

Townshend was more supportive of punk rock than the members of the Rolling Stones, going so far as to say in Pat Gilbert's book *Passion Is a Fashion* that he understood why some punk musicians rebelled against the lifestyles of the Stones and operatic aspirations of the Who's music in the mid-'70s. According to Townshend, the Clash "expressed annoyance that the bands that went before them—like the Who—had not been militant enough."

Townshend could appreciate being a Godfather to the punk band. In the booklet accompanying the boxed set *The Clash: The Singles*, he says, "I adore the Clash, as I adore the Sex Pistols. Different, incompatible, not really comparable, they both felt to me like bands who . . . had travelled a route laid by the Who more than any other band."

So it's not surprising to learn that on January 9, 1980, at the Top Rank in Brighton, a red-jacketed Townshend joined the Clash for one of their encores, guesting on "Bankrobber," a rare public airing of "Louie Louie," and "Garageland." The guitar he borrowed from Jones malfunctioned during "Bankrobber." Pete was a fan. His publishing company even published *The Clash: Before and After*, Pennie Smith's book of photos of the Clash.

In September and October 1982, the Clash signed on as an opening act for the Who's first "farewell" tour, along with David Johansen, formerly of the New York Dolls. Townshend has said this idea was the brainchild of a "Junior Manager" named Chris Chappel. Townshend was trying to pass the mantle to the Clash, and he had succeeded: "By the end of the tour, they had broken the USA."

Unfortunately, Joe now had other worries. What was the future of the Clash? "We did eight gigs in super-stadiums, all the biggest joints—LA Coliseum, Oakland Coliseum, Shea Stadium," he told *Uncut*'s Gavin Martin in 1999. "I realized that was where we were heading and it didn't look good." (This fear that Clash megastardom would compromise his integrity resulted in Mick's firing the following year.)

Joe Strummer and the Mescaleros supported the Who during their 2000 tour of Great Britain, and Joe even persuaded vocalist Roger Daltry to participate in a recording session for "Global a Go-Go," the title track of his second album with the Mescaleros. During the song's second verse, when Joe name checks Buddy Rich, Big Youth, Nina Simone, and Bob Dylan, he also includes the Who. When he sings of "*Quadrophenia* in Armenia," Daltry belts out "Armenia city in the sky!"—a not-so-sly reference to the 1967 opening track from *The Who Sell Out.*

And during the Who's thirty-fifth anniversary tour of *Quadrophenia*—where Townshend's best rock opera was performed in its entirety—for a brief moment Joe's face flashed on the huge screen behind the band.

Captain Beefheart

Joe Strummer was not the first lyricist to put down the Beatles and the Rolling Stones in the same song. That would be Don Van Vliet, a songwriter/musician/artist better known by his stage name, Captain Beefheart. "Beatle Bones 'n' Smokin' Stones" was a 1968 recording mocking both bands as supposed leaders of their generation but was not released until years later because Vliet's label, Buddah, saw no commercial potential in his second album, *Strictly Personal.*

To many future British punk rockers, it was Captain Beefheart and Frank Zappa who were the original punks, not Lou Reed or Iggy Pop. Gaye Advert of the Adverts, Don Letts of Big Audio Dynamite, UK Subs vocalist Charlie Harper, Siouxsie and the Banshees bassist Steve Severin, Stranglers' bassist/vocalist J. J. Burnel, and Johnny Rotten have all cited Captain Beefheart as an important influence. Add to that list Joe Strummer, who would often name *Trout Mask Replica*—Beefheart's 1969 album, produced by Zappa—as being a personal favorite.

Joe Strummer's lyrics morphed over the course of the Clash's recordings. While he was a realist on *The Clash*, by *Sandinista!* he was as surrealistic as Captain Beefheart, and this is where he eventually settled as a lyricist. His lyrics in his work with the Mescaleros are doubly Beefheartian. Beefheart's absurdist worldview matched Joe's, but even more so his humor, an often overlooked attribute of Strummer's lyrics.

Mott the Hoople

Perhaps the most influential act on not only the Clash but the course of British rock 'n' roll in the second half of the '70s was Mott the Hoople. But just as most Americans are ignorant of the Clash pre–"Train in Vain," so too most Americans are unaware of Mott the Hoople pre-Bowie. Mott only caught the attention of American rock 'n' rollers when Bowie produced *All the Young Dudes*, for which he also penned the title track. Subsequent LPs *Mott* and *The Hoople* were also US hits. But before that they were popular throughout the UK via albums such as *Mad Shadows* and *Brain Capers*.

Mott the Hoople was the brainchild of future Clash producer Guy Stevens. Mott can be seen as the link between the Rolling Stones and glam rock, and they attracted a passionate following of teenagers that included Mick Jones and his Strand School classmates. They would follow Mott the Hoople from town to town via British Rail. The Fall guitarist Marc Riley is quoted in John Robb's oral history of punk rock as saying that according to Mott vocalist/lyricist/guitarist Ian Hunter, "Mick Jones was a Marshall for Mott the Hoople."

In that same book, Mick says, "Mott were very nice, the way they treated us." Mott's interaction with Mick and his friends rubbed off on the Clash, who would be just as welcoming to their fans, letting them into concerts for free via the back door and inviting them to sleep on their hotel floors after a concert.

The Mott influence abounds within the Clash canon. Echoes of Mott guitarist Mick Ralphs can be heard in Mick's solos, especially on the 1978 recordings. "All the Young Punks" obviously cops its title from Mott's "All the Young Dudes"; "Stay Free" has its roots in "Hymn for the Dudes"; and there are lyrical similarities between "Gates of the West" and Mott's "All the Way to Memphis." *NME*'s Nick Kent wrote in 1977 that "the Clash take up exactly where Mott the Hoople left off."

Deflecting criticism in later years that the band were getting too political, Joe told the *Los Angeles Times*' Richard Cromelin that he "used to say to journalists—'Hang on, don't get the wrong idea that we're carrying around *Das Kapital* and loads of pamphlets.' We had Mott the Hoople records and reefer, you know?"

The New York Dolls

Brian Eno famously said of the Velvet Underground's debut album with Nico that "everyone who bought one of those 30,000 copies started a band."

The same could be said of the impact the New York Dolls had on British rock fans: everyone who saw the New York City–based thrash and glam-rock band's single appearance on *The Grey Old Whistle Test* started a punk-rock band. One of those viewers was Mick. Though the New York Dolls' effect on Mick was strongest during his London SS days (Paul remembered in an interview with Caroline Coon that "they were into the New York Dolls and they all had very long hair"), when he could finally afford it, Mick bought himself a Gibson Les Paul Junior with a P-90 pickup because it was the same type of guitar that Johnny Thunders of the New York Dolls played. This is the guitar you hear Mick playing on the earliest Clash recordings.

Bruce Springsteen

If you look closely, you can see how Joe is the British Bruce Springsteen. The two rockers who came of age in the 1970s have a lot in common. They saw rock music as a means to lift the working class and correct society's ills. And what Joe Strummer saw at Bruce Springsteen and the E Street Band's debut UK performance on November 18, 1975, at the Hammersmith Odeon was a front man who worked as hard as he did but had a wider range of moves. He promptly purchased a longer guitar cord so he could move more freely around the stage like Springsteen. And he also started manipulating objects in service of a song—an act that would peak in 1979, when Joe would hold a candelabra while singing "Armagideon Time."

Many years later, in the mid-'90s, when the Glastonbury Festival organizers were considering inviting Bruce Springsteen and the E Street Band to headline, Joe sent off a handwritten fax (reprinted in the *Guardian* in 2009) fulsomely supporting the idea.

"BRUCE IS GREAT . . . IF YOU DON'T AGREE WITH THAT YOU'RE A PRETENTIOUS MARTIAN FROM VENUS," he begins, writing in all caps. After praising Bruce's looks and tenacity, he continues, "HIS MUSIC IS GREAT ON A DARK & RAINY MORNING IN ENGLAND, JUST WHEN YOU NEED SOME SPIRIT & SOME PROOF THAT THE BIG WIDE WORLD EXISTS, THE DJ PUTS ON "RACING IN THE STREETS" & LIFE SEEMS WORTH LIVING AGAIN." He ends his passionate fax by returning to his original theme: "BRUCE IS GREAT . . . THERE AIN'T NO WHINGING, WHINING OR COMPLAINING. THERE'S ONLY GREAT MUSIC, LYRICS & AN OCEAN OF TALENT. ME? I LOVE SPRINGSTEEN!!!"

Of course, Bruce was as much a fan of Joe as Joe was of Bruce, and the man from Asbury Park, New Jersey, has done his bit to keep Joe's music alive. When the Clash were inducted into the Rock and Roll Hall of Fame, Bruce offered his vocal services to the surviving members if they wanted to perform. They declined, but Mick must have been touched, since he was known to wear a T-shirt depicting the Boss and study his recordings for studio production insights.

Later that same year, Bruce got his chance to pay homage. As the "In Memoriam" portion of the 2003 Grammy awards neared its conclusion, an image of Loving Spoonful guitarist Zal Yanovsky gave way to an early video clip of Joe singing and playing guitar. Then the screen with Joe's image descended into the stage, revealing a band that was hard to identify because of the blinding white light, and yet the song they played was easily recognizable. It was the opening marching chords of "London Calling." "This is for Joe!" Bruce Springsteen shouted out. There were four guitarists and a rhythm section. Elvis Costello got the first lines, followed by Bruce, E Street Band guitarist Little Stevie, and David Grohl of the Foo Fighters and Nirvana. For the first time in decades, a memorable, skin-tingling rock 'n' roll moment was occurring at the Grammys. You could see now a backdrop of screens showing the Union Jack and World War I warplanes and images of the Clash. As Little Stevie took the lead on his black Gibson Les Paul, No Doubt bassist Tony Kanal jumped up on the drum riser and faced Attractions drummer Pete Thomas, just like Joe would Topper. The guitarists continued taking turns singing the lines, but Elvis got the final one: "I never felt like like like like."

Bruce has played "London Calling" on several other occasions, such as at Rock and Roll Hall of Fame Anniversary events (with Rage Against the Machine guitarist Tom Morello) and a 2009 concert in Hyde Park, London. He's also been known to play "Coma Girl" from Joe's posthumous album *Streetcore.*

The Ramones

"It can't be stressed how great the first Ramones album was to the scene because it gave anyone who couldn't play the idea that it was simple enough to be able to play," Joe Strummer is quoted as saying in *The Clash,* their 2008 coffee-table book. "We all used to practice along with it. Paul and I spent hours, days, weeks playing along to the record. Anyone could see where the

"It can't be stressed how great the first Ramones album was to the [UK punk] scene," Joe Strummer said, "because it gave anyone who couldn't play the idea that [music] was simple enough to be able to play."
Stephen Graziano

notes went and it gave everyone confidence. It was the first word of punk, a fantastic record."

Original guitarist Keith Levene agreed, telling Jason Gross, "The Ramones especially, more than they ever realized, had it down. They were punk rock IN-FUCKING-CARNATE before the London thing happened. They had it before the Pistols were doing it."

The Clash clearly stole their musical intensity from the Ramones, and that's not the only thing they took: Mick copped the "1, 2, 3, 4!" shouted intros; Paul held his bass at arm's length near his knees, à la Dee Dee Ramone; and Terry adopted similar drum patterns. The Ramones were the only contemporary band that the Clash covered, as in 1977 when, during the White Riot tour, they'd occasionally spotlight the reggae-punk axis by morphing "Police and Thieves" into "Blitzkrieg Bop."

The Clash were disappointed with the Ramones' subsequent musical indirection, however. "[The Ramones'] first album was great," Paul told *Creem*'s Iman Lababedi, "then they brought out their second album and it sounded just the same as the first. But come the third, I never bothered buying it, 'cause I knew it would be the same."

Patti Smith

Asked by *NME*'s Paul Rambali in late 1981 if any famous people had lived up to his expectations, Mick replied, "I haven't met that many, but I'd have to say, . . . Martin Scorsese, Robert De Niro and, um, Patti Smith."

The Patti Smith Group were not a punk rock band, but Patti had the punk attitude down pat, and for this she is rightly known as the Godmother of Punk. When her debut album, *Horses*, was released in the UK in December 1975, it was one of the tiny fires that ignited punk rock a year later. Mick Jones bought *Horses* and attended the Patti Smith Group's legendary Roundhouse concert on May 17, 1976, as did vocalist Ari Up of the Slits, Viv Albertine of the same band (they in fact met at Patti's concert), and Penny Rimbaud of Crass. Patti's high on rebellion attitude appealed to Britain's restless, disenfranchised youth. Her first single "Hey Joe (Version)" b/w "Piss Factory" had been a DIY affair; it showed other unsigned acts that they could make records without the big boys, too.

Patti was passionate about fashion, and her most lasting contribution to punk rock and new wave was the skinny black tie draped around her long neck in the Sinatra-esque pose captured by photographer Robert Mapplethorpe for the album's cover. In early Clash photos you can see Mick wearing a tie, too, and on their debut album there's Joe Strummer, dead smack center, wearing a tie open at his neck. Though his is wider, the source is unmistakable.

When the Patti Smith Group returned to Britain in the autumn of 1976 promoting *Radio Ethiopia*, Joe, Mick, and Paul attended the first of two London concerts staged at the Hammersmith Odeon. They could not have expected Patti to repay the favor the following evening, October 23. Mark Stewart (later of the trend-setting band the Pop Group) had talked up the burgeoning punk scene to Patti and took her to the Clash's concert at the Institute of Contemporary Arts, where she surprised everybody by leaping onstage as the Clash played "I'm So Bored with the USA." Funnily enough, the Clash's in-house photographer Rocco McCauley didn't recognize Patti—mistaking her for some anonymous hippie—and refused to take photos until the ICA's bouncers threw her off the stage. Years later, Joe laughed that McCauley had missed out on photos of Patti dancing at a Clash concert that he could have sold to the British music press.

It was on this night that Patti struck up a relationship with bassist Paul Simonon, who was whisked away by Patti to Birmingham, where her band was performing the Odeon Theatre on October 24. One can easily see the attraction for Patti. Physically, Paul was Patti's type, and he bore some resemblance to other men who factored in Patti's life, such as Television leader Tom Verlaine, playwright Sam Shepherd, and MC5 guitarist Fred "Sonic" Smith, whom Patti married in 1980. Patti and Paul's relationship was to be a long distance one, however, as by October 30 Patti was back in the States, joining Bruce Springsteen on the Palladium stage in New York City for Bruce's "Rosalita" and her own "Land."

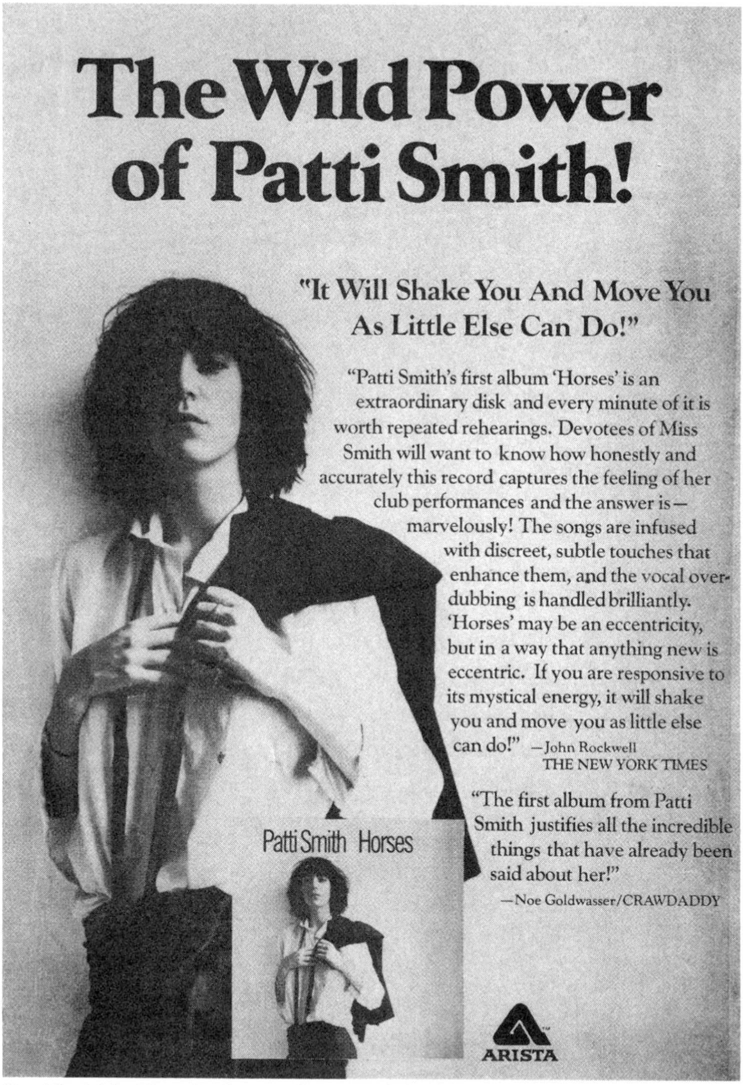

Patti Smith's *Horses* invigorated many of the future punk rockers in the UK, including Mick Jones. *Author's collection*

Patti Smith is one of the few rock 'n' rollers who actively petitioned journalists about rock's acceptance as a valid art form, and undoubtedly this was something Paul found appealing about Patti. In the music press it was reported that Paul had shown up at a concert wearing Patti's fifteen-year-old high school T-shirt, and in photos from 1977, Paul can be seen wearing one of Patti's ART/RAT T-shirts. Likewise, Patti appeared on the cover of *Melody Maker* on August 12, 1978, wearing a Clash T-shirt featuring an image of police charging at the Notting Hill Carnival. (This photo was itself made into a T-shirt back in the day.) Paul can also be seen in 1977 photos playing a paint-splattered Rickenbacker bass guitar with Patti's image from the *Horses* cover affixed to his instrument. Patti also provided the funds for the boiler suits seen in the cover art for the Clash's first single.

Johnny Green, the Clash's road manager between 1977 and 1980, writes in *A Riot of Our Own: Night and Day with the Clash*, co-authored by Garry Barker, his remembrance of days Clash, that during the recording of *Give 'Em Enough Rope*, he often fielded transatlantic calls between Paul and Patti. Another *Give 'Em Enough Rope* connection is the presence of Patti's former boyfriend, Blue Öyster Cult's Allen Lanier, who was pulled in by his producer Sandy Pearlman to redo the piano track originally recorded by New York City lounge lizard Al Fields on "Julie's Been Working for the Drug Squad."

Patti Smith retired in 1980 to marry and raise a family, and by the time of her return to stage and studio in the mid-'90s, the Clash had long since stopped running. But by then the Patti Smith Group and the Clash were indelibly linked by the roles they played in salvaging rock 'n' roll music in the latter half of the 1970s. At Joe Strummer's shows with the Mescaleros, Patti's latest music could be heard before sets. And when Patti served as the curator of the Meltdown Festival in London in 2005, Mick's latest band Carbon/Silicon (with former London SS and Generation X bassist Tony James) were invited to participate. Patti even joined Mick on June 17 for a spirited rendition of "Hey Joe," a version of which had been the A-side of Patti's first 45.

It was three years earlier, however, that Patti paid the Clash the sincerest compliment she could. It was December 28, 2002, in the legendary Stone Pony in Asbury Park, New Jersey. Six days earlier, Joe Strummer's heart suddenly gave out. It was Patti's first concert since his death. Fans expected her to say something, to perhaps perform a song, to perhaps perform "I'm So Bored with the USA," the song she had danced to once before. Instead she played "Land."

"Land" is a rocking tone poem featuring a boy who looks at the universal rebel Johnny. Every time Patti performs "Land" nobody knows what is going to happen to either the boy or Johnny because Patti ad-libs new lyrics. On this December night "Land" began with its standard opening line: "The boy was in the hallway drinking a cup of tea." (Then again the Clash may have been British punks but they were still known to enjoy their cups of tea, especially Mick and Joe.) From there, Patti diverged, continuing to talk about the boy:

> Sometimes he had trouble talking to people. Sometimes he had to turn away when he was talking to them. He had trouble relating. He might just emanate rays up from his heart. He was truly nobody. Just another woebegone rocker living at the world's end. The world's end where he couldn't get any peace. He couldn't get anything. Nothing was going right. He didn't have nothing. He sat on the floor and he was hungry. But he had one thing . . . one place to go. His mates were waiting. A band of young men at world's end. He . . . he just wanted to get a chance to get his words out of his mouth. Just once, just spit them out once and not get laughed at. He . . . he just wanted to be able to express himself in a way that meant something to somebody. He was hungry . . . hungry . . . went into a little practice room. Led his band and . . . and he . . . and he did it. He saw it. He saw it all happen. He got through. He really saw it. He got through until only a half century's old his heart gave out. But for a while he was on top of the world man! He made at the world's end. He made it to the twelve great stages of Europe. He made it into the Hall of Fame. He fuckin' made it. He was everything. He was no one and he made it. He was everything. He was nothing. He was Joe Strummer. He was everything. And the boy looked at Johnny. . . .

3

An' When Some Punk Come A-Looking for Sound

The Sex Pistols and the Birth of British Punk Rock

Whereas several strains of American rock 'n' roll predate the slang word "punk" being applied to the music, in Great Britain there was none, except perhaps the Rolling Stones' attitude, which was truly nothing more than a brilliant piece of marketing by their manager Andrew Loog Oldham to set his act apart from the Beatles and therefore get whatever leftover scraps of press were available and hopefully appeal to the British youth rejecting the wholesomeness that the lads from Liverpool exuded. Punk rock in Great Britain did originate with the Sex Pistols. This is why—even without hearing them perform—Joe Strummer was transfixed by four unruly youths looking more like a gang than musicians who were booked to open for his pub rock band the 101'ers at the Nashville on April 3, 1976.

The Sex Pistols and the Clash

The relationships between the members of the Sex Pistols and the Clash are complicated, and understanding them is not aided by the way Johnny and Joe spoke of one another. "Me and Rotten never got on. Couldn't be expected to, really," Joe told Jon Savage in an unpublished interview from 1988. Eleven cryptic words.

Johnny's persona is rooted in shock, so it's no wonder that Joe was always more sympathetic. For example, when Peter Silverton said in a June 1978 *Sounds* interview that Joe handled fame better and that it had "freaked" out

"They were on another planet in another century," Joe Strummer said of seeing the Sex Pistols for the first time. "It took my head off." *Ian Dickson/Getty Images*

Johnny, who "locks himself away in a house," Joe was diplomatic: "Well, you can't really compare me and him because he went through the whole heavy thing. Suddenly everybody in the world descended on him. He went through something, a lot more pressure, a million tons more. You can't compare."

But if Joe was sympathetic to Johnny, Johnny was caustic about Joe. "I gave Joe Strummer a career when he was a tosspot," John Lydon says in a fan-captured interview available on *YouTube*. Johnny's dislike for Joe is well known; even when he tries saying something kind about Joe, he can't avoid being uncomplimentary. "Joe's a very nice bloke," John said in a June 2001 interview with Film4. "He's just ashamed of his own class roots. Which is of course the antithesis to me. You are what you are, and you should work accordingly with the tools you've been given. But to pretend to be working-class drives me crazy."

Thirteen years later, in his autobiography, *Anger Is an Energy*, John was still slagging off Joe, despite stating that "I loved Joe. At the beginning he was friendly, friendly, friendly but that soon changed once he started taking the Clash too seriously." Johnny's main arguments do have some merit. "For some strange reason . . . the Clash started setting themselves up as our competition." This is true. Both Joe and Terry Chimes saw the Sex Pistols as rivals (Mick and Paul, however, did not).

"I never liked any of the Clash stuff," John told *Spin* in 2007. "And I never considered the Clash punk. Joe [Strummer] was alright. He was very sweet-natured. But he came from a different music background. He'd already tried the pub-band circuit, so he hopped onto punk."

In his aforementioned autobiography—there are several—John observes that the Clash's most enduring contribution to punk rock was "every song at a hundred miles an hour"—not the Ramones, who are generally the band credited with injecting increased tempo—but that on the negative side, "through (the Clash), punk grew into a standardized uniform."

The truth is that while Johnny saw Joe as a pub-rocking opportunist, Joe never forgot that seeing the Sex Pistols open for the 101'ers had shown him a way forward, and except for some heated words circa 1980, he usually held himself above the fray.

So if Joe had been around in 2014 to read that, according to Johnny, he "began to lack a sense of humor about himself. He took himself too serious as purveyor of some kind of weird socialism, and was definitely out to grab himself a crown," Joe would have probably agreed. He was quoted in the July 24, 1976, issue of *Melody Maker* saying, "Before I used to think I was a crud. Now I realise I'm the King and I've decided to move into the future."

Among the key differences between the Sex Pistols and the Clash was their perception of "the future." For the nihilistic Sex Pistols, there was "no future for you," as they sang in "God Save the Queen." Society was broken and beyond repair. For the humanistic Clash, however, "the future is unwritten," as indicated in the open book on the cover of the "Know Your Rights" 45. Society may be malfunctioning, but with change it could be repaired for the betterment of the masses.

The Sex Pistols

The Sex Pistols date back to 1973, when an aspiring vocalist named Steve Jones approached a rock 'n' roll boutique shop owner about finding musicians to supplement his band, the Strand. The shop owner would go on to be one of rock music's legendary band managers, but that is not the career Malcolm McLaren had in mind when he arranged for one of his employees, Glen Matlock, to play bass with Jones and his friend, a drummer named Paul Cook. It was McLaren's occasional business partner, Bernie Rhodes, who actively encouraged the band to take their endeavor seriously.

Fate stepped in when McLaren and his boutique business associates Vivienne Westwood and Gerry Goldstein were invited to participate in the

National Boutique Show being held in New York City in August that same year. McLaren crossed paths with the New York Dolls, a notorious glam-rock outfit that may have been the talk of the underground in the Big Apple but were too glam for America's music industry. The Dolls wore high-heeled shoes long before the Cramps' Lux Interior did, and this was a turnoff for homophobic America. Yes, Alice Cooper was selling out stadiums, but he was masculine—a killer. The Dolls were too transsexual, and Bowie had yet to popularize the androgynous look for the young Americans.

The New York Dolls were aware of McLaren's shop, having gone there during a previous visit to London, and when guitarist Sylvain Sylvain found out that McLaren and his associates were in Manhattan, he paid them a visit. McLaren was soon living at the Chelsea Hotel, attending concerts at Max's Kansas City, palling around with Andy Warhol. It was a small "in scene," but one with a ridiculously adventurous flamboyancy McLaren found himself longing for when he was back in London.

It's no wonder then that when the New York Dolls "swooned into London" (as Nick Kent phrased it) on a return visit, McLaren wormed his way into their entourage, cementing his connections with the band and discovering that rock 'n' roll decadence suited him quite fine. The New York Dolls received far better press in Great Britain, but their flirtation with stardom was undermined by a lifestyle that led to heroin addiction and alcoholism. They had become the "New York Floozies" by the time McLaren reappeared in New York City in 1975, offering life support.

McLaren—who in the interim had reinvented his counterculture boutique as a SEX, a store specializing in risqué clothing—thought the best way to instill new life into a band as weakened as the Frankenstein monster the Dolls had once sung of was shock treatment. He got bassist Arthur Kane into detox and prescribed a new look with red patent leather outfits that shouted out "COMMUNISM!" They would even have the hammer-and-sickle flag onstage. McLaren got a reaction all right, but it was one from which the New York Dolls would not recover for decades. Their former supporters may have been decadent, but they were not communists, and—feeling outraged—they withdrew what little support the Dolls had left.

The person who personally triumphed from this morass, however, was McLaren. Infected by the management bug, he returned to London hoping to jumpstart Sylvain's career by transforming Steve Jones' band into Sylvain's. Since this meant the vocalist would be playing second fiddle, McLaren bribed Jones by giving him Sylvain's white Gibson Les Paul guitar. But when Asylum Records founder David Geffen offered the New York

Dolls a tour of Japan, Sylvain accepted, and all McLaren was left with was Steve Jones's band. Only Jones by now had played Sylvain's guitar along to Iggy and the Stooges and New York Dolls records for days on end, and he considered himself a budding guitarist. What his band needed was a vocalist. Could a green-haired teen whose jib Bernie Rhodes had liked be the answer?

They only knew him as John. He was a young squatter who had been thrown out of his home because of his short haircut—not the norm in 1975 for Britain's youth. He had been hanging around SEX—drawn there by the sadomasochistic attire being sold as clothing to be worn outdoors—when McLaren asked if he could sing. His wiseass answer is legendary: "What for? No: only out of tune and anyway, I play the violin." This was classic Johnny Rotten even before he was so christened, the surname given in honor of his 'orrible teeth. McLaren sensed the young man's latent charisma, and even after John's initial meeting with the band did not go well—John had wandered in with a friend and proceeded to ignore the band and act superior—he auditioned John by having the young man sing along to Alice Cooper's "Eighteen," a song on the SEX jukebox.

John's yelping was not the epiphany to the Strand that it was McLaren, who felt certain he'd found the band's singer. McLaren insisted they rehearse together, and that they change their name to the Sex Pistols. Ever the salesman, he thought the band might drive clothing sales at his boutique. And what was in it for John? The Londoner of Irish decent sensed a way out of the dead end he'd been born into, and so he went along with it, even if he didn't get along with the others in the band. McLaren liked this, too. Tension between members of the Sex Pistols would surely generate controversy.

Their first gig was at St. Martins Art College on November 6, 1975. Dragging in stolen equipment, the Sex Pistols opened for Bazooka Joe, a band that included the future Adam Ant, who would triumphantly lead his Ant Invasion in five years. On this evening, however—and even though this was their first gig—the Sex Pistols were already polarizing. Someone literally pulled the plug on the belligerent band's equipment. Ant's bandmates didn't think much of the Pistols and even got into a ruckus with them, but as Ant later told British music journalist Jon Savage, "They had the look in their eyes that said, 'We're going to be massive.'" Adam Ant quit Bazooka Joe the next day. The Sex Pistols had their first convert.

And so it went for roughly the next six months. The Sex Pistols would upset patrons, antagonize headlining bands, and bicker among themselves in performance, *but* they'd also win over a few new rabid fans at each gig. John was metamorphosing into Johnny Rotten. The new fans were taken as much by his clothes as by his attitude, which was just as well, as the band was still in its formative stages, and Johnny's vocals were not yet on par with his controversial stage comments.

Although Johnny is known for his wit, it was Steve Jones who made the statements that most affected the band's direction. In the Sex Pistols' first published interview, he told *Sounds* music journalist John Ingham, "Actually we're not into music. We're into chaos." And it rang true. Disaffected youth started attending their gigs. After their second concert, opening for the 101'ers, Joe Strummer was their latest convert.

"As soon as I saw them, I knew that rhythm and blues was dead, that the future was here somehow," Joe told *Melody Maker*'s Caroline Coon in late 1976. "Every other group was riffing their way through the Black Sabbath catalogue. But hearing the Pistols, I knew. I just knew. It was something you just knew without bothering to think about."

It was at a Sex Pistols concert at the 100 Club—the only London venue that would book the Sex Pistols as headliners, despite their violently unpredictable performances and the unbridled behavior of their fans—that Joe Strummer was approached by Bernie Rhodes and Clash guitarist Keith Levene about joining the band Bernie was managing. When Johnny told John Ingham, "I hate pub bands. I want to change it so there are more bands like us," he never anticipated his biggest rival emerging from one of those bands.

The British Punk Movement

The Clash were never Situationists, but their manager certainly was, and this movement—an avant-garde strand of Marxism—was part of the philosophical indoctrination Bernie Rhodes was peddling to the five youngsters in whom he saw musical potential. Founded in 1957, the overarching doctrines of the Situationist International had shifted over the decades from artistic expression to political theory. Its role in the May 1968 demonstrations in Paris affected both Rhodes and McLaren, the latter seeing a need for a movement if the band he was managing were ever to be a cultural phenomenon. McLaren put Rhodes's band the Clash on same bill as the Sex Pistols at the Black Swan in Sheffield on July 4, 1976, and was vocal in his support of two Manchester youths who, after seeing the Sex Pistols in London, had staged a concert in their hometown and opened for the Londoners. Their name? Buzzcocks.

The burgeoning movement was even given a name by *Melody Maker* staff writer Caroline Coon (who would temporarily play a guiding role in the Clash's management). In an article published on August 7, she described the Sex Pistols as a "band [that] play exciting, hard, basic punk rock." Further, she explained, "Punk rock was initially coined, about six years ago, to describe the American rock bands of 1965–68 who sprung up as a result of hearing the Yardbirds, Who, Them, Stones. Ability was not as important as mad enthusiasm, but the bands usually dissipated all their talent in one or two splendid singles which rarely transcended local hit status."

Without acknowledging her source, Coon was building on the mushrooming word of mouth coming from New York City about bands such as the Ramones, the Patti Smith Group, and Television revolutionizing the Downtown music scene. Two Connecticut teens—"Legs" McNeil and John Holmstrom—had published a new magazine nine months earlier called *Punk*, with a crude, cartoonish drawing of Lou Reed on the cover. It was only a matter of time before what was coming out of New York City collided with what was happening in London.

It must also be noted that Coon's article includes probably the first published reference to the Clash, as Mick Jones is quoted as saying of punk rock, "It's wonderfully vital." The Clash's private performance for the British press, which got the band their first published article, took place six days later, on August 13.

The Punk Special at the 100 Club

In retrospect, it has been called the Punk Festival, but flyers from the era call the two shows, staged on September 20 and 21, 1976, a "Punk Special." (McLaren was emulating a similarly staged rock festival at CBGB that presented thirty bands over six nights.) That these were Monday and Tuesday nights is a clear indication that "punk rock" was not yet the musical tsunami that would engulf the cliffs of Dover.

The opening night lineup featuring the Sex Pistols and the Clash outdrew the second night, no doubt due to the Pistols' notoriety. Tuesday night featured the Vibrators as headliners, burying the Damned and Buzzcocks, the two punk-rock bands on the bill. But not all attendees were drawn to punk rock because of the music. A fair number were drawn by how punk rock also encouraged a revolution in fashion, eventually influencing the

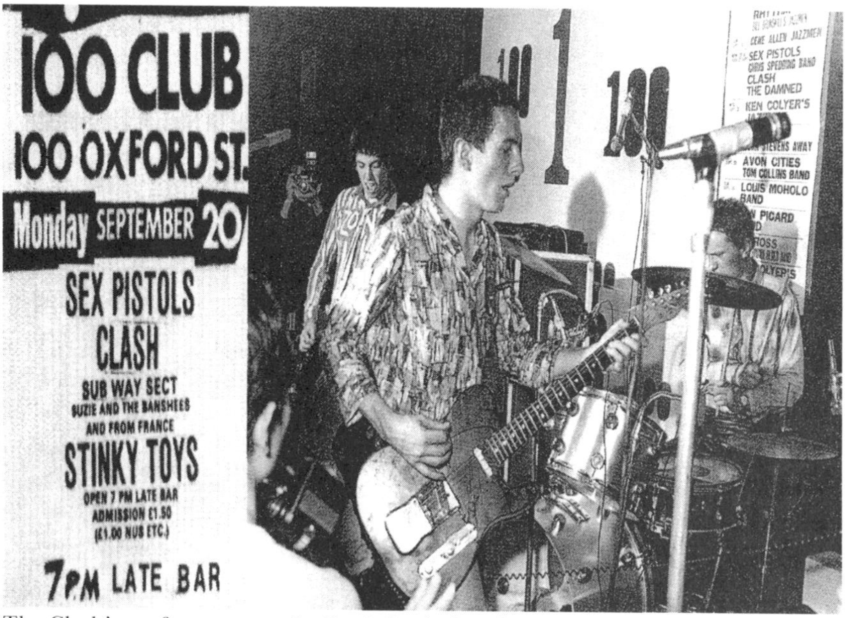

The Clash's performance at the Punk Festival at the 100 Club is one of their earliest bootlegged recordings. *Author's collection*

work of more mainstream designers. Part of this was the role that McLaren's SEX boutique played in the punk scene but attendees also brought their own DIY approach to what they wore to punk concerts, whether it be Soo Catwoman's distinctive feline hairstyle and handmade clothing or the buxom Jordan's wild bouffant and cubist makeup or Siouxsie Sioux's Nazi imagery. The stereotypical outfit of a punk rocker in a black leather jacket and Doc Marten boots—which the Clash did popularize—was not what attendees of the Punk Special wore. And, in fact, many of those initially attracted by the fashionable freedom punk rock espoused dropped out of the scene when it became a national fad.

But I digress. The second night was also marred by Sid Vicious (more noted at this point for having invented the "pogo" than being the infamous Sex Pistols bassist or alleged murderer of his girlfriend) expressing his disapproval of the Damned by throwing a glass at the stage; the glass shattered, and splinters from it struck a young woman in her eye. *Sounds* staff writer Giovanni Dadomo was so dismayed at the violence he witnessed that evening that he wrote, echoing John Lennon's "Revolution," that "if all the indignation about the mess the world's in only results in some poor chick getting her eye chopped up then count me out." But he did also give his "apologies therefore to all the people who played good rock 'n' roll those two nights (and I'd include the Pistols alongside Chris Spedding, the Vibrators, Damned and Clash)."

The Clash's performance was their first without lead guitarist Keith Levene, who had been sacked in an act of "Year One" punk purity less than a fortnight earlier. (He was deemed not sufficiently committed and therefore disruptive to the band's cohesion.) Caroline Coon's review noted that the Clash "pitched like rockets" and "are a fine, visionary rock band with a wild style . . . their humour and spontaneity is uncontrived and, now that they've settled into their new line-up, they'll be a cornerstone for the developing punk rock scene."

In retrospect, it's insightful that Coon took note of the Clash's humor—a psychological quality the Sex Pistols lacked. Still, at the Punk Special—staged in part by McLaren so that the Sex Pistols would be signed to a lucrative major-label record contract—the Sex Pistols were clearly at their peak. Matlock's melodic basslines locked in with Cook's beats, creating a sonic bedrock for Jones's layered rhythm notes and Rotten's braying vocals. Dressed in black bondage gear with swaying crucifixes, Rotten had put the finishing touches on his persona. He was more than just a riveting figurehead for the punk movement—he was a talented vocalist tongued with barb-wired wit. The rampant thirteen-song set began with "Anarchy in the UK" and ended with a version of the Stooges' "No Fun." "Anarchy" was revived for a one-song encore.

As attendee Michelle Brigandage wrote decades later, on a Sex Pistols website, of seeing Johnny Rotten, "I practically fell to my knees—it was like a religious experience—here was someone who understood what I was feeling inside—we no longer felt alone—we were individuals but with others, not some mindless gang, but a group of people who had found their way home."

And the Sex Pistols had found the first record company willing to take a chance with them. The four members of the band signed a management contract with McLaren the same day they played the 100 Club and signed with EMI—home of the Beatles back catalogue—on October 8, 1976, unknowingly setting in motion the events that would produce the rousing closing track on their debut album, *Never Mind the Bollocks, Here's the Sex Pistols*, recorded for another company.

The Anarchy in the UK Tour

Four of the Clash's first five concerts were in support of the Sex Pistols, but after the September "Punk Special," the bands largely went their separate ways for the next two months. The Sex Pistols played eighteen dates and had their initial recording sessions, while over the course of sixteen concerts the Clash refined their act as a four-piece.

"The Clash taking the stage was like an injection of electricity into the smoky air," Kris Needs wrote in *ZigZag* of the October 9 concert at Tiddenfoot Leisure Centre. "They charged headlong into 'White Riot' with shattering energy, strutting and leaping like clockwork robots out of control. They never let up for half an hour."

"White Riot" was to become a lightning rod even between members of the Clash but during this tour almost all surviving reviews mention the punk classic. For example, as John Ingham wrote of the October 27 show at Barbarella's in Birmingham, "'White Riot' was superb. The Clash's anthem . . . contains all the Clash's best trademarks: great hooks and chorus, a storming rhythm, and a Clash trick of everything dropping out except for Mick Jones's guitar, dropping back in two bars later behind a thundering crack from Terry Chimes's baseball bat sized drumsticks."

Terry Chimes's formative role in the Clash, as acknowledged in the above press clipping, has been diminished by innuendoes spread after he unexpectedly informed Joe, Mick, Paul, and Bernie of his intention to leave the band. The Clash disparaged Chimes by saying he was too materialistic and lacked the proper militant worldview essential to members of the band. In reality, Chimes was wearying of Bernie's mind-melding tactics and the Clash's own fascistic mindset during their "Year Zero." And so the November 29 concert at Lanchester Polytechnic in Coventry, when the Clash supported the Sex Pistols for the fifth time, was Chimes's last public appearance with Joe, Mick, and Paul until May 29, 1982.

The band scurried for a replacement drummer to ensure their first nationwide tour in support of the Sex Pistols, due to begin two days later in Dundee. Despite being relegated to the opening act on a four-act bill, the Clash wanted to be part of the first "punk" package traveling through Great Britain. The other two acts were to be the Damned—second billed due to the fact that they had released "New Rose," the so-called first punk single—and former New York Dolls guitarist Johnny Thunders with his new band, the Heartbreakers.

The Pistols' debut single, "Anarchy in the UK," was decimating the charts, and they were planning on promoting the single throughout December and generating Christmas sales when their December 1 television appearance on *Today*, a live program featuring Bill Grundy, set the nation's Christmas trees aflame. Reportedly the most requested television clip from

Thames Television (part of the British ITV network), the appearance saw the Sex Pistols and members of their entourage (including a pre-fame Siouxsie Sioux) unintentionally shock the nation when they were booked as a last-minute replacement for Queen.

Grundy, whose television career was jumpstarted by broadcasting the Beatles before anyone else, was inebriated when he sat down to the left of the Sex Pistols and friends. He began his interview by telling his viewers that the Sex Pistols are "the new craze, they tell me. Their heroes? Not the nice, clean Rolling Stones . . . you see they are as drunk as I am . . . they are clean by comparison." After a clip of the Sex Pistols in performance, the unimpressed moderator taunted the Pistols over their musical ability and flirted with Sioux, prompting Steve Jones to defend her honor by calling Grundy a "dirty old man." With five seconds left to the broadcast, Grundy goaded Jones, telling him to "say something outrageous." And so Jones, escalating his foul wit, went on to make his second legendary quote by saying of Grundy, "What a fucking rotter."

That did it. Grundy's career was over, and the Sex Pistols became the nightmare of a nation when the British press made Jones's comments front-page news. Grundy was suspended for two weeks over "sloppy journalism" and, as the *Guardian* reported, "a tour arranged by Rank Leisure Services" was canceled. "They . . . did not wish to be associated with the punk rock group's type of stage presentation."

"It put Punk on the map," Joe recalled in the Clash's 2008 coffee-table autobiography.

"It always seemed to be night time on that tour," Paul added. "I think that was because we'd drive somewhere to play a gig and it would be cancelled, so we'd drive on to the next place. I remember being in a room constantly with the Pistols, waiting for sandwiches to turn up, or beers or whatever."

It wasn't until December 6, on what supposed to be the fourth date of the tour, that a concert was actually staged. By now the Damned had been relegated to opening act because Bernie insisted his band was better. There was dissension in the ranks anyway, because when the city fathers of Derby had offered to let the other bands play without the Sex Pistols, the Damned were the only act willing to do so, therefore severing the punk solidarity even the out-of-town Heartbreakers seemed to share. The Damned were kicked off the tour before the second concert was held at the Electric Circus in Manchester on December 9. The Buzzcocks opened in their stead.

Of the twenty-five scheduled or rescheduled dates, only eight went ahead, and half of these dates were in the final week around the holidays.

The tour took a toll on the Sex Pistols. Although they were not household names, it was the Clash stealing the shows. In Manchester, the Clash "was probably the best received band of the evening," according to *Sounds* staffer Pete Silverton. Of the December 14 show in Wales, a fan named Dave Smitham remembered, "The band launch immediately into an abrasive thrash of noise with lyrics barked like angry dogs. I never caught a single lyric in their twenty minute set, but what a rush. . . ."

The Clash and the Sex Pistols never shared the same stage again. The rivalry between the bands' managers affected the musicians. Their career trajectories differed as well. EMI dropped the Sex Pistols, while the Clash signed with CBS. Both bands lost members, but while new drummer Nicky Headon's jazz and soul roots offered the Clash new directions in their music, Sid Vicious's only contribution, when he replaced bassist Glen Matlock, was "image." This was—and remains—a powerful element in the Sex Pistols' appeal—and Sid has gone on to supplant Johnny as the face of British punk rock—but Matlock was an important contributor to the band's songs. (Joe later compared Matlock's knack for melody to that of Paul McCartney.) The songs Sid Vicious is partially credited with (i.e., "Holidays in the Sun," "Bodies," and "Belsun Was a Gas") reek of Nazism and violence.

And while the members of the Clash bonded, the Sex Pistols splintered. It may have been Steve Jones who offended a nation but it was Johnny Rotten—the one with the more colorful name—who bore the brunt of the backlash. This what Joe was getting at when he said in that interview with Peter Silverton that "you can't really compare me and [Johnny] because he went through the whole heavy thing." Suddenly Johnny Rotten was front-page news for Great Britain's many tabloids, held up in editorials as an example of what was wrong with England's youth. He was viciously attacked by Teddy Boys and largely abandoned by his manager. It's no wonder that he quit in San Francisco following the Sex Pistols' only American tour in January 1978. As he left the Winterland Ballroom stage after performing the Stooges' "No Fun," he asked the audience, "Ever get the feeling you've been cheated?" He was expressing how he felt about the whole experience of being a Sex Pistol.

Johnny returned to England and "lock[ed] himself away in a house." Paul was invited to bring his bass over. Paul only saw it as helping a friend get through a transition period, but in reality Johnny was on the lookout for a bassist for the band that would become Public Image Ltd. Johnny thought Paul's reggae roots would mesh with the music he was plotting. He was probably encouraged by former Clash guitarist Keith Levene, who was already onboard, but the spot eventually went to another self-made bassist named John "Jah" Wobble.

Sid Vicious

The Sex Pistols carried on for a time with the idea of Sid Vicious as their front man—an idea that surprisingly the heroin addicted Sid Vicious did not want any part of. Sid was in a downward spiral that saddened his friends, many of whom were in the Clash. There's a short clip of a pink-faced John Simon Ritchie in Julien Temple's documentary *The Clash: New Year's Day 1977* before he morphed into Sid Vicious that gives you a glimpse of the teenaged youth they all liked. (Sid's stage name was coined when he said "Sid is really vicious!" after his friend Johnny's pet rat bit him.)

Joe remembered meeting Sid on the night he saw the Sex Pistols for the first time at the Nashville Rooms. Sid wasn't a Sex Pistol yet—he was just a member of their entourage—but Joe told him he liked the gold lamé jacket he was wearing. It was of the type Elvis Presley wore on the cover of *50,000,000 Elvis Fans Can't Be Wrong*. Joe was shocked when, instead of giving a wiseass answer, Sid enthusiastically told the 101'ers' front man that he'd gotten the jacket at Kensington Market. The two became friends, as did Sid and the other members of the Clash.

Keith Levene was already a friend of Sid's. They had squatted in the same abandoned house and played together in the Flowers of Romance. In recent interviews, Keith has forcefully defended Sid, noting his friendly demeanor before the public taunted him into living up to his punk image. Sid was also the original drummer in the earliest lineup of Siouxsie and the Banshees. Despite his little musical ability, he had undeniable charisma and a bracing sense of style; he was unwittingly working his way up the punk rungs to a place onstage next to punk's figurehead.

In the interim, Sid could often be found in the Clash's audience, and he even helped Joe and Paul fight unruly members of the crowd at the November 5 concert at the Royal College of Art while Mick stayed onstage and in tune. By early 1977, he was often in attendance at Rehearsal Rehearsals, the Clash's home base. Paul and Sid were tight friends, bonded by a common interest in punk fashion and the occasional petty theft. Members of the Clash even appeared in court on Sid's behalf and supported his contention that he had played no role in the thrown glass at the Punk Special.

After the Sex Pistols' implosion and Sid and his girlfriend Nancy Spungen's relocation to New York City, the Clash's second drummer, Nicky "Topper" Headon, moved into Sid's vacated flat, which he found splattered with blood. Barry "The Baker" Auguste, the band's drum technician between 1976 and 1983, quickly noted the ominous symbolism to the drummer whose own after-show partying would one day get out of hand. Later that same month, while in New York City putting the finishing touches on *Give 'Em Enough Rope,* Mick—with Joe's encouragement—agreed to played guitar with Sid's pickup band of former New York Dolls and Heartbreakers for a poorly attended gig at Max's Kansas City. Nancy was murdered in the Chelsea Hotel three weeks later. Sid maintained his innocence, and the Clash must have believed him because they headlined a benefit concert for the Sid Vicious Defense Fund at the Music Machine on December 19, 1978. No tape of this performance exists, but they allegedly played an instrumental version of Sid's last single, "My Way." "We were the only ones who stuck up for [Sid] when it all happened in New York," Mick told *Sabotage Times* in 2011.

Sid soon followed Nancy by overdosing on heroin at the Chelsea Hotel on February 2, 1979, just as the Clash were beginning their first American tour. His death greatly upset Joe and Paul and drove home the point that the Clash truly were the last of the original UK punk bands still standing.

4

Are You Taking Over or Are You Taking Orders?

"White Riot"

The square silver sticker with a blue box stating "IGNORE ALIEN ORDERS" in red lettering on Joe Strummer's Fender Telecaster above and mostly behind the guitar's bridge is as iconic to Clash fans as the image of the Notting Hill Riots on the back cover of the debut album. Strummer acquired the guitar while fronting the 101'ers. Though it was originally sunburst-colored, Strummer had the instrument coated with gray primer and automobile paint during the band's Jackson Pollock phase of stage gear. Although he could easily have upgraded guitars after signing with CBS Records, this is the guitar he primarily played for the next quarter-century, including his final tour in November 2002. By then, the Fender was quite weathered, but that sticker had survived all of Joe's lightning strums. For some fans, seeing "IGNORE ALIEN ORDERS" flashing behind the man's strumming forearm always reminded them of the closing verse on the Clash's first single, the punk classic "White Riot."

The Notting Hill Carnival Riot of 1976

The date is August 30, 1976. The Clash have played two public concerts thus far. Tomorrow night they open for the Sex Pistols at the 100 Club. Now, on a night off, Joe, Paul, and Bernie attend the Notting Hill Carnival—celebrating its tenth year—which has its starting point at Emslie Horniman's Pleasance, a park in Ladbroke Grove, near the Clash's Rehearsal Rehearsals base.

The Notting Hill Carnival promotes cultural unity—an objective the Clash will similarly embrace. Tonight, however, there is tension in the air that the sound of calypso music cannot dissipate, possibly as a result of the significant white police presence in what is a black part of London. The police have been accused of abusing the "SUS" (suspected person) law, found in section 4 of the Vagrancy Act 1824, which permits officers to stop any person they suspect of criminal activity or intent. This also grants them the power to search and arrest at will. The black community has grown upset at this practice and is particularly unhappy at the sight of thousands of policemen at the carnival. Into this environment walk Joe, Paul, and Bernie. The riot that inspires their punk classic begins soon after.

The cause of the riot is unknown, but it is said to have begun with the arrest of an alleged pickpocket. When bystanders made their disapproval known both vocally and by throwing empty beer cans, police officers charged at them. According to a BBC news report, "Windows were smashed, fires were lit and ill-equipped police officers picked up dustbin lids and milk crates to charge the rioters. More than 100 officers and 60 other people were taken to hospital." During the melee, Joe and Paul were separated from Bernie.

Paul, who came from this same neighborhood, immediately started throwing bricks as well. Joe is said to have disappeared into the Elgin, a pub the 101'ers had often played at; after being fortified with some of the proprietor's product, he went back out and found Paul. The two Clash members attempted to set alight an overturned automobile, but without success. Joe and Paul were then confronted by a group of young black men, and things got heated when Joe refused to give them the transistor radio he was carrying. They were only spared injury when one of the neighborhood leaders told the band of black youths to leave Joe and Paul alone.

"We participated in the riot," Joe said afterward, "but I was aware all the time that this was a black man's riot." Bernie had been advising Joe and the others to write about their own first-hand experiences, and here was ideal subject matter. One of the most overt themes of the Clash's earliest material was the suppressed lifestyles of London's white youth. Black youth—according to Joe at least—had had the nerve to strike back at the government. He would write a song urging white youth to do the same. The universal appeal comes from the fact that Joe doesn't reference the Notting Hill Carnival Riot in his lyrics.

"White Riot" (Single Version)

Appropriately enough for a band whose songs would often take umbrage at police actions, the single version of "White Riot" begins with the sound of an approaching siren as a police car responds to a riot. Then the band leaps in, the rubbery bassline pogoing madly before settling into a walking pattern, almost carrying a melody as the other musicians thrash about in riotous abandon. It has been rumored—and denied—that Paul did not play the bass at the sessions resulting in the debut album and single, but this is one instance where it appears Mick *did* overdub the bassline, a prominent feature in the 45 mix. The walking pattern adds drama when Joe shouts out how the poor white oppressed masses "walk the street too chicken to even" riot.

This version was cut on January 28, 1977, during one of the weekend recording sessions that resulted in the Clash's debut album. Other characteristics of this version include Mick's guitar struggling to be heard in the cacophonous rhythm, submerged Strummer vocals, and stomping . . . lots of stomping,

The Clash's first single, "White Riot," was released on March 18, 1977. *Author's collection*

courtesy of the footwork of the band's entourage, including the roadie Steve Connolly (better known as "Roadent") and Sebastian Conran. There are other sound effects as well, including breaking glass and a fire alarm.

The single was released on March 18, 1977, the cover featuring a black-and-white photo of Joe, Mick, and Paul in stenciled clothing with their hands up against a wall. This concept is similar to the artwork from *State of Emergency*, a 1976 album released by Joe Gibbs and the Professionals. (Born Joel A. Gibson, Gibbs was a Jamaican reggae producer along the lines of Lee "Scratch" Perry, who worked with many of the era's most important reggae recording artists, including two name-checked on Clash 45s: Delroy Wilson and Prince Far I.) But whereas the Clash have often acknowledged the influence of Jamaican artwork, Paul Simonon has said he didn't remember seeing the Gibbs cover before taking the photo used as the cover of "White Riot."

NME's "Singles" section led with a review of the Clash's first release and made clear this was obviously an important 45: "'White Riot' isn't a poxy single of the week, it's the first meaningful event of the year." Caroline Coon was noticeably cooler in *Sounds*, writing, "The overall sound is a little safe and the lyrics between verses are sadly unintelligible." Even so, she predicted hit status.

Frequent Clash concert attendee and future Pogues vocalist Shane McGowan wrote of the "White Riot" single in the *Singles Box* booklet, "All the Clash singles come down to 'White Riot.' It was the first single, it wasn't on the album, it's got '1977' on the B-side and I'll always remember the day I bought it—which was the day it came out. It was March '77 and you could really see that the party was already over."

The recording peaked at #34 on the UK charts. Recording engineer Simon Humphrey told *Sound on Sound* in 2013 that "no one was more amazed than [CBS, the band's label]. It had no idea what it had unleashed at that point."

"White Riot" (Original Album Version)

Three weeks after the single surged up the charts, *The Clash* was released with a new take on "White Riot" as the album's fourth track. Disappointed with the version recorded at CBS Studios, the Clash reached back for an 8-track recording they had made at the National Film and Television School in Beaconsfield in November 1976, when student and future director Julien Temple offered to film the as-yet-unsigned band.

There are notable differences. First, the police siren is replaced with Mick Jones counting off "1-2-3-4!," and the other sound effects do not appear either. Joe's vocals are pushed forward in the mix, as is Mick's guitar track, which now snarls around Paul's bassline. Most notably, Strummer's classic line asking the listener "Are you going backwards or are you going forwards?" is substituted with: "Yeah, and instead of all that, all we get is someday maybe."

The White Riot Tour

The Clash's first tour as headliners was christened after their single, and henceforth every tour would have a name associated with it. This tour began on May 1, 1977, at the Civic Hall in Guildford, a Surrey town draped in English history. The tour spanned the entire month, with the Clash playing virtually every single day as they raced through England and dipped into Amsterdam for the legendary concert referenced in "Complete Control," arguably their greatest punk rock song.

This was Topper Headon's first tour with the Clash. Supporting acts included Buzzcocks, the Jam, the Prefects, the Slits, and Subway Sect. The Jam were on the bill for the first nine shows but quit shortly after punk rockers in the UK trashed the seats inside the Rainbow in London. (It was never clear why the Jam left the tour, although there were rumors they were unhappy with the lighting they were getting during sets.) Total damages were £28,000. It was, in Joe Strummer's memory, the Clash's finest hour.

And it probably was an hour, because the set was comprised of songs from the Clash's debut album, the "White Riot" single, and an NME flexi-disc. A band's mindset is best reflected in their set list, and for this reason throughout this tome I will present the standard set list for each tour. What was notable about the White Riot tour is that the Clash would sometimes play "1977" twice each night. After the year ended, the song was never played again, except during soundchecks.

As with Clash performances, there were variations—for example, during the first dates, "Pressure Drop" was played early in the set—but the following is the latest known set during the White Riot tour. Typically, the Clash's sets hardened toward the end of a tour, as if they had sharpened it like a diamond, the best they could give their fans:

1. "1977"
2. "I'm So Bored with the USA"
3. "Hate and War"

4. "48 Hours"
5. "Deny"
6. "Police and Thieves"
7. "Capital Radio"
8. "Cheat"
9. "Protex Blue"
10. "Pressure Drop"
11. "Remote Control"
12. "Career Opportunities"
13. "Janie Jones"
14. "White Riot"
15. "What's My Name"
16. "Garageland"
17. "1977"

Presumably the set ended with "White Riot" and the last three numbers, including the second airing of "1977," were the encore.

The Controversial Content of "White Riot"

"White Riot" was soon misconstrued as promoting the political views of white supremacists and racism. This was a ripe concern in Great Britain in 1976. The National Front—a white nationalist, far-right political party founded in 1967—had recently won nearly 20 percent of the local vote in Leicester. A few music journalists were worried that, with "White Riot," the Clash were aligning themselves with the racist views of the National Front and supporting its opposition to non-white immigration and the repatriation of non-whites living in Britain.

In December 1976—even before the song had been released—Joe and Mick were defending themselves in an *NME* interview with staff writer Barry Miles. Joe offered this defense: "Primarily we gotta be concerned with young white kids because that's what we are. But we ain't nothing like racist, NO WAY."

Actions speak louder than words, of course, and the Clash's anti-racist rhetoric was substantiated by their appearance at the 1978 Rock Against Racism event in Victoria Park, a hotbed of National Front activity. (A clip of their performance before an estimated crowd of 80,000 can be seen in the movie *Rude Boy*.) Over time, the Clash's absorption of black musical genres such as reggae, hip hop, and funk into their songbook persuaded the press that the Clash were not and never had been advocating a white nationalist state.

"Joe wanted to challenge people, he wanted to force people to think," road manager Johnny Green told biographer Pat Gilbert. "He wasn't scared of getting people to confront (racist ideas and language), however uncomfortable it would make them feel. He wanted people to work it out for themselves."

The song, however, had ramifications within the band. "White Riot" convinced guitarist Keith Levene that Joe's agitprop lyrics would have a dominant role in future Clash material and, if so, the Clash was not a band he wanted to be in. Joe wasn't pleased with Keith's dwindling commitment to the band anyway, and he used Keith's reluctance to play on "White Riot" as a reason for sacking him (as discussed in more detail in chapter 5).

Mick Jones also took issue with the lyrics to "White Riot," but not because they were racist. He knew they were not. He had been as forceful as Joe in the aforementioned interview with Barry Miles in insisting "White Riot" was being misunderstood: "We're completely antiracist, we want to bridge the gap. They used to blame everything on the Jews, now they're saying it about the Blacks and the Asians . . . everybody's a scapegoat, right?" What Mick objected to, however, was the song's call for a violent resolution to the problem.

Mick also increasingly believed the song was the instigator of unnecessary violence at Clash concerts. This may have been the cause of the only

The Acton benefit concert was quickly bootlegged because of Mick's surprise guest appearance during the three-song encore. That's Tymon Dogg standing between Mick and Joe. *Author's collection*

punch-up between band members. On January 27, 1980, at the Top Rank in Sheffield, just as the band were about to go out for their second encore, Mick suddenly announced he wasn't playing "White Riot." With no time to talk it out, and probably wired from the concert performance, Joe struck Mick in the mouth. With blood everywhere, Mick was bandaged up; the Clash retook the stage, but halfway through the song, Mick dropped his Gibson and walked off the stage. "White Riot" was rarely played by the Clash afterward.

Shoot forward twenty-two years and Joe Strummer and the Mescaleros are playing Acton Town Hall on November 15, 2002, at a benefit for the Fire Brigades Union. Mick Jones is in attendance, celebrating the birth of his second daughter. When the Mescaleros take the stage for their encore, they begin with "Bankrobber," a song that was not included in the handwritten set list, and Mick impulsively joins them. Joe and Mick have not shared a stage for nearly nineteen and a half years.

They play a long version that stretches to almost nine minutes. The next song on the set list is "A Message to You, Rudy" but Joe—as if having the last word in a long-running argument—turns to Mick and says, "You know this one. It's in A." Mick smiles and joins Joe and the Mescaleros in bashing out "White Riot."

Joe Strummer died thirty-seven days afterward.

There's Five Guitar Players but One Guitar

Keith Levene, the Original Third Guitarist

In the earliest written accounts of the Clash, Keith Levene is often labeled the "original third guitarist" who has left the band under mysterious circumstances. With Stalinist vigor he was being written out of a history that might not have been, had he not been present. Levene had been the second musician to offer his loyalty to Mick's as-yet-unnamed musical enterprise. He was playing guitar alongside "Rock 'n' Roll Mick" before art student Paul undertook an apprenticeship on bass or no-nonsense Terry auditioned to be the drummer.

In addition, it was Keith who aggressively took action and persuaded the singer in one of London's most popular pub bands that abandoning playing "Telecaster rock" for a lead role in whatever the Sex Pistols were stirring up was the right artistic choice. That Levene went on to play nursemaid to the Slits and the Red Hot Chili Peppers, as well as having a central creative role in Public Image Ltd. (PiL) with John Lydon, makes you wonder what the Clash would've sounded like, had he remained onboard as the band's original lead guitarist, which is how he should have been identified in those early written accounts.

Roundabout

Julien Keith Levene was born in Wood Green, London, on July 18, 1957, making him the youngest member of the Clash. Growing up in Southgate, which despite its name was in northern London, he was obsessed with music from an early age—so obsessed that when his mother found him one day staring endlessly at a vinyl record going round and round on a turntable she took him to see a doctor; the doctor diagnosed Keith an orchestra conductor in the making. As with Mick and Terry, the Beatles were an early influence, but Keith never renounced them. He thought the line in "1977" about there being no Beatles in 1977 was ridiculous. In his fifties he was even often photographed in a brown T-shirt with a white Beatles logo, while once, when he was asked to name his ten favorite recordings, *Sgt. Pepper's Lonely Hearts Club Band* topped the list.

By eight years of age, Keith was working for a tailor. By fifteen, he was working in a factory and debating the merits of Yes over Humble Pie with co-workers. Sensing (as Joe was to say) that a factory is no place to waste one's youth, he took his admiration for Yes guitarist Steve Howe and talked

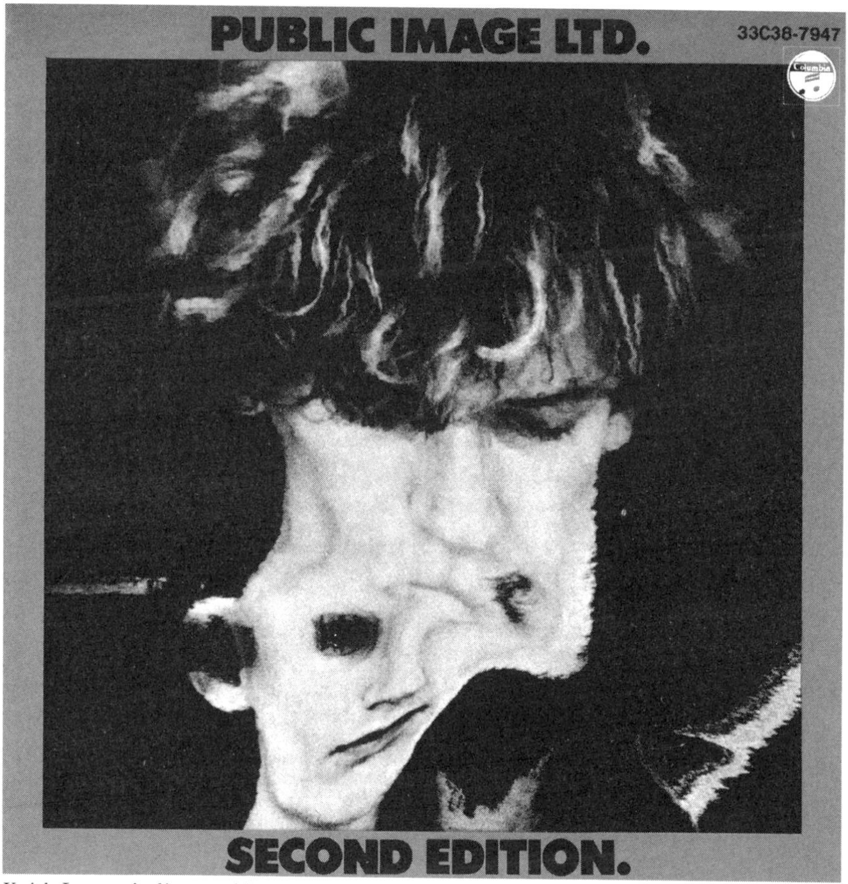

Keith Levene's distorted image graced the cover of PiL's *Second Edition*. It was the apex of his recording career.
Author's collection

his way into a job as a roadie for the band during part of their Tales from Topographic Oceans tour in 1973. When he inquired about being a roadie for Rick Wakeman's subsequent Journey to the Center of the Earth tour, however, Wakeman himself pointed out Keith was too busy asking questions about synthesizers and playing Yes's instruments to function effectively as a roadie. Wakeman explicitly called out Levene's true calling, telling him not to touch his "synths" and to form a band of his own—an idea that had never crossed Keith's mind previously. He went home, plugged in his copy of a Gibson SG and practiced daily in his room like Mick was doing in west London.

Keith Was a Teen Guitarist 4 the Clash

In 2014, Keith began issuing a series of books presenting a perspective on his days with the Clash—the polar opposite in tone of what he had been saying for almost thirty-five years. Co-written with Kathy DiTondo, the books were the result of "a ton of interviews . . . talking about the times, the people, the places and it was quite fucking heavy therapy" as Keith told *Louder Than Bombs*' Phil Singleton. For the first time, Keith presented a positive view of his role in the Clash's formation.

He was also more honest. For example, after decades insisting he should have received credit for writing *all* of the songs on the Clash's "lame" debut album—which never made sense because a few songs such as "Garageland" and "Remote Control" dated from after his departure—Keith now admitted he had received credit for the only song he contributed the chorus to: "What's My Name." He also came up with opening line. Of course, "What's My Name" is more metallic than any other Clash song except for "Workin' for the Clampdown"—especially the *Rude Boy* version—so you can hear Keith's strumming hand in it.

What follows is a digest of Keith's perspective of his eight or so months in the Clash.

It was Mick, he says, who introduced Keith to Bernie Rhodes. They had met previously through a mutual friend (Alan Drake) and even recorded together on future Roxy operator Barry Jones's 4-track reel-to-reel tape recorder. Because Keith played bass on that occasion, Mick mistook the north Londoner for a bassist, but Keith's turn on an acoustic guitar lying nearby one day corrected that impression. Mick was really pleased: Keith was the rare individual whose enthusiasm for music matched Mick's.

Bernie engaged Keith in the type of challenging conversation he was to become known for and agreed Keith was a good candidate for the new band's second guitarist. Bernie liked the young man's ideas. Keith, too, was fully onboard. "When I started out, all I knew is that I wanted to be in a band—that was my Clash phase," Keith told Jason Gross in 2001.

Terry Chimes has said Keith was the Clash's most dedicated member when they started out, having had endless discussions with Bernie about the band's direction. One thing Keith knew had to change was the singer, Billy Watts. Paul couldn't play bass, but he had the cheekbones, and Terry was reliable. Keith concurs with Terry's memory of the first singer Billy Watts as being a Jagger wanna-be. As he told Kathy DiTondo, "He was nice . . . a big guy . . . but all wrong for [the Clash]."

Luckily, Keith knew who could be the key to the band's future. "Joe Strummer looked good. He used to wear these mid-'50s rockabilly styles, baggy suits and crepes, and was pure white heat energy on stage. It was me that got Joe into the Clash when I stole him from the 101'ers," Keith said, in an interview with *3AM*'s Greg Whitfield. In his book *Meeting Joe: Joe Strummer, the Clash, and Me!*, Keith revises the myth of Joe's entry into the band. "I used to go to a lot of pubs to see bands. When the 101'ers came on your attention went straight to Joe." Keith could already see elements of Elvis Presley, Bruce Springsteen, and Johnny Cash in Joe. He reeked of American rhythm and blues. "Joe would have wanted to be at any given bus terminal in America with his sunburst guitar with five strings," he writes.

Mick and Paul and Bernie had all seen Joe strumming that sunburst guitar wildly at the Nashville Rooms the night the Sex Pistols went on before the 101'ers—the night that was an epiphany for Keith. "I opened the door . . . just as the fuckin' Pistols got going. My eyes looked forward. There stood one Johnny Rotten with a big snot rag in his hand," he remembers, in *I WaS a TeeN GuiTariST 4 the CLaSH!*, another of his books with Kathy DiTondo. In his memories of first seeing Johnny on the Nashville's stage, Joe also mentioned the snot rag because he too, like Keith, was having an epiphany—only Joe didn't know that, as his band the 101'ers rocked the stage after the Pistols, his performance also caught the attention of Mick's new bandmates and their manager. They conferred in their rehearsal studio: was there any way they could poach the 101'ers' front man for their band?

According to Keith, Mick was unsure if Joe was the right front man. He wanted someone "Bolan-esque." Perhaps this indifference explains why it was Keith—not Mick—who Bernie took along when the 101'ers were playing the Golden Lion Pub to make Joe an offer he could refuse.

Memories differ on what transpired next. According to Joe, Bernie met him outside the pub and gave him forty-eight hours to join this new band he was managing. Keith says that's just another myth. According to the future PiL guitarist, Keith and Bernie were in the Golden Pub after the 101'ers' set, milling about, when Bernie asked him if he's "going to do it, then?"

Keith had been the most strident about Joe Strummer being the right man for the job. A denizen of London's rock clubs, he had been on nodding terms with Joe well before Bernie ever saw him. Keith knew he should do it, then.

This sounds like something that manipulative Bernie would do. And calculating, too: wouldn't a young musician have a better chance than an older, balding man once mistaken for being an R&B piano thumper? This also strikes one as an incident that the Clash camp would erase once Keith was no longer a member and just an "original third guitarist."

Keith sidled up to Joe in the pub. The other 101'ers were nowhere to be found. He knew that asking Joe to leave his bandmates was a delicate matter. These were more than musicians he played with; the 101'ers were people he squatted with at 101 Walterton Road and considered friends. They were the only family Joe had in London. An offer from an acquaintance in a pub would not work. Keith instead invited Joe to the squat he was staying at on Davis Road.

When they met the following Saturday, according to Keith, he was brazen. Guiding Joe into the squat's home studio—a small walk-in closet—he picked up his guitar and began playing 101'ers numbers and saying audacious thing like "You're too old to be in the wrong band, Joe" while seducing the older man with his guitar playing. (As their *Elgin Street Breakdown* album attests, the 101'ers were competent, but no one in that bad could play a satisfying guitar solo.) Keith played better versions of Joe's songs than the 101'ers did and then previewed the Mick Jones songs the new band were kicking into shape. Joe was wavering. What Keith didn't know was that Johnny Rotten had gotten under Joe's skin, too.

"I'm facing him at close range, right in his face, and playing a bunch of tunes on my Les Paul Deluxe," Keith told Kathy DiTondo, in an interview printed in the *Mudkiss* fanzine. "I then played 'Keys to Your Heart,' one of Joe's songs, to him. That nailed it. He said he would join us."

Having coerced Joe into the fold, Keith focused on implementing other ideas for the unnamed band. It was, as Keith writes, "a dynamite situation where there would be no-holds-barred collaborations as far as the music was concerned or at least, that's what I thought was going on." Keith was successful in making the band play faster—seeing and hanging out with the Ramones at Dingwalls helped—but met turbulence in getting other ideas their fair shake—ideas that came to fruition in PiL. Bernie couldn't see where Keith's ideas about guitar synthesizers fit in. To the manager, it seemed "too *Doctor Who*." Metallic guitars didn't have a place either. The band was finding a "comfort zone"—fast versions of Mick's music with Joe's increasingly agitprop lyrics—that Keith was uncomfortable with.

Of course, you could see that as being Keith's high-tempo vision of Mick's music with Joe's lyrics, but the seventeen-year-old skateboarder did not. He admits today that perhaps he reacted rashly because of his young age. He was too impatient with not having his musical ideas listened to. Still, he hung in there, tolerating the band's name, which everyone else liked, because he knew he was in the best band on the burgeoning scene. Bernie had even found them an impressive three-story building that had previously belonged to British Railways that would be renamed Rehearsal Rehearsals and serve as the band's rehearsal space and center of their manager's varied operations. And he still got on well with Bernie, agreeing with him that the Clash shouldn't play every chance they got. A Clash concert should be an event. But for Keith, there would only be five of them.

The sequence of events Keith presents in his books does not hold up to research, but it does appear that the Clash's arrangement of "White Riot" was what caused him to throw the final brick. Following the riot at the Notting Hill Carnival, Joe wrote lyrics that Mick set to music. Turning up at Rehearsal Rehearsals, Keith found Joe alone and presented an alternative arrangement for "White Riot." Writing today that his concept was similar to PiL's "Theme," Keith recalls telling Joe that the music should sound like the riot he was singing about. Keith found Joe agreeable but was dismayed when "White Riot" was attempted at a subsequent rehearsal, with Keith's ideas for the song nowhere to be heard.

There's a difference of opinions over what happened next.

In Joe's version, as quoted in Jon Savage's *England's Dreaming*, "[Keith] rang up when we were doing 'White Riot,' and he said, 'What you working on? "White Riot"? Well, there's no need for me to come up then, is there?' I said, 'Make that never, man.'"

In Keith's version, as told to Greg Whitfield, "I'm late as usual. We plug in and start playing, and I remember Joe Strummer poking me in the arm and going, 'Look Keith, just what is wrong with you man, are you into this or not.' I'm not into it, so I just leave my guitar up against the amp, feedback howling back like mad, like white noise, and I just walk out."

In the version in his books, Keith leaves with his Mosrite Venture guitar feeding back, but only after a meeting in an office upstairs from the rehearsal room, where it is mutually agreed it is in everyone's best interests if he leaves the group.

Keith's books omit any reference to his speed habit, which he copped to in earlier interviews, and which some Clash insiders thought contributed to his becoming ostracized from the other band members. He does include his final appearance at the Roundhouse on September 5, 1976, however, writing that—like Terry Chimes afterward—he played the gig because he didn't want to let the band down, even though the decision had been made that he should go. Besides, the Clash were opening for the Patti Smith Group. Who'd want to miss that?

Except that never happened, historically. Yes, the Patti Smith Group played London's Roundhouse; they even played there in 1976, but that was on May 17. Joe wasn't even in the Clash yet. On September 5, Patti Smith and her Group were in New York State, where they occasionally played concerts. And while the Clash were in the Roundhouse, they were third on a bill with the Kursaal Flyers headlining. Keith's fifth and final performance with the Clash is preserved on the bootleg recording *5 Go Mad in the Roundhouse.*

"White Riot" had not yet made it into the set, which leads one to conclude the new song composed after the carnival riot on August 30 was not ready for the September 5 gig. Sometime soon after, Keith, unhappy with the new song's arrangement, either quit or was pushed out. "White Riot" debuted on September 20—the first concert without Keith in the lineup—and was the opening number. "White Riot" was a song Joe Strummer felt strongly about. It could certainly be the song causing a riot within the band. Didn't Mick eventually rebel against it, too?

Careering

Joe may have stenciled "HEAVY MANNERS" after Prince Far I's album title onto his black boiler suit, but it was Keith who played with the Jamaican reggae DJ during his long and winding recording career following his departure from the Clash. Reggae and dub and old Blue Beat records had seeped into him as much as anyone on the British punk scene, and they were instrumental in the role he played nurturing the musical career of Viv Albertine, his squat mate at David Road, and the Slits, the first formidable girl group to emerge from punk rock. The Slits beat the Police in rooting their sound in reggae. Their debut album, *Cut*, was voted #58 on a list of the 100 greatest British albums in 2011 in the *Observer*, and even Keith will admit that the opening track, "Instant Hit," was about Keith and his friends and their drug addictions.

After the Clash, Keith played with the Quickspurts and then had a dalliance with Sid Vicious in the Flowers of Romance. Like London SS before them, the Flowers of Romance never performed live but included many future punk rockers. The saxophone-playing Sid left to join the Sex Pistols, and Keith then played with Terry Chimes in the Ken Lockie–led Cowboys International before learning that Johnny Rotten—now the former lead singer of the Sex Pistols—was seeking him.

Flashing back to the Clash's very first concert at the Black Swan in Sheffield on July 4, 1976, Keith found himself looking at Johnny Rotten, sitting apart from the other Sex Pistols, and sensed the singer's isolation within his band was similar to his own within the Clash. Not one to leave an idea without acting on it, Keith approached Rotten, sarcastically told him "you look happy," and mentioned that if Rotten was ever looking to form a band after the Sex Pistols, Keith was interested.

Almost two years later, Johnny was ready to begin collaborating with Keith. Rehearsals began in May 1978 with Jah Wobble on bass and Canadian Jim Walker on drums, and the most rewarding musical period of Keith's career was underway. He was PiL's maestro: editing Wobble's basslines, turning dub into a post-punk art form, experimenting with guitar synthesizers and metallic guitars—ideas he couldn't bring to fruition with the Clash. Johnny Rotten reverted to John Lydon. PiL debuted with the classic single "Public Image." Drummers came and went—including Richard Dudanski from the 101'ers—as PiL put out *Public Image: First Edition*, the legendary *Metal Box* (three 45 rpm 12-inch records later repackaged as *Second Edition*), and a live album. Wobble left and PiL resolved this by issuing *The Flowers of Romance*, a mostly bass-less recording. You had to admire the impunity.

Sadly, the "bromance" between Keith and John wilted. The band had relocated to New York City in May 1981, just in time for Keith and John to turn up at several Clash concerts during the Bond's residency. Sessions for the band's fourth studio album, *Commercial Zone*, were hampered by contractual issues, lineup changes, and Keith's deepening heroin addiction. Keith left the band and John carried on with drummer Martin Atkins and session musicians. Keith stole back the master tapes, continued to work on the songs, and gave them to Virgin Records president Richard Branson, saying they were PiL's next album. Lydon, however, decided otherwise. He wanted to re-record the songs, and as Lydon was the band's figurehead, Virgin sided with him. Keith countered by releasing his mix of *Commercial Zone* in January 1984. An initial run of 10,000 copies quickly sold out. Lydon's version was the polarizing *This Is What You Want . . . This Is What You Get.*

It was now July 1984. A month later, Keith printed up another 30,000 copies of *Commercial Zone.* Virgin took legal action, and Keith was prevented from issuing further pressings. Keith headed west, to Los Angeles, where he worked with guitarist Hillel Slovak and bassist Flea, fledgling members of the Red Hot Chili Peppers. Over the decades, Keith has come to see himself as more of a composer than musician. He has worked with a varied array of recording artists, including Dub Syndicate, Glen Matlock, Mark Stewart, and Pigface.

As a final note, Keith waited thirty-eight years before recording "What's My Name." He released it as part of *Commercial Zone 2014* and on a four-song EP supplement to *Meeting Joe.* Fittingly, his version is an instrumental. He says in *Meeting Joe* that it wouldn't have been right with anyone's vocals but Joe's.

Now the Boys and Girls Are Not Alone

The Clash

The Clash's eponymous album is regularly included in "best of" lists of not only the best punk albums but also the best debut albums, alongside luminous works such as the Jimi Hendrix Experience's *Are You Experienced*, Guns N' Roses' *Appetite for Destruction*, and Arctic Monkeys' *Whatever People Say I Am, That's What I'm Not.* Not bad for a recording hurriedly made over three winter weekends by four studio novices, a musically challenged manager, a live sound engineer playing producer, and a company recording engineer only assigned to the sessions because he was the youngest CBS Records had on staff.

The Polydor Demos

The road to *The Clash* began in mid-November 1976. In between concert dates, the four band members found themselves in Polydor Records' Marble Arch Studios, recording five songs in hopes of landing a recording contract. Record companies were anxiously pursuing punk bands, moving quickly to sign, record, and release punk music before the fad faded . . . because they viewed the grassroots movement emerging from London's tower blocks as having as much staying power as glam rock had had a few years earlier (which is to say not much: glam only produced one worldwide star, David Bowie). The Clash were also anxious to release records before the other bands featured at the 100 Club Special could. They knew the Sex Pistols had already signed with EMI; even more worrisome was that the Damned had released "New Rose," the so-called first punk single, on Stiff Records on October 22.

The handpicked producer was a legend whose best days were behind him. Guy Stevens's bio can be found in chapter 14, but through the first two-thirds of the Clash's existence he was a specter—a ghost from British rock 'n' roll's past glories—materializing at odd moments. He may have orchestrated Mick Jones's exit from Little Queenie the previous year, but this did not prevent Bernie from selecting Stevens as the producer for the session. Bernie knew how Stevens had helped the Small Faces and the Who during their formative years with his industry connections and musical suggestions. Working with Polydor recording engineer Vic Smith and A&R man Chris Parry, he believed Stevens could do the same for the Clash.

"It was great recording with Guy Stevens . . . fantastic when we were doing it," Mick told *ZigZag*'s Kris Needs in April 1977. "He was really inciting us, but when it came down to the mixing, it was a bit untogether." Stevens had begun his descent into alcoholism, and his ideas did not mesh with the Jam's future production team. Joe was instructed to carefully enunciate syllables, thereby removing his bite from the lyrics. The band members were disappointed when they heard the playback: was this what they really sounded like? Joe thought the demos were "flat and dull." It certainly wasn't punk rock.

Given this reaction, it's somewhat surprising that all five tracks are preserved for posterity on *Sound System*'s *Bonus Disc 3* (with incorrect session dates), but this at least allows fans to make up their own minds about how the demo session went. The five tracks are "Janie Jones," "Career Opportunities," "London's Burning," "1977," and "White Riot." The biggest drawback is the tightened tempo. Not only is Joe carefully enunciating, so too are musicians. For example, "Janie Jones" is so evenly paced that it lacks its natural bounce. Twice in the song the bassline hops for a high note—it's a hidden highlight—but at Polydor it's just a carefully played note lacking any rock 'n' roll spark. The band's humor is also absent. All those Strummer asides worthy of Hendrix (such as "Fill 'er up, Jacko") are missing. Even the drums on "Career Opportunities" forget to knock. It's telling when the funniest thing about the Polydor demos is Joe singing "London's burning with boredom, *babe*."

Not their finest minutes.

"We Were Never Your Toy to Begin With"

And yet they were still in the running to be signed by Polydor Records in January 1977. Having had the Sex Pistols snatched out his grasp by EMI, Chris Parry was determined to sign the Clash. His offer even matched that of EMI to the Sex Pistols: a £40,000 advance. But unbeknown to Parry, CBS Records was looking to cash in on the new musical craze sweeping Great

Britain and made an offer of £100,000. Despite the stories spread thereafter, it wasn't Bernie's decision. When the band learned an offer was on the table that exceeded what any of the competition was getting, Mick spoke up and said they'd sign with CBS.

This signing, on January 27, 1977, resulted in the DIY fanzine *Sniffin' Glue*'s founding member Mark Perry writing, "Punk died the day the Clash signed to CBS." (In reality, British punk rock never recovered from the self-inflicted wounds made during the Sex Pistols' infamous interview on *Tomorrow* with Bill Grundy.) While still being complimentary of *Sniffin' Glue* and Perry's faith in the DIY punk-rock work ethic, Joe later noted in *Westway to the World*, "I remember thinking, 'But we were never your toy to begin with.'"

The fact is the Clash were being held to higher standard. The Sex Pistols had signed with the Beatles' former label, and the Damned's label, Stiff Records, had a distribution deal with Island Records. If bands such as Buzzcocks were releasing records on their own, it's because they had not been approached by a major label. Like most musicians—and perhaps even more so with the Clash—they wanted their music heard so desperately that they signed to CBS without considering the consequences. They later presented the label's worldwide distribution as motivation, but this was unlikely. In January 1977, they were simply focused on keeping pace with the other punk acts.

It was, however, a bad deal for the Clash.

"We took a hundred grand and that brought the Clash to the attention of the people; we invested it in that," Joe told *Melody Maker*'s Paolo Hewitt in December 1980. "Yet it wasn't our hundred grand; we had to pay them back, and that meant we were fucked."

It seems that nobody explained to Joe or the others that the £100,000 was an advance that had to be recouped by CBS before new pounds flowed into the Clash's bank accounts. In addition, neither Bernie nor CBS Records UK chairman Maurice Oberstein had shown the Clash the fine print in the five-record contract where it said CBS had the right to exercise an option for five more albums.

The Whitfield Studios Recording Sessions

If the Clash were wary of making a punk rock album at a corporate label's recording studio—CBS Studios at 31–37 Whitfield Street—the apprehensions of the band members were mollified when they learned the building they found themselves standing in had also been used by Iggy and the

Stooges for the Bowie-produced punk classic *Raw Power.* Perhaps inspired by this, the resulting recording was the rawest and most powerful the Clash ever released.

Sessions were scheduled for Thursday through Sunday for three consecutive weekends, beginning on February 10, 1977. The plan was to have the first single released in mid-March, with the album following four-to-six weeks after the final session. With the band having not yet found a suitable replacement, original drummer Terry Chimes kindly agreed to temporarily return and sit behind the kit. "I didn't want to ruin everything because if I had walked out it would have damaged the progress at a crucial time," he told *Guardian* reporter Herpreet Kaur Grewal in early 2014. For this act of maturity, Terry was rewarded by being named "Tory Crimes" on the album's back cover and badmouthed in the press.

Studio 3 was located at the top of the building. "Without a doubt, the Clash were very deliberately booked into there," remembered Simon Humphrey, the recording engineer. "The record company wanted them out of the way, four floors up, where those unruly punks couldn't cause any trouble." Except with Humphrey, that is.

Humphrey remembered Paul as being reluctant to talk, Terry having to be told what to drum, and Joe and Mick constantly reworking lyrics in the studio. This was especially true of the band's newest song, "Garageland." When it was obvious the running time of the album was going to be under thirty minutes, Mick worked up a six-minute arrangement of Junior Marvin's "Police and Thieves" that hinted at new directions in music for the band. Mick was the musician most interested in the possibilities that double-tracking guitars might have in enriching the sound. This was important because Joe's guitar was so tinny sounding and needed to be camouflaged, if used at all.

"I was only interested in recording them the way they wanted to be: the truth of how they sounded and what they wanted to be, in the raw," Humphrey told *Sound on Sound* in 2013. "As a result, that first album sounded raw beyond belief—shockingly raw—whereas the Sex Pistols' records sounded fantastic. They were very radio friendly and very well produced. Well, the Clash record didn't sound like that at all, but it did sound like them."

Produced by Mickey Foote

Having been credited as producing an album that course-corrected rock music's direction in the late '70s, you'd think Mickey Foote would have worked with at least half a dozen British punk bands. You'd expect him to have a discography similar to Spot, the house producer for SST Records, who worked with Black Flag, Hüsker Dü, the Minutemen, Minor Threat, and many others. But no, Mickey Foote is only credited with having worked with the 101'ers, the Clash, and Subway Sect, acts associated with Joe Strummer and/or Bernie Rhodes.

Joe and Mickey had met in Newport, Wales, where Joe had sought out an old girlfriend studying at the Cardiff School of Art and Design in an unsuccessful attempt at rekindling a vanquished flame. After Joe relocated to London, Mickey and his girlfriend followed and shared the squat where Joe was living. In time, Joe moved to another squat at 101 Walterton Road, which is where Joe's pub-rock band (the 101'ers) began taking shape. Mickey got involved as the 101'ers' road manager, roadie, and sound mixer. This latter role was the same one he was to fulfill during the Clash's earliest days.

Determined that their debut album replicate their sound in concert and not the lifeless Polydor demos, the Clash insisted that Mickey sit in the control room and monitor the recording session with CBS recording engineer Simon Humphrey. He had overseen the recordings at Beaconsfield to the Clash's satisfaction. Foote told biographer Pat Gilbert that his job "was to make sure [*The Clash*] sounded like *we* wanted it to, not how [CBS] wanted it."

Having succeeded in this, Foote was credited as the album's producer. In actuality, this was a throwback to the 1960s, when a manager such as Andrew Loog Oldham would claim production credit of Rolling Stones singles when recording engineers had a played a larger role in committing the sound to tape. The main difference between Oldham and Foote, however, is that Oldham did instinctually know what take or arrangement would make a song a pop hit. This was not Foote's forte. In fact, if anyone was producing *The Clash*, it was Mick Jones, who had a personal interest in ensuring the songs that often originated with him—and that he had arranged—were improved with some studio trickery. Soon it was Mick and not Mickey who was working closely with Humphrey.

Mickey Foote's career as "producer" of Clash recordings came to an end with the band's fourth single, "Clash City Rockers." The single was cut in October and November 1977, again at CBS Studios. The Clash were happy with the result. Then Mickey made an error by suggesting they varispeed the recording a little faster while cutting the master take. Bernie thought the original version lacked the oomph needed to be a hit. Mick was livid when he heard what had been done to his song, and the Clash—who were not entirely pleased with Bernie's management at the moment—felt Mickey had betrayed them and was not to be trusted. It was an act bordering on insubordination. Mickey Foote never entered a recording studio with the Clash again.

Simon Humphrey, Recording Engineer

Simon Humphrey was hired as tape-op/tea boy at CBS Studios in 1973. By January 1977 he had had a hand in recording sessions for a cornucopia of actors, comedians, poets, orchestras, jazz performers, and pop/rock recording artists, including ABBA, Rod Argent, and Marc Bolan, when he got the nod to record CBS's first punk rock act.

"My education as an engineer taught me to be very open-minded about who I worked with," Humphrey told *Sound on Sound* in 2013. "It didn't matter if I liked or understood the material I was recording, I just had to be professional and do the best possible job for whichever client walked through the door." This attitude came in very handy when the Clash came walking through those doors.

The band arrived at the sessions with their dander up. Smarting from the criticism they were receiving in the press for having signed with CBS Records, they were determined that the sound of their first record reflect the principles of punk rock. When the band questioned him about how he went about recording ABBA, Joe made it clear that the engineer must throw out anything he'd ever learned if he was going to record the Clash to their satisfaction. Humphrey was willing to try it the Clash way: "The idea of not doing what I'd learned before was really at the heart of how I approached recording the band. I felt there was some relevance to what they were saying; they didn't want to sound like what had gone before."

And so Humphrey's role in the album's perpetual success is not to be overlooked. He balanced the Clash's desire for capturing the band's live, raw sound with studio techniques that improved the songs, such as double-tracked backing vocals or the phased guitar on "Cheat" (a precursor to the large role phased guitars would have on later Clash albums, especially *London Calling*). With the band playing live in the studio, the recording engineer quickly discerned they'd stubbornly keep the tracks he said could be better when asked, and—conversely—they'd redo what he praised; so if he thought a vocal or guitar lead needed work, he'd tell the Clash that it was a great take.

Humphrey received his first gold album for his contributions to *The Clash*. While he never worked with the band on another album, he was the recording engineer for "Complete Control," "Clash City Rockers," and "(White Man) In Hammersmith Palais" and the accompanying B-sides. His post-Clash work includes the Vibrators, XTC, Culture Club, David Byrne, and Tom Verlaine, among others. In 1989 he formed his own band, Beijing Spring. After the band dissolved he opened Radar Rooms Studios in West Yorkshire, which was later renamed ChairWorks. The Fall partially recorded *Your Future Our Clutter* at ChairWorks in 2009.

Steve Levine, Tape-Op

There was a third presence in the control booth operating the tapes for Foote and Humphrey. This was Steve Levine. Hired by the label in 1975, Levine began working with the Clash while demos were being recorded at CBS in preparation for the album. Supertramp were also in the studios, taking considerably more time finessing their sound. The Clash's demos were done in a day.

Levine's memories of the session color in some of the shadows in Humphrey's recollections. For example, when Joe famously told Humphrey he didn't know what "separation" was but didn't like it anyway, "we immediately moved the screens and that was the difference between the old and new bands at the time," Levine told John Robb, in an interview for *Louder Than Words*. "We thought differently from [the Clash] but we were willing to work in their way."

According to Levine, the first song recorded was "White Riot," and as the tape-op it was up to him to find the sound effects. "I remember going to get . . . the police siren for the beginning of 'White Riot.' The CBS studios had a massive sound archive." He wound up using a BBC recording. The second song recorded was "Janie Jones."

In between the Clash's first two albums, Humphrey and Levine continued working with the Clash on their singles up until the February–March 1978 sessions that resulted in "Time Is Tight," "Jail Guitar Doors," and "(White Man) In Hammersmith Palais," the latter track being Levine's personal favorite.

In addition to session work with the Clash, Levine recorded the Vibrators and XTC before producing Culture Club's biggest-selling singles and first three albums.

The Clash and the Gray Lyricism of London

The Clash was released on April 8, 1977, approximately one year after the band's formation, and shot up the charts to #12. It has since been named to over fifty "best of" lists. This is because *The Clash* captures a time and a place. Thirteen of the fourteen tracks are essential Clash recordings (only "48 Hours" fails to make the grade), including five punk classics ("I'm So Bored with the USA," "White Riot," "Hate and War," "London's Burning," and "Career Opportunities"). But from the very first track ("Janie Jones") through the last ("Garageland"), Joe Strummer with his "Year Zero" fervor has tapped into the alienation of dispirited British youth: young men and women who are either on the dole or trapped in pointless jobs. The city is burning with boredom, not flames caused by a white riot. Even love is disappointing. The nearest they get to love songs on the album are "Deny" (about a heroin-addicted girlfriend) and "Protex Blue" (a song about a prophylactic brand young men could purchase in their pub's restroom as Mick did in the Windsor Castle).

Mick sings of how "it's so grey in London town" in "Remote Control," the first song reflecting the real-life collective experiences of the Clash as a band and the oppression they faced during the Anarchy in the UK tour. The popular punk haunt the 100 Club is mentioned in "Deny." There's mention of the Westway and Westbourne Park and the BBC. Just about the best thing for a Brit to be proud of is London's "traffic system," because "it's so bright." And yet these young men and women are somehow going to make things better—even if they have to cheat to do it. "Use the rules you stupid fools," Joe advises: you've got to do something. It's a central theme of the Clash to their fans. Start a band. Do something creative with your lives. Don't be the bored office worker in love with Janie Jones.

Cover Artwork

Bassist Paul Simonon may have been the quiet one in the band, but he had a lot of say about the band's "look," be it clothing, stage backdrops, or cover art. When CBS's artistic director, Roslaw Szaybo, showed Paul and Bernie the cover art the record company planned to use for the debut album—"a picture of a cobbled street with a pair of dodgy old boots," as Paul puts it in the Clash's coffee-table book—Paul knew it was awful. Scouring Jamaican album covers, he noticed that "there was a lot of green," which he thought worked for a Clash cover. "Green seemed slightly militaristic, and with the black and white photo it was striking."

The band knew which photo they wanted to use: an image that *Sounds* staff photographer Kate Simon had snapped of Paul, Joe, and Mick—the recording sessions had not changed Terry's mind about quitting—just outside Rehearsal Rehearsals' front door. Simon was on friendly terms with Mick and Paul and had attended the Sex Pistols' performance at the Nashville Rooms, so this was not just another band shoot for her. "A strange thing happened to me during the shoot. I started crying," Simon told journalist Paul Gorman decades later. "Maybe I knew that I was doing something which wasn't just important to me, but was going to be significant for a lot of people. It never happened to me before, and hasn't since."

The similarity to the front cover of *The Ramones* is obvious. The way the band members are lined up, the brick wall, the urbanity; *The Clash* artwork is almost an homage to an album the Clash considered tremendously influential. It was no accident that both albums bore eponymous titles.

So Paul and Bernie went back to Szaybo, a Polish artist who had led the record company's art department since 1972, with their suggestions. The result would appear on thousands of T-shirts sold the world over. The back cover of the police charging at the Notting Hill Carnival Riot was taken by Rocco Macauley, and was the same image as the Clash would use as the backdrop for their White Riot tour.

American Version

Twenty-seven months after its UK release (and nine months after *Give 'Em Enough Rope*), *The Clash* was finally issued by Epic Records in America, with the band's name no longer in lower right-hand corner, but dangerously close to Mick's head; it's as if he's ducking. The Columbia Records honchos that had not released the album in 1977 because they thought the production too tinny for American ears and that Joe Strummer's voice would never have commercial potential, were finally yielding. According to urban legend, 100,000 copies of the debut album had crossed the Atlantic and been sold in record stores everywhere across America from New York City to Los Angeles. Obviously there were some Americans interested in what this punk-rock band had to say.

To drive up sales, "I Fought the Law" was issued as a single simultaneously with the album's release on July 26, 1979. The Clash version of the old Bobby Fuller hit was one of six UK single sides included on the album. The original album clocked in at 35:20, but the US version was 43:29. Four songs from the original album ("Deny," "Cheat," "Protex Blue," and "48 Hours")

When the Clash's debut album was finally released in the US, the artwork was subtly changed: the band's name was moved into the upper right-hand corner and the color of the type tweaked. *Author's collection*

were omitted; the album version of "White Riot" was replaced with the single version, the police siren, smashing glass, and ringing alarms all kept intact. The American version has five songs not on the UK version.

Is it a better album? It's hard to argue against an album that opens with "Clash City Rockers" and wonderfully re-sequences its tracks by pairing "Remote Control" with "Complete Control" (complaining about the former's release as a single), and "White Riot" with "(White Man) In Hammersmith Palais." The anti-police theme is stronger, too, with "I Fought the Law" and "Jail Guitar Doors" complementing "Hate and War" and "Police and Thieves." What gets lost in the reissue is London. The sense of time and place is gone. You could almost characterize the US version as the Clash's first greatest hits package.

7

Let's Hear What the Drummer Man's Got to Say

The Many Myths of Terry Chimes

"A paradiddle really," is how the drummer behind the beat matter-of-factly described it to me. "Two beats, one beat, two beats, one beat. Just get the energy going." Terry Chimes was being exceedingly modest. "Janie Jones"—the opening track from *The Clash*—kick-started a musical genre; his energetic drumbeat sounding like the punk rockers in the UK rushing the stage after bouncers have unlocked the front doors of the Locarnos and Town Halls they've been waiting outside of for hours.

Terry Chimes was the Clash's original drummer, and as such he helped lay down the bedrock on which the Clash's towering body of work has been built. He was behind the kit for the band's first nineteen studio recordings. Originally known to most fans as "Tory Crimes" because he was thus credited on the back of the debut album, Terry's role was marginalized in early interviews when band members explained their formation. But then his vital contributions came into sharper focus when—after the dismissal of Topper Headon due to his deepening drug addiction—Terry returned in late May 1982 and helped salvage the band's impending American tour. He was one of the five men inducted into the Rock and Roll Hall of Fame in 2003 as members of the Clash.

Terry Chimes

Terrence "Terry" Chimes was born on July 5, 1956, the second son of Bill and Donna Chimes, and raised in London's East End. Other members of the Clash may have feigned a Cockney accent in their earliest interviews to exaggerate their street image, but Terry's tongue was his own. Although

Terry's father was a photographic plate maker for the *Sunday Times*, he was also a talented musician, and as a saxophonist and clarinetist he played in dance bands on weekends. This passion for music rubbed off on his three sons, who all pursued musical careers.

Beatlemania wasn't phony to eight-year-old Terry. Seeing John, Paul, George, and Ringo on television convinced him that playing in a band could be a successful career, even if he wouldn't begin playing music until a year later, with his younger brother Bryn.

Still, Terry's interest in science and nature prevailed over music until he happened to catch the Jimi Hendrix Experience's live appearance on *The Lulu Show* on January 4, 1969. This was a historic performance, culturally and musically. Here was the Experience playing "Voodoo Child (Slight Return)," one of their noisiest rockers, pleasing to even the die-hardest fan. The fact that *Electric Ladyland*'s closing track wasn't even a single and the show's producers were allowing the power trio's performance did not, however, mollify Hendrix's attitude about the song he was asked to perform next. By 1969, Hendrix was tired of "the song that absolutely made them," as Lulu dubbed "Hey Joe."

Hendrix's tremolo-barred intro threw his Fender Stratocaster's tuning out of whack, but after turning and grinning to his fellow Experience makers, he soldiered on, singing a verse or two (while his guitar notes wryly quoted the Beatles' "I Feel Fine") and playing a tuneful solo before signaling to drummer Mitch Mitchell and bassist Noel Redding to cease. Announcing to the television studio audience that "we'd like to stop playing this rubbish and dedicate a song to the Cream, regardless of what kind of group they may be in," he then took the Experience off on a spirited—if truncated—instrumental rendition of "Sunshine of Your Love." Television programmers truncated the unexpected third number because the Experience were exceeding their allotted time limit. Decades later, it is still exciting television—arguably the greatest televised performance by a rock band—and it is palpably clear why it so viscerally affected Terry.

Terry's musical interests were nurtured by Alice Cooper's *Killer* and Led Zeppelin, and after trying his hands at several instruments, he discovered a natural affinity for drumming. This was not unusual for the Chimes siblings, as Terry's older brother John was well on his way to becoming a classical percussionist. His brother's success convinced Terry that he could do the same, but in a rock band. That televised performance of the Jimi Hendrix Experience having fun had made a lasting impression.

Upon his graduation, Terry had a choice to make. He was still very interested in science and wanted a career in medicine as well as in music. He chose the latter, reasoning that medical studies left little time for being in a band. Terry found employment in a school laboratory, moved out, purchased a car, and was soon searching *Melody Maker* ads for drummers, including one placed by Mick Jones and Tony James for the London SS. The young graduate attended one audition, but neither Terry nor the London SS were overwhelmed by one another's musical abilities, so each went their separate ways.

The Early Days of the Clash

While promoting the definitive Clash package *Sound System* in 2013 and explaining why the Clash, Round Two (the lineup that Joe led for nearly two years after his dismissal) was not represented, Mick told the *Guardian*, "It's not the Clash. The Clash is the three of us, and the two drummers." In other words, Joe, Mick, and Paul ("the three of us") and Terry and Topper ("the two drummers"). It was refreshing to hear Terry get his due, because too often his contributions to the Clash are overlooked, distorted, or—even worse—dismissed. Others were asked to sit in with the green outfit, but it was Terry's hard beats that brought the Clash cohesion in the early days.

Approximately half a year had passed since the London SS audition, and Terry still hadn't found a band with his drive and ambition when he answered another *Melody Maker* ad for a drummer. Dialing the number, he recognized the voice on the other end as belonging to the same manager who had arranged the London SS audition. Bernie told Terry that Mick had an entirely new band and that Tony James was no longer involved. Arrangements were made, and after an initial meeting with Paul, Keith, and vocalist Billy Watts, the five young men ran through some songs.

Terry told me what he liked about Led Zeppelin drummer John Bonham—Terry's biggest influence—was his "hard-hitting but simple style"—a style well-suited for this new band. He had finally found a band with standards high enough to meet his.

"When I met the guys, there was no discussion about whether they were going to make it," Terry told the *Guardian*'s Herpreet Kaur Grewal. "They had an attitude that said, 'We are going to do this and it will work.'"

He was surprised several weeks later, however, when he was called back for another audition and found Billy replaced by a new bloke named Joe Strummer. He didn't know what to make of Joe; he didn't seem like a rock singer.

The original four-piece Clash lineup in action, with Terry Chimes behind the drum kit.
Julian Yewdall/Getty Images

Bernie had acquired the defunct Gilbey's Distillery, centered in a railway yard in Camden Town in north London, from the local council, and this is where Terry's second audition was held. Without explaining that the building was to be used for his new venture into band management, Bernie had persuaded the council to lease the property to him so that the space could be used by aimless youth who demonstrated an interest in mastering their musical instruments. The space would be named Rehearsal Rehearsals, and the aimless youth that would master their instruments within its confines were the Clash.

Bernie was eager to drill into the five members of the Clash a sense of purpose and devotion to the band. His was a method of divide and drive. He would divide each member from their friends: Mick for example was not allowed to fraternize with Chrissie Hynde or Tony James. Only Mickey Foote had followed Joe Strummer when the front man left the 101'ers. Paul, Terry, and Keith were loners. By isolating and then instilling in the young men the validity of being a rebel rock band with a cause, he was driving the Clash apart from bands whose goals were merely *Top of the Pops* appearances and #1 records.

Foote became Bernie's right-hand man, which permitted the band's manager to remove himself from the grueling, seven-days-a-week rehearsals the Clash were putting themselves through after Bernie convinced the young men that nothing less would suffice. The Sex Pistols had an approximately seven-month head start, and there was a lot of ground to be covered if the Clash were going to complement or compete with what McLaren's upstarts were up to.

The First Nineteen Studio Recordings

"[Terry] was cool enough to come and do the album with us, 'cos we'd rehearsed the numbers with him," Joe told Jon Savage in an unpublished interview from 1988, now available on the Rock's Backpages website. Substitute drummer Rob Harper had not survived past the Anarchy in the UK tour (although there is some disagreement if the choice was Harper's or the band's) and so Bernie reached out to Terry to sit in during the recording sessions for the first single and album for CBS.

It has been recalled by others that Terry was told what to play during the sessions, but that doesn't mean that the drummer didn't have a say in the sound. "I wanted a very live, echo-y drum sound," Chimes said in 2013. "I couldn't bear these awful disco records at the time, where the drums were full of cotton wool and played this really dead, contained sound. So as long as the drums sounded like drums and they went BOING! I was happy."

When I spoke to him, Terry downplayed his nickname, Tory Crimes. "At the time it was a nickname. I don't know who came up with it." (Research reveals it as coined by someone who had a fairly unflattering nickname himself: Steve "Roadent" Connolly.) "Never thought of it as something I'd discuss forty years later. It was bit of a fashion then, having a stage name." If you notice, punk stage names emphasized a perceived negative aspect of the person: Damned drummer Rat Scabies was thus nicknamed because he looked like a rat and had a bad rash; Johnny Rotten had rotten teeth. Terry was Tory Crimes his political views were "fairly right-wing." Only Joe Strummer's name accentuated the positive, but that was because it predated Year Zero Joe.

Other misinformation was spread. Former *NME* journo Barry Miles reported in *Time Out* in 1978 that Terry quit when, at the Lanchester Polytechnic gig in Coventry on November 29, 1976, he "watched as a wine bottle smashed into a million pieces on his hi-hat." The implication being that he couldn't handle the violence at punk concerts. Not true. Then it was reported that Terry was booted for saying he hoped the band was successful enough for him to purchase an expensive luxury sports car made in Italy.

(Paul always remembers Chimes mentioning a Lamborghini, while Joe said it had been a Maserati). The inference being that Terry wasn't sufficiently committed to the Clash's mission. Also not true. What troubled Terry about the Clash was band's inability to enjoy themselves: the political arguments, the subtle brainwashing, the daily rehearsals. "I liked the music," Terry told me, "but it was all too miserable."

Decades later, in his e-book, Terry wrote that a Jaguar E-Type was the expensive car he had expressed an interest in buying. He also revealed that Joe had offered to buy Terry the car out of his own money from signing with CBS Records, if he'd only reconsider leaving the band. Terry felt that his decision had been made, however, and that Joe never ever truly forgave him. The band's original drummer has compared Joe's feelings to that of a jilted lover, and there's a bit of truth in that observation.

Terry's Best Beats

The fact remains that, in retrospect, Terry Chimes doesn't get his proper due for his contributions to the Clash's early work. He wasn't even properly compensated (he was paid only £100 for his work on *The Clash*!), and just as Bo Diddley couldn't copyright his signature rhythm, Terry couldn't copyright the drum characteristics that were copied by countless punk rock and hardcore punk drummers. There are those who posit the Clash never released a good record after "(White Man) In Hammersmith Palais," Topper's sixth recording with the Clash. What those critics may miss is Terry's thunderous involvement in the punk era recordings.

Peter Silverton put it best in a 1978 *Trouser Press* article: Terry Chimes was the drummer who "didn't give a flying one about the politics (in the widest sense) of the Clash but made up for it by being one of the best drummers this side of Jerry Nolan."

Terry's discography is full of stellar performances, including the opening bounce of "Janie Jones," the rock-steady drive of "Police and Thieves," and the dancing beat he created for Billy Idol's "Dancing with Myself." Here are his "best" performances from the Clash's first nineteen recorded songs.

"I'm So Bored with the USA"

"I'm So Bored with the USA" begins with just Mick's guitar. Then, via a series of well-timed double beats descending across his drum kit, Terry provides a gateway to Joe's first verse about the drug addicted "Yankee soldier."

Walloped drumbeats as a means of shifting between verses and choruses and codas are a defining characteristic of early Clash songs, and therefore a trademark of Terry's early drumming. Where most drummers throw in drumrolls, Terry wallops. He puts this trait to good use at the conclusion of "I'm So Bored with the USA." The Clash are enjoying playing the chorus so much that as the final note semi-fades, Terry throws in a beat to reignite it. After the third go-around, the listener begins expecting a fadeout, but no, just as the guitars fade for a third time, Terry throws in a series of beats and the song shifts into the coda where Joe evokes famous television detectives from the USA. When I asked Terry about the song structures of the Clash's early songs and how they never wasted an outro, Terry told me this was a conscious decision: "Someone—I don't know who—said a fadeout is an easy way out. We have to end it."

"White Riot"

The start of "White Riot" is so uproarious that the Clash sound in full thrash mode from the very first beat. Much of the credit for this thunderbolt of sound is Terry's. He leaps from silence to pure muscular rage in one beat. He would often compare himself to John Bonham, but Bonham never banged on his drums as hard as Terry does throughout "White Riot," a song that never lets up for its 1:55 duration.

Despite the pounding beat, it's three strategically placed drumrolls that give the song added oomph. First, Mick barks out "1-2-3-4!" and stomps through the intro, then Terry throws in a drumroll as Joe makes an exclamation and Mick hits some lead notes to heighten the tension. Joe sings a chorus and then, just before the first verse, Terry throws in his second drumroll, setting the stage for Joe's controversial point of view. (He doesn't do this before the second verse.) Finally—but only midway through the song—Terry plays his third drumroll under Mick's guitar solo as the bass notes link up with that of the guitar, sidestepping and pivoting like dancers. It just wouldn't work without Terry's drumroll.

"Career Opportunities"

It was fitting that "Career Opportunities" was revived during Terry's second stint and gained popularity when it was one of the two songs filmed during the band's appearance at Shea Stadium and released as a promo film. It was fitting because, despite some funny lyrics, it's Terry's drumming that makes the song. Whenever Joe sings about the career opportunities "that never knock," Terry humorously mimics the sound of someone knocking.

"Cheat"

I have to include "Cheat" because, along with "Garageland," Terry said it was his favorite to play. And, from a drummer's perspective, it's easy to see why. Terry often ran drum clinics in the 1980s, and "Cheat" is a drum clinic unto itself. Terry's drumroll under the opening chord gives way to a frantic beat. Using dropouts, dynamics, and at one point a pounding bass drum, Terry helps shift an intricate song through many moods, ending with well-placed beats that accentuate Mick's police siren–like guitar outro.

"Capital Radio"

Consider this Terry's swan song, as it was released exclusively as part of an EP with "Listen" and a band interview as an *NME* giveaway that was available via mail-order only. Interestingly, there are two versions of "Capital Radio," and each reflects the drummer's talents. The version of "Capital Radio" released as part of the *The Cost of Living EP* features Topper's breakneck tempos and endless drumrolls, whereas the April 1977 version features Terry pounding away, reflecting Joe's anger about Britain's airwaves.

The 1977 version of "Capital Radio" begins with Terry banging out a one, one, one-two-three beat that the band hops onto. Terry switches to a straightforward 4/4 beat but reverts to the intro pattern whenever Mick sings the end of the second and fourth verses. Then, in another example of the classic Clash dropout, Terry and everyone else stop playing as Mick scratches out a new guitar rhythm; Terry throws in a drumroll and leads the shift to the outro, where Joe rants about Capital Radio; and then just as the song ends, Terry incrementally slows down the beat until a final cymbal crash for Joe to scream out "Don't touch that dial!" without any musical accompaniment.

Inter-Clash Activity

With punk rock boiling over, there was no shortage of group activity in London, and, being the ex-drummer of the Clash, Terry found many doors open. After "managing" an all-girl French band's tour of Italy at Bernie's suggestion, Terry was behind the kit again, touring as one of

Johnny Thunders' Heartbreakers. Refreshingly, with the Heartbreakers there weren't any political discussions, just sex, drugs, and rock 'n' roll . . . and wine, lots of wine.

With the Heartbreakers being New York City–based, however, Terry was soon looking for another band. He met a Newcastle singer who was working on material with former Clash guitarist Keith Levene and soon the three were in a band named Cowboys International with bassist Jimmy Hughes. Cowboys International's electro-pop brand was novel enough, but despite earning a deal with Virgin Records, they failed to break through. Terry rejected an offer to join the unsigned Pretenders, left Cowboys International, and recorded with Bernie Rhodes protégé Vic Godard, formerly of Subway Sect.

After marrying his wife, Maxine, Terry became a member of Gen X, a later generation of Generation X now built around founding members Billy Idol and former London SS bassist Tony James. Sifting through guitarists, they settled on Jamie Stevenson and signed with Chrysalis Records. The first song this lineup recorded was to become one of Idol's signature songs: "Dancing with Myself." It's one of Terry's best studio performances. Incredibly, "Dancing with Myself" was not a hit for Gen X—it's the 1981 remixed version credited solely to Billy Idol that most rock fans have danced to, but not by themselves. After lackluster sales for the band's *Kiss Me Deadly*, Gen X was no more. "Dancing with Myself" is one of the most iconic songs from the early '80s, heard often in Manhattan's rock clubs and throughout the world and probably the most popular song Terry has drummed on.

The Call Up

May 30, 1982. Approximately fifty minutes into the second of the Clash's three shows in the Convention Hall in Bruce Springsteen's old stomping ground of Asbury Park, New Jersey, Joe points to where Mick is standing and says, "On June 10th 1965, Brian Jones stood over there." Pointing at Paul, "Bill Wyman stood there." The crowd cheers. Joe's got the date wrong—the Rolling Stones actually played the Convention Hall on July 3, 1966—but the implication is clear. Joe doesn't point out where Charlie Watts sat, but sitting in Charlie's spot this foggy Sunday night is Terry Chimes, who's been introduced before "Car Jamming," as he will throughout the tour. Five years after showing Topper the ropes, Topper did the junkie slip one time too many at the Lothem Festival outside Amsterdam on May 21, 1982, and within days Terry had returned to the fold.

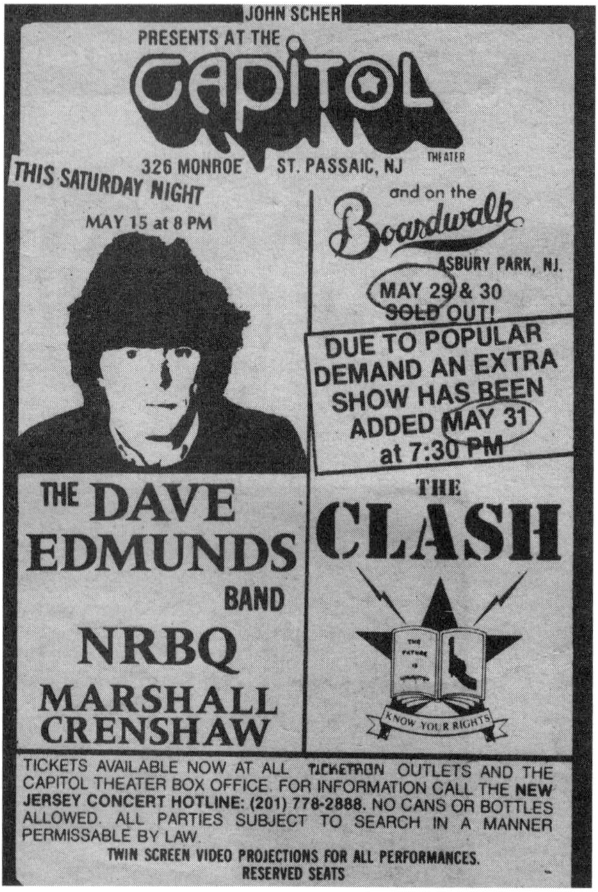
JOHN SCHER
PRESENTS AT THE
CAPITOL
THEATER
326 MONROE ST. PASSAIC, NJ
THIS SATURDAY NIGHT
MAY 15 at 8 PM
and on the
Boardwalk
ASBURY PARK, NJ.
MAY 29 & 30
SOLD OUT!
DUE TO POPULAR DEMAND AN EXTRA SHOW HAS BEEN ADDED MAY 31 at 7:30 PM
THE DAVE EDMUNDS BAND
NRBQ
MARSHALL CRENSHAW
THE CLASH
KNOW YOUR RIGHTS
TICKETS AVAILABLE NOW AT ALL TICKETRON OUTLETS AND THE CAPITOL THEATER BOX OFFICE. FOR INFORMATION CALL THE NEW JERSEY CONCERT HOTLINE: (201) 778-2888. NO CANS OR BOTTLES ALLOWED. ALL PARTIES SUBJECT TO SEARCH IN A MANNER PERMISSABLE BY LAW.
TWIN SCREEN VIDEO PROJECTIONS FOR ALL PERFORMANCES.
RESERVED SEATS

An advertisement for the Clash's shows in Asbury Park in late May 1982, which marked the return of Terry Chimes as the Clash's drummer. *Author's collection*

It was Bernie who contacted Terry, who immediately agreed. With only a week left before the thirty-three-date Casbah Club USA tour of America and Canada and Paul already stateside, Terry rehearsed with Mick and Joe.

Many myths and misconceptions have arisen around the eighty-five shows Terry performed with the Clash in 1982. For example, it is said that half of the Clash's set list from the first weekend in Asbury Park derived from debut album tracks. Not true. Yes, "Police and Thieves" was unusually played second and "Career Opportunities" fifth, but the only other song from *The Clash* to be played during Terry's first show back with the band was "Janie Jones." The following night was more of a standard set, with only "Career Opportunities" and "Janie Jones" performed from the debut album.

Rock journalist David Fricke highlighted Chimes's contributions by writing in *NME* that the drummer "played this show like he'd been rehearsing the set for a year instead of less than a week. He was the boot in band's pants during 'Clash City Rockers' and even the hall's trashcan acoustics couldn't deaden the crack of his machine gun drum fill in 'I Fought the Law.'"

This was true. Listening back to bootleg recordings of Terry on "I Fought the Law," it always sounds as if he's carrying two six-guns to Topper's one.

Fricke also called this show "the best show I have ever seen [the Clash] give."

Live at Shea Stadium

"I knew we recorded the gig, but it never occurred to me that the tapes were sitting in someone's wardrobe," Clash drummer Terry Chimes told Ian Croft of *TRAPS*, a magazine devoted to everything drums, in early 2009. "I'm pleased that it has been released, as it is really the pinnacle of what we did [in 1982]."

Discovered by Mick Jones during a house move, *Live at Shea Stadium* was released on October 6, 2008, and is one of only two live albums officially released by the Clash. It is generally considered superior to 1999's *From Here to Eternity: Live*, but because of sequencing rather than quality. *From Here to Eternity: Live*'s seventeen tracks are more or less presented in the order the studio versions were first released, so the album does not replicate the true experience of a Clash concert. *Live at Shea Stadium* at least presents a full Clash concert, even if it is only a fifty-minute set featuring Clash hits from

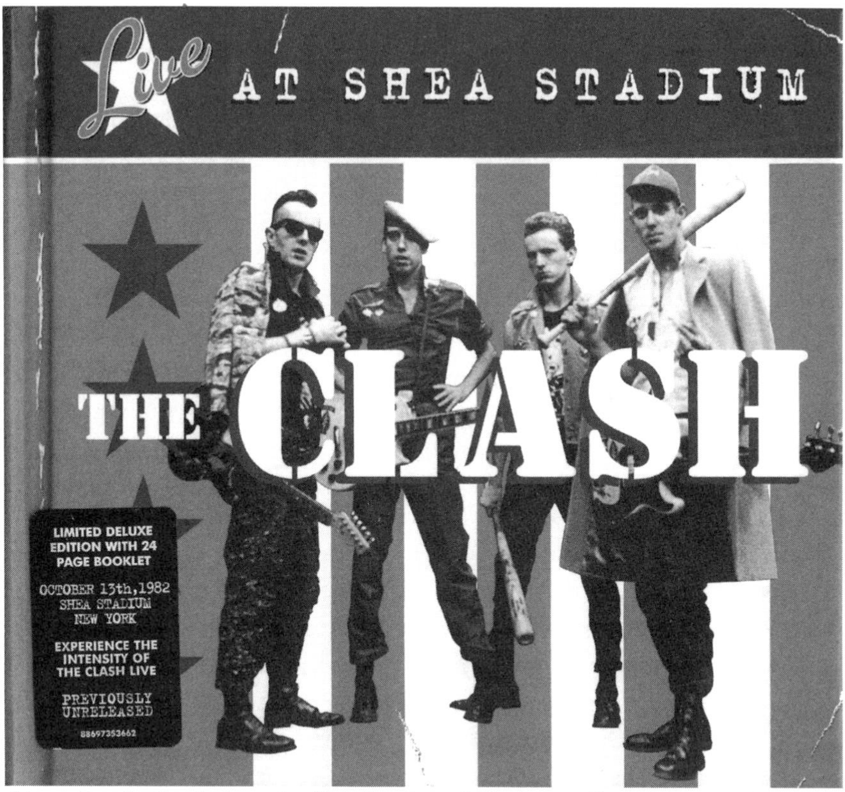

Live at Shea Stadium is the only officially released Clash recording with Terry Chimes on the cover. *Author's collection*

the second of their two appearances opening for the Who at Shea Stadium in New York City.

It is also a perfect artifact of Terry's second stint with the Clash.

As such, *Live at Shea Stadium* is—to use the words attributed by Horace Walpole to Oliver Cromwell when he was having his portrait painted—a recording with "roughnesses, pimples, warts, and everything." Clash publicist/consigliore/yes-man Kosmo Vinyl's introduction trying to rouse up a crowd of Who fans is retained, and after Joe says, "Welcome to the Casbah Club," he misses the mark for the first verse of "London Calling." Any other band would have spliced the tape, but not the Clash.

Anyway, one of Terry's favorite words to describe what he hoped to restore to rock music is "energy," and it was an energetic performance the Clash put on that rainy night in Shea. They race through fifteen songs and Terry very capably adjusts his style to mimic Topper when necessary, such as on the rat-a-tat-tat drum bursts of "Tommy Gun" or the tribal beats of "The Guns of Brixton." Some might hold it against Terry that "The Magnificent Seven" rocks more than it funks, but the Clash had rockified much of the *Sandinista!* material in concert as far back as the Bond's residency. Only on "Armagideon Time" is Topper's sensitive touch missed.

Rock 'n' Roll Doctor

A lack of activity due to a lack of communication forced Terry to leave the Clash once again in early 1983. He played over the next five years with Billy Idol, Hanoi Rocks, the Cherry Bombz, and finally Black Sabbath, during their Eternal Idol tour. It was during his stint in Black Sabbath that Terry found his second calling. They were in Sun City in South Africa when Terry hurt his shoulder and was unable to raise his arm after playing ten-pin bowling. Black Sabbath leader Tony Iommi arranged to have a chiropractor treat his drummer. As Terry writes in his memoir *The Strange Case of Dr. Terry and Mr. Chimes*, "I did not at that point leap up and decide to have an immediate career change but it did plant a further seed that was to germinate over the next year or so."

As the title of Terry's memoir implies, he did finally get around to pursuing the medical career he set aside to be a drummer in a rock 'n' roll band. After approximately fifteen years and several near-death experiences, and having noticed that the lifespan of rock 'n' roll drummers to be on the short side, he decided to hang up his drumsticks. He truly had an urge to heal others as the chiropractor in Sun City had healed him. After enrolling in a school in Bournemouth and studying for his chiropractic degree (as well as a degree in acupuncture), Terry graduated in 1993 and opened a successful chiropractic clinic in London.

The Rock and Roll Hall of Fame Induction Speech

When the Clash were announced as Rock and Roll Hall of Fame inductees in late 2002, Terry, as the original drummer, was one of the five inductees invited to the ceremony. Ever the gentleman, Terry in his short induction speech in March 2003 deliberately shone a light on Topper Headon, who, at the last minute, chose not to attend.

"There are two drummers being inducted tonight, and I don't want to pass up the opportunity to pay tribute to my friend and fellow drummer, Topper," Terry said, pausing as the crowd of assembled music-industry honchos clapped for the absent drummer, before resuming with, "I love those early songs from the first album. I love them still. But I had no idea back then the extent to which the band would develop and diversify. In fact when I rejoined five years later it was a bit of a shock to have to play all these different styles, suddenly. And much of the credit for that goes to Topper, I think, not, just because of his undoubted skill as a drummer, but also because of his contributions on the creative side helping with some of the songwriting, for example on 'Rock the Casbah.' So I'd like you to all join me now to salute the contribution of Topper Headon." Then after another round of clapping and cheering for Topper, Terry modestly acknowledged his own induction. "We heard earlier that the whole is always greater than the sum of its parts, well, this particular part would like to express gratitude for being recognized this evening and I'd like to thank the Hall of Fame very much indeed."

As of this writing, Terry continues to run his chiropractic clinic in East London, but he has also picked up his drumsticks once more and is drumming with the Crunch, a super-group of sorts featuring former members of the Cockney Rejects, the Diamond Dogs, and Sham 69, in addition to Terry. They released the albums *Busy Making Noise* in 2013 and *Brand New Brand* in 2015.

8

This Is Radio Clash

The Clash Help Revive the 45

"Revive the 45!" could almost be the clarion call of punk rockers in the UK and all their musical offshoots. Once a commercial means of remaining in the public eye between long-playing albums, the 45 had also served as a vibrant stepping stone in the musical development of the Beatles, the Rolling Stones, the Who, and the Kinks, until it once again reverted to a vast teenage wasteland of vinyl, a mere marketing tool for promoting the LP, the 33⅓ rpm disc that in the early 1970s was now cited as the apex of the recording artist's work. And from which 45s almost always derived.

UK punk rockers and other recording artists who between 1975–78 had little hope of signing with major labels resorted to the do-it-yourself (DIY) ethic of paying for not only studio recording time, but actually the pressing of the 45s; the unsigned recording artists had the covers designed, Xeroxed, folded, and pasted together, and then peddled them to local and faraway London record stores. The relative success that Stiff Records and Chiswick Records had with their 45s convinced punk rockers throughout the UK that they could do it themselves. Bands such as Swell Maps, the Desperate Bicycles, and the Mekons really did it themselves, while others such as Buzzcocks created their own label to get their music heard but entered into deals with larger labels for distribution.

The Clash (you may have heard) killed punk rock by signing with the major label CBS Records and not resorting to the DIY method, but they did play their part in reviving the 45 by issuing three singles between their first and second albums that documented not only their musical growth but the permutations punk rock was undergoing in the UK in the wake of national uproar caused by the Sex Pistols' appearance with Bill Grundy.

This was an important recording period for the Clash but one that is hard to grasp decades later because not only have the nine songs from this period rarely been presented together, the A-sides are usually separated from the B-sides. Recorded between August 1977 and March 1978, the work from this period includes the earliest studio recordings with new drummer Nicky "Topper" Headon and features two A-sides that are generally considered among the Clash's ten best songs.

"Complete Control"

Newly armed with Topper, the Clash set off on their first headlining tour in May 1977. Christened the White Riot tour, it was a twenty-six-date thrust through England, Scotland, Wales, and even one show at Brakke Grande in Amsterdam that was to be referenced in their next single. The blistering, road-honed magnificence of "Complete Control" belies the fact that the Clash were mostly off the road when they stepped into Sarm East Studios on Brick Lane in the London Borough of Tower Hamlets in August 1977 to record their third single.

It was the only time the Clash recorded at Sarm East, and the reason the studio was picked appears to be because of the involvement of legendary Jamaican producer Lee "Scratch" Perry, who had remained in London after working with Bob Marley. The previous month, Perry had produced Marley's "Punky Reggae Party," a B-side recording released in December 1977, with "Jammin'," that has over time gained popularity largely because during the song Marley name checks punk groups, including the Damned, the Jam, and the Clash, that went on to have notable successes. "Punky Reggae Party" was eventually released as a standalone 12-inch single featuring a 9:19 vocal version and an 8:49 dub version. Marley is said to have recorded the song after hearing the Clash's version of Junior Murvin's "Police and Thieves," a song that Perry co-wrote and produced.

("Punky Reggae Party" was the first song to name check the Clash. It was not the last. Other songs that the Clash or Joe Strummer are mentioned in include Aztec Camera's "Walk out to Winter," Crass's "The Feeding of the 5,000," the Hold Steady's "Constructive Summer," Rancid's "Indestructible," Richard Thompson's "Tear Stained Letter," the Stingrays's "Joe Strummer's Wallet," and Throbbing Gristle's "Death Threats," while both R.E.M. and Courtney Love made references to "London Calling" in their songs in the wake of Joe Strummer's death in 2002.) Still, the best reference is found in the Minutemen's "History Lesson—Part II."

It is likely that Perry himself first played the Clash's version of "Police and Thieves" for Marley because British journalist Vivien Goldman had played it for Perry. An arranged meeting between the Clash and Perry at Island Studios went well, and Perry agreed to produce the Clash with Scratch at the controls for two recording sessions for £2,000. On paper, it seemed like a match made in heaven considering the Clash's genuine interest in reggae roots music, and there was no stronger root than Perry. The only problem was that, as Mick Jones said in 2003, "At that point it was the only non-reggae record Lee Perry had made."

Perry himself has downplayed his involvement with the recording session. "When I got involved with that record, most of it was already done," he told *NME* in November 1984. "I liked the Clash, they were nice boys, I taught them to turn down their guitars in the studio." Perry's late arrival is supported by Paul's memory in 2003 of working with one of his heroes, as noted in Nick Johnstone's *The Clash: Talking*: "It's a bit difficult for me to talk about Lee Perry because by the time he was there I had a really bad flu. I recorded my bass part, only saw him for half an hour then had to go lie down. Missed the whole thing."

With Perry present, a disagreement from the Clash's debut album's session was revived: Paul's bass sound. Paul wanted his bass guitar to sound like what he heard in on Jamaican reggae records: he wanted the bass booming and the walls shuddering. Mick Jones had argued against this previously, believing that what worked on a reggae recording would not on a rock 'n' roll record. According to Terry Chimes's memoir, they argued for hours about this during sessions for the first album while Joe and the drummer waited. Finally, Simon Humphrey suggested recording the bass part in both styles and the band got on with the recording session. Apparently Jones's point was proved during the playbacks. But with a real reggae producer at the controls of what was said to be the largest mixing console Perry had ever encountered, Mick gave in and let Paul have his way. "[Perry] nearly blew the control room up trying to get Paul a bass sound," Mickey Foote told biographer Pat Gilbert in 2004. Perry left with a dub mix completed after his two sessions that the Clash respected but felt lacked the drive needed if the song's powerful diatribe against everything that was bugging them about CBS and Bernie Rhodes was to be convincingly conveyed.

Led by Mick, who was beginning to assert himself in the studio, the band worked with Mickey Foote to remix the tracks. This made perfect sense, as the song was Mick's to begin with, lyrics and all. (Joe suggested referencing the concert in Amsterdam.) He had written it in June, following the White Riot tour. Paul's bass sound was brought back to London. Mick's guitar pushed up. It's hard to believe that the band did not save a copy of Perry's mix, even if only for the B-side, but there's no questioning the results.

Beginning with an intro that is a direct descendent of "I'm So Bored with the USA," "Complete Control" is the Clash's fiercest recording. As Robin Banks put it in his *ZigZag* review, "Ain't heard a single with this impact since 'I Can't Explain,' 'Jumpin' Jack Flash,' or 'Anarchy in the UK.'"

When the single was released on September 23, 1977, the production credits for "Complete Control" on the label named Lee Perry and Mickey Foote. After Foote's ostracizing from the Clash camp in early 1978, however, it would subsequently be credited simply to Perry. The single rose to #28 on the British charts. Some critics point to the song's inability to crack even the Top 20 as proof of its lack of quality, but let's face it: an angry song about record company squabbles played at a breakneck pace—this may be the very first hardcore punk recording—was never going to reach the Top 10 on the pop singles chart. My guess is that—as bassist Steve Hanley said of the Fall's mid-'80s releases—in midweek "Complete Control" was in the Top 10, only for it to be knocked down by the Saturday shoppers.

The song pokes fun at manager Bernie Rhodes's declaration that he wanted complete control of the band. The Clash then twisted this statement into a reflection of the lack of control they had at the hands of CBS records executives. They complain about how "Remote Control" was released as the band's second single without their input, and about how CBS told them to focus on an upcoming show in Amsterdam instead. Joe cites the line in their contract about having complete artistic control in his defense, but he found little industry support when he complained about the record company wanting to make money.

At the time of its release, the Clash issued a statement to the press that "Complete Control" "tells a story of conflict between two opposing camps. One side sees change as an opportunity to channel the enthusiasm of a raw and dangerous culture in a direction where energy is made safe and predictable. The other is dealing with change as a freedom to be experienced so as to understand one's true capabilities, allowing a creative social situation to emerge."

This prompted perhaps the first astonishment at Joe Strummer's naiveté regarding the music business. (Late British DJ John Peel famously said that it could not be a surprise that CBS was not a foundation for the arts.) It was not to be the last criticism of the band as such self-mythologizing references began piling up in their recorded output. In Joe's defense, let us consider Marcel Proust's observation in *The Guermantes Way* that "Everything great in the world is done by neurotics; they alone founded our religions and

It's fitting that Mick's amplifier with its torn speaker is shown in the artwork for the "Complete Control" 45, because he wrote the anti-CBS Records diatribe.
Author's collection

composed our masterpieces." Is this not a similar to the naiveté common in overachieving artists?

"Joe is a bit naïve," Clash biographer and music journalist Chris Salewicz says in the documentary *The Rise and Fall of the Clash.* "That's an important point, you know?" And that's an important point in understanding how the Clash created universal music, just as you'd have to be a bit naïve like John Lennon to pen and record a song called "All You Need Is Love."

In late 1979, Joe conceded to *Melody Maker*'s Chris Bohn, "I must agree it's not the point at all, fighting record companies. It's a waste of time, but with 'Complete Control' I thought strongly about it, and the phrase kept cropping up everywhere after we seized on it, so I think, looking back, it was worth latching on to."

"Complete Control" features Joe's best ad libs this side of "Janie Jones." As Mick takes his first extended guitar solo, Joe responds with, "You're my guitar hero!" (Some cite this as the first usage of a phrase now most widely known to the public through the music rhythm games created by RedOctane and Harmonix, though it must be pointed out that Sex Pistols guitarist Steve Jones had "GUITAR HERO" spray-painted on his amplifier.) Then he's "Joe Public," a performer who's "controlled in the body, and controlled in the mind." Then he stands up for a tarnished musical movement on its last legs by proudly declaring of the musical roar you are listening to: "This is punk rockers!" Finally, in a verbal fury worthy of Little Richard, Joe shouts out the punk equivalent of "Wop bop a loo bop a lop bom bom!" The words, however, are so buried beneath Topper's thumps and the rhythm's galloping pace that they have never appeared on any lyric sheet.

Building on a theme first heard in "Garageland," the Clash were doing what Bernie told them to: writing about what was affecting them. This was central to the Clash's lyrics of the time: punk rock's growing pains; a depressed London (financially and culturally) where gangs fight and the National Front is gaining strength; and the effect of rock 'n' roll on lives. Almost every song from this period is in some way about rock 'n' roll. Even "City of the Dead," described below, contains advice from "New York Johnny," who is none other than the Heartbreakers' Johnny Thunders.

Also recorded at the two sessions with Perry were an early arrangement of the Clash's take on "Pressure Drop," a 1969 recording by the Maytals they were familiar with from the soundtrack for the 1972 film *The Harder They Come* and had played during encores in concert; an embryonic version of "(White Man) In Hammersmith Palais"; and "The Prisoner." All three songs had been debuted at the Mont de Marsen Punk Festival on August 5, 1977 (as well as "Clash City Rockers"), and would be re-recorded during the eight-month period that produced their three most important 45s.

Lee Perry, by the way, crossed paths with the Clash again at Bond International Casino where, for several of the eventual seventeen shows they played in the Times Square disco, he was the middle act preceding the Clash's performance. On June 5, 1981—and supported by the Terrorists, the white reggae band from New York City—the dub master shook his tiny black frame and transformed a mostly mild-mannered crowd of white, middle-class American kids from Jersey and Long Island into Jamaican rude boys and girls for one night as one dub toast doubled into another. I watched as one kid threw an empty plastic beer cup onto the stage and then a copycat did the same. Someone then threw a T-shirt and a balled-up piece of paper, and then more plastic cups followed. The empty plastic beer cups piled up at the feet of the bearded performer. Like Grandmaster Flash, who according to newspaper reports had picked up a similar cup and tossed it behind him exactly one week earlier, Perry picked up a cup that had been thrown at him. But—unlike Grandmaster Flash—Perry refused to be driven from the stage before his allotted time was up. Ignoring the impatient audience, he calmly sang about the plastic cup he held in his hand. Spoke into it. Displayed the idiosyncratic behavior he became better known for than all the inventive and revolutionary music he had produced at his Black Ark Studios in Kingston, Jamaica in the 1970s. (And where the Clash were the only white recording act whose image adorned the studios walls.) Perry was always a man hearing a different drummer's beat, and his indifferent behavior mollified the crowd, who sensed his obliviousness to them and their debris, and so Perry's set proceeded without further incident.

"City of the Dead"

The B-side to "Complete Control" was also recorded in August 1977, but back at CBS's recording studios on Whitfield Street, where Mickey Foote was once again supported by recording engineer Simon Humphrey and tape-op Steve Levine. The assumption is that since members of the Clash were disappointed that the "Pressure Drop" session with Lee Perry hadn't resulted in a finished track, and were anxious to record something to pair with "Complete Control" on a 45, they used Mick's newest, as-yet-unheard song. This was an extremely prolific period for Mick as a songwriter.

The title is stolen from an obscure 1960 British horror movie starring Christopher Lee, making "City of the Dead" the first cinematic allusion in a discography that would contain many. There would be references to actors Montgomery Clift ("The Right Profile"), Errol Flynn ("If Music Could Talk") and Lauren Bacall ("Car Jamming"); *Sandinista!*'s "Charlie Don't Surf" quotes a line by Lieutenant Corporal Bill Kilgore in *Apocalypse Now.* The Clash would even name another song from the same album after a motion picture ("The Magnificent Seven").

Another boastful first "City of the Dead" can lay claim to is the involvement of outside musicians. In the first of his many collaborations with the Clash, Gary Barnacle—Topper's school friend from his days growing up in Dover—plays saxophone. *NME* also identified Steve Nieve from Elvis Costello's Attractions as the pianist on the song.

Being a depressing song about city life, the lyrics are dear to many of the original UK punkers who lived through the summer of 1977, a summer of punk rocker–bashing that the song tells of.

Robin Banks's *ZigZag* review of "Complete Control" made sure not to neglect the strong B-side, pointing out the "Bossa nova–type chorus" and how "the clever, catchy nature of the tune almost belies the reality of Joe's words." Another tuneful arrangement of Mick's, "City of the Dead," with its poppy "ooohs" and Springsteenian sax, softens Joe's blow-by-blow account of lifeless sex, kick-less kicks, and Teddy Boys beating up punkers. Mick's arrangement alleviates Joe's despair and what should be depressing winds up being uplifting. The paradox of the Clash's songs was the music's stirring effect on the soul, despite what was often being said.

A roadie and fan favorite that the band themselves were less fond of, "City of the Dead" was first played live in September 26, 1977, at Amsterdam's infamous Paradiso Club, a converted church. A live version can be heard on *From Here to Eternity*, the Clash's first live album, released on October 4, 1999.

"Clash City Rockers"

"Clash City Rockers" is a Mick Jones composition that was recorded at CBS Studios on Whitfield Street during October and November 1977. It was the last A-side produced by Mickey Foote, who was abetted once again by Simon Humphrey and Steve Levine.

The third of the Clash's self-mythologizing songs, the title is an obvious parody of the Scottish pop, pseudo–glam rock band Bay City Rollers, but the musical references don't end there. The intro is a modification of the Who's "I Can't Explain," and the outro mirrors Status Quo's "Caroline." A song in three parts, its middle echoes the traditional British nursery rhyme "Oranges and Lemons," which is said to date back to the reign of Henry VIII. In the Clash's adaptation, "the great bell of Bow" becomes the "bells of old Bowie." The bells of glam rocker Gary Glitter and reggae toastmaster Prince Far-I are also mentioned. (The nursery rhyme's melody is alluded to again in the opening notes of "Ivan Meets G.I. Joe" on *Sandinista!*)

With its release sandwiched between that of "Complete Control" and "(White Man) In Hammersmith Palais," "Clash City Rockers" is one of the most underrated Clash compositions, somewhat akin to the Rolling Stones' "It's Only Rock 'n' Roll (but I Like It)."

While away on the Get Out of Control tour in late 1977, the Clash's management found the song lacking and tinkered with the tapes. "CBS wanted this single and Bernie thought it was too flat," Foote is quoted as saying in the booklet that accompanied 1991's *The Clash on Broadway* boxed set. "We couldn't get the group back in the studio, so I suggested we varispeed it. We varispeed'd the master about one and a half percent."

Proudly playing the test disc for friend, Mick immediately heard the difference and was aghast that someone within the Clash camp would betray the band in such a manner. He demanded Mickey Foote's ouster. Joe agreed at the time, and his former soundman from the 101-ers was never allowed in the studio with the Clash again. Years later, however, Joe told Jon Savage that the song "wasn't bad speeded up, I think Mickey was probably right."

The "Clash City Rockers" 45 was the last to feature Rocco Macauley's photography.
Author's collection

Judge for yourselves. The varispeed'd mix was used as the opening track for the US version of *The Clash*, but all subsequent releases on other compilations use the original, slightly slower version. Both versions have their charms. On the original, Mick's guitar work is more distinct and Joe's voice more natural. But Foote's version provides the live rush experienced when the Clash opened shows with "Clash City Rockers" between 1978 and 1980, Topper's drums have more smack, and Mick's feedback during the outro is more dramatic. (Actually, I should mention that this is the first Clash recording featuring feedback.)

"Jail Guitar Doors"

The B-side to "Clash City Rockers" was also recorded at CBS Studios on Whitfield Street during September 1977, with Foote, Humphrey and Levine at the controls. One of two songs the Clash performed that originated with Joe's pub band the 101-ers, "Jail Guitar Doors" was a reworked version of "Lonely Mother's Son."

The three verses are like a courtroom artist's sketches of Mick's guitar heroes facing or doing time for drug offenses. The first verse, "'bout Wayne and his deals of cocaine," is about MC5 guitarist Wayne Kramer, who would serve over two years prison time at Lexington Federal Prison for selling cocaine to undercover law-enforcement agents.

The second verse is about Peter Green, founding member of Fleetwood Mac, who in 1969 began abusing LSD and expressed his disinterest in making money (hence the line "gave all his money away") and was arrested in 1977 for threatening to shoot his accountant for sending him money from his royalty checks and committed to a London psychiatric institution, where he was diagnosed as a schizophrenic.

And then there's the third verse, which is obviously about Keith Richards's arrest in Toronto in 1977 and the trial he faced for trafficking narcotics. Mick sings of the Stones' rumored intention to "carry on anyway," a notion that offends Mick's ethics about band members banding together when faced with adversity, and so of the remaining Stones he says, "Fuck 'em!"

(Keith Richards's 1977 criminal charges were reduced to possession of twenty-two grams of heroin, and when Richards pleaded guilty on October 24, 1978, presiding judge Lloyd Graburn stated that, although "the Crown seeks a jail term . . . I will not incarcerate him for addiction and wealth." He then sentenced the guitarist/songwriter to a year's probation and ordered him to continue his drug treatment throughout the probationary period. The judge had been moved by a blind woman's letter asking the court to spare Richards the potential seven years in prison, and so Richards was instructed that, as the last part of his punishment, within six months he had to perform a benefit concert for the Canadian National Institute for the Blind, a commitment that the Rolling Stones honored on April 22, 1979. Mick must've been proud.)

In concert, Mick later reworked lyrics to comment on his own drug arrest for marijuana possession.

Appropriately enough, on the outro of "Jail Guitar Doors," Joe sings "54-46 was my number," copping the refrain from a 1969 Toots and the Maytals song about Toots's arrest for marijuana possession.

"(White Man) In Hammersmith Palais"

Generally considered the Clash's finest work song, "(White Man) In Hammersmith Palais" was the final recording the band would make at CBS Studios on Whitfield Street with recording engineer Simon Humphrey and tape-op Steve Levine. With Mickey Foote ousted from Clash recording sessions, the band themselves—which mostly meant Mick—received the production credit. The sessions took place in March and April 1978.

Levine cites this as his favorite session with the Clash. He was also happy to be working with Terry's replacement. "Topper was a great drummer; I knew him from before the Clash when he was actually a session drummer and had come in and worked on some sessions I had been working on."

The band had finally forged a song of "punk reggae" (they disliked the characterization of their reggae numbers as "white reggae") that the Clash referred to as "London Reggae." Their version of "Police and Thieves" was a first step in the right direction with its clever arrangement and Joe ominously repeating "police, police, police" during the fadeout, but the song never skanks. The two songs begin similarly with crashing chords, but whereas "Police and Thieves" settles into a rock beat, "(White Man) In Hammersmith Palais" skanks. "For this one, you move your arse sideways instead of up and down," Joe once said when introducing the song in concert.

"(White Man) In Hammersmith Palais" is a song about disappointment. Accompanied by reggae DJ/filmmaker/future Big Audio Dynamite member Don Letts and roadie Roadent, Joe attended a reggae all-nighter at the Hammersmith Palais on Shepherd's Bush Road in Hammersmith, London.

On the bill were three Jamaican reggae acts: toaster/vocalist Dillinger, vocalist Leroy Smart, and Delroy Wilson, a ska/rocksteady singer who began recording at the age of thirteen.

The Jamaican acts disappointed Joe. They were giving watered-down, choreographed performances, not the "roots rock rebel" music Joe had gone out to hear. He was expecting a reggae variant of the Clash, but instead he found many "black ears here to listen," making Joe question first his conclusions about the Notting Hill Festival riot and then everything else around him. Riots wouldn't work, because the "British army is out there." Punk rockers were preoccupied with getting close to the stage, and the new groups were selling out. And then came the final disappointment with "people changing their votes": the racist National Front was gaining in popularity.

"I have listened to this song hundreds of times and I'm still not entirely sure how [Joe] gets us from a reggae show at the Palais to Adolf Hitler in a limousine," novelist Nick Hornby writes in the booklet accompanying *The Singles*. The answers lie in the arrangement. "Simon and I were, by then, recording on multi-tracks, and we recorded a lot of overdubs on that song," tape-op Steve Levine later told interviewer John Robb. "There is a piano and acoustic guitar and a harmonica somewhere in the mix on that one."

The Clash only played two dates at the Hammersmith Palais toward the end of the 16 Tons tour in June 1980. I was in attendance for both, but I only have notes from the first night. The support acts were Spartacus and Holly and the Italians. The concert on June 17, 1980, was sabotaged by poor sound. The Clash were fleshed out by keyboardist Mickey Gallagher, but Gallagher's organ wasn't loud enough. The same complaint could be made about Mick's guitar. Things settled down, however, as they played the usual 16 Tons set, omitting only "Clampdown," which was swapped out for "Wrong 'Em Boyo." They saved "Clampdown" for the opening number of the only encore of the evening. Sound problems arose again during "Armagideon Time" (which closed the set), and it plagued the encore. It was a good crowd: swaying and hopping and dancing. Joe was talkative, such as when he introduced "(White Man) In Hammersmith Palais" as "a song about this building. Let's all get sentimental." During "Wrong 'Em Boyo," somebody fainted, and as the intro ended and Paul took up the bassline, Joe—seeing the stage crew helping a fellow up out of the crowd—said, "Hold it. Come to dance? Take a spot on the left." Later he mentioned, "We've got a Top 20 single in America" as the band roared into "I'm So Bored with the USA." And, of course, "Stay Free" was dedicated to familiar faces in the crowd:

The label of the "(White Man) In Hammersmith Palais" 45 marked the first time the Clash used gun imagery in their artwork. It would not be the last. *Author's collection*

"The few who were in Newcastle and those who waited all these months"—a reference to postponed dates. Speaking of fans, there was a Japanese girl standing next to me on the balcony, and the way she squealed, I could've sworn we were seeing the Beatles in 1964.

The Hammersmith Palais closed its doors on April 1, 2007, after a rambunctious performance by the Fall (preserved on *Last Night at the Palais*).

There is an alternate version of "(White Man) In Hammersmith Palais" with different lyrics and mix on *Rock Against Racism—RAR's Greatest Hits*, an album issued in the UK in 1980 on RAR Records. It can also be found on the *Clash on Broadway 4* bootleg recording. This version was recorded during the *Give 'Em Enough Rope* sessions and produced by Sandy Pearlman.

Many years later, when touring with the Mescaleros, Joe told *Punk*'s Judy McGuire, "It suddenly occurred to me that the songs aren't just stuff that's written on a bit of paper or put on a record. What if a song is like a person? Like a song might . . . have a store of kinetic energy of a kind we . . . haven't managed to quantify or identify. And it felt to me, like when we play '(White Man) In Hammersmith Palais,' it plays itself. It wants to be played." Joe was right.

"The Prisoner"

The B-side to "(White Man) In Hammersmith Palais" was recorded at Marquee Studio in Richmond Mews during March 1978 (as were future B-sides "1-2 Crush on You" and "Pressure Drop," and a cover of the Booker T. and the M.G.'s instrumental "Time Is Tight"). "The Prisoner" was one of the two songs Mick sang lead on at these sessions due to the lingering effect on Joe's vocal chords of a recent bout with Hepatitis B. Joe is only heard making the plaintive appeal "I don't wanna be the prisoner," as repeated four times at the end of each chorus.

"The Prisoner" is a tight vehicle featuring Topper's sharp drumming and Mick's layered guitars. Said to be influenced by Patrick McGoohan's 1960s television series of the same name, the first verse is practically an homage to television, as it also references *The Muppets* and *Coronation Street*, a British soap opera that premiered on December 9, 1960, and is still being broadcast as of this writing. As such, the prisoner in the Clash song is imprisoned not by a judicial system but a dead-end society. And when Mick references how "the rude boys get rude," here is the Clash's first citing of a Jamaican image that they would go on to appropriate for their own use.

9

If They Wanna Get Me, Well, I Got No Choice

The American Debut of the Only English Group That Matters

"The Only English Group That Matters" was the US advertising pitch Epic Records placed in the inner cover of *Trouser Press*'s January 1979 issue. And with *The Clash* having been deemed unlistenable by record company executives and never released stateside, *Give 'Em Enough Rope* was the Clash's *de facto* debut album in America, and so naturally perceptions about *Give 'Em Enough Rope* differ among not only music journalists but fans, too. In Great Britain, the sophomore effort may have shot up to #2 on the charts—the top spot was held by the *Grease* soundtrack—but reviews were mixed. *Sounds* gave it five stars; *ZigZag* was equally positive, but its objectivity was questionable, since the review was by Robin Banks, who was both Mick's childhood friend and also the subject of one of album's the songs. Nick Kent in *NME* approved of the improved production but took issue with Joe's naïve view of a violent world.

It was Jon Savage's unflattering review in *Melody Maker*, however, that struck, and stuck in, Britain's collective consciousness. Wielding a musically imbued Jingoism, Savage pointed out that the album's producer was American, that overdubs had been made in San Francisco and New York City, and that the album was aimed at American audiences. The Clash, it seemed to Savage, were bored with the UK. This was untrue. *Give 'Em Enough Rope* was about England, not America, but for many the damage was now done.

Patti Smith had told *Sounds* reporter Sandy Robertson that producer Sandy Pearlman would give the Clash's second album the "technical competence" needed to establish beachheads for the band on both American coasts. (Patti knew Pearlman's work quite well, since she was romantically involved at the time with Allan Lanier of Blue Öyster Cult, the Long Island–based heavy-metal band Pearlman not only produced but managed.) And Pearlman delivered. Much of American punk rock is based on *Give 'Em Enough Rope*, not *The Clash*. Just check out Green Day, Rancid, or Rage Against the Machine, and you can hear them hoisting their sound systems up with *Rope*.

Enter "The General"

He wouldn't have admitted it in 1978, but being Bruce Springsteen's stablemate on Columbia Records in America would have thrilled Joe Strummer—except CBS had moved the Clash's American contract to another subsidiary, Epic Records. The marketing philosophy of Muff Winwood, the A&R man for CBS in Great Britain handling the Clash, was that the way to groom hit makers in the British market for greater success was via promotion in Europe. "And once you have the hit in Europe," he told *Billboard*, "you can really start developing that artist." In other words, you could then market that artist in America.

Epic Records, however, was eager to push Clash product in America. Its A&R man was Bruce Harris, a self-described "avid Clash Fan" who had justified not releasing their debut album stateside by saying its production quality was "an enormous drawback." Writing to Paul Doherty, a fan of the band, in November 1977, Harris took issue with the band's approval of the production: "The band's live performance is many times better than what is on [*The Clash*] and one has to question the artistic integrity of creating an inferior sounding album." Harris defended himself by writing that the band cannot dismiss his criticism by stubbornly saying that *The Clash* is what punk rock truly sounds like because the production on the Sex Pistols' debut album proves otherwise. *Never Mind the Bollocks, Here's the Sex Pistols* sounds "really strong and captures the band's power," Harris wrote, before adding, "I believe the Clash are better than anyone in in the field except the Sex Pistols and I have been getting very involved in guiding the production of their second album."

Enter "The General," the nickname Joe gave Sandy Pearlman during the Automatt overdubbing sessions in San Francisco. Epic Records knew of Pearlman's FM-radio production standards from the Blue Öyster Cult material he had delivered to Columbia Records, including "Don't Fear the

Reaper," which had been a mega-hit in 1976, but is this why Pearlman was recommended? This author doesn't think so. Word must've filtered across the Atlantic about the Clash's mulishness in the recording studio. Pearlman had just produced his third album for the proto punk New York City–based Dictators. The reasoning must have been, "We've got a producer we're comfortable with who's worked with bands 'in the field,' let's have him work with the Clash"—and so Pearlman was recommended to Bernie Rhodes for the Clash's next long-playing project.

"One day I was in Bernie's car and he was playing Blue Öyster Cult," Joe told *Sounds*' Pete Silverton in June 1978, "and I said, 'What are you playing this shit for?' . . . 'cos he's usually got some doo-wop or some reggae of something, and he goes, 'Oh, it's well produced,' and I said, 'So what? It's a load of shit.' 'But I'm listening to the production,' he said. He was checking it out."

The next thing Joe knew, Bernie had booked a three-date swing in late January 1978 through the Midlands so Pearlman could see and hear the Clash in action. Set lists are incomplete for these three dates, but two songs that would be on the sophomore album ("Tommy Gun" and "Last Gang in Town") were debuted during these shows.

New York Rocker's Jack Basher wrote of seeing Pearlman at the January 26 show at Lanchester Polytechnic in Coventry. It was an energetic performance: "After half a bar of music it was as if they had been playing for fifteen minutes; it's like they start at an energy level that most bands have trouble building to"—a description that brings back memories of the Clash concerts with Mick I experienced twenty-four times.

It's at the Lanchester Polytechnic where the story originates of Mick's friend Robin Banks punching Pearlman in the face for entering the Clash's dressing room minutes before their performance. It has been said that the Clash then calmly stepped over Pearlman's prone body as they walked out to play, leaving Bernie to rush forward with a handkerchief for Pearlman's bloody nose. Another version has it that the band was apologetic, especially Mick, who admired Pearlman's production on the Dictators' albums. Pearlman himself has described the legendary punch as an exaggeration, which seems true, considering his subsequent agreement to produce the Clash's next long player. Pearlman even says he got a punch in at Banks.

Unfortunately, Joe landed in Saint Stephens Hospital on Fulham Road in Chelsea the following day, suffering from Hepatitis B. Joe's illness postponed plans for Pearlman to begin recording the Clash at CBS's Studios on Whitfield Street in March.

This may have been a blessing in disguise. Short of new material for the second album, Joe and Mick had been flown by Bernie to Kingston, Jamaica, for songwriting inspiration in December 1977, but little came of it. "We were so overwhelmed," Mick remembered in *Audio Ammunition*, a documentary produced for YouTube to promote the re-release of Clash albums in 2013, "we didn't get much writing done." The Lennon/McCartney songwriting team for the punk set only worked up two new compositions: "Safe European Home" and "Drug-Stabbing Time." Upon their return, the band kept working up new material, but without Paul, whose disappointment at not having gone to Jamaica with Joe and Mick was the impetus for him flying off to Moscow with his girlfriend, Caroline Coon, the blonde *Melody Maker* journalist who was ten years his senior. In his absence, Joe and Mick continued working up new songs with Topper for the second album. The bassist was handed a cassette of the demos upon his return and banished to the top floor of Rehearsal Rehearsals until he learned the basslines.

Biding their time, in March the Clash entered Marquee Studio in Richmond Mews with Sex Pistols producer Bill Price to record four songs as potential B-sides (see chapter 7). Then at the end of the month came the infamous pigeon-shooting incident where Paul and Topper—along with Robin Banks and Topper's friends Pete and Steve Barnacle—went up to Rehearsal Rehearsals' rooftop and with an air pistol and air rifle shot several expensive homing pigeons that belonged to a garage mechanic.

A fracas ensued between the Clash's rhythm section and two of the mechanics sent up to investigate, but that was nothing compared to what occurred next, when a helicopter suddenly materialized in the sky. Rehearsal Rehearsals was near railway tracks, and one British Rail employee had thought Paul and Topper were shooting at passing trains. The fear was that the shooters were terrorists, which was rather ironic given the material that would appear on *Give 'Em Enough Rope*. All five young men were arrested. Paul and Topper owned up to being the shooters, and their bail was set at £1,500 each.

In a scene recreated in *Rude Boy*, Mick and Caroline Coon are shown bailing out Paul and Topper. Bernie repeated the mistake of Rolling Stones manager Andrew Loog Oldham in 1967 when Mick Jagger and Keith Richards were busted for drug possession at Richards' home Redlands: he disappeared when the musicians he managed needed him the most. Oldham did not last out the year, and neither would Rhodes. Paul reacted angrily by painting a large mural in Rehearsal Rehearsals of a naked Bernie being shat upon by pigeons. This schism between Bernie and the band was one of the unexpected hassles Sandy Pearlman had to overcome while making the album.

Produced by Sandy Pearlman

Looking over Sandy Pearlman's production credits, one is struck by how few acts he has produced: twelve albums by Blue Öyster Cult, three albums by the Dictators, two each by Pavlov's Dog and Shakin' Street, and one each by the Clash and the Dream Syndicate (*Medicine Show*). This indicates a man who only produces recording artists he believes in.

In the Clash documentary *Audio Ammunition*, Pearlman says he was contacted by Dan Loggins, CBS's A&R man: "He said, 'Hey we need to come to London as soon as possible' . . . so we went in and apparently the sound dude signaled the Clash that I was in the house. So they began by announcing, 'We're going to do a song and we want to dedicate it to Journey and Ted Nugent'—a bunch of AOR bands that were big in the late '70s—'and most of all the Blue Öyster Cult. This is "I'm So Bored with the USA!"'"

Pearlman wasn't offended. "I think Pearlman definitely saw in us all the possibilities of that black side of rock 'n' roll," Mick told Chris Salewicz in a July 1978 *NME* article. "He immediately seemed to see in us another possibility for what he really wanted to do with the Blue Öyster Cult. He knows the Cult don't really do it. And he knows we know it, too."

Pearlman went to bat for the Clash by meeting with Columbia Records executives and acquiring better equipment before recording commenced. As he told *Trouser Press*'s Ira Robbins, "The object was to make them sound as fiery and spirited as they do live, only better . . . they had bad equipment that was run down and poorly maintained. They just didn't sound that good. They couldn't make a good record with the equipment they were playing through." Mick got a Gibson Les Paul Special, Joe rented a Gibson 345 (the type of guitar his hero Chuck Berry used), and Paul acquired the Fender Precision bass fans now associate with him.

"The Glutton Twins"

"Sandy's just a knob-twiddler. Well, not even that—he oversees others twiddling knobs," Joe would tell *Melody Maker*'s Chris Bohn, a year after *Rope*'s release. The knob-twiddler for Pearlman during his only recording sessions with the Clash was fellow American Robert "Corky" Stasiak, a recording engineer with a far more extensive discography than Pearlman. Beginning with Jim Croce, Stasiak went on to work with Aerosmith, Alice Cooper, Bruce Springsteen, Lou Reed, and many others, including Kiss (for which Pearlman teased him).

In an obvious pun on the Glitter Twins (the name used by the Stones' production team of Jagger and Richards), the two Americans were christened "the Glutton Twins" by the Clash for their late night ordering of Indian food as the band were forced to do take after take after take until they laid down tracks that met the exacting producer's approval.

The Utopia Studio Sessions

Initial sessions with the Glutton Twins took place at Utopia Studios, which was near Rehearsal Rehearsals. This studio was booked because Paul and Topper were required to visit their bail officer daily in Kentish Town until sentencing for shooting the homing pigeons was set down.

The Clash had already demoed their new songs for what would become *Give 'Em Enough Rope* but Pearlman insisted on having his own demos made. Pearlman loved the drum sound Topper was getting at Utopia, but plans for further recording were abruptly dashed when Paul and Topper—unaccustomed to the grade of ganja the Glutton Twins smoked—knocked over some flowerpots in the lobby and created an obstacle course to ride motorbikes around. Dirt and tire tracks were everywhere. Seeing the mess, Pearlman knew they wouldn't be welcomed back for a second session, so he made sure the Clash recorded the new demos in one night.

The Basing Street Sessions

Opinions of the *Rope* sessions are split along the natural fault lines of the Clash. Joe told Jim Shelley he had "no fond memories of it." For Paul, "it showed my flaws in my bass playing because before I met Mick I never played an instrument in my life," as he says in *Audio Ammunition*. They are the instinctual musicians of the band, the true punks in terms of musical ability.

Mick and Topper, however, are pegged as "musos"—a critical piece of British slang defined by the Free Dictionary as "a pop musician, regarded as being overly concerned with technique rather than musical content or expression." So it's not surprising that Topper's view differs dramatically from Paul's. "I really enjoyed working with Sandy Pearlman," he says in *Aural Ammunition*. "He was very complimentary about my drumming, which meant there some affinity between us and he got a great drum sound." In fact, if there is one reason to give a fresh listen to *Give 'Em Enough Rope*, it is the sound of Topper's drums.

He's wavered since, but immediately after making *Rope*, Mick was quoted as saying he wanted Pearlman to produce the Clash's third album. It's easy to hear why. Mick guitars are stacked on track after track. His counterpart in the Sex Pistols—Steve Jones—had been praised for his layers of guitar on Pistols tracks, and one has the impression that Mick was itching to demonstrate he could outdo his fellow punk guitarist. A famous quote Sandy Pearlman made to Greil Marcus at the time was that there were "more guitars per square inch on [*Give 'Em Enough Rope*] than in anything in the rest of Western civilization." But because Mick's guitar playing was rooted in Mick Ronson and Keith Richards, the result was more rock 'n' roll than punk rock, and an album that reflects Mick's true rock 'n' roll sensibilities:

Give 'Em Enough Rope was released in the US with a bonus 45 containing "Groovy Times" b/w "Gates of the West." *Author's collection*

it's everything Hoople. So it's no surprise to learn that Mott the Hoople had recorded *Wildlife* and *Brain Capers* at the studio Pearlman was forced to relocate to.

Basing Street Studios was owned by Island Records. The building was originally a chapel that had its foundation stone set in July 1865. By the 1920s the churchgoers were congregating elsewhere, and the building was being used by the makers of wax figures for Madame Tussauds. It transitioned to a recording studio in the late 1960s. A who's who of classic rock albums were completely or partially recorded at Basing Street Studios, including Jethro Tull's *Aqualung*, Led Zeppelin's *Led Zeppelin IV*, and the Rolling Stones' *Goat's Head Soup*. It was also at this studio that Bob Marley recorded "Punky Reggae Party" and that the Clash first made the acquaintance of Lee "Scratch" Perry.

The sessions were seemingly interminable—the antithesis of *The Clash*, which was recorded in three four-day weekends—but Pearlman felt he had been hired by CBS to deliver an album by the Clash that was played by the Clash, which accounts for his insistence Paul keep redoing his basslines. Rumors have persisted that Mick redid Paul's parts but this seems unlikely, given Pearlman's work ethic. He was not averse to using unplanned errors that improved a song—he has cited Joe bursting a blood vessel in his mouth during a take of "Guns on the Roof" kept in the recording Joe saying "Got blood in me mouth!"—but mistakes that were "off the scale" had to be redone.

Despite all the retakes, the London sessions were productive, and the Glutton Twins produced ten new songs for the second album, an alternate version of "(White Man) In Hammersmith Palais," and the basis for two songs that would find a home on *The Cost of Living EP*, which some consider the Clash's finest recording.

The American Sessions

Things were not well with the Clash during the first half of 1978. Original members of the inner circle, such as Roadent, Sebastian Cochran, and Mickey Foote, became disenchanted and left or were ostracized. Joe had been ill and was unsure of how to move forward artistically after punk rock in the UK fizzled. Mick became more assertive, but he too was ditching punk rock and beginning to live out his teenage dreams of the rock 'n' roll lifestyle, which included a coke habit.

Then there were the simmering problems with Bernie, who had disengaged from the day-to-day running of the Clash, leaving that to Johnny Green, the band's new road manager, and seemed to be more actively promoting Subway Sect. Bernie refused to believe in January that Joe was truly ill and had to be hospitalized—he thought Joe was drinking too much alcohol—and failed to materialize when Paul and Topper were arrested. Mick was exerting more influence over the group and advocated ousting their manager. Arguments over management would break out at the recording sessions and interrupted what the Glutton Twins were in London to accomplish. There were too many extraneous matters for the record to be properly wrapped up—a record that American executives at CBS and Epic Records were not happy with when they heard the initial mixes. Over £100,000 had been spent on the sessions in the UK, and they were worried that their investment would never be recouped. They discussed replacing the Glutton Twins, as they wanted something more polished than what they were hearing from a band already worried their second album was too polished.

For Pearlman, the solution was flying Joe and Mick in August to San Francisco after the July dates of the Out on Parole tour, as he explained to Ira Robbins, "I recorded part in San Francisco because . . . the Automatt is the best sounding studio that I knew of in the US. I felt it was the best studio to do the guitar overdubs."

The Automatt at 827 Folsom Street had opened two years earlier and originally shared space with Columbia Records, but in 1978 founder David Rubinson, a freelance producer who had gotten his start with Columbia, subleased the entire building following a pay dispute between Columbia and its engineers. The Automatt was used primarily by jazz musicians (Herbie Hancock, Ron Carter) and rhythm-and-blues acts (Patti Labelle, the Meters) when the songwriting half of the Clash entered its doors for three weeks of intense re-recording. The two worked with the Glutton Twins twelve hours a day, seven days a week. There was even a short write-up in *Billboard* noting their activity. The only relief Strummer/Jones got was hanging out at night in the San Francisco punk scene they had helped spawn, especially at Mabuhay Gardens—nicknamed the Fab Mab—a Filipino restaurant that became San Francisco's version of CBGB in the late 1970s. Several local acts were launched there, including the Dead Kennedys, a punk band whose influence on the genre arguably matches that of the Clash. They also caught performances of Mike Bloomfield and Emmy Lou Harris.

Once these sessions were completed, final mixing was scheduled at the Record Plant in New York City a week later. Joe and Mick went their separate ways for the week. Joe fulfilled a lifelong dream of driving cross-country, by way of New Orleans. Mick flew to Los Angeles and then New York City. Reunited in the Big Apple, Joe and Mick caught pianist Al Fields's act in a bar and invited him to play boogie-woogie piano on "Julie's Been Working for the Drug Squad." Pearlman wasn't happy with the results, however, and brought in Blue Öyster Cult's Allan Lanier to redo the solo. Stan Bronstein—best known for his work with John and Yoko in the early 1970s—was hired to blow sax on "Drug-Stabbing Time." Considerable work was done on "Gates of the West," but it was left off of the album. Joe and Mick then picked up Paul and Topper at the airport so they could hear the final mixes.

Something About England

The chasm of opinion of *Give 'Em Enough Rope* remains wide, decades later. There are often journalistic calls for a major reassessment, which implies the negative reviews have prevailed. The album is sandwiched between the Clash's two unqualified critical successes and thus suffers by comparison. But on the basis that that major reassessment does not appear to be imminent, let's take a crack at it.

Several reviewers in 1978 bemoaned the absence of a lyric sheet, because deciphering Joe's words under Pearlman's loud production was impossible. It's no secret that Pearlman was no fonder of Joe's voice than some of the executives at their record company, but for many fans Clash lyrics contained messages, so it was a negative that the production had sacrificed Joe's voice in favor of Mick's multi-layered guitar tracks and Topper's thundering drumbeats. Thankfully, this has been rectified with the mix of *Give 'Em Enough Rope* included in 2013's *Sound System* boxed set.

Somewhat defensively, Joe admitted to journalists that Bernie Rhodes's lack of input during the recording of *Rope* had left him flailing for subject matter. Left to his own devices, Joe avidly read the newspapers and interacted with fans coming to Clash shows. What he found was a dreary ol' England on the brink of a war between terrorists and totalitarians, with his confused fans caught in the middle.

The first beat of *Give 'Em Enough Rope* rings out like a gunshot. This is perfect for an album riddled with gun imagery.

On the face of it, "Safe European Home" is about Joe and Mick's journey to Jamaica, but rewritten as if it's the average Brit's holiday in the sun gone awry. Instead of finding the reggae music the tourist has gone for, they find a place where "every white face is an invitation to robbery" and they "can't take the gunplay." They are happy to be back in their safe European home. But the final third of the song is about how the rude boy can't fail. Without the lyric sheet, it seems to contain further description of the rude boys in Kingston, but that's not what the outro's about. Looking up and saying "What?," the Brit realizes that "Rudie come from Jamaica." In other words, the Jamaicans are emigrating to his no-longer-safe European home. This influx to England is the very thing swelling the ranks of the racist National Front.

This is the perfect lead-in to the next song, "English Civil War," Joe and Mick's adaptation of Louis Lambert's "When Johnny Comes Marching Home," first published during the American Civil War. Joe wrote new words for a song he recalled from his earliest school days. The new lyrics foresee a civil war that will erupt in England because of the rising popularity of local fascist organizations such as the National Front. "It's already started," Joe pointed out to *NME* writer Chris Salewicz in the summer of 1978. "There's people attacking Bengalis with clubs and firing shotguns in Wolverhampton." (The Clash pointedly unveiled "English Civil War" during the Anti-Nazi League Carnival in Victoria Park.) But Joe doesn't foresee victory. The totalitarian state will win. Johnny's coming home, but his female relatives are getting his coffin out.

The rat-a-tat-tat drumming of "Tommy Gun" effectively reminds the listener of Jimi Hendrix's "Machine Gun." The drumrolls were Topper's idea—a concept that he later felt was his first contribution to the band's music. If any band member should have been pleased with Pearlman's production, it was Topper, the subject of so much of the producer's praise. Pearlman called Topper "the rhythm machine" and "the human drum machine," telling Pete Silverton, "What have we done? A hundred tracks? And [Topper's] only screwed up once." Topper's drumming alone is a major reason to revisit *Give 'Em Enough Rope.* With the drums perfectly miked—Pearlman devoted three days to achieving and perfecting the drum sound—the producer makes good on replicating the bollocks of the band's live fury. In concert, almost every song began with Topper, and so does almost every song on *Give 'Em Enough Rope.*

Lyrically, "Tommy Gun" builds on the anti-terrorism theme begun in "English Civil War," with Joe mocking the terrorists and comparing them to pop stars as he describes how a hijacked airliner is to be swapped for "ten prisoners." With the song's references to "standing there in Palestine, lighting the fuse," the Clash could be singing of today's turmoil. The first single from the album, "Tommy Gun" is a marvel of an arrangement. It begins with Topper's machine-gunnery drumming answered by explosive guitars and Joe setting up the scene, moves to a chorus echoing the 101'ers' "Silent Telephone," another verse and chorus, and then Mick's Morse code guitar lead is screaming for help. There's a rhythmic buildup and then, during the final verses, Topper shoots off volleys of drumbeats, the sound of tommy guns going off at the airport.

The final line of "Safe European Home" states that "no one knows where the policeman goes," and that theme finally gets picked up and developed in "Julie's Been Working for the Drug Squad," the fourth track of Side 1. Based on "Operation Julie," a two-and-a-half-year police investigation in Wales that resulted in the smashing up of a large LSD operation, this song must have been influenced by Joe's reading of the newspaper for ideas. Referencing the Beatles' "Lucy in the Sky with Diamonds" in the first line, Joe paints a surrealist picture of undercover cops getting high in the name of the law. On an album generally lacking the Clash's satirical humor, we finally get a laugh when Joe says, "Everybody's high, high, high," and is answered with Mick going, "Hi, man!"—which Mick was always sure to say during concert performances. Still, this is serious stuff, because it is the policeman's role in a totalitarian state to keep the people in their place. You can fight the drug laws, but the drug laws will win.

With a musical arrangement seemingly out of place on this album, if "Police and Thieves" was a forerunner of the reggae numbers that would increasingly form the bedrock of the Clash's music in 1980, "Julie's Been Working for the Drug Squad," with its New Orleans–style piano, predicts *London Calling*'s wide musical palette.

The Side 1 closer "Last Gang in Town" was often cited as one of the album's low points in record reviews, and it is. The fact that the song exceeds five minutes didn't help. Neither did the press mistakenly inferring that "Last Gang in Town" was another of the band's self-mythologizing efforts. Rather, the song is about what the Clash were seeing on the streets or in concert halls or train stations, where "kids fight like different nations." "Last Gang in Town" is not a great Clash song; they had handled this subject matter in much catchier fashion on "City of the Dead." In the studio, Joe had a tough time doing vocal take after vocal take of this song for Pearlman. Written from his insider status, Robin Banks's review in *ZigZag* revealed that Joe's shouts of "I might as well give up!" and "Useless!," heard at the end, were aimed at the producer. Turning frustration into art, Pearlman weaved the outbursts into the final recording.

While Side 1 begins with a loud crack of the snare, Side 2 begins with whispering guitar noises. Then Mick does a count-off and slashes away at a clipped version of the Clash's favorite Who riff ("I Can't Explain," here being used for the third and final time in a Clash tune). Topper adds the beat said to have been the impetus for this composition, the first credited to Strummer/Jones/Simonon/Headon. Joe swears himself into the court of public opinion before Joe's rhythm guitar and Paul's bass come crashing in. If "Tommy Gun" was aimed at terrorists, "Guns on the Roof" targets totalitarian regimes where systems "built by the sweat of many" are abused by "legal rapers." No one is innocent in Joe's eyes; the USSR is plotting and the USA is "pretending that the wars are all done."

"Guns on the Roof" was seen by the British music press as a misguided reference to the pigeon-shooting incident at Rehearsal Rehearsals. While the song was worked on in the days after Simonon and Headon shot the homing pigeons, Joe in his ad libs had taken the incident as a starting point for chords and a beat in need of lyrics. In retrospect, he would have been wise to revise a set of words that only encouraged further derision from the press.

The manner in which "Drug-Stabbing Time" follows "Guns on the Roof" is one of the most powerful one-two punches on any Clash long-player. Mick's squirrely notes are cut off by a rhythm guitar being strummed at a hardcore pace. Other instruments pile on, rushing forward only to abruptly stop as a bass note skids. The hardcore pace is revived and the chorus sung. "Drug-Stabbing Time" is one of the Clash's fastest songs. Upon its release in America, *Give 'Em Enough Rope* was very popular in San Francisco and Los Angeles, the punk strongholds of the West Coast, and part of the appeal was the album's brisk pace. Pearlman captured not only the sound of the Clash in concert, but the tempo: the Clash in 1978 could play fifty-minute sets that were sixty minutes on paper. *Give 'Em Enough Rope* is actually their hardcore punk album, and the album was influential on the American hardcore punk movement spread by the likes of the Bad Brains and the Dead Kennedys in the early 1980s.

"Drug-Stabbing Time" was another target of record reviewers in 1978. *Trouser Press*'s Ira Robbins thought it "the only lame cut on the album." While it is true that the chorus is repeated six times, the arrangement is livened by a bracing sax solo courtesy of Stan Bronstein, the Elephant's Memory leader, and after a false ending there is a dramatically played reenactment of a police bust—Joe's vocals screeching like a police car—which pairs this song thematically with "Julie's Been Working for the Drug Squad." Not lame at all.

Heading into the album's home stretch, we have what has been referred to as "the trilogy": three songs where the Clash of 1978 recount recent life experiences in hopes of imparting lessons on their fans. "Stay Free" is the closest they came to Mott the Hoople balladry, and features Mick's only solo vehicle on *Rope*. Drawing on his childhood friendship with Robin Crocker (*né* Banks), Mick embellishes the facts with precise poetic strokes and provides a cautionary tale to fans that a life of crime does not pay. If Joe on the closing cut will state that a factory is "no place to spend your youth," then neither is a jail cell. The organ on this track is sometimes erroneously credited to the Attractions' Steve Nieve, but it was the Rumour's Bob Andrews who played it.

"This song was written by a used car salesman that lives up Camden Road," is how Joe introduced "Cheapskates" at the London Lyceum on January 3, 1979, taking a knock at the band's former manager Bernie Rhodes and drawing laughs from those in the know. He continues in an atypically lengthy, almost Springsteen-like manner (at least for Joe, who usually introduced songs with a cryptic one liner or by stating the first lines of the opening verse). "He gave us the idea for it. He goes, 'Why do you always sell yourself dirt cheap?' The answer? Because it's the only price we can get."

"Cheapskates" is the first of the two songs on *Rope* about the Clash. Highly praised in reviews, it nevertheless was quickly dropped from the set list. In fact, it appears the aforementioned London Lyceum performance was its last ever airing. *Rope*'s penultimate track finds the Clash in a rare defensive posture, lashing out at formerly supportive rock critics who thought Joe a hypocrite for living in Sebastian Conran's white mansion. (Conran was a member of the band's inner circle during the first few years.) These same critics are surprised to still find Joe in London clubs "trying to hear a tune" because he's a rock star now.

"All the Young Punks" also begins with a scene out of the Clash's past, although this one is from the myth of the Clash. It was often said that Joe met Mick and Paul in the road one day before he joined the Clash and told that they liked him but not his group, the 101'ers. It never happened. But Joe recreates this mythical meeting and uses it as a stepping-off point to impart a message to the band's fans. "It's important that people don't see it as a kind of corny bio pic," Mick told Ira Robbins. "Some do—some see it as a system of living. That's not all it is—we're more than that. It's all for them as well as us; it's for their imaginations. We're raising consciousness. It's the only thing that young people can do for other young people that's worth doing."

The message then of *Give 'Em Enough Rope* from the Clash to young people is that they should not turn to racist organizations or terrorism or drugs or thievery or factory jobs for their future. They should do something creative, like Mick had done: they should "practice daily in (their) room." Caroline Coon had challenged the Clash in November 1976, when they were mocking the career opportunities society offered, by noting, "But somebody's got to work in a factory." Joe, Mick, and Paul disagreed, with Paul countering, "We can inspire people. There's no one else to inspire you. Rock 'n' roll is a really good medium. It has impact, and, if we do our job properly then we're making people aware of a situation they'd otherwise tend to ignore. We can have a vast effect!"

As daunting as it seems, the Clash were determined to try and improve the lives of their fans. They do not want to see their youth wasted, and so advise in the album's closing track, "Live it now, there ain't much to die for."

The Cover Art

The Clash's sense of self-depreciating humor is evident in the title chosen for their second album. Said to have been inspired by a line in "White Punks on Dope" by the Tubes, the saying "Give a man enough rope and he'll hang himself" can be traced back to the Old Testament story of Haman in the Book of Esther (7:10: "So they hanged Haman on the gallows that he had prepared for Mordecai") and is so common that the band only used the first clause, expecting fans and music journalists to understand their intent, which was probably aimed at the record company executives they often found themselves at odds with. It's likely that the title was also inspired by a similar album title by a band Mick once enthusiastically followed: the Faces' *A Nod Is as Good as a Wink . . . to a Blind Horse.*

The source of the image used for the album cover was a painting by artist and punk aficionado Hugh Brown, first sighted by Joe and Mick inside Mubahay Gardens. (Brown befriended and photographed Mick and would go on to become an award-winning art designer for recording artists and the creative director at Rhino Records.) Its title would have appealed to Joe's socialistic sensibilities: *End of the Trail for Capitalism.*

Featuring brilliant flat colors, the cover artwork by CBS designer Gene Greif was based on a photograph by Adrian Atwater of buzzards feasting on a dead American cowboy portrayed by Wallace Irving Robertson that was printed as a postcard in 1953. Greif added a Chinese horseman staring down at the American cowboy's body. The back cover was of Chinese horsemen holding red flags. (Greif, who died in 2004 from Hepatitis C, also designed album covers for the B-52's and Phoebe Snow.)

The lettering was done in a faux-Chinese style. In America, Epic replaced this with block capital lettering, which displeased the Clash and was rectified on subsequent pressings. The original album also had incorrect song titles, with "That's No Way to Spend Your Youth" being used for "All the Young Punks (New Boots and Contracts)." This error was originally blamed on CBS and Epic Records, but Pearlman told Ira Robbins, "The Clash did all the credits that appear on the album. Remember, they didn't have a manager at the time"—Bernie having been fired on October 21, 1978. "Usually managers look after this stuff, and they submitted a list to the record company that had the wrong title of the song and a few other things left off, and they forgot to send a corrected list. Somebody noticed the error on a proof and the record company said they'd fix it, which they did in the UK but not in the US."

The Playback

If I may paraphrase Joe Strummer: "Fuckin' loud, innit?" But *Give 'Em Enough Rope* hasn't been this loud since the dawn of the CD age. In explaining the motivation for the release of the *Sound System* boxed set, Tim Young—credited with remastering the set along with the Clash—told www.mixonline.com that "Mick had been a lifelong Beatles fan, and when he heard the Beatles reissues, he was knocked out with the fact that there was lots of detail in the tracks he hadn't heard before. And that was his brief to me: 'I want people to listen to this and hear things that might have been buried before.'"

This turns out to be especially true with *Give 'Em Enough Rope.* "This is the first time that the masters on the second album . . . have ever been used for CD, because we never had the master tapes at CBS studios in London," explained Young. "That was cut in San Francisco at the Automatt. An EQ'd copy tape was sent across to England, and the original masters disappeared into the Sony library somewhere. Of all the five albums, that's the one where people will hear the biggest difference: in the guitar sounds and the whole aggression of the songs."

So this is the perfect time for new fans and old fans alike to give the Clash another chance to hang themselves.

As the Wind Changed Direction

The Cost of Living EP

The title of the Clash's second EP reflected their skewed sense of humor. "There was something on the TV or in the newspapers going on about the cost of living," Paul recalled, in the Clash's coffee-table book, "and for some reason me and Joe saw humor in those words and we were getting on our knees laughing going, "Oh no! The cost of living!'"

As was becoming common with Clash releases, *The Cost of Living EP* encountered turbulence on its way to market. It contains the first four songs the Clash recorded at Wessex Sound Studios, a converted church hall located in Highbury New Park in London, and was also the first record made with recording engineer Bill Price, who would be their studio accomplice for the next two years, and was probably recommended to the band by CBS's Muff Winwood. Price had produced the Sex Pistols' singles and various album tracks but, perhaps more importantly, he had engineered a number of Mott the Hoople recordings. For *The Cost of Living EP*, he received a co-production credit alongside the Clash.

Recorded in mid-January between the London Lyceum dates and the band's first American tour the following month, this was the Clash's attempt at wresting control of their recordings after the unsatisfying sessions with Sandy Pearlman. They were eager to commit to tape "I Fought the Law," a new cover tune that had already crept into their live set in Belfast, Ireland, on October 13, 1978; two songs left unfinished from the *Give 'Em Enough Rope* sessions; and a re-arranged version of the obscure punk gem "Capital Radio," newly transformed by Topper's drumming.

Pleased with the results—and no doubt happy that the Clash had funded the sessions with money from the producers of *Rude Boy*, who thought they were working on the forthcoming film's soundtrack—CBS Records nonetheless informed the Clash they'd have to hold off releasing the EP. The record company wanted to capitalize on the marketing for *Give 'Em Enough Rope* by releasing "English Civil War" as a second single from the album.

The Packaging

The Cost of Living EP was finally released on May 11, 1979, which was election day in the UK. If he had known who would be elected as prime minister, Mick might not have objected to the original cover proposed by Joe, who described it to Jon Savage in 1988 as featuring an image of Margaret Thatcher holding a basket of dirty laundry.

With Thatcher vetoed, Joe and Paul worked with design agency Rocking Russian on creating a cover that was a parody of a box of laundry detergent. The cover promised "EXTRA POWER" and "Clash INTENSIFIED," while the back assured customers that you'd "GET THE BEST RESULTS BY ALWAYS USING NEW CLASH." The image within the EP's gatefold was of football fans fenced into a stadium—one of the subjects of "Groovy Times," the second song on the A-side.

The Clash wanted the EP to sell for the standard 45 price of £1.00, but CBS insisted on setting the cover price at £1.49 because of the two additional tracks and the clever, intricate gatefold design. It was not released in the US at all, but this was not a surprise. The Clash may have been on the Epic Records roster for over two years, but thus far no singles had been issued stateside.

The Content

The Cost of Living EP is an important recording in the Clash's discography. Its running time of 13:48 altered the course of the band's career. Having spent the previous year wrestling with punk rock's legacy, they had finally found a way forward: by merging their four pre-punk personalities, they had birthed a Clash fluent in multiple musical idioms. The British press was too distracted with championing the Jam to notice its once favorite sons going global. Even Epic Records didn't realize this EP contained the song that would break the band in America.

And yet "I Fought the Law" *was not* the song promoted on the EP's front cover. That was "Capital Radio," and this makes sense because if *The Cost of Living EP* is about anything, it is about the dire state of radio in the late

1970s. "I Fought the Law" is a cover of an old radio hit. In "Groovy Times," the radio says that "Groovy times are number one," and there's mention of someone in a "dog suit like from 1964" (allegedly Elvis Costello). "Gates of the West" find the Clash singing about finding themselves in the Record Plant, making songs that will be played on the radio and give "something new" for Eastside Johnny and Southside Sue. There's also a reference to Little Richard, that old hit maker from the 1950s. Then we have the new recording of "Capital Radio," and while the lyrics are identical to the 1977 version, the song now includes an ad lib from Joe as he strategizes about how the Clash can get played on the radio. He even parodies 1978 radio hits from the *Grease* soundtrack.

Some fans consider 1979's *The Cost of Living EP* to be the Clash's best recording.

Author's collection

"I Fought the Law"

When the plane carrying Buddy Holly crashed on a snowy Iowan cornfield on February 3, 1959, he left behind his former band the Crickets, who had split up with the singer/guitarist after siding with manager Norman Petty over a money dispute. Double bassist Joe B. Mauldin and drummer Jerry Allison were in Texas with a recently hired rhythm guitarist while Holly—newly married and in need of cash—toured the Midwest as part of the Winter Dance Party tour with a backing band that included future outlaw country-and-western musician Waylon Jennings. The rhythm guitarist's name was Sonny Curtis; he was a friend of Holly's and a pallbearer at his funeral.

(A little known factoid is that the Clash made a late-night visit to Buddy Holly's gravesite in Lubbock, Texas, after performing an unannounced gig with Joe Ely at the Texan musician's local club, the Rox, on October 7, 1979. Ely and the Clash drank beer, strummed acoustic guitars, and serenaded Lubbock's favorite son. Later, the ride to Ely's ranch where the Clash were crashing for the night was interrupted when Topper—turning blue following a heroin overdose—had to be walked around until the crisis passed.)

With Earl Sinks in as the replacement vocalist, the Crickets traveled to New York City to record songs for their first album without Holly. During the car ride north for the sessions, the Crickets discussed what material to record, and Curtis mentioned a new song in a country vein he had written in twenty minutes in his living room while a sandstorm pounded his house in West Texas. The name of the song was "I Fought the Law." Curtis told interviewer Gary James that when he first wrote the song, it had "kind of a Johnny Cash feel."

The Crickets liked the idea of the song, so Curtis "transcribed it into a straight-eight feel," as he later told the Nashville Songwriters Association's Bart Herbison, "and that's how we recorded it when we got to New York." The date of the recording session was May 18, 1959, but the song would not be released until December 1960, as part of *In Style with the Crickets*. It was also released as the B-side to "A Sweet Love," the fifth and final single from the album.

The song that would become Curtis's "most important copyright" did not receive any radio airplay at the time, but was subsequently picked up and recorded by Paul Stefen and the Royal Lancers for the A-side of their Citation Records single released on August 4, 1962. *Billboard* described the single as a "Regional Breakout" in the Milwaukee area. Two years later, two solo acts took their shots at the song, with Bobby Fuller's version enjoying more success than Sammy Masters's did. Masters's version was the first version to be named "I Fought the Law (and the Law Won)," however.

Bobby Fuller was from the same part of West Texas as Sonny Curtis and was not satisfied with being a regional success, so he relocated with his band to California, where they signed with Del-Fi Records and were marketed as the Bobby Fuller Four on their own label, Mustang Records. For their fifth single, they re-recorded "I Fought the Law," which rose to #9 on the US *Billboard* Hot 100. Continued success for Fuller seemed certain when his next single, "Love's Made a Fool of You," also charted, but on July 18, 1966, Fuller's lifeless body was found by his mother in an automobile parked outside of their apartment.

According to the autopsy, Fuller was "found lying face down in front seat of car—a gas can, ⅓ full, windows rolled up and doors shut, not locked—keys in ignition." His body and clothing were soaked with gasoline. The index finger on Fuller's right hand was broken, and there were bruises on the chest and shoulders. Obviously something had happened to Fuller after he answered a midnight-hour telephone call and gone out, but the official verdict ruled the twenty-three-year-old's death a suicide.

Over the next twelve years, a few recording artists recorded "I Fought the Law," including Roy Orbison and Kris Kristofferson with Rita Coolidge, but it was Fuller's Mustang single that Joe Strummer and Mick Jones heard on the Automatt's jukebox between overdub sessions for *Give 'Em Enough Rope*. Both took a shine to the song and heard how—with judicious rearranging by Jones—"I Fought the Law" would fit comfortably with their work. The rhythm section was uncertain, however, with Topper ironically saying, "Oh no, I'm not doing that, it sounds terrible," when Strummer and Jones played an acoustic version of the song that would become one of his signature performances.

The Clash's version is almost cinematic. The song fades in with galloping tom-tom drums, and because the song was written by a Texan and made famous by another Texan, the galloping drums suggest a galloping horse. Topper comes to a full stop, slams a beat, and Joe, Mick, and Paul come crashing in. Joe's vocals are prominent in the mix as he sings about working on a jail gang and then gives the song's catchphrase a punk touch when he sings, "I fought the law *and-uh* . . . the law won." (Previous versions had the phrasing as "I fought the law and the . . . law won.") Adding "uh" to a word is a Johnny Rotten vocal tic, one that Mark E. Smith of the Fall shamelessly stole and exaggerated on so many songs that it is now a vocal mannerism associated with Smith, not Rotten.

The first verse and chorus are followed by a guitar solo. But it's no ordinary solo, though, as Mick—having learned well at Sandy Pearlman's elbows—layers a symphony of guitars that would make "Wall of Sound" producer Phil Spector proud. Then, as Joe sings about "robbin' people with a six-gun," Topper hits his snare six times like a six-shooter going off, adding drama to the performance. (This is part of the song's signature arrangement, as it dates back to the Crickets' original version.) Putting all their tricks to good use, Mick and Paul drop out, leaving Joe to sing the catchphrase with only Topper's accompaniment and handclaps. Paul—his bass guitar finally receiving the reggae boom he's been searching for since *The Clash* sessions—hops back in, and a few bars later he's joined by Mick. The song ends with Joe no longer singing and the musicians bashing out four chords that suggest the song's title—another touch that's a holdover from the Crickets and Bobby Fuller Four versions.

"Groovy Times"

"Groovy" is a hard word to get away with saying. It is so comically associated with 1960s stereotypes that the only person you can take seriously saying "groovy" is Jimi Hendrix—he has this tone that doesn't make the word the joke it has become. Joe Strummer, too—somehow—manages to get away not only with using it but using it in the title of a song released in 1979! The fact that he is using the word satirically helps. "Groovy" was still in Sandy Pearlman's vocabulary when he was producing the Clash, and since the original tracks for "Groovy Times" were laid down during the *Give 'Em Enough Rope* sessions, I'm assuming that that is who Joe picked up the word from.

"Groovy Times" is about the hard times the people of England were facing in the late 1970s: boarded-up shops, fenced-in football fans, mobs shot at by the police. Mick plays acoustic guitar and turns in a splendid Flamenco-infused solo. He plays harmonica as well, crediting himself as "Bob Jones," which was an inside joke about Bob Dylan, even though his playing is nothing like Dylan's. Mick's harmonica, by contrast, is played almost like a trumpet.

The "extra high vocal" by Dennis Ferrante (misspelled as "Ferranti" on the EP sleeve) is a holdover from the *Rope* sessions at the Record Plant with Sandy Pearlman. A legendary recording engineer who worked with John Lennon and Yoko Ono, Ferrante did not lend his voice to many recordings, but the ones he did are of high quality (see Alice Cooper's *Muscle of Love* and Lou Reed's *Berlin*). He passed away on June 6, 2015, from heart failure.

The demo version of this song was known as "Groovy Times Are Here Again."

"Gates of the West"

The production credits for *The Cost of Living EP* are misleading. First, the Clash are credited as co-producers, when in actuality it was Mick Jones who handled the production. Second, there is no mention of Sandy Pearlman and Corky Stasiak, who not only recorded the basic tracks for "Groovy Times" and "Gates of the West" but spent time in America adding overdubs.

"Gates of the West" was a retread of one of Mick's earliest compositions, "Ooh Baby, Ooh (It's Not Over)," which he had worked on with Chrissie Hynde before forming the Clash. It was remodeled as "Rusted Chrome" during the London sessions for *Give 'Em Enough Rope*, but the final lyrical content clearly indicates considerable effort was put into the track in New York City in October 1978. References to Eastside Johnny and Southside Sue make the listener think of characters from Bruce Springsteen's albums.

"Gates of the West" is the perfect vehicle for Mick, as it is all about his childhood rock 'n' roll aspirations coming to fruition. And, once again, he references Mott the Hoople. When he sings that he "should be jumpin' shoutin' that I made it all this way from Camden Town station to 44th and 8th," he's clearly echoing Mott's "All the Way to Memphis."

Probably the most boring song in the Clash's discography is their version of "Time Is Tight," the Booker T. and the M.G.'s song that the Clash had recorded the previous March—there's a reason why it wasn't issued until the *Black Market Clash* compilation—but at least it served a purpose, because Paul's bassline in "Gates of the West" bears more than a passing resemblance to it.

The Clash almost never waste an outro, and "Gates of the West" is no exception. The chorus is repeated multiple times, but your interest is held as, in the background, Mick plays one of his most stirring guitar solos, giving a wonderful display of crescendo. The song then abruptly slinks away via a loop of Mick playing wah-wah guitar.

"Capital Radio"

"Capital Radio" appears on both of the Clash's first two EPs, but in drastically different arrangements and dressed up in radically opposing production. You could almost chart the band's musical growth by comparing these two versions. The original, with Terry Chimes's powerful drumming setting off a Strummer's diatribe against the sorry state of radio programming in the UK, is 2:08 in length. The latter version clocks in at 3:20 and begins with Mick fingerpicking a short acoustic-guitar intro. Then he shouts out "1-2-3-4!" and the Clash attack their punk classic at a hardcore pace.

The reason given for recording and issuing a second version of "Capital Radio" was that the original version was out of print. It had only been released on a free flexi-disc available to anyone who sent in a coupon from the April 9, 1977, issue of *NME*. By 1979, it had become a valuable collector's item and was selling in record stores at exorbitant prices. (In one interview, Joe hinted that then former manager Bernie Rhodes had hundreds of copies stored away and was the main beneficiary of this.) The Clash re-recorded the song so that a more affordable version would be available for fans.

The lyrics are identical in both versions until Joe begins ad-libbing, addressing Mick Jones with "Hey Jonesy!" "Yeah, wot?" Mick replies. "You know, I've been thinking," Joe continues. "We'll never get on the radio this way." He then explains as the band jams how the Clash can get that elusive hit record. Topper plays an extended drumroll as Joe describes the drummer "in the box office with all the money," and then—above a metallic explosion—Joe yells out, "You guys know just what to do!"

The Clash are a pure propulsive force at this point. Joe's ample humor is on display as he tells the band "on four," and then, without a pause, shouts, "Four!" The other musicians are in step with him, however, and they don't drop the beat as they segue into a groove and Joe mimics several hits from *Grease* before fading out.

(Both versions of the song are given the same title on the first disc of *Sound System Extras*. The use of "Capital Radio One" and "Capital Radio Two" to differentiate between the two versions began when *Black Market Clash* was issued in 1980.)

"The Cost of Living Advert"

"Train in Vain" is not the only hidden track in the Clash's discography. There is an unlisted fan favorite track on Side 2 of *The Cost of Living EP* that follows on the heels of the "Capital Radio" fadeout. And although it is known as "The Cost of Living Advert," it is in actuality a reggae reprise of "I Fought the Law." Its presence thematically wraps up the EP as a whole. It is inexplicably missing from the *Singles* boxed set, a collection of all the

Clash's singles on CD in carefully reproduced packaging, however. Nor is it on *Sound System*.

Without this forty-eight-second track, the compact disc version of the EP has its artistic message undermined. It is like seeing the Mona Lisa without her smile. This is because, seconds before, during "Capital Radio," Joe has been going on about how he has found a way for the Clash to have that elusive hit single. As the song fades away with Joe shrieking—the first appearance of the atomized seagulls from "London Calling"—"I Fought the Law" comes crashing back in, only now it has a reggae beat for a radio ad featuring Joe toasting about how this hit single is now available on the very EP you are playing.

"The Cost of Living Advert" is a satisfying summation of the thirteen minutes of music preceding it. (The reggae beat also hints at what was to be a dominant musical influence on *London Calling*, *Sandinista!*, and the "Bankrobber" 45.) Without it, "Capital Radio" is satire; with it, "Capital Radio" becomes a prediction fulfilled, because when the US version of *The Clash* was released on July 26, 1979, "I Fought the Law" was simultaneously released as the Clash's first single in America. It never charted, but "I Fought the Law" was played in major markets in the US. The Clash had gotten themselves on the radio.

Mick Jones's Ten Greatest Hits

Sing Michael, Sing!

In any band other than the Clash, Mick Jones would have been the featured vocalist. This is especially true in America, where two Mick vehicles—"Train in Vain" and "Should I Stay or Should I Go"—were the radio-friendly hits generating their initial commercial success. Even with its revamped, electrified, ass-kicking live arrangement, Joe only played "Train in Vain" in concert grudgingly . . . but he knew it had to be played.

You could tell around 1981 that this shortage of moments in the spotlight was eating away at Mick. On every side of *London Calling* and *Sandinista!* (except Side 6), he had gotten a song to sing lead on. And yet, in concert, he was still only taking two or three star turns in sets that could at times exceed thirty songs. He started sharing vocals more often with Joe; he even sang the Robin Hood verse in "(White Man) In Hammersmith Palais."

So it's surprising that after getting only one vocal on *Combat Rock*, Mick hadn't lit out on his own before being fired. That he should have better chart success with Big Audio Dynamite than Joe and Paul had with the Clash, Round Two probably didn't surprise him. Hadn't he already sung lead vocals on a greatest hits album's worth of songs?

"Hate and War"

Simply put, "Hate and War" is Mick's punkiest song. By 1976, punk rockers in the UK no longer viewed hippies as the counterculture. Hippies were a cause of the cultural malaise. Hence "Hate and War" is a clever inversion of the wilted hippie plea for peace and love. Joe even had the words stenciled on the boiler suit he wore during this time period. "The hippie movement was a failure," Joe told early champion Caroline Coon in November of that year. "All hippies around now just represent complete apathy." Having written the lyrics, Joe then handed them off for Mick to sing. It was not the last time that Joe was to write lyrics for Mick.

As this chapter will demonstrate, Mick's vocal showcases generally fall into three categories:

1. Lovers being torn apart;
2. Rock 'n' roll lifestyle;
3. The Londoner's viewpoint.

The protagonist of "Hate and War" is a young, disaffected Londoner feeling abandoned by his society and angry about the hate and war he feels surrounds him. But he's a survivor who will cheat to win, will combat aggression with aggression, and will not leave, "even when the house fall down." He's a Londoner through and through.

Just as Mick is usually a vocal foil in Joe's songs, Joe has a similar role in Mick's numbers. In "Hate and War," he is the voice of hate in the protagonist's head, the evil angel. This is why Joe has the final verse about hating "wops" and "cops" and "kebab Greeks" all to himself: he is expressing the all-consuming racist hatred being felt by the protagonist. Though few made an issue of it during the punk era, in 1995's *The Last Gang in Town*, Marcus Gray slams the Clash for using such ethnic slurs in "Hate and War." The biographer overlooks the fact that the usage of these slurs is necessary if the song is to accurately capture the anger young British men harbored within them. Young men with these same bigoted thoughts were swelling the ranks of the racist National Front. The Clash's usage is a characterization, not an endorsement of bigotry. The Clash's performance at the Rock Against Racism Carnival in April 1978 was proof of their anti-racist stance.

Played sporadically throughout the band's tours after 1977, "Hate and War" was revived for the Pearl Harbour tour in February 1979 and the US Festival gigs of 1983, Mick's final shows with the Clash.

"1-2 Crush on You"

Apparently a holdover from as far back as the London SS rehearsals, Mick finally got his chance to commit "1-2 Crush on You" to tape during the March 1978 sessions at Marquee Studios. In between, it had been an encore vehicle for Joe at the Clash's earliest shows. Describing an explosive early gig at Barbarella's in Birmingham on November 26, 1976, *Sounds*' Jonh Ingham wrote that "it was the encore, 'I've Got a Crush on You', that clinched it. Joe sings about being handsome and does his visual best to look

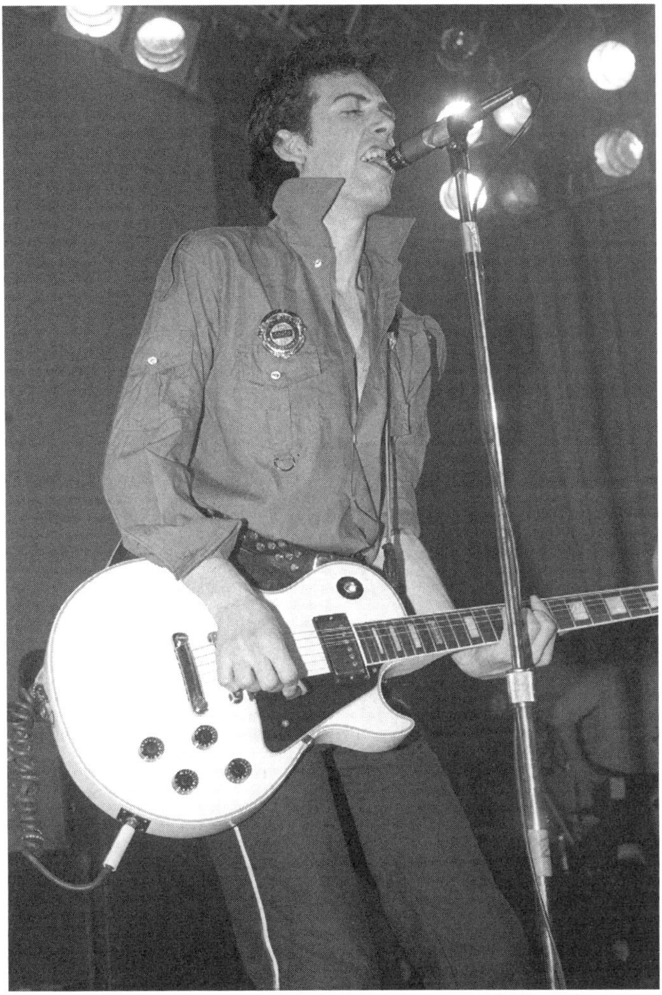

In any band other than the Clash, Mick Jones would have been the featured vocalist. *Peter Noble/Getty Images*

anything but pretty. This time, he excelled himself, and with Mick racing between mikes and Paul exploding and jerking, it had powerful effect."

And you can see how, after a set about cops and boredom and riots, the Clash closing with a pop love song could be effective, although in concert it probably wasn't so poppy. Roadie Roadent remembered it being played at an incredible pace. Never comfortable singing love songs, however, Joe soon tired of "1-2 Crush on You," and with the band prolifically knocking out new songs, it was dropped from concert performances, because, as Joe told *Sounds*' Pete Silverton, "There was no room for it."

At the March 1978 recording sessions, however, with Joe still weak and recovering from hepatitis, Mick sang lead on two of the four songs recorded. With an intro based on the Beatles' version of "Twist and Shout," "1-2 Crush on You" is the Clash's only unabashed upbeat love song. Every other Clash love song is about a strained relationship or a breakup, "Train in Vain" and "Should I Stay or Should I Go" being perfect examples. The protagonist in "1-2 Crush on You" is just a guy heads over heels in love, although the line about how "I gotta cum clean" implies a more prurient intent than the arrangement. In this way, it echoes "Protex Blue," Mick's song about condoms.

Released as the B-side to "Tommy Gun" on November 24, 1978, "1-2 Crush on You" includes a guest appearance by saxophonist Gary Barnacle—the second B-side he is featured on. Joe plays piano and has the lead vocals on the coda—a sonic blast that hints at the Knack's "My Sharona," released the following year. Joe's voice is that of the doubting conscience, wondering, "Why should I get a crush on yet?" So maybe it's not totally unabashed after all.

"Stay Free"

Mick Jones was regularly getting the B-side on 45s by the time *Give 'Em Enough Rope* was released on November 10, 1978, but he only sang lead vocal on one of the ten songs on the Clash's second album. As was to become the norm, however, one turn was enough as he almost steals the show from Joe. "Stay Free," a heartfelt performance about friendship and a slice of London life, is arguably Mick's best song.

"Stay Free" gets its starting point from Mick's childhood friendship with Robin Crocker, whom he met at a strict grammar school for boys called the Strand. Crocker was two years older than Mick, but they found themselves in the same grade after Crocker was been held back a year for unsatisfactory behavior. A dust-up in math class over who was better, Chuck Berry or Bo Diddley, led to a lifelong friendship.

Twenty years of age and newly laid off from the *West London Weekly*, Crocker engaged in a few petty crimes and was eventually arrested for armed robbery. He was sentenced to three years, which he served first at Wormwood Scrubs (where Mick Jagger had briefly been jailed in 1967) and later at a prison on the Isle of Wight.

"By the time I got out," Crocker told Dave Simpson, in a 2008 *Guardian* article, "Mick had formed the Clash. One evening he came over with an acoustic and played me 'Stay Free.' Somebody once said to me it's the most outstanding heterosexual male-on-male love song, and there is a lot of truth in that." Robin was welcomed with open arms into the Clash camp upon his release from prison, and he parlayed his connections into a *Sounds* writing gig with the pen name of Robin Banks, a pun on his notorious past. "Stay free" is Mick's closing line—the only time the phrase is used in the 3:40 song—and his advice to his friend to keep out of jail. (Unfortunately, Robin did not, as he was later jailed in Sweden for robbery.)

Music journalists upset with the ways the Clash mythologized their past took Mick to task for stretching events and making it sound like he was a tough kid thrown out of school (when he wasn't) and that Robin served time in H.M. Prison Brixton (when he didn't). Mick didn't help matters when he told *NME*'s Chris Salewicz that the song was "about all my gang in Brixton," but certainly a songwriter has license to romanticize and dramatize events to aid a song's universal appeal. The song struck a chord with young British men, with Mick telling *Trouser Press*'s Ira Robbins that "even the skinheads cry over it. It really moves them." And while the song dropped out of American set lists after 1979, it remained a staple of British concerts for the remainder of the band's career.

"It's like our ballad," Mick told Robbins, and he was onto something. It was the first Clash song that hinted that the Clash might have emotions other than rage and anger. "Stay Free" was Mick at his most Mott, and Ian Hunter was known to write very touching power ballads that avoided being maudlin. There's a reason "Stay Free" is derived from Mott's "Hymn to the Dudes"; and the solo is pure Mott guitarist Mick Ralphs—and Mick's best to date. The bouncing bassline and keyboards by the Rumour's Bob Andrews help pace an action-packed fadeout.

In concert, the outro was extended, with Mick given more room to play the guitar hero. It also served as the framework for a similar guitar blast at the end of live versions of "Train in Vain."

"Rudie Can't Fail"

American music journalists quickly compared *London Calling* to the Rolling Stones' *Exile on Main St.*, citing the music found on both double albums. *Exile on Main St.* refracted American rhythm and blues so exquisitely that the Stones sounded like an American band. Similarly, the New Orleans flavor of "Julie's Been Working for the Drug Squad" on the Clash's previous album, *Give 'Em Enough Rope*, had opened the door for exploration of other

American musical idioms such as rockabilly ("Brand New Cadillac"), the Bo Diddley shuffle ("Hateful"), and Phil Spector's Wall of Sound ("The Card Cheat"). But whereas the Stones sang on *Exile* of Tampa, Buffalo, and sweet Virginia, too, the Clash were still singing squarely of London. Despite a blitzkrieg bop through America in February 1979, they were still very much a Britain-centric band as they created *London Calling*.

Belting out "On the route of the 19 bus!," Joe puts us on the top of the double-decker bus he rode every day to Vanilla Rehearsal Studios in Pimlico, London, where the music for *London Calling* was kicked into shape in sessions sandwiched around football games in a nearby field. Written for *Rude Boy* (discussed in chapter 18), "Rudie Can't Fail" harkens back to the use of the same phrase during the last third of "Safe European Home," proving that Joe's usage of the "rude boy" image in Clash songs predates by at least eighteen months the popularization of that same image by the Specials. So, with the release of "Rudie Can't Fail" in December 1979, the Clash were not just hopping on the latest craze being trumpeted by the music weeklies. They had, in fact, fostered its rise by having the Specials as a support act on the Out on Parole tour during the summer of 1978, when the Specials were still named the Coventry Automatic and managed by Bernie.

Joe probably sketched out the song's chords and lyrics and then handed them off to his songwriting partner because, as previously indicated, Mick's voice sounds more like the average Brit's. In "Rudie Can't Fail" he portrays the archetype of the young British male who probably missed out on the punk era and the Jam's mod revival but is ripe for the crazy ska revival of 1979–81, with its porkpie hats and fly blazers. So, like the Jamaican rude boy of legend, the song's protagonist is castigated by society for being an unemployed hooligan who drinks "brew for breakfast"; the British rude boy answers by saying that what society is offering for employment is not sufficient. (The line about not being a doctor born for a purpose is a reference to Doctor Alimanato's *Born for a Purpose*.)

Then comes a key verse about the British rude boy going "to the market to realize [his] soul." This not only sets up Mick's next song on *London Calling*—"Lost in the Supermarket"—it also reminds the listener of the subject matter of "Career Opportunities" from *The Clash* and a centerpiece of the Clash message that society will not hand you the job that will allow you to live up to your potential. You need to do it yourself.

"Rudie Can't Fail" concludes with the rude boy mocking an employer for his "chicken-skin suit" and the employer mocking the young man for his porkpie hat. The rude boy struts out as the song ends, certain that he can't fail.

"Lost in the Supermarket"

Drawing on the normally guarded emotions he felt as the son of distant parents, Joe Strummer merged his feelings of childhood abandonment with what he imagined his songwriting partner had gone through as the son of divorced parents when he wrote "Lost in the Supermarket," his most sensitive song. Then he gave it to Mick to sing, correctly believing the lead guitarist's voice would make the sentiment ring true.

Joe's parents worked for Her Majesty's Foreign Service, and after posts in Kenya and Germany, they were transferred to Ankara, Turkey, where Joe was born. They were subsequently assigned to positions in Egypt, Mexico, England, and Germany, coming back to England when Joe was eight years old. His parents managed to stay in London for three years after that, but when they were reassigned, they left Joe and his older brother David to fend for themselves in the City of London Freemen's School, a posh boarding school. Since it was a fashionable school attended by the children of wealthy parents, when the facts of Joe's childhood became better known, some journalists took him to task for this presumed life of privilege. It became clear in subsequent interviews, however, that attending a school for the rich had not left Joe feeling privileged. If anything, he had felt abandoned. But at least he had survived. His withdrawn brother had committed suicide.

Mick's abandonment was a more familiar story: his parents had divorced when he was young, leaving him to be largely raised by female relatives who—unlike Joe's parents—showered the young boy with affection.

"Lost in the Supermarket" takes the "Stay Free" perspective of the previous album but through refraction admits the frailty of growing up abandoned in post–World War II England. Joe merges his own memories (the verse about the hedge he could never see over) with that of Mick's living in a towering block flat (the verse about people living on the ceiling). The final images were inspired by going shopping with his future common-law wife, Gaby Salter, in the supermarket near their flat.

Building upon the image of "the market" in "Rudie Can't Fail," "Lost in the Supermarket" is the Clash's tuneful exploration of how consumerism leads to alienation. Once again, Mick is the voice of the Londoner: he's shopping in the supermarket with coupons, buying the "hit discotheque album," anxious to purchase a "guaranteed personality." Paul's disco-fueled bassline alludes to the "hit discotheque album" that the lonely Londoner is emptying a bottle of liquor to. Unlike Joe, Mick was quite willing to sound fragile on record, and Charles Shaar Murray's *NME* review of *London Calling* called attention to the way his "still small voice" effectively conveyed the childhood images the song was built upon. More than a few reviewers noted it was Jones's increased confidence in his voice—which had previously been described as "weak" and "wobbly"—that accounted for *London Calling*'s commercial success.

Joe would return to the theme of abandoned children in "Straight to Hell" on *Combat Rock*.

"Train in Vain"

In order to avoid confusion with Ben E. King's iconic hit "Stand by Me," Jones was quoted as saying in a Johnny Black article for *Blender* that he chose to call *London Calling*'s closing number "Train in Vain" because "the track was like a train rhythm, and there was, once again, that feeling of being lost." This may be a contributing factor, but a more likely explanation is that it is a reference to Mick's desperate train rides during the summer of 1979 to see Slits guitarist Viv Albertine in hopes of salvaging their on-again, off-again relationship, which had begun in 1977.

Albertine offered this viewpoint in a BBC 6 Music interview with Cerys Matthews that aired on October 5, 2010. The Slits' debut album, *Cut*, contains a well-known song called "Typical Girls" that is critical of typical girls who "stand by their man." The Slits were looking for "the new improved model" of a girl, which is what Albertine proved to be when Mick asked her if she would "stand by me." The answer was "no."

Written in one night and recorded the next, "Train in Vain" was reportedly originally intended for an *NME* flexi-disc, but when that option fell through, it was added to *London Calling* at the last minute, even though the album artwork had already been approved and was being printed, hence its reputation as the infamous "hidden" track. (Though not in France, where *London Calling* was released *without* "Train in Vain.")

Mick later told Clash biographer Tony Fletcher, "I did ['Train'] the night before, I did a demo at home, came in with the song the next morning, into the studio, and we recorded it. Just like that. And Chrissie Hynde was upstairs, I was looking up at her through the window, the upstairs lounge, she was there. I recorded the song looking up at her." Also joining the Clash in the studio for Mick's Motown-influenced song about heartbreak was Mickey Gallagher, on organ. Mick Jones plays the loopy harmonica outro.

"Somebody Got Murdered"

One of the ironies of the post–*London Calling* period is that although it was Mick who discovered New York City's hip-hop culture while the band held the initial sessions at Jimi Hendrix's Electric Lady Studios for what would become the triple album *Sandinista!*, it wasn't he who sang the hip-hop inspired songs the Clash subsequently recorded. Mick gets the only two rockers that would not have sounded out of place on their previous albums: "Somebody Got Murdered" and "Police on My Back."

It has been said that Joe received a phone call in March 1980 during the American swing of the 16 Tons tour from musician and composer Jack Nitzsche, who asked him to write a heavy rock song for the William Friedkin–directed film *Cruising*, starring Al Pacino, that Nitzsche was scoring. This cannot be true, however, because *Cruising* had already been released on February 8, 1980. It is more likely that it was during the Take the Fifth tour of America in September and October 1979 that Nitzsche made his request, because *Cruising*, a movie about a murderer targeting gay S&M clubs, had been shot that summer in New York City.

The misconception probably arises from the fact that "Somebody Got Murdered" must have been started at the Electric Lady Studio sessions in March and April 1980, because it was debuted at a one-off date in Hollywood's Roxy Theater on April 27, 1980—the same weekend that the Clash had played a four-song set on *Fridays*, ABC's attempt at imitating *Saturday Night Live*. It was then a staple of sets when the 16 Tons tour resumed in Europe in May, making "Somebody Got Murdered" the first *Sandinista!* track to find its way onto the set lists.

"The car park attendant in the World's End housing estate, where I was living, was murdered over five pounds," Joe says in the *Clash on Broadway* booklet, adding that after getting the call from Nitzsche, "I went home and there was this guy in a pool of blood out by the car parking kiosk. That night I wrote the lyric." Joe was living in World's End while recording *London Calling*, substantiating the theory that Nitzsche's request was made during the Take the Fifth tour, the first tour featuring songs from the legendary double album.

Mick must have been delighted that Nitzsche had contacted the Clash; the keyboardist and arranger had worked on some of Jones's favorite Rolling Stones recordings between 1965 and 1971. But after Nitzsche never followed up on the request, the Clash kept the song for themselves. It was decided that Jonesy could turn in a more sympathetic performance than Joe. Experimenting in the studio, Mick added some synthesizer-created whooshing sounds, but when it came to the "sounds like murder" part featuring Joe, they had to be a little more creative.

Sandinista! is awash with sound effects—there are vacuum cleaners and clocks and trains—and for the end of "Somebody Got Murdered," the band wanted the sound of a dog barking. In an overdub added at Wessex Studio in London, Topper's dog Battersea was coaxed into action. Battersea was tremendously protective of the Topper, so the band knew he'd bark whenever someone struck his master. And so, after bringing Battersea into the studio, Joe feigned attacking Topper, and they caught the sound of him barking. Battersea received credit in the liner notes.

"Up in Heaven (Not Only Here)"

The second track on the third side of the triple album *Sandinista!*, "Up in Heaven (Not Only Here)" is the truest indicator of how far the Clash had moved musically since their debut album only four and three-quarter years earlier. Lyrically, with its references to "the towers of London" and how "children daub slogans to prove they lived there," "Up in Heaven (Not Only Here)" fits in thematically with *The Clash*. What differs now is Mick's delivery. Where in 1977 there would have been anger, there is now sadness.

Mick wrote this tune after his stay in New York City in March 1980. Visiting his grandmother in the Wilmcote House flat he used to share with her (number 111 on the eighteenth floor), he was dismayed. This was a council high rise, something "built by the bourgeoisie clerks who bear no guilt." The building was crumbling, the broken elevators smelt of piss, and the inhabitants lived in fear.

Ira Robbins's review of *Sandinista!* for *Trouser Press* noted how "the Clash is becoming the only rock band doing protest (or what used to be called 'topical') songs," and so who do the Clash echo in this wistful complaint? Deceased protest singer Phil Ochs. The closing verse about Allianza dollars is lifted from Ochs's "United Fruit." The Clash then take a rare extended outro, with Jones's guitar feedback suggesting the high-rise buildings swaying to and fro in London's gray skies.

"Police on My Back"

The Clash hit that wasn't.

"Police on My Back" is similar to the Rolling Stones' "Under My Thumb": a catchy album track so memorable that many fans incorrectly remember the song as being a 45. There are also Clash fans who insist they first heard the Eddy Grant cover played at Bond International Casino in New York City, but this is not true. The Clash did not play "Police on My Back" at any of the seventeen concerts in their late-spring residency at Bond's in 1981. In fact, one of the Clash's best covers did not get a public unveiling until January 28, 1982, at Sun Plaza in Tokyo, Japan. It seems the Clash did not know how popular this song was with fans.

This despite "Police on My Back" being one of the few songs consistently receiving critical raves in what were otherwise dismal reviews for *Sandinista!* Likening the song to "Somebody Got Murdered," Van Gosse of the *Village Voice* called "Police" one of "two all-out 4/4 guitar based shoot-'em-ups"; Ira Robbins found "Police" to be one of the album's "more direct songs" and wrote in *Trouser Press* of how the "two-note riff imitating a European police siren increases tension; train noises add ambience"; even Nick Kent in *NME* thought Mick's track "comes close to being an ideal vehicle for the Clash's instinctual attack" before lambasting the album's production.

The Clash had been touring for the previous two months in support of *London Calling*, eventually finishing up in New York City. Wanting to build on what was arguably their best tour, they did a session at the Power Station and then moved to Electric Lady, where they could more easily book blocks of time. Having recorded their only new song ("Bankrobber") the previous month during a day off from the tour, they did not have a large backload of unrecorded songs to develop. For this reason, Eddy Grant's "Police on My Back" was one of the few songs recorded at the Power Station. The Clash knew it from a version by the Equals that was on one of the cassette mixtapes often played on their tour bus.

"Police on My Back" is an aberration among Mick's songs. First, it's the only cover song he sang lead on that was released while the band was active. Second, you could characterize the recording as Mick's "I Fought the Law." It's a song about the police and the law. Yes, Mick had sung about jailed prisoners in "Jail Guitar Doors" and "The Prisoner," but here he is crossing over into Joe's lyrical territory. It was no surprise then when Joe began performing "Police on My Back" as early as his 1989 tours with the Latino Rockabilly War, and he continued to do so through his shows with the Mescaleros.

"Should I Stay or Should I Go"

Seven years after Mick's dismissal from the Clash, the band had their only #1 hit. Spurred by its use in a television ad for Levi's jeans, CBS re-released "Should I Stay or Should I Go," and it rose to the top spot on the British charts, supplanting the Simpsons' "Do the Bartman."

Rather than a cause for celebration, however, the 1991 single created more disharmony among former Clash members because Paul was upset that Mick insisted on having "Rush," a song by Big Audio Dynamite, on the B-side, rather than another Clash song. CBS sided with the recording artist still generating revenue at the time.

"Should I Stay or Should I Go" is the Clash's most ubiquitous song. It still gets radio airplay, and all the bar bands know it. Despite this, exactly what spurred Mick to write this song during the summer of 1981 remains somewhat of a mystery. (The song debuted during the Clash's residency in Paris in September 1981.) Was it about his relationship with singer/actress Ellen Foley? Was it a clever allegory about America's possible invasion of Nicaragua (hence Ronald Reagan's image on the cover artwork of the 45 sleeve)? Or was it Mick wondering if he should stay in the Clash or should he go?

The song has striking similarity to "Little Latin Lupe Lu," which might explain the lines in Spanish in the third verse, sung by Joe with Texan singer/songwriter Joe Ely, whom the band had befriended in 1978 after hearing Ely's *Honky Tonk Masquerade*. Ely had opened for the Clash in 1979, 1981, and 1982 and found himself in Electric Lady Studios when the Clash were working on Mick's number. "I think [singing in Spanish] was Strummer's idea," Ely told www.songfacts.com in 2012, "because . . . when it came to that part, he immediately went, 'You know Spanish, help me translate these things.' My Spanish was pretty much Tex-Mex, so it was not an accurate translation." Sound engineer Eddie Garcia was also asked to assist in the translation, and he telephoned his Ecuadorean mother for help. Therefore the Spanish lines sung by the two Joes are a mixture of Tex-Mex and Ecuadorean Spanish.

Ely in his Songfacts interview also solved the mystery behind Mick shouting "Split!" in the song's middle. According to Ely, when Mick was doing his vocals, "me and Joe had snuck around in the studio . . . and we snuck in and jumped and scared the hell out of him right in the middle of recording the song, and he just looked at us and [said], 'Split!' So we ran back to our vocal booth and they never stopped the recording." So, just as during the recording of "Armagideon Time," when the Clash kept in Joe's

Mick Jones at the microphone during the Clash's debut at the Palladium in New York City on February 17, 1979. *Stephen Graziano*

instruction to Kosmo Vinyl not to "stop us when we're hot," they once again kept an unplanned line in the final mix.

Some hear a Cramps influence in "Should I Stay or Should I Go." This is not as far-fetched as it sounds. The Cramps had opened for the Clash at New York City's Palladium on February 17, 1979, and at other shows later that same year, and Joe was known to be a big fan of Lux, Poison, Bryan, and Nick. He even told Jon Savage that the Clash, Round Two played Cramps songs during the busking tour of 1985.

12

You See He Looks Like Ivan

Paul Simonon, Punk's Most Stylish Bassist

What Paul Simonon brought to the Clash had everything to do with looks. Holding his Fender Precision bass at arm's length below his crotch in a Dee Dee Ramone homage, he looked wholly the part of the punk rock bassist. The image of the six-foot, blue-eyed Simonon was, in turn, copied by other punk bassists such as Joy Division's Peter Hook, who in an interview with *GQ* magazine said that after seeing the Clash he wanted to "emulate the strap length of Paul Simonon." (Notice how Hook doesn't mention Paul's bass playing or sound. He says he got his sound from Stranglers bassist Jean-Jacques Burnel.)

Likewise, Fall bassist Stephen Hanley, in his memoir *The Big Midweek*, admits he "never particularly considered [Simonon] to be one of the world's greatest bass players," but says he did admire the way he moved and looked onstage. The Fall opened for the Clash once, on June 9, 1981, at Bond International Casino in New York City, and, crossing paths with the band backstage, Hanley took note of each Clash member's appearance, but none so much as Paul's: "black leather pants, studded belt, black sleeveless jacket, dirty-blond quiff, cigarette hanging out of his mouth at a James Dean angle. Now there's style."

Unlike Joe and Mick, Paul was photogenic offstage as well as on, and so became a focal point for their punk image. His innate charisma compensated for his limited abilities as a bassist while, being a real DIY musician from a real broken home, Paul provided the band punk cred whenever they needed it. He was tall, angular, and mysterious onstage as he exchanged sides with Mick and said little. His short, spiky, often dyed hair was the blueprint for Billy Idol's image a few years later.

Over time, by working hard and through years of touring, Paul brought forth and contributed to punk rock music a unique bass style derived from the Jamaican music he heard in the neighborhood homes and clubs of Brixton.

Paul Simonon

Paul Gustave Simonon was born on December 15, 1955, in Thorton Heath on London's south side in his mother Elaine's childhood home. Less than two years later—by which time the family was living in the seaside town of Ramsgate—his brother Nick was born. The Simonons returned to London and were living in the neighborhood of Brixton that we now associate with the bassist when his parents divorced. Paul was ten years old. His stepfather, who was of Belgian descent, moved in shortly thereafter. Though not credited as an influence on Paul's future direction, his stepfather was a pianist and composer, and when he won a scholarship and was invited to Italy to study baroque music, the family lived in Rome and Siena over the course of approximately one year, where Paul encountered the masterpieces of Italian renaissance painters, including Leonardo da Vinci, which made an enduring impression on the young boy.

Paul Simonon: punk rock's coolest-looking bassist. A photo of Patti Smith is taped to the body of his Rickenbacker bass guitar. *Erica Echenberg/Redferns/Getty Images*

"I just want to transfer that simplicity from drawing and painting to bass playing; to say an incredible amount with just one flowing line of notes just like Leonardo used to paint," Paul told *NME*'s Chris Salewicz in July 1978.

But what Paul Simonon brought to the Clash was not limited to the movie-style profile that saw him being selected in 1982 as one of *Playgirl*'s ten sexiest men in the world. Unlike Mick, who attended Art College because he thought it was a stomping ground for future rock 'n' rollers, Paul had a genuine interest in painting. He also had a natural talent for art, stemming from his father Gustave's own interests. By the time Paul and Nick (later a drummer with Whirlwind, the UK rockabilly band, and Pearl Harbor and the Explosions) had moved in with him after the sojourn to Italy, Gustave was "a Sunday painter" (as Paul put it in later interviews) who worked as an art teacher at a junior school.

Paul applied for a scholarship and attended the upscale Bryan Shaw School of Art. ("It was really good there. All the other kids had really rich parents, so you could just nick their canvas and paints and they'd get their fathers to buy them replacements," Paul told Chris Salewicz in 1981.) Despite the role he would play in revolutionizing rock 'n' roll, however, when it came to art, Paul was a traditionalist more interested in formal drawing than the abstract art methods preached by his instructors. He would end up dropping out, but with his eye for artistic detail, Paul played a leading role in designing the Clash's onstage gear, their concert backdrops, and the artwork for the band's earliest singles and albums.

Their first look—even before the leftist, stenciled slogans—was acrylic-splattered clothing that in interviews they tied to Jackson Pollock. But as Joe admitted to Jon Savage in 1988, "All the stuff about Pollock was a bit of a veneer on it, 'cos what actually happened was . . . we got all covered in paint and we saw it was a good cheap way to put an image together, something to wear onstage . . . Paul knew something about Pollock; he'd just come from art school." And it was Paul who first sensed that name checking a famous American abstract artist who died in a car crash would appeal to journalists' sensibilities.

Another unusual way Paul applied his painting talents was in learning the bass guitar. He had only made Mick's acquaintance through happenstance when he accompanied a drummer friend of his girlfriend to a London SS audition for moral support. The drummer did not catch the band's eye, but Paul's looks and manner did, and Mick—at Bernie's suggestion—asked Paul to sing a few rockers he did not know, including the Standells' "Barracuda" and Jonathan Richman's "Roadrunner." As Paul's later vocal turns with the Clash attest, it was not his unfamiliarity with the material that led the London SS to conclude that he would not do even if he looked the part. ("Roadrunner" was played at the Clash's earliest soundchecks, but with the phrase "Radio One" sung instead of "Roadrunner.")

When Mick mentioned a chance meeting he'd had with Paul to Bernie after the dissolution of London SS, Bernie told him that Paul was who he needed in the ranks if his band was to click, not Tony James. (Input such as this explains the importance of Bernie's instincts in the Clash's success.) The original idea was that Mick would groom Paul as a guitarist, but after one frustrating lesson, Mick suggested Paul might be better suited to the bass because he'd only have to master four strings, not six.

"I always wanted to be a guitarist, he's the one [who] looks really excitin', but when I first met Mick I couldn't sing, I couldn't do fuck-all—I was useless," Paul told *Creem*'s Stephen Demorest in 1979. He proved himself a hard worker and put in copious hours playing along to the Ramones' debut album, Sex Pistols singles, and reggae albums, but to make sure he got things right in concert, Paul painted the letters of bass notes on the fretboard of his Rickenbacker 4001.

Wanting his bass sound to replicate the heavy, shuddering basslines heard on reggae records, Paul early on switched to a mid-'70s model of the Fender Precision as his instrument of choice. The heavier models could withstand being violently swung about during each live appearance. (In fact, The Baker, in his foreword to Randall Doane's *Stealing All Transmissions*, writes that Paul nowadays has chronic hip pain stemming from his many live performances with the Clash.) Paul's basses were almost always white and stenciled or carved with words such as "PAUL" and "PRESSURE" and "POSITIVE." Sometimes he would tape someone's picture to the body, such as Patti Smith's image from *Horses*. Despite the influence reggae had on his bass playing, he usually struck the strings with a plectrum instead of using a fingerpicking style. He played through an Ampeg SVT amplifier.

When Bernie met Alex Michon at the Clash's performance at the Royal College of Art on November 5, 1976, he found the woman who along with Paul would design the majority of the band's stage gear through 1983. An art student, she had lied to Bernie about her abilities as a seamstress and said she could sew the trousers he asked about and anything else the band might need. And so, when the Clash took the Coliseum stage in Harlesden, London, on March 11, 1977, they had a new look to replace the Pollock-style splattered clothing. It was to be Terry Chimes's final appearance with the Clash for over five years, but while he wore a T-shirt Paul made for him with "GOOD-BYE" stenciled across the chest, the other members wore their new punk military gear, designed by Paul, Alex, and Sebastian Conran, an early Clash enthusiast from the upper classes. The new clothing featured zippers at odd angles, D-rings, and breast pockets made from screen prints of photographs.

During this time period, Paul found himself involved with older women, whether it be a long-distance relationship with Patti Smith or a very close-distance relationship with Caroline Coon, the *Melody Maker* journalist who served as "not the Clash's manager" (according to Joe) between late 1978 and the summer of 1979. When Joe and Mick flew off to Jamaica in search of creative inspiration for new songs needed for *Give 'Em Enough Rope*, Paul and Coon holidayed in communist Russia, a trip whose impact was more lasting on the Clash than that of Strummer/Jones. This is because Paul brought back as gifts Russian badges of red stars. And stars would be found on just about every Clash product issued afterward.

As Bernie's input was on the output through 1978, stage gear and its design fell to individual members. In the beginning, photographs taken by Rocco Macauley were magnified and manufactured by Conran as the stage backdrops for concert performances. When Joe began getting flak for squatting at Conran's "white mansion" and therefore betraying punk orthodoxy, Conran was squeezed out of the Clash's inner circle and Paul began designing the stage backdrops, including the "flags of the world" image preserved in Don Letts's "Tommy Gun" video, and another of a Junkers Ju 87 Stuka, a German World War II aircraft. The latter derived from Paul's interest in World War II. He was known to own a German machine pistol, too. It was a replica, but his possession of this and the tattooed pistol poised between his left nipple and shoulder—in an era when rock 'n' rollers were not routinely tattooed—reflected an interest in guns that led to one of the more notorious arrests during the Clash's existence: the shooting of three racing pigeons by Paul, Topper, and three friends on March 30, 1978.

Described in more detail in chapter 10, this violent episode can be viewed as the prankish act of five immature, young men toying with an air pistol and an air rifle and certainly nothing as serious as the charge of terrorism that the Clash rhythm section momentarily faced. It is certainly portrayed as such in *Rude Boy*. That Paul was the band's prankster cannot be denied. He was known for tying together his friends' shoelaces, engaging in food fights, and so on. Life on the road can be tedious, and this was a way of livening up the passing time.

There were certainly occasions, however, when this behavior did cross a line, such as the time recounted in American critic Lester Bangs's epic—and recommended—55,000 word, three-part piece on the Clash's Get Out of

Control tour, "Six Days on the Road to the Promised Land," written for *NME*. While praising the band as the real rock 'n' roll deal, Bangs was disturbed after witnessing members of the Clash's entourage roughing up a fan after a food fight and Paul and Topper not interceding. Another unsavory incident occurred when Paul and Topper desecrated DJ Barry Myers's record collection with swastikas. Myers, who was Jewish, could not believe that members of a band preaching humanistic values would do such a thing. When this was mentioned to Joe, the band's singer did what he normally did in such situations: left it up to the victim to retaliate. It was seen within band circles as a code of honor: you give as good as you got.

For our purposes, however, we appreciate Paul for his contributions to the Clash, a musical endeavor and not a committee on political correctness. Artists are complex people; sensitive yet often cruel. French author Marcel Proust, after all, was said to have enjoyed watching rats being tortured. Seen in such a light, we can view some of Paul's pranks as being insensitive but not malicious.

When Blackhill Enterprises took over management of the Clash's day-to-day operations in spring 1979, employee Kosmo Vinyl—whom both Joe and Mick knew previously—began ingratiating himself with the band. Vinyl's girlfriend at the time was Pearl Harbor, a Filipino singer who had danced for the Tubes and fronted her own group and toured with Elvis Costello, Graham Parker, and others. After Pearl and Vinyl broke up, she and Paul hooked up, and she became part of the entourage. She was the Clash's DJ during the Bond's residency and her band Pearl Harbor and the Explosions opened for the Clash in Japan during the Far East tour in 1982. Later that same year, Paul and Pearl wed; they divorced in 1989.

When discussing Paul's bass playing, original Clash drummer Terry Chimes stressed to me that "Paul is a very hardworking, dedicated man. Never screwed up, never showed up drunk. Didn't mess around." Topper has said the reason he really enjoyed performing as half of the Clash's rhythm section is that Paul never improvised, thereby allowing Topper the freedom to do so. Now, this approach to rock 'n' roll rhythm where the bassist—not the drummer—is the timekeeper was advocated by none other than Jimi Hendrix, but Hendrix's approach to song composition has never been cited as a model by any member of the Clash. It is implied then that Paul was "a very hardworking, dedicated man" because playing did not come naturally to him, and in concert he didn't stray from a song's basslines because he was uncertain if he could get back to where he belonged.

But Paul still made significant contributions to bass culture. Interviewed by Chris Salewicz for a February 1981 *Face* feature, Paul admitted, "It was probably true that I wasn't a very good musician at first. But I also think that situation's changed a lot now. I've been working very hard at it for some time. Playing along to reggae records has been one of the ways that I've bettered my playing."

It was with his genuine love and affinity for reggae that Paul created a punk rock bass style all of his own. Being in the Brixton area teeming with a Caribbean immigrant community had exposed Mick to reggae music, but it was his fellow Brixtonite Paul who felt the music he heard in friends' homes and later in local clubs during the skinhead phase of his teenager years pulsing in his blood, as he revealed in the following interviews:

> "I used to hate all that Deep Purple and Hawkwind stuff and just listened to reggae 'cos I was a skinhead. Those reggae records really used to say a lot to me. Some of them really meant quite a lot." —to Chris Salewicz, *NME*, 1978

> "I listen to a lot of reggae. Something about that beat that really gets to me. It's really close to our own stuff. You know, what they talk about, everyday occurrences." —to Iman Lababedi, *Creem*, May 1981

> "Listening to reggae had shown me that you have contemporary political content in music, so I was always aware of political systems from a young age. For Joe, it was folk music—Woody Guthrie, Bob Dylan. By the time of *London Calling* there was a lot of cross-referencing going on. We all knew that music can be about things other than love, kissing and having a nice dance." —to Ben Myers, *Record Collector*, October 2004

Paul makes it clear he felt the message in reggae music was akin to that of the Clash, and this may have encouraged him to move his Clash basslines in that direction. Beginning with *The Cost of Living EP*, the basslines reflect Paul's bearings, not Mick's—something Mick has acknowledged. Paul was finally transferring the simplicity of line drawing to bass playing, and his basslines were one flowing line of repetitive notes played over and over. It was so much Paul's trademark style by 1980, in fact, that when Mick looped Norman Roy-Watt's bassline for "The Magnificent Seven," many fans thought it was Paul playing.

No one has summed up Paul's singing as well as Mick, who sarcastically described it as "Jamaican Marlene Dietrich" (as cited in several of Marcus Gray's well-researched, if mean-spirited tomes on the Clash). And it is Paul's lead vocals on "The Guns of Brixton," "The Crooked Beat," and "Red Angel

Dragnet" that reveal clues to Paul's self-image, a blend of Ivanhoe "Ivan" Martin from *The Harder They Come* and Pinkie in Graham Greene's *Brighton Rock*, though he seems more familiar with the 1947 movie adaptation than the novel. It's no surprise that Paul plays Earl, a character with similar sensibilities, in the Clash's home movie *Hell W10*, as described in chapter 26.

Over the course of the Clash's eight-year existence with Mick in the ranks, Paul gradually drifted over to Joe's musical worldview. Mick may have offered Paul a way forward in 1976, but over time Mick's lifestyle and selfish habits, and the endless arguments between the two, led to Paul siding with Joe and Bernie when it was decided to sack Mick. It could not have helped that from *The Clash* through *Combat Rock* he engaged in arguments with Mick over the sound of the bass on Clash recordings and only seemed to get his way on the various mixes of "Armagideon Time" and "Bankrobber." Paul was the only member of the Clash to join Joe in the Clash, Round Two. And while the final lineup of the Clash was better in concert than the players are given credit for, Paul's presence is missing on *Cut the Crap*, where Norman Watt-Roy plays bass on all the tracks, even if he is uncredited. Often, in photos from this period, Paul—wearing enough rings to be the second coming of Ringo—is shown looking off into the distance, as if wondering where his future lay.

"It was a weird time," Paul said, recalling the end of the Clash to *Guardian* reporter Sean O'Hagan in 2008. "I guess I was a bit dazed. Bewildered. The thing was, Mick lived just around the corner, and he had formed Big Audio Dynamite. I'd see his tour bus heading off, and I wasn't going anywhere. It was tough, after all those years of the constant Clash agenda." Paul made peace with Mick by appearing along with Joe as policemen in Big Audio Dynamite's video for "Medicine Show." He later provided the cover design and artwork for the band's album *Tighten Up Vol. 88*.

Paul tried to recover his musical equilibrium by forming Havana 3 a.m. in 1986 with Whirlwind lead singer Nigel Dixon and former Figures guitarist Gary Myrick. (The band's name came from an album by Prez Prado.) In all of his previous musical enterprises for the likes of Ellen Foley, Pearl Harbor, and Janie Jones and the Lash, Paul had had other members of the Clash by his side, so now he was in new territory. Only the sessions for Mikey Dread's *World War III* had not involved his former bandmates.

Bernie Rhodes agreed to manage Havana 3 a.m., a rockabilly outfit with Latino sensibilities. "I got quite into rockabilly when I was a kid," Paul told *Rolling Stone* reporter Andy Greene in 2013, "because I was trying to find something that represented me as a white person." Paul's interest in rockabilly strayed with punk rock and his role in it, but it was renewed around 1979. This was a passion Joe had shared, too, and both hoped that the Clash, Round Two could be rebuilt from its hot-rod chassis. When that crashed, Paul tried again with Havana 3 a.m.

During this period, Paul appeared on Bob Dylan's *Down in the Groove*, an odd connection since, as Paul told *Creem*'s Iman Lababedi in a May 1981 interview, "I'm not really into Bob Dylan's work." Maybe he thought it would impress Joe, who was. Apparently, Dylan had turned up quite often at Clash shows, and after Paul relocated to El Paso in the late '80s with Havana 3 a.m. bandmate Nigel Dixon, they motorcycled to Los Angeles, where ex-Pistol Steve Jones invited Paul to a recording session Dylan had asked him to set up, for which Jones needed a bass player. The one-night session at Sunset Studio held in March 1987 resulted in six songs recorded and one used; Paul can be heard on Dylan's version of Arthur Alexander's "Sally Sue Brown."

Havana 3 a.m. finally released an album on IRS Records in 1991, with all twelve songs credited to Simonon/Myrick/Dixon. They toured in support of it, and even played "The Guns of Brixton" as the set opener. The single "Reach the Rock" was a minor hit, but after the deaths of drummer Travis Williams and then Dixon from cancer on April 3, 1993, Paul took a break and picked up his paintbrushes again.

Paul focused on his first artistic love and worked hard on establishing himself as a painter, building on, of all things, the Westway mural of a car dump that he had painted at Rehearsal Rehearsals shortly after moving in (as can be seen in photos of the Clash's "press only" concert on August 13, 1976). Paul's artwork is decidedly realistic and is said to be influenced by the American Ashcan School and the British "Kitchen Sink" art movements. His subject matter has included the Thames River, Spanish bullfighters getting the worst end of it from the bulls, leather biker jackets, and burning cigarettes.

By the mid-2000s, a return to music seemed unlikely for Paul. It has often been rumored that it was his refusal that prevented the Clash from reforming; he was determined to be taken seriously as a painter. But in the interim, Paul had made the acquaintance of Blur front man Damon Albarn at Joe's wedding to Lucinda Tait; a few years later, when Albarn played some recordings he had made in Nigeria to Paul, the Clash's former bassist found a kindred spirit. Damon had been working on a solo project with Danger Mouse that he wanted to expand into a group effort. "We shared ideas about people, musical styles and where we live," Paul told the *Observer Music Magazine*. "With the music, I wanted to complement Tony [Allen]'s drums.

I'm not into over-complication—I'm not capable of it, to be honest. The lyrics, the London atmosphere, all that evolved as we played. There's a lot of craftsmanship on the record, and Damon has a vision for arrangements, and everyone slotted in around them."

The result was 2007's *The Good, the Bad & the Queen*, the same name that has also been given to the band that recorded it (whose other members include Verve guitarist Simon Tong and drummer Tony Allen, who had performed with Nigerian legend Fela Kuti), although the band does not officially have a name. *The Good, the Bad & the Queen* won well-deserved awards. It is the rare supergroup of musicians that succeeded; a wonderful blending of talents. If anything, it is the Specials record that the Specials should have made after releasing "Ghost Town."

It was also the perfect music project for Paul. Albarn spins musical projects like plates, so Paul knew that the band that made *The Good, the Bad & the Queen* would not be required to do excessive touring, which would interfere with his painting. He has contributed to Albarn's cartoon group Gorillaz, an endeavor that saw him team with Mick on "Plastic Beach," the title track from the group's 2011 album. Paul and Mick also participated in Gorillaz's 2011 tour from which the 2012 album *The Fall* was manipulated and culled. Paul is featured on "Aspen Forest."

"I can dip in and out of music when I feel like it but it's not my life any more," Simonon told Sean O'Hagan. "There was a point after the whole intensity of the Clash finally subsided when I just found that painting grounded me in a way that music didn't."

Paul married his second wife, Tricia Ronane, a former model who graced the cover of Havana 3 a.m.'s album, on July 28, 1990, at St. Pius X Church, located in St. Charles Square, Kensington. They have two sons, Louis and Claude, both of whom have followed their mother into her (former) line of work. Paul and Tricia separated in 2006 but, as of this writing, she continues to serve as the Clash's manager.

Paul continues painting and, fittingly enough, his art studio is located under the Westway.

13

There's a Move into the Future for the USA

The Clash Take New York City by Storm

In Joe Boyd's documentary about Jimi Hendrix, Mick Jagger says of the left-handed guitarist's meteoric rise in London in late 1966/early 1967, "I thought he had just come out of nowhere and, like, we had just adopted him. We felt in England, like, 'cause he was great and, like, he wasn't big in America and he'd come here. I mean, he'd come to England and we were there and, like, he had his first big record in England and he was ours, you know?"

Punk rockers in the USA felt the same way about the Clash: they were ours, you know?

What we didn't understand is what was taking them so damn long to cross the Atlantic. We didn't know that their American label, Epic Records, was stalling on the idea of an American tour, more focused on promoting the likes of Toto and Dan Fogelberg. But Joe and Mick had spent considerable time in San Francisco and New York City in the summer of 1978 while applying strategic overdubs to *Give 'Em Enough Rope*. They had hung out with the punks at Mabuhay Gardens in San Francisco and watched Bob Gruen's personal films of the New York Dolls in New York City. They knew the country was ripe for the taking.

Caroline Coon, acting as the band's manager after Bernie's dismissal, contacted Epic and pushed for a tour, even a short one of major cities. She put up $6,000 of her own money—Bernie had frozen the Clash's cash flow pending legal resolution—and Epic agreed to provide the remaining $30,000 needed. Even after *Give 'Em Enough Rope* had sold 40,000 copies in America (despite a minuscule marketing budget) and was voted the fourth best album of the year in the *Village Voice*'s annual "Pazz & Jop" critics' poll, the record company was not convinced of the band's commercial appeal. Promoter Ron Delsener, who staged shows at New York City's Palladium, scoffed when approached about the Clash appearing there. Delsener didn't think they'd sell more than 400 tickets; normally, new acts from the UK with good press made their Manhattan debuts at the Bottom Line, where the building capacity was 400. No way did he think the Clash would sell out the Palladium, where the capacity was 3,600.

The Palladium

Constructed in 1927, the structure on the south side of East 14th Street between 3rd and 4th Avenues, near Lüchow's restaurant, may have been named the Academy of Music, but, after the depression that struck in late 1929, it was soon converted into a cinema, as well as the site of occasional boxing matches.

Radio DJ Alan Freed, who popularized the phrase "rock and roll" for the new music taking America by storm in the 1950s, staged the first rock 'n' roll show at the Academy during the Christmas season of 1955. According to the blog Streets You Crossed Not So Long Ago, the lineup included the Cadillacs, LaVern Baker, the Valentines, the Heartbeats, the Wrens, the 3 Chuckles, the Bonnie Sisters, and the Count Basie Orchestra. Thereafter, similar rock 'n' roll shows were staged each Christmas season, but it wasn't until the mid-1960s that rock concerts were regularly scheduled at the Academy of Music. (The Rolling Stones played there during 1964 and 1965, for example.)

When Bill Graham closed the Fillmore East in June 1971, a rival promoter named Howie Stein began booking rock shows at the Academy of Music. Seating capacity at the mid-size venue was an ideal stepping-stone for bands such as Alice Cooper and Black Sabbath who had outgrown the clubs but were not quite popular enough for Madison Square Garden. The theater was well known for its acoustics, so several popular live albums were recorded at the 14th Street venue during the first half of the decade, including the Band's *Rock of Ages* and Lou Reed's *Rock 'n' Roll Animal* and *Lou Live.* After it was renamed the Palladium on September 18, 1976, Frank Zappa recorded his double album *Zappa in New York* and filmed *Baby Snakes* in the concert hall.

February 17, 1979

The Clash finally performed in the American city they would be most closely associated with—a city so great they used the same name twice, as Joe once said, probably having heard Gerald Kenny's song "New York, New York (So Good They Named It Twice)," which was released in England in 1978—on February 17, 1979. They had been playing together for over two and a half years, but their show that evening at the Palladium was their penultimate gasp as a punk band. They would return in seven months a very different outfit after recording *London Calling*.

According to road manager Johnny Green's memoir, *A Riot of Our Own*, the Clash knew their debut New York City performance would be important if they were going to secure a successful future in America. It was, after all, where many of the major rock publications were headquartered. So "that night in the Palladium we did a soundcheck and a half. Every light was focused, every speaker double-checked, every spare guitar tuned, every drumstick sanded."

The previous night at the Palladium, a number of artists including Meat Loaf, Patti Smith (without her Group), Rick Derringer, Blue Öyster Cult, David Johansen, and Utopia had gathered for the Indochinese Refugee Concert. It was a good event but lacked the electricity engulfing the Clash show. Elvis Costello and the Attractions had played four sold-out shows at the Bottom Line in January, but this was the first big concert event in the City in 1979. You could sense it. There was Lenny Kaye of the Patti Smith Group, standing near the balcony staircase, come to play spectator, not performer. You saw Debbie Harry. You saw members of the Ramones. As an anonymous newspaper clipping reported, "The audible excitement for the New York debut of the Clash ran high right through Bo Diddley's opening set. Dozens of the droogiest-looking concert-goers milled around the Palladiums lobby, tanking up on whatever."

Decades later, I feel sorry for those milling about in the lobby. While "tanking up," they had missed the local opening act, the Cramps at their punkabilly best. It was the classic lineup with vocalist Lux Interior, lead guitarist Poison Ivy Rorschach, noise guitarist extraordinaire Bryan Gregory, and drummer Nick Knox. Lux's image was still in flux, but the showmanship was palpable as the Cramps made their way through their soon-to-be infamous, gravest hits. Poison Ivy shimmied as her fingernails flicked out killer riffs and Bryan bandied huge slabs of feedback about.

Then, legendary R&B guitarist Bo Diddley, whom the Clash personally lobbied for as their opening act, came and went. The Clash's DJ served up the platters as the crowd waited impatiently, the electricity rising. I was seventeen rows back, near the center. Finally, as "Riot in Cell Block No. 9" rocked, the Flags of the Nation backdrop unfurled and the Clash came walking out. Mick's Keef-style locks were gone and he was wearing a red shirt and white pants. Joe had on a yellow shirt and black pants. Paul wore a light blue shirt and white pants. Mick and Paul were wearing black motorcycle boots, which according to Paul would later become known as "Clash boots." (I'm not sure about Joe.) Then, as Jim Farber wrote in his review for *Sounds*, "The band moved better than any group this side of the old New York Dolls. Joe Strummer and Mick Jones flash their long legs, making them seem like elongated nerve endings with their mouths as synapses. Altogether they have a light footed energy." Farber singled out "Tommy Gun" as being "movingly redemptive."

China had invaded Vietnam on the same day as the Clash's performance, and *New York Rocker*'s Roy Trakin noted the effect this event had on the Clash, stating that "the apocalyptic international situation was seemingly mirrored in the dramatic desperation of Joe Strummer's vibrating, vein-popping vocals and Mick Jones's dedication of 'Hate and War' to the Red Menace. The Clash's act was not only the epitome of an exciting rock 'n' roll show; it served as the climax of a twenty-five-year era of peace, prosperity and a booming entertainment industry. The Clash shook and rumbled like the giant atomic generator in *The China Syndrome*; working at 110 percent capacity, they threatened to explode and take half the world with them." Because Joe continually scrambled the set lists through 1982, the

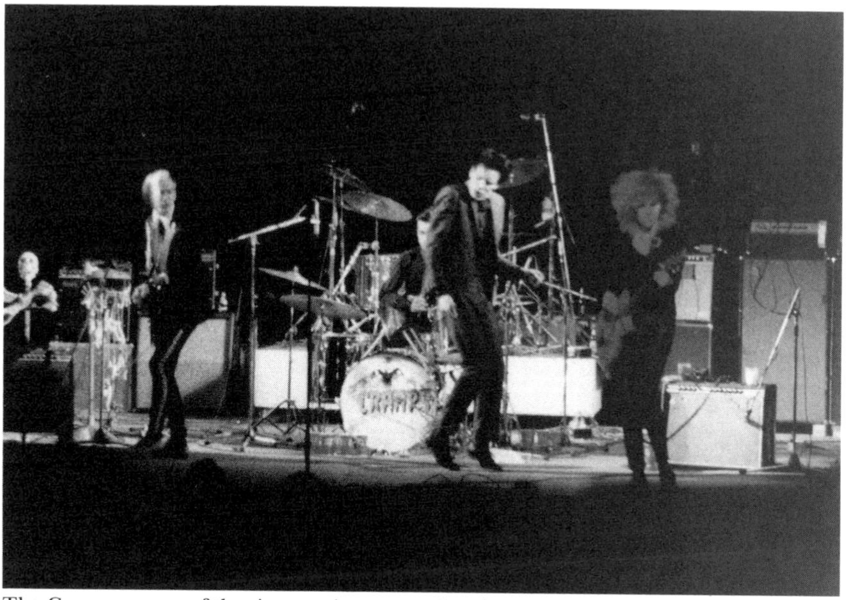

The Cramps—one of the six most important bands to emerge from the CBGB scene—open for the Clash at the Palladium on February 17, 1979. *Stephen Graziano*

The Clash perform to a sold-out crowd at the Palladium on February 17, 1979.
Stephen Graziano

mistaken impression has arisen that Clash sets changed night after night after night. This is incorrect. After the second or third performance at Bond's, for example, the set hardened like a piece of sculptor's clay, with surprises generally reserved for the encores. It was as if the Clash had determined that if a fan was only going to catch one show at Bond's, it was going to be what the band believed was the best they had to offer.

Another example was the second half of the blitzkrieg of the Clash's Pearl Harbour tour in February 1979, where they bopped and baptized America. For the last five shows, including this one at the Palladium, the set list was:

1. "I'm So Bored with the USA"
2. "Guns on the Roof"
3. "Jail Guitar Doors"
4. "Tommy Gun"
5. "City of the Dead"
6. "Hate and War"
7. "Clash City Rockers"
8. "(White Man) In Hammersmith Palais"
9. "Safe European Home"
10. "English Civil War"
11. "Stay Free"

12. "Police and Thieves"
13. "Capital Radio"
14. "Janie Jones"
15. "Garageland"
16. "Julie's Been Working for the Drug Squad"
17. "Complete Control"
18. "London's Burning"
19. "White Riot"

Encore:

20. "What's My Name"
21. "Career Opportunities"

Rolling Stone's Tom Carson noted how the crowd was standing even before the Clash stormed the stage. He said they were still standing two hours later, but Roy Trakin wrote the show's length was a little over an hour, and the sixty-nine-minute CD-R recording of it that is in circulation today confirms this. I remember the show being a real blast of punk rock that was perfectly capped when Sid Vicious's rendition of "My Way" came wafting over the PA system as we slowly exited the sold-out venue. (He had died a fortnight earlier, following a heroin overdose.)

"By gig time the place was packed and all the top liggers in town were there. We were plenty nervous," Joe admitted, in a tour diary he wrote for *NME*. "Halfway through the show I checked the audience and became convinced that we were going down like a ton of bricks. But like they say it's a tough town and by the end of the day we managed to whip it out and give 'em some of our best."

"We felt we'd achieved something there, definitely. A night of nights," Joe told *Q*.

The *Village Voice*'s Robert Christgau, one of band's few champions in 1970s New York City, summed up the debut performance thus: "No one has ever made rock and roll as intense as the Clash is making right now—not Little Richard or Jerry Lee Lewis, not the early Beatles or the middle Stones or the inspired James Brown or the pre-operatic Who, not Hendrix or Led Zep, not the MC5 or the Stooges, not the Dolls or the Pistols or the Ramones."

The Clash spent the next day chatting up journalists in an Indian restaurant, the night dancing to "YMCA" in Studio 54, and woke up on the 19th to a city-crippling blizzard through which they made their way north to the tour's final show, in the Rex Danforth Theatre in Toronto, Canada, on the 20th.

14

You Won't Succeed Unless You Try

London Calling

In 1979, while staring out over Edith Grove, where three Rolling Stones had lived pennilessly seventeen years earlier, Joe Strummer wrote the anthemic "London Calling." Somehow, a Stonesian vibe had seeped into his composition, and this connection might account for the song's swagger, as he theorized years afterward. It's an interesting fact, given that the album *London Calling* is most often compared to is the Rolling Stones' *Exile on Main St.* And it's easy to see why. Both are double albums with a running time under sixty-eight minutes. Both contain dust covers adorned with black-and-white band photos that have handwritten liner notes stuffed to album jackets without gatefolds. And the music on both albums is rooted in American musical idioms.

For the Rolling Stones, this was no surprise. Their music, from their debut recording of Chuck Berry's "Come On" onward, had always been rooted in Americana. For the Clash, however, this was a growing influence that would soon cause British music journalists to turn their sharpened wit on the band they had earlier championed. Soon they'd be railing at and mocking the Clash and writing that they had abandoned Britain for America's big bucks.

In a year's time, Paolo Hewitt in *Melody Maker* would even compare the Clash unfavorably to the Jam, a band who basked in their Britishness. It was the Jam, he wrote, who "grew strength to strength," not the band they once opened for. Many British fans agreed. But on the Clash's third LP, it's London that's calling, not New York City; it's the guns of Brixton, not Brooklyn. The British music journalists and fans were wrong. Despite drawing on Americana, *London Calling* was all about Britain.

The Vanilla Sessions

Years later, many people call *London Calling* the Clash's "finest hour." But for the Clash, the making of the album took place during desperate times. "Desperation. I'd recommend it," Joe told *Melody Maker*'s Chris Bohn, in an interview promoting *London Calling* and published a fortnight after the British release. Bernie Rhodes, their former manager, had their monies tied up in legal knots and barred them from their former base at Rehearsal Rehearsals. Johnny Green and The Baker, the faithful dynamic duo of their crew, had been dispatched to find a rehearsal space the Clash could call their own.

They checked out Nomis in Earl's Court, the Who's Eel Pie in Shepperton, and a series of small studios that had placed advertisements in *Melody Maker*. None were acceptable. Then they struck gold. Another advertisement took Johnny Green and the Baker to Vanilla Rehearsal Studios at 36 Causton Street, off Vauxhall Bridge Road in Pimlico, near the Houses of Parliament. It was a converted rubber factory and car repair shop that had two things going for it: a stage and cheap rent. Johnny persuaded CBS Records to front the rent money. The Clash were back in business, and it was at Vanilla that they wrote, rehearsed, and demoed the collection of songs that would be known the world over as *London Calling*.

Produced by Guy Stevens

In the five-part documentary *Audio Ammunition*, Paul recalls something Guy Stevens told him: "In this world there are two Phil Spectors. And I'm one of them." His gap-toothed smile is as wide as can be, and he's flanked by Topper and Mick, who are as joyous with this memory as their bassist is. The Clash loved Guy Stevens. But did he really "produce" *London Calling*? That's difficult to answer, and the question implies another *Exile on Main St.* connection. Did Jimmy Miller really produce *Exile on Main St.*? There are some recording engineers who thought he didn't, that he just provided "ambience." The engineers did the production work. But then the Stones made their best albums with Miller's "ambience." And isn't that what Stevens provided for the Clash? By throwing around chairs and ladders, pouring beer over a piano, and wrestling in the recording booth with the Wessex Studio engineers, he conjured a carnival-esque ambience that the Clash thrived on much more than they had the clinical ambience of the Glutton Twins. In this sense, yes, Guy Stevens produced *London Calling*. When Paul said he had flubbed a note, Guy told him not to worry. When Topper told him that his tempo on "Brand New Cadillac" sped up, Guy said that all great rock 'n' roll songs sped up. And for this, the Clash loved recording under Guy Stevens's guidance.

Guy Stevens was one of those souls who lived for music. "Every musical entity, record, group, or individual performer he's ever recommended me to, has turned out to be a gas," the *International Times*' Mark Williams wrote in late 1969. By then, Stevens had been a music journalist promoting rhythm and blues artists and legendary Sun Records performers, had spun discs as the DJ at the Scene Club, and had assisted the rise of the Rolling Stones, the Who, and the Small Faces by recommending R&B material to play before they found their way as songwriters.

He had also bailed Chuck Berry out of a British jail in 1964; worked for Island Records, overseeing a subsidiary specializing in blues acts (licensed from Sue Records in the US); and worked with Traffic. He advised Procol

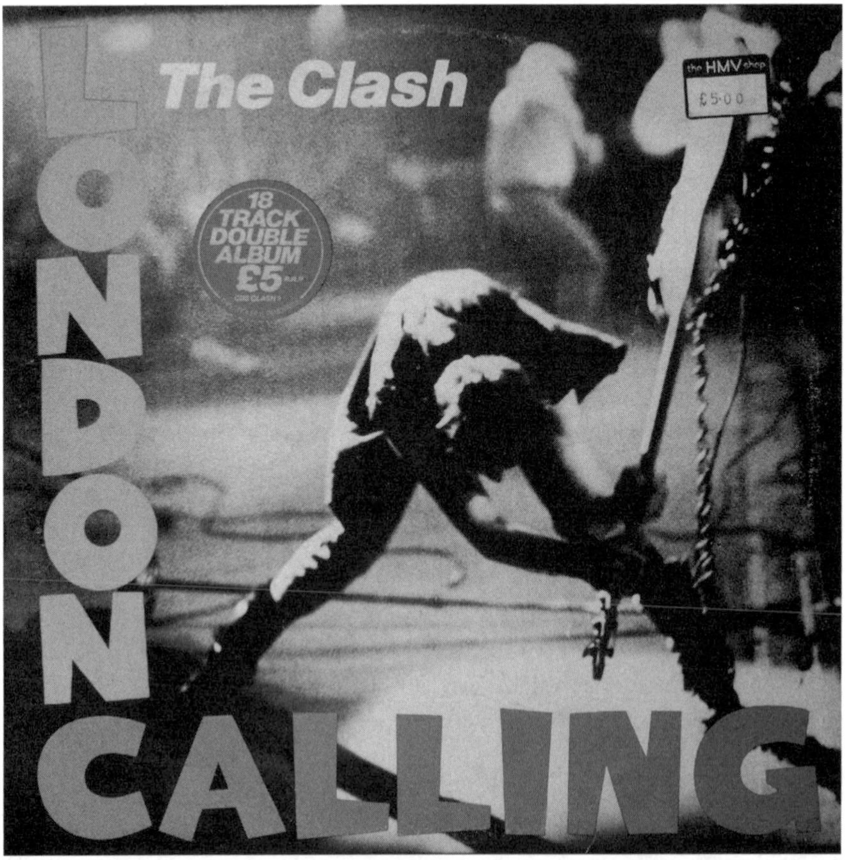

The Clash gave their fans their money's worth: the double album *London Calling* sold for a fiver! *Author's collection*

Harem (named after Stevens's cat) and signed and produced Free, as well as Spooky Tooth. But it was as manager and producer of Mott the Hoople—a band he had selected prospective members for, including front man Ian Hunter—that Stevens was best known. He named them, too, after a book by Willard Manus that he'd read.

By the mid-1970s, however, he was out of control. He'd been arrested for drug offenses and served time at Wormwood Scrubs Prison in 1967, and afterwards drug addiction dovetailed into the alcoholism and general mayhem that made him *persona non grata* within the British music industry.

It's the stuff of fiction, but Guy Stevens seemed fated to produce the Clash. A young man buys his first record: a greatest hits collection with liner notes written by the president of the Chuck Berry Appreciation Society in the UK. The young man grows up to be Joe Strummer. The liner notes were by Guy Stevens. Mick Jones crosses paths with Stevens more directly. There's a photo of Mick at the Rolling Stones' 1969 concert in Hyde Park, and there on the stage is Stevens (who allegedly suggested *Sticky Fingers* as an album title). A few years later, Mick is one of a band of fans following Mott the Hoople around England, and is thrilled when Stevens agrees to manage Little Queenie, one of Mick's pre-Clash efforts—only to have his hero orchestrate Mick's ejection from said group. You would think this would have made Mick unwilling to work with Stevens, but for Mick it was an opportunity to demonstrate the error of Stevens's previous decision.

It is Stevens who fails the test the first time he works with the Clash, on the demos for Polydor Records in November 1976. By now, although he is still held in high esteem by Joe, Mick, and Bernie Rhodes, Stevens is seen as an out-of-control alcoholic by industry insiders. The sessions do not go well. Polydor's recording engineer Vic Smith and A&R man Chris Parry are looking out for diction when Stevens is striving for ambience. Stevens doesn't have the authority to truly "produce" the session.

It comes as something of a shock, then, when the Clash inform CBS Records they want Stevens to produce their third album. As Strummer would tell Shaar Murray in a December 1979 interview in conjunction with *London Calling*'s release, "They hate his guts! They said they wouldn't use him again until he was bankable." But the Clash are insistent, and, for once, CBS gives in.

"It's been tremendously refreshing working with the Clash," Stevens told Shaar Murray. Recalling the effect rock 'n' roll had on him, Stevens added, "There's a quote from Jack Kerouac's *On the Road* . . . something like, 'All my life I've been chasing after people who are mad, mad to talk, mad to play.' . . . And I suppose that applies to rock and roll . . . I've always felt that way about making records. Making a record is an event. Big letters: AN EVENT. It's not just 'another session': I hate people with that attitude. It's electricity. It's got to be." And so Guy Stevens helped the Clash create an event that's still reverberating today.

When Stevens died from an overdose of prescribed drugs meant to curb his alcoholism on August 28, 1981, aged thirty-eight, the Clash were in the middle of their London sessions for *Sandinista!* But it was not until over a year later—on September 17, 1981—during the *Combat Rock* sessions, that the Clash recorded "Midnight to Stevens," a touching tribute to him. The song was then forgotten for ten years before appearing on 1991's *The Clash on Broadway*. (Strummer and Jones even state in the boxed set's liner notes that they had forgotten recording the song entirely.)

Produced by Guy Stevens (and Mick Jones)

One of the worst kept secrets in rock 'n' roll is that Mick Jones deserved at least a half-credit for the production of the album regularly cited as one of the best of all time. Stevens was so pleased with the guide vocals Joe recorded while laying down the basic tracks that the maverick producer wanted to retain them. Joe wanted a few extra takes. While the Clash were more than satisfied with the ambience whipped up by Stevens, they saw the need to have Johnny Green steer Stevens away from Wessex Studios each day while overdubs were made, guide vocals replaced, and guest musicians brought in. This phase was overseen by Mick.

Guest Musicians

Although the idea would probably have turned their stomachs as they recorded their debut album in February 1977, the Clash quickly adapted to the concept of session musicians, and Topper's childhood friend Gary Barnacle—who would go on to have a long career as a session man—turned up on sax on "City of the Dead," "1-2 Crush on You," and the demo version of "Drug-Stabbing Time."

Under the twiddling thumbs of the Glutton Twins for *Give 'Em Enough Rope*, Joe and Mick had worked with session musicians in both London and New York City, so they were not averse to working with musicians who could help flesh out *London Calling*. The Baker provided the whistling heard on "Jimmy Jazz," but for brass and organ they turned to new faces.

Mickey Gallagher

For one year approximately—between August 1979 and September 1980—organist Mickey Gallagher seemed well on his way to becoming the fifth member of the Clash. That he found his way into the Clash's camp was a bit of surprise, given Joe and Paul's commandment that thou shalt not perform with rival band members. Gallagher was one of Ian Dury's Blockheads, a band Joe and Paul had sneered at when Mick had performed "Sweet Gene Vincent" onstage with them at the Concerts for the People of Kampuchea the previous December.

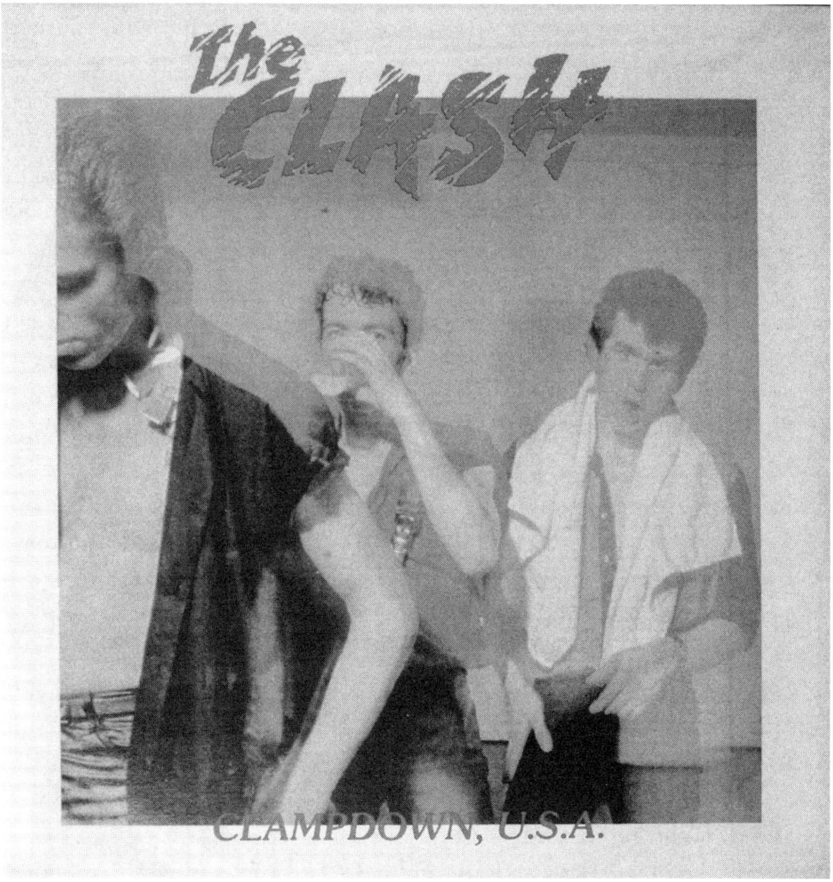

The cover art for the bootleg recording *Clampdown, U.S.A.* shows Mickey Gallagher standing next to Joe during his first tour with the Clash. *Author's collection*

But following the Pearl Harbour tour, the Clash had parted ways with interim manager Caroline Coon and hired Blackhill Enterprises, run by Peter Jenner and Andrew King. One of the acts they handled in 1979 was Ian Dury and the Blockheads. In an *NME* piece that ran on October 20, 1979, about the Clash's second US tour, Joe told Paul Morley, "I never envisaged this kind of development. Mick said to me six months ago we'll get a piano player for the British tour and I said, 'Oi leave it out, we're a four-piece group,' and then we got Mickey down to play in the studio. Organ's so much cooler than piano!"

Press agent Kosmo Vinyl came onboard along with the Clash's new managers, and he was tasked with enlisting Gallagher, who was first given a copy of *Give 'Em Enough Rope* to acquaint himself with the Clash's music. He couldn't imagine where his Hammond B-3 organ fit in, but he agreed to participate in the *London Calling* sessions, where the Clash gave scant instruction and left him to his own devices. Despite this, he ended up contributing mightily to several tracks, especially "Wrong 'Em Boyo," "Revolution Rock," and the B-side "Armagideon Time." The Clash thought the experiment enough of a success to bring him over to the USA, where he caught up with them in Boston at the Orpheum Theatre on September 19. He sat out the first few songs before joining for "Jimmy Jazz" and remaining onstage for the remainder of the set and encores. It was the first time he'd ever seen the Clash live! Morley wrote of that concert that "usually Gallagher is an interference, musically superfluous, but he's a necessary experiment."

Strummer agreed. "If people are going to stand there saying this ain't punk or whatever then they'll be the fucking losers," he said in the same article. "They're gonna miss the point. Because it feels good to me."

So, for the next year, Michael William "Mickey" Gallagher, who was born in Newcastle upon Tyne on October 29, 1945, and had been a working musician since 1963, including stints with the Animals and (Peter) Frampton's Camel, was on loan to the Clash. He would be the fifth member of the Clash throughout the various legs of the 16 Tons tour, appear in a few videos, and contribute to the recording of *Sandinista!* He was upset when he did not receive the partial songwriting credits for "The Magnificent Seven," "Hitsville UK," "Lightning Strikes (Not Once but Twice)," and "Charlie Don't Surf" that he thought Joe had offered him during a between-session bathroom break. He sued the band, but it was not these legal proceedings that ended his tenure with them. In fact, it was injuring his leg during one of the Clash's pickup football matches between demo sessions for their fifth studio album that resulted in the termination of Gallagher's services with El Clash Combo.

The Irish Horns

Johnny Green's *A Riot of Our Own* contains an entertaining vignette about him "chauffeuring" Joe and Mick to Bob Dylan's concert at the Picnic on July 15, 1978, where they finagled their way onto the guest list. Also on the bill that evening were Graham Parker and the Rumour. Little did they know that, fourteen months later, the Rumour's brass section would be overdubbing horns onto several *London Calling* tracks. The brass musicians by this time were no longer members of the Rumour, and this may account for why they are credited on *London Calling* as the Irish Horns. It was, in fact, their only recording credit as the Irish Horns. They are far more commonly known as the Rumour Brass.

The Irish Horns comprised Chris Gower (trombone), Dick Hanson (trumpet), John Earle (saxophone), and Ray Beavis (saxophone), and their role is fundamental to the success of songs such as "Jimmy Jazz," "Wrong 'Em Boyo," and "Revolution Rock." Earle even double-tracked his baritone saxophone on "The Right Profile," his horn providing the perfect complement to the timbre of Joe's voice.

As the Rumour Brass, this foursome can also be heard on the DB's' *Repercussion*, Shakin' Stevens's eponymous album from 1978, and Katrina and the Waves' seminal summer hit "Walking on Sunshine."

Post-Production of *London Calling*

America was calling as the Clash wrapped up the *London Calling* sessions by recording "Armagideon Time" and "Train in Vain" on the same evening. They would have to leave post-production efforts in the capable hands of Bill Price and Jeremy Green, the Wessex Studios recording team. Much care was taken by those left behind in London. For example, Green later told www.mixonline.com interviewer Chris Michie that Joe wanted the title song to sound like "London fog swirling off the river Thames, with seagulls circling overhead"—a concept Price honored by slowing down and repeating sounds via delay.

"Once the band got to New York," Price added, "I had a few phone calls with Joe and the rest of the band about how they wanted it mixed—I remember asking if it was okay for 'Jimmy Jazz' to sound like a live recording from a smoky old jazz club. So basically I mixed it totally on my own . . . and flew to New York with it. I was very nervous at the time, I must admit. I met up with the band, who were about to do a gig, and we played the mixes backstage at the Palladium, and basically they were happy with them."

Bill Price

You cannot recount the Clash's middle recording period without mentioning Bill Price. Not only is he is the constant studio presence on the Clash's recordings between producers Sandy Pearlman and Glyn Johns, he is the recording engineer who ably assisted the band in breaking free of CBS Records' interference. No doubt the record label felt comfortable knowing that a seasoned professional whose experience dated back over fifteen years was working with the Clash. Price was guitar-neck thin with the long hair that was a prerequisite for 1970s recording engineers and what Johnny Green wonderfully described in his memoir as "late night eyes."

Born on August 8, 1943, Price started his career in 1962 at Decca's West Hampstead Studios. He never worked with the Rolling Stones but he was soon engineering sessions for vocalists such as Tom Jones and Engelbert Humperdinck. It wasn't until a 1970 session with Marmalade, however, that he started working with rock bands. Hired by George Martin, the Beatles producer, he moved to Air Studios, where he recorded film soundtracks and sessions with Paul McCartney and Wings, Harry Nilsson, Sparks, and Mott the Hoople. When punk broke in the UK, he found himself working with the Tom Robinson Band, the Saints, XTC, and the Sex Pistols before the Clash booked time at Wessex Studios in January 1979, where Price was now the chief recording engineer.

Pleased with Price's contributions to *The Cost of Living EP*, the Clash asked him to assist with the re-recording of the soundtrack for *Rude Boy*, their only feature-length movie, which had been filmed by a talented crew who had nonetheless inadvertently botched the sound captured on film. This trying process of the Clash playing to filmed projections of themselves is described in detail in chapter 17; it would have been all the more trying without Price's expertise, so it was no surprise that he was subsequently recruited for the sessions for the band's third and fourth studio albums. He also worked on Mikey Dread's *World War III*, Ellen Foley's *Spirit of St. Louis*, and Ian Hunter's *Short Back 'n' Sides*, which Mick produced.

Inexplicably, Price was not involved in any of the sessions for *Combat Rock*, possibly because he was in such high demand. In the 1980s, he worked with Pete Townshend, the Pretenders, Elton John, Big Country, the Human League, and the Jesus and Mary Chain. He would later be reunited with Mick for work on Big Audio Dynamite's *Megatop Phoenix*. Said to be extremely affable, he demonstrated this by working in the 1990s with the notoriously difficult and unreliable Guns N' Roses. That same decade he mixed or produced recordings with the Cult, the Waterboys, and the Stone Roses, but a session with Joe Strummer and the Mescaleros was a bust.

Clash management brought Price back into the fold to work on the 1999 live collection *From Here to Eternity* and Sony hired him for the remastering of the Clash's catalogue. Price told www.mixonline.com that his goal in working with the original tapes of the Clash's recordings was the recreation of the vinyl experience fans had when hearing the Clash for the first time. He was highly complementary of Simon Humphrey's efforts on *The Clash.* He has also contributed to various reissues since the band's dissolution in 1985. In 1999, he mixed a few tracks for Joe Strummer and the Mescaleros that remain unreleased. And in the 2000s, Bill worked with Mick on recordings by the Libertines and Carbon/Silicon.

Jeremy Green

Jeremy Green was Bill Price's assistant engineer at Wessex, and as such he contributed to many of the same acts and recordings, including Public Image's debut album. Unlike Price, however, he would later be whisked by Joe to Electric Lady Studios in New York City to record his vocals for *Combat Rock.* He also worked with Mick on Big Audio Dynamite's debut album, *The Bottom Line.* His discography credits for engineering generally fall between 1978 and 1985, except for Death Cult's *Ghost Dance* in 1996. He also worked with Lene Lovich, Fun Boy Three, and the Special A.K.A. He resurfaced in the 1990s and 2000s as a drummer and producer.

The Best Rock 'n' Roll Cover of All Time

September 21, 1979. The Palladium. New York City. My girl and I were sitting in the back of our fifth-row seats. I felt someone tapping my shoulder but I didn't look back. Out of the corner of my eye I saw a hand touch my girlfriend's shoulder. "When the show starts, could you two both sit down?" a girl in the row behind us asked. Clearly she had never been to a Clash concert before. Nobody sits. My girl said we would, knowing full well that as soon as the house lights dimmed and the neon Mateus sign hovering over the stage was raised up, we'd be vacating our seats for the aisle anyway. There was some concern over a nearby usher who was trying to fulfill his obligation of keeping the aisle clear. But then the concert hall suddenly darkened, and I gave my girl a push. "Let's go," I said, and we ran down the aisle and became part of a mass of fans rushing the stage. Taped music was still playing. The longer we waited, the more worried I became. Believe it or not, the usher was trying to make everyone in the aisle return to their seats. Two girls pushed through the crowd. One kept saying, "Emergency! Emergency! Emergency!" Just then, the Clash emerged from the stage shadows, and the bashing chords of "Safe European Home" detonated the audience. The kids were pushing and shoving forward and dancing and jumping and landing on toes and waving fists in the air and shouting along with Joe Strummer. The usher fought back. Tiny battles broke out, usually involving an overly enthusiastic Clash fan and a bemused concertgoer who couldn't fathom what all the fuss was about. The dancing crowd would sway back and forth and someone would feel threatened and bark out angry words. I jumped wildly, swinging my wrists to Headon's drumbeats. My girl was lost in the crowd. The temperature was rising. I was sweating, but so was everyone else. The Clash were so bored with the USA. Same two opening songs as the previous night. Safe to assume then that it's the same set list. That meant "Complete Control" was next. I jumped as Jones landed. The guy in front of me jumped and smashed me in the face. I caught my flying glasses. My eye was sore. I was positive I'd cut it. My eye hurt. The usher was still fighting with concertgoers. He was causing more trouble than we were. As the song ended, I felt a sudden rush of pain from my right shoulder. A girl had bit me—a cute blond who screamed at me, "Keep moving up!" Yeah. Right. So I can get punched by the usher? But then the usher was suddenly gone, and we all moved a little closer to the stage. A frantic calm descended. The fights subsided. Songs roared by like the cars of a subway train. "Sorry man, if I keep stepping on your toes." "It's all right. I'm used to it." He laughed. "Were you here last night?" "Sure." "I love his voice," he said. "He sounds like a cement mixer."

The band was dressed the same as at Thursday night's show—Jones and Simonon in black, Headon in white—except for Strummer, who wore a blue shirt and black pants. Mick had an acoustic guitar for "Guns on the Roof" and Strummer held up the day's *New York Post*, which bore the following headline: "The Beatles Are Back!" The crowd booed and yayyed. The concert was on the radio: WNEW-FM, which Strummer called "WNSHIT." "Clash City Rockers" was the next song, and it brought out the crowd's best. This reaction was only matched (and perhaps surpassed) during "I Fought the Law," "Tommy Gun," and "White Riot." Sweat-drenched, I would jump above the bobbing heads and steal a few breaths of fresh air. My hair dripped and I checked my cheek occasionally for signs of blood. There was only sweat. My girl reappeared only to vanish throughout the concert.

Three songs were added to Thursday's output. They were "Tommy Gun," "What's My Name," and another unreleased song. The energy in the crowd was unbelievable. The Clash draw a good crowd, unlike Patti Smith and Debbie Harry, whose crowds have been mediocre the past year. The back of my arm rubbed against the tit of the girl behind me, but she didn't seem to mind. "White riot. I want to riot! White riot. A riot of my own!" Yelling. Shouting. Many in the crowd. And then the last chord in this town, and only the screaming and the whistling and the cheering and the clapping and the ringing remained. My girl was near me. "That's it," I said to her, "if we use last night as a precedent." She agreed. I lit a joint that we shared as we waited for the Palladium to empty and I scribbled down the set list:

1. "Safe European Home"
2. "I'm So Bored with the USA"
3. "Complete Control"
4. "London Calling"
5. "(White Man) In Hammersmith Palais"
6. "Koka Kola"
7. "I Fought the Law"
8. "Jail Guitar Doors"
9. "The Guns of Brixton"
10. "English Civil War"
11. "Clash City Rockers"
12. "Stay Free"
13. "Clampdown"
14. "Police and Thieves"
15. "Capital Radio"
16. "Tommy Gun"
17. "Wrong 'Em Boyo"
18. "Janie Jones"
19. "Garageland"

Encore:

20. "Armagideon Time"
21. "Career Opportunities"
22. "What's My Name"
23. "White Riot"

That's my slightly edited notes from the Clash's third appearance in New York City. Little did I know that, at that very moment, *NME* photographer Pennie Smith was possibly snapping the iconic image of the Clash that

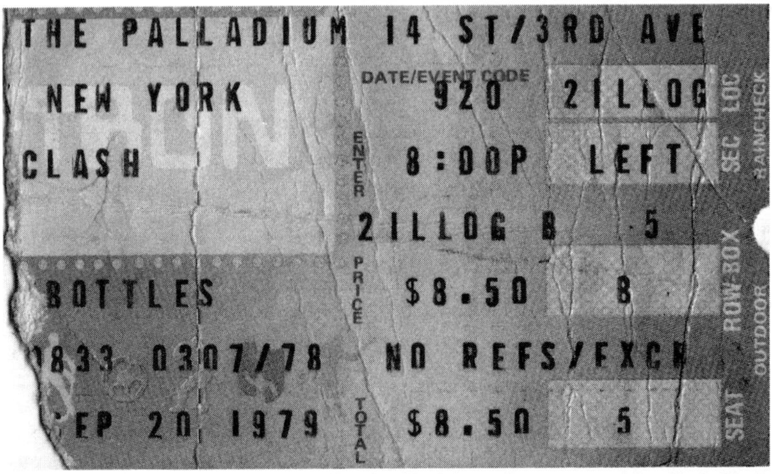

The author's torn Ticketron ticket for the Clash's performance at New York City's Palladium on September 20, 1979. *Author's collection*

would appear on the cover of the album that housed the five new, unreleased songs heard that night in the Palladium.

Now, the Clash were justly known for physical, over the top performances. Mick would leap; Joe would strum his Fender Telecaster so abusively that he would take to inventing a strum guard, which he wore on the lower half of his right forearm to prevent bleeding and rash burns; Paul would frenetically exchange places with Mick; but they were not known for smashing their equipment. They couldn't afford it. But on this Friday night, the Clash had given a performance that satisfied everyone but Paul. He says he was frustrated that the fans were so far away from the stage (which doesn't match up with my notes), and started swinging his bass. Johnny Green says in his memoir that Paul did this to impress his girlfriend, Deb, who was standing in the wings. Randall Doane, in *Stealing All Transmissions*, questions whether or not this happened on Thursday night and not Friday. All I can add to this debate is my memory of Mick rescuing the girl being chased across the stage by the bouncer and escorting her off the stage. It's not in my notes, which leads me to believe that Mick's gentlemanly act and Paul's destruction happened on Thursday night.

"I was watching Paul," Smith recalled to Pat Gilbert in *Passion Is a Fashion*, "and realized his guitar was the wrong way up. He started coming toward me. I had a wide-angled lens that made him look further away and when I looked up he was right on top of me. I took three shots and ducked." Smith objected when her photo was being considered as the album's cover. She rightly noted it was somewhat out of focus, but the band better understood the power of her image. (That blurry figure in the background is the bouncer!) Smith's *NME* cohort and illustrator Ray Lowry, who was part of the Clash's Takes the Fifth entourage, designed the cover in homage to Elvis Presley's first RCA album, *Rock 'n' Roll.* Apparently, Lowry and Johnny Green had picked up a battered copy in Chicago during the tour. Doing so established a lineage between *London Calling* and the world's first rock 'n' roll album, what Lowry, in *The Clash: Rock Retrospectives*, co-authored by Ben Meyers, characterizes as an album that "had so impressed me a hundred or so years earlier as the most down and dirty rock-and-roll album that was ever thrown together."

Lowry's only regret about the cover art was the pink "wasn't quite hot enough."

Pennie Smith

Pennie Smith has photographed everyone from Siouxsie Sioux to Lily Allen and the Jam to the Babyshambles, but she is probably best known for her work with the Clash, who permitted her unfettered access between 1979 and 1982. Not only did she shoot the cover for *London Calling*, she did the same for *Sandinista!* and *Combat Rock*, and she published the first book of photography of the band (*The Clash: Before & After*) in 1980. Scenes from Joe Strummer's 1983 film *Hell W10* were even filmed in her offices.

A Londoner, Smith was born in 1949 and studied graphics and fine art at Twickenham Art School in the Swinging London days. Her earliest contributions were to *Friendz* magazine between 1969 and 1972; her first *NME* commission was shooting Led Zeppelin's 1973 tour. She would be a member of the *NME* staff for a decade and would develop a well-deserved reputation for her black-and-white photography. Eleven of her portraits are in the permanent collection of London's National Portrait Gallery, including one of the Clash and another of Joe Strummer. In 2002, *Q* magazine voted the cover shot of Paul smashing his bass against the Palladium stage as being the "Greatest Rock 'n' Roll Photograph."

At the time of this writing, Smith lives in an abandoned train station in west London that she bought as a student and converted into her house.

Ray Lowry

Likened to a "War Artist" by Joe in Johnny Green's memoir, Ray Lowry was born on August 28, 1944, in Cadishead, a suburb of Salford, Greater

Manchester. His mother died when he was sixteen, but by then the self-taught Lowry—exhibiting the punk attitude he would admire in bands in the mid-'70s—had already landed jobs at local advertising agencies. He moved on to work with the radical underground fanzine *Oz* and the *International Times*, and then more mainstream publications such as *Mayfair*, *Private Eye*, and *Punch*. Using a Gillott nib with Indian ink and wash, his style was as loud and brash as the content.

Harnessing his passion for rock 'n' roll, he eventually became an in-house illustrator for *NME*. It was during the Sex Pistols' legendary Anarchy in the UK tour in December 1976 that he first crossed paths with the Clash. He would catch the Clash over the next several years before finally paying

Ray Lowry's artwork for the back cover of the *Rude Boy* DVD booklet is a good example of his "war artist" style of illustration. *Author's collection*

his own way onto the Clash Take the Fifth tour and the connections that found him designing the Clash's next album cover.

Lowry had the rock 'n' roll heart Lou Reed sang of, and he knew his finished design "had to feature the infamous pink and green rock-and-roll lettering" found on Elvis Presley's album. "God made me do that," he later wrote. It was Joe who deemed the cover was the "War Artist's" to design. "Why the hell I thought I was even going to get near the cover is a bit of a mystery. Sod it, let's just have a go. We couldn't do worse than Hipgnosis." (Hipgnosis was the English design team responsible for the cover art of Pink Floyd's *Dark Side of the Moon*, Led Zeppelin's *Houses of the Holy*, and many other albums from the '70s.) Lowry remembered that "Joe and I were the only ones to share that exultant, 'Yihaa! This is it' moment," when they spotted Smith's photo of Paul smashing his Fender Precision to smithereens. "His Strummership and moi saw a fantastic rocking moment." Returning to Lancashire after the tour, "Plagiarinspiration strikes!!!," as one of Lowry's own drawings details, and he came up with retro design. He also wrote out the lyrics and liner notes on the *London Calling* dust covers.

It's puzzling that, as someone so affected by rock 'n' roll and who worked for *NME* and who designed a legendary album cover, Lowry did not design album artwork for any band other than the Clash. Given how striking his one attempt was, you'd think other bands would have hired him. Instead, he began writing a column for the *Face* in the early 1980s before changing mores led to limited publication. The rock 'n' roll illustrator was no longer in demand. Not the healthiest of men, Lowry died suddenly on October 14, 2008, in Waterfoot, Lancashire, aged sixty-four, a month after the first exhibition devoted to his work.

In addition to liner notes and CD booklets for various reissues of *London Calling*, Lowry's illustrations of the Clash can be found in Johnny Green's *A Riot of our Own*, a recommended inside look by the road manager of the band's activities between 1978 and 1980; *The Clash: Up-Close and Personal*, Lowry's own book of sketches from the 1979 tour in America; and Ben Myers's *The Clash*.

"London Calling to the Underworld"

Much was made about Joe romanticizing the criminal element in "Bankrobber," but as a lyricist he had been doing so for years. There's the rich being mugged in "1977," the cat burglar in "What's My Name," the Mafia contracts in "All the Young Punks," and throughout *London Calling* the underworld responds to Joe's call in the third line of the title track. Side 1 alone has the police looking for Jimmy Jazz, drug dealers, and rude boys. Here, then, is a roll call of all the criminals crawling over the four sides.

"Jimmy Jazz"

So who is this Jimmy Jazz the police are looking for? He is a Rastafarian assassin who has murdered Jimmy Dread and has just given the police the slip, possibly thanks to the song's narrator. In an interview with *Best* magazine's Bruno Blum, Mick said the initial idea came from the police actually walking into the studio while he was alone with The Baker, recording potential ideas for songs: "[I looked up and] there were policemen all over the room and . . . we did the parallel between them and the mafia in the song."

"Jimmy Jazz" references *Satta Massagana*, the 1976 recording released by Jamaican roots reggae artists the Abyssinians. The ten-track album also includes a track titled "Satta a Massagana." What "satta massagana" means has been open to debate, but according to Abyssinians vocalist Donald Manning, "When you say Satta Massagana, you give thanks to God. It means 'give thanks.'" But in Joe Strummer's lyrics it takes on a darker connotation, one that Mick explained to Blum: "If you re-read 'Satta Massagana,' you can notice that you can also pronounce it 'Sat on My Cigar,' you know. Imagine a big chief of the mafia . . . who suddenly learn[s] that Jimmy Jazz has just arrived in town and he's playing by his own rules and . . . he yells to his men to leave right now and to go get Jimmy Jazz and to bring his head back."

Often likened to a number by Tom Waits or Mose Alison, in concert "Jimmy Jazz" (the Clash's bluesiest tune) became a vehicle for Joe's ad libs about Lenny Bruce or rock songwriting or being gobbed on or whatever was on his mind that evening. Regularly played fourth in the set during the 16 Tons tour, thereafter "Jimmy Jazz" became one of those songs, like "Junco Partner" or "Spanish Bombs," that would be performed infrequently in concert.

"Hateful"

There was little doubt the Clash would adopt Bo Diddley's infamous and infectious rhythm somehow after they shared life on the road with the rhythm-and-blues legend in America during February 1979, and they did so in "Hateful," a song about drug addiction, perhaps influenced by Topper's shenanigans. Even so, with the chugging rhythm changes and vocal interplay between Joe (as the junkie) and Mick (as the voice of his conscious), this is no mere rethread. An updated tale of Lou Reed waiting for his man, the drug addict's plight is so bad that his drug dealer is his only friend; he even says, "This year I've lost some friends." Drug addiction is a common theme on *London Calling*, and will recur in "The Right Profile," "Koka Kola," and "Revolution Rock."

"Rudie Can't Fail"

Much of "Rudie Can't Fail" echoes the rude boy–centered songs popular in Jamaica in the 1960s. According to Jamaican slang, rude boys were unemployable youths—either through lack of opportunity or attitude—who turned to a life of crime in order to subsist. The songs were parables about good and bad lifestyles. (Stranger Cole's "Ruff and Tough" from 1962 is considered the first song about this type of Jamaican youth.) Even the phrase "Rudie Can't Fail" is directly lifted from Desmond Dekker's "007 (Shanty Town)" and means that the rude boy will survive and thrive. In 1948, the first of a wave of Jamaican immigrants were detained by the British government before being allowed to settle in Brixton, where the community took root. The children of these immigrants identified with the characters in the songs of the music coming out of Jamaica and some adopted the lifestyles of the rude boys being sung of. Latter-day white rude boys were found in the Clash's London as described in chapter 11.

"The Guns of Brixton"

"The Guns of Brixton" is arguably the epitome of all the Clash's work. For some, it is the center, the "x" where all that is Clashical intersects, and it is easy to see why: the subject matter is a remnant of the *Give 'Em Enough Rope* era, but the music reflects the dominant strain of London Reggae that imbued the Clash's ego from the summer of 1979 until Mick's departure—what *Sounds*' Mark Cooper described as "the new Clash sound in which the rhythm section leads." (Through April 1979 and the recording of the *Rude Boy* soundtrack, the dominant aspect of the Clash's collective ego had been London punk.)

Initially lambasted as an indicator of all that was wrong with the *London Calling*–era Clash by British journalists, it was later described as "very true and relevant" (Paolo Hewitt) and "topically prophetic" (Mick Farren). "The

Guns of Brixton" is a song about authoritarianism, painting a picture of British authorities closing in on Brixton revolutionaries who are leading the riots of the early eighties. The intent of the song is emphasized by the references to Ivan and *The Harder They Come*, Paul's favorite movie about ghetto resistance in Kingston, Jamaica. These characters from the underworld are coming out with their guns blasting.

"Wrong 'Em Boyo"

"A living lesson of where not to put your feet-boyo!" Joe wrote in the *Armagideon Times*, a self-produced band zine, the first of which was included in the initial British release of *London Calling* (and reprinted as part of *Sound System*). "Wrong 'Em Boyo" was written by Clive Alfanso, who had died in a car crash, but Joe notes that "his next of kin will cop some royalty."

"Wrong 'Em Boyo" was a favorite of Paul's, and the band knew it well from the Rulers' version on the jukebox in Rehearsal Rehearsals. The Clash version loosely mirrors the Rulers', including the false beginning about Stagger Lee, the nefarious character that Mick in his *Best* interview likened to Jimmy Jazz. Both are murderers from the underworld. Stagger Lee, however, has a far longer history than Jimmy Jazz.

Bluesman "Mississippi" John Hurt is credited with keeping the Stagger Lee legend alive through his 1928 recording of "Stack o' Lee Blues" for Okeh Electric Records. Stagger Lee's historical name was Lee Shelton. He was an American pimp and gambler who entered into folklore with the Christmas 1895 murder of William Lyons—the Billy threatening "to leave [a] knife in [Lee's] back" in "Wrong 'Em Boyo."

According to a contemporary report in the *St. Louis Globe-Democrat*, the two were gambling and drinking buddies who argued over politics; when Lyons "snatched" the dapper Shelton's hat, he was shot dead. Soon after, the murder became the stuff of work songs sung by field laborers. Lee Shelton's infamous nickname has been attributed to several sources, the most colorful is that of the Stack Lee, a Mississippi riverboat known for its role in the prostitution trade.

"Death or Glory"

"Death or Glory" begins with a reference to how "every cheap hood strikes a bargain with the world," in an effort to liken the Clash's situation with that of the underworld. And with the constant harassment the Clash received from the British authorities, it is easy to understand why Joe might feel like a hood, especially since the first half of the song describes how his belief in punk rock left him feeling spiritually bankrupt.

"The Card Cheat"

Amid imagery of "the opium den" and "barroom gin," "The Card Cheat" harkens back to the scuffling gamblers at the beginning of "Wrong 'Em Boyo," because just like Stagger Lee's victim Billy, the card cheat is "shot dead."

"Revolution Rock"

As *London Calling* comes to close, Joe gives a parting, cautionary shout-out to the underworld. As part of a series of ad libs, Joe almost dedicates the album "to the coolest mobsters in Kingstown with the hardest eyes and the coolest nose" who he continues to address and then, as if to make a final point, he yells out, "Young people shoot their days away / I've seen talent thrown away!" He is lamenting the tragedies that befall so many young people marginalized by life.

The Call of the Wildebeest

Ever wonder about the sound Joe is making in "London Calling," just as Mick's backward-sounding guitar solo bursts forth? The one that conjures up the cries of nuclearized seagulls flying over the River Thames after the narrator says he lives "by the river"? This particular vocal tic of Joe Strummer's is the "call of the wildebeest." Rather than a cry, it's supposed to be a howl.

On March 20, 1979, Mick and Topper (and bassist Tony James) contributed to a one-off single by British music journalist Kris Needs. Prior to the Clash's Pearl Harbour tour of America, Mick had agreed to produce a single for Needs's band the Vice Creems, only to find they'd disbanded on the eve of the planned recording session at Olympic Studios. Mick said he'd find Needs a band, and he did, even if the musicians couldn't use their real names on the "Danger Love" sleeve, so Mick Jones is listed as Michael Blair and Nicky "Topper" Headon as Nicholas Khan.

One giveaway to the true identities of the personnel is Mick's friend Robin Banks, who is credited with the animal noises on the B-side "Like a Tiger." Topper loved the sound and would often imitate it. According to Needs's book *Joe Strummer and the Legend of the Clash*, Robin informed him in 2004 that it was the animal noises on "Like a Tiger" that had given Joe the idea for "the wildebeest noise."

This is incorrect, however, because Joe first makes this sound during the fading moments of the version of "Capital Radio" heard on *The Cost of Living EP*, a recording made in January 1979. But it is possible that hearing Needs's single and Topper's imitation of the animal noises may have encouraged Joe to revisit the cry and develop it further for "London Calling." In fact, the best version of Joe's "call of the wildebeest" is on the demo version on *The Vanilla Tapes* (described later), where the call is heavily echoed. Joe also employs this vocal idiosyncrasy of his on "Death and Glory."

The *25th Anniversary Edition*

In 2004, *London Calling* was remastered for a *25th Anniversary Edition* with a thirty-six-page booklet, a foldout lyric sheet, rare Pennie Smith photos and Ray Lowry artwork, and a DVD containing not only promos and *The Last Testament*, a documentary on the making of *London Calling*, but also a private home movie running almost fourteen minutes shot in Wessex Studios during the recording sessions. There's Mick testing out leads to "Jimmy Jazz," the Clash running through numbers and pointless jams, and rock 'n' roll maverick Guy Stevens "producing" the Clash by coaching Joe on vocals and jumping about to ensure the songs have energy.

But it was Disc 2 that made this edition a must have for fans. In *A Riot of Our Own*, Johnny Green writes of demos The Baker had made at Vanilla Rehearsal Studios on a Teac recorder—a copy of which Johnny had left on London's Underground. *The Vanilla Tapes* were long considered lost, until Mick found another copy during a house move. Finally, fans could hear the twenty-one track tape of songs that made the grade (and didn't) for the formal recording sessions for *London Calling* at Wessex a month later.

Just about every track is worth hearing. "Paul's Tune"—obviously "The Guns of Brixton" in embryonic form—has a busier bassline; you'll wish Paul's shouts of "You're a naughty boy" could have been kept in the finished version of "Rudie Can't Fail"; "Koka Kola, Advertising & Cocaine" is almost a folk song. Then there are surprises like the Clash performing the allegedly despised "Remote Control" or Mick Jones performing the previously unreleased "Oh, Lonesome Me," a C&W hit for Don Gibson in December

1957. Makes you wonder why the Clash never did record a C&W number. Probably too American.

Other previously unreleased tracks include "Walking the Sidewalk," an instrumental that sounds like a *Let It Be* outtake. It's followed by the instrumental "Where You Gonna Go (Soweto)" and a version of Bob Dylan's "The Man in Me," which the Clash try unsuccessfully to make Clashical. Another unused song, "Heart and Mind," has the most potential of the unreleased songs, but Joe's singing is tuneless until he segues into the 101'ers' "Keys to My Heart." With its catchy chords, it might have been a good vehicle for Mick.

15

The Bells of Prince Far-I

The Punky Reggae Party

That Jamaican music would be a significant Clashical influence was evident from the revamped look of Joe Strummer's 1966 Fender Telecaster guitar the very first time he walked onstage with the Clash. The sunburst guitar was now repainted with gray primer and black automobile paint. Even the pick guard was repainted, above which—reflecting the Clash gear of the day—"NOISE" was stenciled in white lettering. Above—but mostly behind—the bridge is the iconic "IGNORE ALIEN ORDERS" sticker in red lettering. The final new touch was made to the horn of the pick guard. There are three small stripes in black, yellow, and red, suggesting the Rastafarian flag. Only green is missing. Even at this early performance, the Clash were at the vanguard of the punky reggae party.

London Reggae

Like the Rolling Stones fifteen years earlier with electrified Chicago rhythm-and-blues artists, the Clash educated their fans on a musical genre from another land that would become an essential touchstone of the British punk scene: roots reggae. Since Paul and Mick hailed from Brixton, a poorer part of London where a large Jamaican immigrant community flourished in the mid-'60s, reggae was not new to them, but Joe had been less exposed. He may have considered playing "The Israelites" by Desmond Dekker while in the 101'ers but he—like many others—soaked up reggae for the first time at the Roxy Club, where Don Letts was DJ'ing.

It was January 1977. There were punk bands but few punk records. Stuck for discs to spin in this central London scene for punk rockers, Letts—the son of Jamaican immigrants—started mixing in the reggae records he spun daily at the Acme Attraction boutique, which Andy Czezowski owned as well as the Roxy. "I soon realized that (the nite klubbers) were turned on by the anti-establishment vibe of the 'Burn Babylon Burn' business," Letts says in John Robb's oral history of punk. "Obviously it was the basslines and the lyrical content that was turning them on, and the fact that these songs were about something. It was the ultimate rebel sound around."

It was a rebel sound that appealed to Joe, too, and one he felt the Clash should appropriate for their songbook. Reggae dropouts—a key trait of Jamaican recording artists—were already part of the band's musical vocabulary. Maybe it was time to take it one step further. As they experimented with Bob Marley's "Dancing Shoes" and Junior Murvin's "Police and Thieves," the Clash convened with the Sex Pistols and Joe let the Pistols know he foresaw how a marriage of the two genres (punk and reggae) could birth a London brand of reggae. It was a touchy subject. Was it blasphemous? Was it just white musicians ripping off black musicians again? Was it a musical dead end?

The Pistols didn't think much of the idea, so the Clash were free to forge this sound on their own terms. The result was what Joe once referred to as "London Reggae," a tributary of reggae music that interestingly no other band was able to sail on. There were other white British bands immersed in reggae, such as the Police and UB40, but their reggae was too light, too nimble, too Top 40, to be taken seriously. When *Trouser Press*'s Ira Robbins pointed out that "most reggae played by white bands is musically upbeat and happy," he was onto something. The Clash's reggae was not something to dance your troubles away to.

It was original, too, because the Clash played reggae instinctively. The Clash's version is like the artwork of Jean-Michel Basquiat, which is child-like but without a trace of innocence. The Clash's playing of reggae was not light, it was heavy, which is not to say that Mick was heaping on lines of distortion or that Topper was pummeling his tom-toms. In fact, their playing is the opposite: Mick would play simple melodic lines while Topper applied supple-wristed jazz techniques. It was Paul and Joe who provided the menace. Paul's bass grumbled as he played repetitive basslines that somehow lost their repetitiveness and began to seem like one continuous line. And Joe's voice—the subject of so much criticism—was in its natural element when he sang reggae. Maybe it was the passion in the voice that explains this, but his heavily treated voice would echo like those of oppressed souls denied the luxury of dying.

Lots of echo was applied to Clash instrumentation, too, resulting in jangly pianos and clicky guitars, as well as Joe's vocals. Another component were sound effects. True, they are present in the form of fireworks in Bill Price's various mixes of "Armagideon Time," but it was a trait of Mikey Dread's aural vision of reggae that the Clash made a signature of their own reggae, having learned at the hands of the master. Dread's contributions are not to be overlooked. (The case can be made that no one affected the Clash's sound more in 1980 than Dread.) Nor is that of Mickey Gallagher, who brought a Londoner's perspective to the sheets of organ or simple keyboard fills he played.

Simply put, the reggae the Clash created is unlike anyone else's because they added their souls.

"Police and Thieves"

As punk rock was incubating in London, Junior Murvin's "Police and Thieves" was released by Island Records in July 1976. It became one of the signature songs of the summer, peaking at #23 on the charts, and was later voted #6 in *NME*'s list of the best singles of 1976. The Clash's version was—as summed up by Mick in the special edition of the *Armagideon Times* included with *Sound System*—"the summer hit, done over."

"It was just a wild idea I had one night," Joe told Caroline Coon in a 1977 interview. "I wanted to do a Hawkwind version of a [reggae] song that was familiar to us, and we just did it within our limitations. If it had sounded shitty we'd have dropped it. But it sounded great. There's hardly any reggae in it at all—just a few offbeat guitars thrown in for a laugh—it's all rock 'n' roll. I think it's an incredible track."

Mick's take on the Clash's version, as told to *ZigZag*'s Kris Needs in April 1977, was, "It's a logical progression. There's obviously a lot of links between us and what's happening with the Rastas. It just seemed right to do it. We had lots of our own material, but we wanted to do one song by someone else. What would we do? Not a '60s rehash . . . let's do something which is '76, right? . . . They can't understand that what we're trying to do is redefine the scene and like make it clear to people the way to move. . . . You've got to take risks all the time. That's why we did it . . . as a risk."

The risk became a staple of Clash sets for the remainder of their touring career. And while much has been made of Mick's arrangement of his and Joe's seesawing, sweet-and-sour guitars that is echoed in the vocal arrangement, Terry Chimes's steady drumbeat has gone unheralded. After the crashing chords during the song's intro he lays down a steady, relentless beat that never lets up through the songs verses and choruses. In this he laid the groundwork for Topper, because in concert, as Mick added lead guitar and Joe piled on the ad libs, that beat kept on a-rollin'. It's the most rock thing about the Clash's version. In concert, when Topper would begin the song, the drumbeat was so familiar to fans that cheering and clapping and whistling began instantly, even before a note was played. Then Topper would bang out the beats under the crashing opening chords before steadfastly resuming the drumbeat—a metaphor for the unyielding presence of the "po-lease," as Joe would intone.

"(White Man) In Hammersmith Palais"

The second of three London Reggae recordings where punk rock is the dominant influence, the arrangement of "(White Man) In Hammersmith" echoes the loud crashing chords of "Police and Thieves" but then settles into a beat that is more skank than rock 'n' roll.

What is extra clever about the arrangement and performance of "(White Man) In Hammersmith Palais" is that the song begins with Joe voicing his disappointment with the roots reggae show he witnessed in the Hammersmith Palais, to which the band responds by demonstrating perfectly the type of "root rock rebel" music he *should've* heard.

By the time of this recording, live versions of "Police and Thieves" ended with a reprisal of the crashing chords heard during the intro, and the Clash borrow that concept for "(White Man) In Hammersmith Palais," where the outro refers back to the intro. (See chapter 8 for a fuller description of this song.)

Blue Beat

When answering a question about the then trending 2 Tone movement from *Creem*'s Susan Whitall in 1980, Joe—without missing a beat—educated the interviewer about how 2 Tone's roots were nothing new. The Clash were ahead of the Specials and Selecter on that one: "Blue Beat? This one summer I'd gone to live with [Don Letts] . . . he gave me this Trojan album, 'cause he was digging the 'now sound of roots rock reggae' . . . they're not interested in the old stuff. They think it's boring if it ain't new, which is quite a good attitude. But anyway—he said he didn't want it . . . so I got hold of it, I put it on . . . and I was just wiped away for six months, 'cause it's just like the cream, in a triple album set, the cream of all the bluebeat stuff."

Blue Beat Records was an English record label singularly responsible for popularizing Jamaican R&B and ska in Great Britain in the 1960s. And, for a period, the Clash were so into old Blue Beat recordings that they were referenced in songs such as "Safe European Home" and "(White Man) In Hammersmith Palais."

"Pressure Drop"

The Clash only recorded one classic Blue Beat song, however: "Pressure Drop," originally released by the Maytals in 1970 and subsequently included on the soundtrack to *The Harder They Come*, which is where the Clash first heard the song that subsequently made *Rolling Stone*'s "500 Greatest Songs of All Time."

The Clash debuted "Pressure Drop" on April 19, 1977, in Paris; recorded it at the Marquee Studios in February 1978; and finally released it as the B-side to "English Civil War" a year later. Much is made of Mick's arrangement of "Police and Thieves," but his intro to "Pressure Drop" is even better. The opening is a stirring orchestration of guitars—both played by Mick—that introduces the chord changes and melody hummed in the Maytals version before Paul and Topper and then Joe leap in. The vocal arrangement is similar to that of "Police and Thieves," with Joe delivering lines that Mick answers with, "Oh ye-ea-ah!"

The Maytals version definitely skanks, so the Clash add their DNA by punking it up. Actually, a key to the Clash's reinvention of reggae is that Mick *does not* play skanking rhythm guitar. Usually this is suggested by the bassline or organ.

Reggae Calling

Except for the references to Blue Beat and how "Rudy can't fail" in "Safe European Home," reggae is completely absent from *Give 'Em Enough Rope*. This was unexpected, since the Clash's previous single was "(White Man) In Hammersmith Palais," arguably their best song and certainly a mature mash-up of punk rock and reggae that no other band could match. Not the Police. Not the Slits. There is a reason why producer Sandy Pearlman had the Clash re-record the song during the *Rope* sessions. He must have wanted to include it on the album, but that was never going to happen, given the Clash's philosophy about not swindling their fans. That was part of the Sex Pistols' credo, not the Clash's. Toots and the Maytals' "Pressure Drop" was a B-side on one of the singles released to promote *Give 'Em Enough Rope*, though, so Clash fans were not surprised when *London Calling* contained four songs—over 21 percent of the record—with Jamaican roots.

"The Guns of Brixton"

Paul Simonon's Sisyphean bassline in his composition "The Guns of Brixton" is probably the most sampled piece from the Clash's canon. (Check

During live performances of "The Guns of Brixton," Joe Strummer played Paul's Fender Precision bass guitar. *Ebet Roberts/Getty Images*

out Beats International's "Dub Be Good to Me.") Today it is a classic; it has even been covered by Paul's hero, Jamaican ska and reggae musician Jimmy Cliff. Brix Smith of the Fall named herself Brixton after hearing the song. (Mark E. must've loved that!) It was a staple of Clash concerts dating back to September 19, 1979, when it was first performed at the Orpheum Theatre in Boston. But in the early days "The Guns of Brixton" was somewhat controversial. For example, while Charles Shaar Murray called it "musically impeccable," he found issue with the lyrics: "We don't need another paean to martyrdom; we've already had enough martyrs."

The music is portentous: scraping guitars, primitive drums, things literally going "boing!" in the night. That bassline, however, which goes up the hill only to run down, is the linchpin. It implies the day-in, day-out drudgery of Brixton's underclass. Then Paul "sings," and his inability speaks multitudes. His inarticulate voice gives the lyrics, with their references to Ivan in *The Harder They Come*, "Black Marias," and guns, their verisimilitude. Paul would "sing" on a few other tracks, but never with the same conviction. "The vocal mike was right up against this glass panel of the control room," Paul says in *The Clash on Broadway* booklet, "and sitting right in front of me, two feet behind the glass, was some sort of American CBS bloke, and it really annoyed me. So that's probably why the vocals came out the way they did!"

In concert, Paul and Joe would swap instruments for "The Guns of Brixton." Topper would start the tribal rhythm as Joe stepped back near the drum riser, stage left. Then he'd leap on with the seesawing bassline, his eyes fixated on the fretboard of the Fender Precision. He looked like he was manning a jackhammer. "The Guns of Brixton" became a feature for Mick and Paul. Mick's guitar drenched the song with voodoo effects as Paul scrapped out chords, but more often he just stood there with his lanky left arm swaying. It was so dramatic that you would have thought a choreographer had staged the performance.

"Wrong 'Em Boyo"

The second of two ska-infused tracks on *London Calling*, "Wrong 'Em Boyo," with the Irish Horns accompanying the Clash throughout, is the closest the band came to sounding like a 2 Tone outfit. Another cover that the Clash made their own, "Wrong 'Em Boyo" was originally recorded in 1967 by the Rulers, an obscure Jamaican band of which little is known. They were a vocal recording act produced by J. J. Johnson for his own JJ label. Musical support was provided by Bobby Aitken and the Carib Beats. The Rulers' 45 was on the Rehearsal Rehearsals jukebox, with Paul the advocate for the Clash's rendition.

The Rulers' original begins with a lengthy piano intro missing from the Clash's version, which jumps right into telling the R&B legend of Stagger Lee's murder of Billy in a saloon over a card game. Both versions abruptly stop, like patrons fleeing, only to have the singer instruct the band to start all over again, but this time the beat is different. The Rulers' version is rock-steady . . . very steady . . . almost slow. The Clash version is neo-ska with an uptown tempo and swinging horns. The Clash used horns throughout their career, from "City of the Dead" to "Sean Flynn," but this is the only recording where the band sounds like a soul revue. Joe's striving voice perfectly complements the horns.

"Revolution Rock"

"Get Up" by Jackie Edwards and the Revolutioners is a reggae original that, like Junior Murvin's "Police and Thieves," dates from Year Zero. It is an infectious song calling for "everyone to get out of your seat" and protest. Later that same year, Edwards produced a record by Danny Ray that borrowed heavily not only from "Get Up's" riddim but its backing tracks as well, which explains why this new recording, called "Revolution Rock," is credited to Edwards/Ray. Although Jamaican-born, Ray had been operating out of the UK since the late '60s. "Revolution Rock" was also the B-side to Ray's 1979 single "Rastaman Live Up." "Get Up" is the better song of the two, but "Revolution Rock" is one of the Clash's best covers.

The Clash version is faithful in tempo, but Joe takes liberties with the lyrics. Just as "London Calling" contains a lyric snippet from Guy Mitchell's "Singing the Blues," here Joe includes lyrics from Bobby Darin's "Mack the Knife." He doesn't stop there. When he says, "Everybody smash up your seats and rock to this brand new beat," he's recalling the mayhem when punk rockers used to tear up the seats in venues with seating up front, such as the Clash's infamous show at the Rainbow on May 7, 1977. In the late '80s, Joe was to remember that show as the band's high point: "A night where you're at the right place, at the right time, doing the right thing, saying the right words, almost without effort, all the seats get demolished. Chance, luck, the effect was magic." You can imagine Joe at the mic, ad-libbing, recalling that magical night as he begins a song that's all about getting up and making things happen.

"Revolution Rock" was a soundcheck favorite that graduated to vinyl preservation. Originally it was planned as the closing track on *London Calling*, which explains Joe's ad libs at the end, asking the listener to follow him, insisting that "this must be the way out." Then, as El Clash Combo jams, he sounds like Frank Zappa during "America Drinks and Goes Home" at the end of *Absolutely Free*: Joe says the band can play "any song you want"; they'll take requests, and bongo jazz is a specialty—something they'd prove a few years later, on "First Night Back in London" and "Mustafa Dance."

"Armagideon Time"

Johnny Green has been quoted as saying of Jamaican reggae and dub musician and producer Willi Williams's 1978 hit "Armagideon Time" that it was "a soundcheck job, that turned into an encore job, that turned into a studio job." This is not entirely accurate, though, as the Clash had recorded their version on September 5, 1979, three days before it was first played live during an encore at the Tribal Stomp Festival in Monterey, California.

An excellent example of the "Real Rock" riddim first produced by Clement Seymour (Coxsone) Dodd at the legendary Studio One in Kingston, Jamaica during a Sound Dimension session, here the Clash brought in keyboardist Mickey Gallagher to refashion "Armagideon Time" at the same session in which "Train in Vain" was cut.

The Clash chose not to include horns, a feature of Williams's version, possibly because they might end up sounding too close to trombonist Rico Rodriguez's solos with the Specials. Instead, the Clash arrangement features Paul's "rub a dub" bassline (which adds an extra bass note to Williams's version), Mick's simple, melodic guitar line, and Topper's turn on the tubular bells.

Again, Joe took liberties with the lyrics. Against Gallagher's organ and soft percussion, he uses a three-line verse to set up a scene of a foreigner in an old town from which it might be better to move on. There's a pervading sense of violence brewing. Then Paul's hypnotic bassline begins pulsing, raising the temperature. Joe is fairly faithful at first to the lyrics, but when he sings the verses, he opts for an American bluesman's edit of the lyrical structure by repeating the first line in each verse (something Williams did not do). Joe also rephrases Williams's line from "Remember to praise Jahovah / And He will guide you in Armagideon time" as "Remember to kick it over / No one will guide you through Armagideon time."

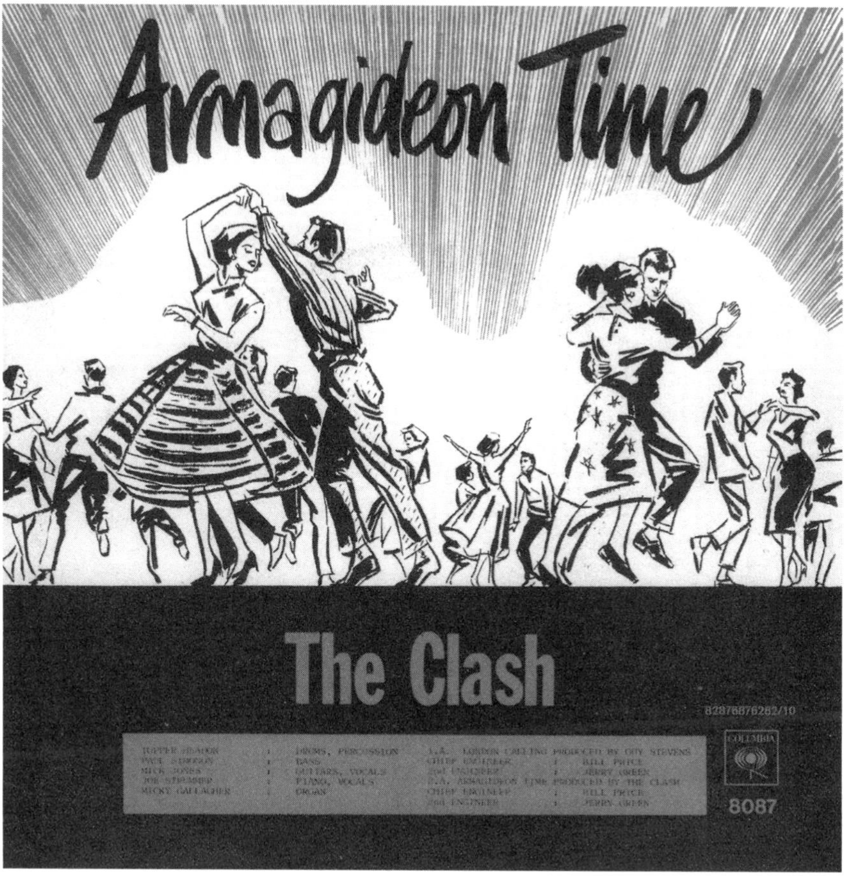

The Clash's version of Willi Williams's "Armagideon Time" was the B-side to the "London Calling" single. *Author's collection*

It's a subtle change, but "Kick It Over" would become the title of the second of two dub versions by the Clash on the 12-inch version of "London Calling" that merge into an 8:54 opus as there is no space between the two versions, and they've always been paired. ("Justice Tonight" / "Kick It Over" was edited and released as a 7:00 version on *Black Market Clash* but then restored to its proper length for *Super Black Market Clash*.) Simply put, this echo-dipped dub mix, featuring Joe's piano chords, is one of the Clash's top twenty recordings.

Various versions have entertaining ad libs, such as Joe saying that it's "not Christmas time, it's Armagideon," and "a lotta people use a calculator," but the best ad lib came from a moment of studio interference that the Clash turned into a musical triumph. Band publicist Kosmo Vinyl was a fervent proponent of the 2:58 pop song and had expressed this thought to Joe, who told Kosmo to let the band know when they were exceeding 2:58 during the session. On the final mix by Bill Price, you can hear Kosmo over the intercom say to Joe, "Time's up. Let's have you out of there." To which Joe—in riddim—steps away from his mic and responds, "Okay, okay. Don't push us when we're hot!" It sounds like the atmosphere's at a breaking point, like a mob responding to police instructions to leave, like the song's pervading sense of dread coming to fruition. It's put to even better use on the "Kick It Over" dub version, where Kosmo's voice is not heard but Joe's heavily echoed retort erupts as rockets whistle through the air.

"Armagideon Time" had true staying power and was virtually played at every Clash concert after September 5, 1979, even outlasting Topper and Mick's departures.

Dread at the Controls

Michael George Campbell was working as an engineer at the Jamaica Broadcasting Corporation (JBC), the first locally owned public broadcasting company in Jamaica, when he saw an opportunity. The JBC's mission when it formed in 1958/59 may have been the promotion of Jamaican culture, but by 1976 the radio network's playlists featured talk shows and pop music from other countries. These pop music shows were hosted by DJs—in the on-air personality sense—but Dread was the person in the studio actually operating the console, the tape machines, turntables, the phone lines, and playing the music.

Mikey was dissatisfied with the playlists, especially since Jamaica's local music scene was so vibrant, but knowing that the radio station was off the air between midnight and 4:45 a.m.—when the JBC resumed broadcasting with a program called *Back to the Bible*—he persuaded the station's management to let him host an overnight radio show, where he would play only Jamaican recording artists.

Michael rechristened himself Mikey Dread, and his *Dread at the Controls* radio program soon became the most popular radio broadcast throughout Jamaica, despite his adhering to an agreement that he not speak on the air, because he was not technically a DJ. Despite this restriction, Dread personalized the music he chose by adding sound effects. "And the kind of sound effects I would use are not discernable sound effects, you could not tell what it is." Record buyers who first heard a song on *Dread at the Controls* would often be disappointed when Dread's sound effects were not on the track they purchased in the music store.

By 1978, Dread was making recordings himself. He won Jamaica's coveted "Top Radio Personality" award for 1977–78, ruffling the feathers of the conservative executives of the state-owned JBC. They began looking for ways to oust Dread, underreporting the size of his overnight audience and asking the top radio personality of 1977–78 to tone down the reggae in favor of tame rhythm-and-blues recordings. Feeling too much pressure, he resigned from the JBC to further his recording career. Dread knew the success of his singles and albums (*African Anthem* and *Evolutionary Rockers*) had spread beyond Jamaica's island shores to London, so he traveled to England, where he gave interviews to promote his music.

Among the many Londoners enjoying Dread's recordings was Paul Simonon, who had borrowed cassettes of Dread's radio broadcasts from Don Letts. Dread came and went from England without encountering the Clash or their music, however, so he was surprised when a telegram found him in Jamaica, requesting his return to London for the purpose of producing their recordings. Glad to be home, Dread declined, but the Clash were persistent. They told him there was a British Airways ticket to London in his name at the airport.

"Bankrobber"

Joe's earliest attempt at songwriting was a twelve-bar rocker called "Crummy Bum Blues" that he committed to tape in the winter of 1973–74, shortly after its composition. In the final verse the singer reveals that his true aspiration in life is to be "an intelligent bank robber." It is the first appearance of the romanticized robber that graces many a Clash original, as well as their versions of "I Fought the Law" and "Police on My Back." In December 1979, just as Mikey Dread was deciding to pick up that airline ticket at Palisadoes Airport and fly to London to hear what the Clash had in mind, Joe was showing his mates a new song entitled "The Bankrobbing Song."

"The Bankrobbing Song" is said to have had a neo-ska beat similar to "Rudie Can't Fail" and "Wrong 'Em Boyo" from the newly released *London Calling* album; the earliest bootleg recordings find the band tampering each night with the tempo. It probably debuted on Christmas Day, 1979, at Acklam Hall in Ladbroke Grove, as a recording of the following night's concert in the same venue has it as the fourteenth song in the sixteen-song set list. Mick plays slide guitar. The Christmas shows were a gift to the locals and a warm-up for the 16 Tons tour, which commenced in Friars Maxwell Hall in Aylesbury on January 5, 1980.

Mikey Dread's thick reggae-roots production of "Bankrobber" paved the way for *Sandinista!* *Author's collection*

"Jamaican dub vocalizer" Mikey Dread (as he was described in the press) joined the 16 Tons tour as a support act on January 20 at the Edinburgh Odeon in Scotland. Mikey would later describe opening for crowds only interested in seeing the Clash and occasionally gobbing at the stage as "the biggest challenge that I ever faced in the '80s." He soldiered on, joined during his set each night by young men donning bank-robber masks, skanking around the toaster. These young men were members of the Clash and their crew. When a gig on February 1 at Victoria Hall in Hanley was canceled, the Clash moved on to Manchester, where their next concert was scheduled, and booked Pluto Studios (owned by two former members of Herman's Hermits) with the intent of recording "The Bankrobbing Song" with Dread at the controls.

In the form it was originally shown to him, "The Bankrobbing Song" was not a composition Dread was interested in producing. He remembered the song as being in the punk-rock vein—although this seems unlikely, given the era—and said that it was his suggestion that it be reggae-fied. As he recounted in his biography at www.mikeydread.com, "I told Paul, 'Let's change this and put a reggae bass line [in]. And he agreed . . . and the song 'Bankrobber' was born, and then Joe Strummer and everybody just sit in and sing it at a slower speed, tempo, and more melodic." Mick was credited with sound effects and slide guitar, Mickey Gallagher ARP synthesizer, and Dread background vocals. The two-day recording session was attended by future members of the Stone Roses.

In one of the great "what-might-have-been's" of the Clash's career, "Bankrobber" was to be the first of a series of bi-monthly singles released by the Clash in Great Britain throughout 1980. This singles campaign was quickly quashed by CBS executives, however: they hated the mixes and, according to Kosmo Vinyl in the *Clash on Broadway* booklet, thought "Bankrobber" sounded like "all of David Bowie's records played backward at once." More than likely this was just a smokescreen, as CBS was probably not interested in having the Clash issue a single every other month. It would set a bad precedent for the label's business model.

Neither side budged. The Clash continued to play "Bankrobber" in concert, but the song went unreleased until its appearance on the B-side of a Dutch release of "Train in Vain" in June. Import copies were quickly snatched up in record shops. CBS finally relented and released "Bankrobber" domestically as a 45 in August. It peaked at #12, higher than any previous Clash single except for "London Calling." The B-side was "Rockers Galore," another track from the Dutch single, on which Dread uses the "Bankrobber" instrumentation to toast over as he describes his initial impressions of touring with the Clash. (It was originally recorded for the 12-inch release of "Bankrobber" that never materialized.)

"Bankrobber" was released in the US in October 1980 as part of *Black Market Clash*, a 10-inch collection of B-sides and outtakes, only here it was paired with "Robber Dub" for a 6:16 mix. This unique mix is only available on this vinyl release, because when *Super Black Market Clash* was released thirteen years later to the month, "Bankrobber" / "Robber Dub" was replaced with just "Robber Dub," a 4:42 recording also intended for the 12-inch release of "Bankrobber." This is what makes you wonder what might have been had CBS just released "Bankrobber" in April 1980. The songs recorded in March and April would not have piled up. "Police on My Back"

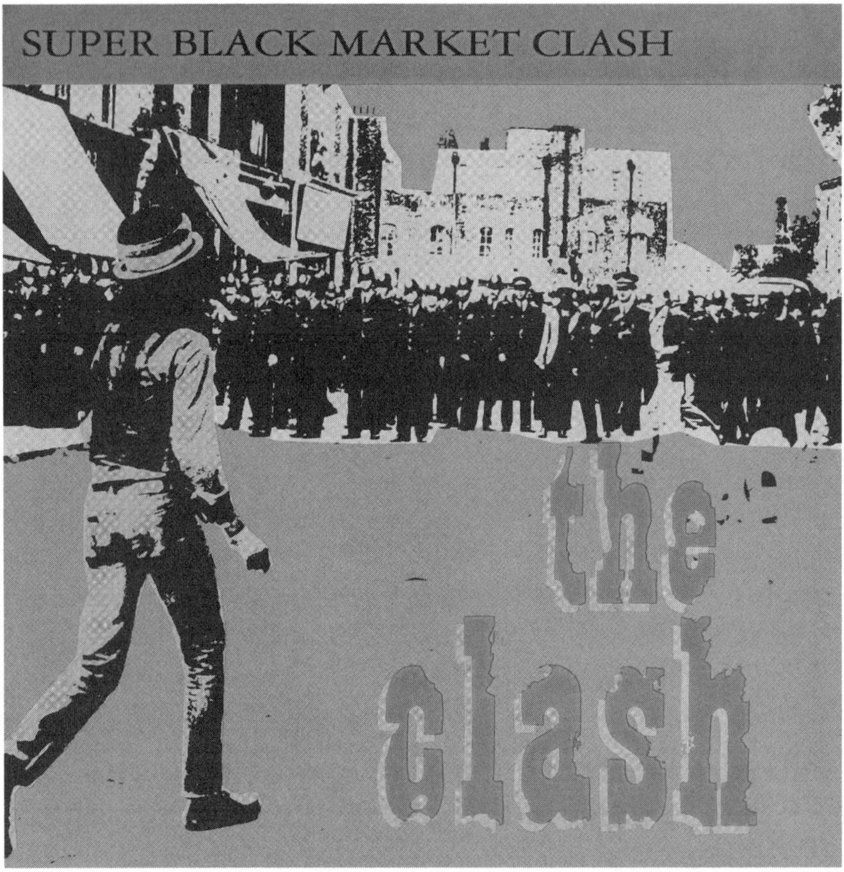

The second half of *Super Black Market Clash* features the Clash's London Reggae.
Author's collection

may have been released in June. The Clash might just have recorded a single reggae album with Mikey Dread in December 1980, and not the triple album *Sandinista!* And if that had happened, the band's history would have been greatly altered.

"Bankrobber" was panned by critics but a fan favorite nonetheless, and Joe was still singing it with the Mescaleros in 2002.

"Junco Partner" / "Version Pardner"

Anyone who attended more than one of the shows on the 16 Tons tour sensed the emergence of reggae as a driving force in the Clash's musical direction; an undertone was becoming an overtone. Barry Myers, the DJ personally selected by the Clash for the tour, exclusively played Jamaican recordings. Mikey Dread was not only a support act: he often joined the band onstage to toast during "Armagideon Time" and "Bankrobber." Unlike the Police—whom the Clash camp openly mocked—the Clash's brand of reggae was not spacy but soupy, like a sonic gumbo. Guitar effects, computerized drums, Joe's voice heavily echoed all meshed like voodoo reggae. It was a dense sound, a dub fusion that mid-'70s Miles would have approved of (and that he might have picked up on, had he not been musically inactive at the time). Their second encore at the Hammersmith Palais on June 17, 1980, consisted of "Armagideon Time," "Rocker's Galore," and "Bankrobber." You could sense the Clash's next album would feature their unique brand of reggae.

Emboldened by the success of the "Bankrobber" sessions, after a quick nine-date swing through America the Clash departed Detroit for Jamaica and recording sessions for their next album at Channel One Studios. Unfortunately, they only laid down tracks for one song, "Junco Partner," an old New Orleans rhythm-and-blues number close and dear to Joe's heart as far back as his 101-ers days. "Junco Partner (Worthless Man)" was originally recorded by James Waynes in 1951. Credited to "unknown" at the time of *Sandinista!*'s release, it has since been determined to have been written by Robert Ellen. Joe wanted to record a reggae-fied version like Dread had done with his tune "The Bankrobbing Song."

"Junco Partner" begins with Joe striking rudimentary chords on the piano. As he tells a cautionary tale about drug addiction, other members join in, including the violin player with Roots Radics, a local Jamaican band formed in 1978 who played on Dread's own recordings. Joe's vocals are full of emotion, and when he sings, "I would have pawned my sweet Gabriella / But the smart girl wouldn't sign her name," he is referencing his girlfriend, Gaby Salter.

Joe was really pleased with the take when the session was suddenly aborted. As he told *Uncut*'s Gavin Martin in 1999, "Mikey tapped me on the shoulder and said, 'Quick we've got to go. The drugmen are coming to kill everyone!' We didn't know, but we were meant to pay tithe of honor to these guys. Of course, being disorganized as ever, we didn't have a bean between us."

That's the often-told version. The Rolling Stones had allegedly just been in town, throwing money around, and the Jamaicans expected the penniless Clash, who were at odds with their own record company over "Bankrobber," to do the same. Dread, however, attributed the sudden scuttling of recording sessions to darker forces. "It was close to election time, and . . . (the

Clash) wanted to use 'Channel One' for the same sound that I used to get on my record. But then, to me, taking them into the ghetto . . . was kinda risky because they're foreigners, and it's like I'm taking them into a really trouble zone because of the tension with elections. So we decided to scrap it and then go back to the United States."

"Version Pardner," buried on the unfairly maligned Side 6 of *Sandinista!*, is the dub version of "Junco Partner" and one of the Clash's finest dubs. And, at 5:22, it is one of their longest, too. Dread dressed up the naked rhythm with sound effects and heavily treated Joe's voice. The result is a harrowing version the aural equivalent of a bad acid trip. At times it sounds like Joe's voice is careening off the rails and into your ears.

Bob Dylan—who once played "London Calling" in concert—took the title of *Knocked Out Loaded*, his 1986 album, from Ellen's lyrics for "Junco Partner."

"The Crooked Beat"

For the second time, the Clash reached far back in English history and used a British nursery rhyme as the source of song. "There Was a Crooked Man" may have been originally notated in the 1840s by James Orchard Halliwell, but the ditty probably dates back to the reign of Charles I, which had ended two hundred years earlier with the king's execution. It is an allegory for Scotland finally accepting English rule. At the time of its release, Paul's second solo vocal, "The Crooked Beat," was one of the better reviewed tracks on the controversial triple album. "Like 'The Guns of Brixton,' it's simple roots reggae," wrote the *Village Voice*'s Van Gosse, "but because of [Paul's] odd child-gangster monotone it sounds like the real thing."

One of the last songs to make the cut for *Sandinista!*, "The Crooked Beat" was recorded at Wessex Studios in London in September 1980. The track is a perfect example of Paul's natural affinity for reggae bass work. Repetitive and persistent, Clash basslines during this period were unlike those heard on recordings by any Clash contemporaries. Paul's bassline provides a supple backdrop for Dread's production tricks and his voice. In fact, "The Crooked Beat" is one of *Sandinista!*'s longer tracks, because the second half—after Mikey interjects, "It's a bird / It's a plane / No, it's the dog white stallion"—is actually the uncredited "Crooked Beat Dub." Paul's song is about nightclubbing in south London and grows increasingly ominous as the police "patrol this crooked crooked beat." The horns stretch like dark shadows and beats echo like gunshots until Mikey Dread begins shouting about a murder that has just occurred. Despite his obvious handiwork all over this track, Dread did not receive co-writing credit on *Sandinista!* for "The Crooked Beat."

Clash material has not been a rich source for reinterpretation, but Wreckless Eric's version of "The Crooked Beat" is a highlight of the recommended *Sandinista! Project*, a labor of love from producer Jimmy Guterman that includes cover versions of every song from *Sandinista!* in the correct running order.

"One More Time" / "One More Dub"

When recording sessions for the Clash's next album resumed after the mad dash out of Jamaica, Dread sensed a change: "When we went to the United States they decided to [record] at the Jimi Hendrix's studio, Electric Ladyland in the Village. Then when it went there I feel Epic Records got another producer instead of me. I was just to be a producer for the reggae tracks on the records." According to Bill Price—flown over from England to handle recording duties—it was never explained to him what Dread's role on the new project was. He is certain he was never told that Dread was the producer.

"One More Time" was, however, one of the tracks Dread definitely oversaw at Electric Lady instead of Mick. It is one of several songs on *Sandinista!* reflecting on the misery of the underclasses, whether it be the "youth of fourteen" shot in Jamaica ("Washington Bullets"), the gang bosses in Central America ("The Equaliser"), or the immigrants in England ("Corner Soul"). "One More Time" concerns the black underclass of the United States, with its references to riots in Watts and Montgomery in the 1960s.

"One More Time" / "One More Dub" is the only instance on *Sandinista!* where the source song segues into the dub version. When "One More Time" ends, Dread says, "Stop wastin' time," to which Joe responds, "Right," and Topper's drums come tumbling back in reigniting the beat.

"One More Time" was a favorite of the Clash's to play in 1981 and was usually the second song of the set by year's end. It was also played during the Far East tour in early 1982, although it appears to have fallen out of favor by the end of that tour. For example, the Clash played a thirty-three-song set at Festival Hall in Melbourne, Australia, on February 23, but "One More Time" was not performed.

"If Music Could Talk" / "Living in Fame" / "Shepherd's Delight"

Whereas "Rock 'n' Roll Mick" had transformed into Whack Attack because of his obsession with New York City's hip-hop scene, Joe was seen as the force within the Clash pushing the reggae and dub connection the hardest, not Paul. But he was also steering the band toward a dub fusion unlike what any other band had played before or since. This dub fusion resulted in songs such as "Rebel Waltz," "The Equaliser," and the saxophone-soaked "If Music Could Talk."

Mikey Dread gets a co-writing credit on "If Music Could Talk," one of the more experimental tracks on the album. It derives from "Shepherd's Delight," an instrumental recorded at Pluto Studios in Manchester, England, during the sessions for "Bankrobber." The track evokes a late night in Electric Lady shared between very stoned musicians. The left and right channels feature double-tracked spiels from Joe Strummer, who references a plethora of musicians—Bo Diddley, Jim Morrison ("a shaman"), Jimi Hendrix ("a voodoo shaman"), Buddy Holly, and Joe Ely and his Texan Men—as well as actor Errol Flynn and Clash lighting engineer Warren "Stoner" Steadman. It's the sound of Joe Strummer dreaming away. He often said it was his favorite Clash track.

Gary Barnacle added the saxophone during the Wessex sessions, which is probably where the backing tracks were recycled for "Living in Fame," the Dread toast on Side 6 that's lyrically similar to the B-side track "Rocker's Galore" as it was another assessment of the British music scene.

So "Shepherd's Delight"—the thirty-sixth and final track on *Sandinista!*—was not only the album's oldest track, but the source of three tracks most critics would have excised from the fabulous single or durable double album version of *Sandinista!* they would have preferred. "Shepherd's Delight" has few fans, but this author is one. (What sounds like sheep bleating was actually Topper playing with squeaky toys.) After the pointless "Listen" and a dull rendition of "Time Is Tight," the Clash finally produce an interesting instrumental that closes a wonderful musical excursion with the roar of an airplane—a metaphor for the global reach of the triple album.

"Silicone on Sapphire"

The dub version of "Washington Bullets" is the only remaining *Sandinista!* track that Dread "produced." Decades later, in *The Clash*, even Paul Simonon says of "Silicone on Sapphire," "I don't understand, don't see the point of [it]."

According to Wikipedia, "Silicon on sapphire (SOS) is a hetero-epitaxial process for integrated circuit manufacturing that consists of a thin layer (typically thinner than 0.6 μm) of silicon grown on a sapphire (Al_2O_3) wafer. SOS technology has helped improve analog-to-digital converters, patch-clamp amplifiers, and temperature sensors among other state-of-the-art electronic devices." This interested Joe enough for him to create another double-tracked, stream-of-consciousness extravaganza of electronic signals speaking and trying to connect. It has some similarity to Jimi Hendrix's conversation with producer Chas Chandler at the beginning of "3rd Stone from the Sun" on *Are You Experienced*, and one suspects being in Jimi's studio inspired Joe's creation of this dub.

Dread received a co-writing credit on this track (as well as on "One More Time," "One More Dub," "If Music Could Talk," and "Living in Fame"). Marginalized by the Clash's management and the band members' increasing inability to communicate with one another, Dread did not work with the Clash again after the August–September 1980 Wessex Sessions for *Sandinista!*, although Paul did lay down some basslines in London for *World War III*, an album featuring the Roots Radics (who had contributed to "Junco Partner") and singers Earl 16, Edi Fitzroy, and Wally Burnett. In Dread's opinion, it was one of his finest, and it has occasionally been cited as one of reggae's best recordings.

The Blizzard of 78 featuring Mikey Dread recorded a version of "Silicone on Sapphire" for *The Sandinista! Project*, which was released on May 15, 2007. Dread died less than a year later, on March 15, 2008, in Stamford, Connecticut, from a brain tumor. He was only fifty-three years old.

Reggae Tracks on *Combat Rock*

It is a misnomer that in the wake of critical miscomprehension of just how innovative their brand of London Reggae was, the Clash entirely abandoned the form on *Combat Rock*. Just as traces of psychedelia can be heard on the Beatles' *White Album* (for example "Glass Onion"), so too do traces of reggae linger on *Combat Rock*. The presence was stronger on Mick's mix for *Rat Patrol from Fort Bragg* and dampened by Glyn Johns for final release, but "Red Angel Dragnet" and "Ghetto Defendant" are the two songs in particular that retain a reggae vibe. The strongest link is Paul's bassline. If Mikey Dread had been on hand, both could easily have received the "Bankrobber" treatment.

16

Following the Clash on the UK Tour

The 16 Tons Tour

If Sean Lennon defended the use of his father's image in a television ad in Great Britain for Citroën cars by saying that we'd be surprised to learn how many young people he meets who have no idea of who the Beatles are, can you imagine how Joe Strummer's family feels? True, in England he is considered something of a folk hero, but in America it's beginning to feel as if Joe Strummer is only remembered by other musicians: Rancid and the Hold Steady name check him; Bob Dylan extraordinarily plays "London Calling" during a London concert; Bruce Springsteen has performed "Coma Girl." But relatively few people in America remember Joe Strummer, let alone the two handfuls of shows the Clash gave when they visited our shores in March 1980. It was the American leg of the 16 Tons tour, and the Clash were at their performance peak. Vindicated by *London Calling*'s critical and chart success, they swept through like Paul Revere in reverse, trying to wake us up. And yet few remember. That is because concert tours are as fleeting as rainstorms: they pass through our towns, replenish us, and are gone.

Elvis Presley in His Gold Lamé Suit Holding *London Calling*

Something I had never done back in 1980 was follow a band around from town to town, and when my parents asked me what I wanted as a college graduation present, I said, "Airfare to England." I wanted to live there for half a year with my granny, read *A la recherche du temps perdu* in its entirety (being a budding author, this was very important to me), and maybe, just maybe, follow the Clash around on their home turf.

My Scottish granny lived in Coventry, England, which I knew was no longer only famous for a naked midnight ride by Lady Godiva. It was now the

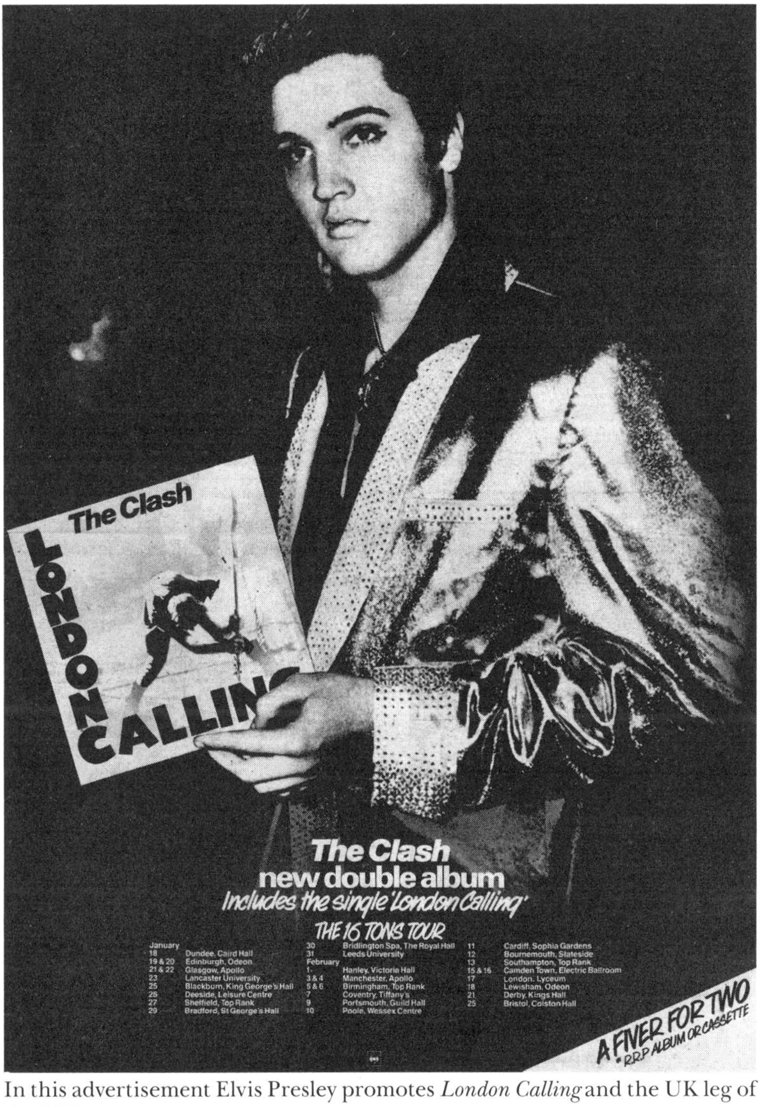

In this advertisement Elvis Presley promotes *London Calling* and the UK leg of the 16 Tons tour. *Author's collection*

epicenter of England's ska revival, the 2 Tone movement best represented by the Specials, a seven-man band hailing from the city, and 2 Tone was affecting the musical direction of the other acts around them. I knew that by staying at my granny's in Coventry, I was sure to be in the thick of Britain's musical stew.

So you will appreciate the auspiciousness I felt when, settling in a seat on a Coventry-bound train, I opened the copy of *NME* I had purchased in Euston Station and saw this full-page ad: Elvis Presley in his gold lamé suit holding *London Calling*. (The album was as yet unavailable in the US of A, although I had secured an import at Colony Music in Times Square's northwest corner just after Christmas.) But this wasn't just an ad for the Clash's latest album. No sirree. At the bottom were listed the remaining dates for the 16 Tons tour. And like me, the Clash was headed for Coventry: Tiffany's on February 7. It was the middle of January. I knew where I'd be standing in less than four weeks!

The thirty-five-date tour was the Clash's first full-fledged tour of Great Britain in over a year. In the interim they'd fired a manager, released a single, toured America, fired another manager, recorded and released an EP, toured America again, and released a double-album to mixed reviews at home. British journalists were upset with the Clash's dalliance with America and—fanning the flames—wondered how loyal or fickle British fans would be. The 16 Tons tour was undertaken to do more than just generate sales of the new album; the tour was an attempt to make amends with the locals.

Tiffany's, Coventry, February 7, 1980

Acknowledging the band's growing interest in reggae music, Jamaican legends Toots and the Maytals were originally scheduled as the opening act during the tour. It wasn't meant to be. Several other acts stepped in to fill the void until Jamaican producer and toaster Mikey Dread joined the tour at Bradford on January 29 and held the second slot on the bill for the tour's remaining dates. (In hopes of promoting unsigned bands, a local band was selected for the opening slot in each town.)

I possess 122 bootleg recordings of the Clash's shows with Mick, but only two from the first few months of the 16 Tons tour—both from January 1980—but one of them contains Mikey's first appearance, in Bradford. The tour was into its fourth week and Bradford the nineteenth show. The recording is generally considered one of the worst from the tour, but it's all I've got, and when you don't have anything else to compare it with, it's pretty amazing: more evidence of the high caliber of the Clash's performances during this period.

The wham bam slam of "Clash City Rockers," the brand new "Brand New Cadillac," (which Topper called "the first British rock 'n' roll song" in the *Armagideon Times*), and "Safe European Home" opened the set. It was standard *modus operandi* for the Clash: they always opened with three fast, furious, flaming rockers that left the pogoing fans up front sweaty and spent ten minutes into the show.

On the Bradford recording, "Jimmy Jazz" gives the band and the fans a little breathing room. But wait . . . where's Mickey Gallagher? "He's a blockhead," as Joe used to say to introduce the organist from Ian Dury's band who filled out the Clash's sound on the 16 Tons tour. He used to join the Clash onstage for "Jimmy Jazz," stage right, as Snagglepuss used to say, before making his hurried exit. His organ is nowhere to be heard on the Bradford bootleg, but he was definitely on the Tiffany's stage when I stood there, pressed up against its lip near bassist Paul Simonon, who stood stage left.

Earlier that day in the Coventry town center, I had hurried past the pigeons cooing near Lady Godiva's statuesque breasts and practically ran to be the first in line. I didn't know that in England fans didn't queue up hours in advance. I was early enough for the Tiffany's employees to give me funny looks as they turned up for work. Later, I looked up from the Capote paperback I was reading to see the Clash and their entourage walk pass me with their ghetto blasters. I didn't say anything to them, but I did notice they weren't wearing punk gear. In fact, with their trilby hats and suits, they looked like jazz musicians. I resumed reading *The Grass Harp*.

> "You from here?" the guy standing next to me in the short line asked later.
>
> "Nope."
>
> "Not many people are, are they?"
>
> I nodded.
>
> "You a Yank?"
>
> "New Yawker."
>
> He started singing: "New York, New York. Forty-second Street!"

I smiled, recognizing the lyrics from "The Right Profile," the Clash tribute to actor Montgomery Clift. We struck up a conversation. He was from Birmingham, about twenty-five miles west of Coventry; had seen the Clash nine times before; and offered to buy me a pint when we got inside. Unfortunately, we were separated in our rush to get in when the doors opened. He ran for the bar; I ran for the stage. I might've been first in line but not knowing the venue I was no match for the fans behind me who did. That's how I found myself near Paul's slice of the stage and not in front of Joe's microphone. Fine by me. I was just happy to be up front.

Actually, I was happy to not be near any microphones. The audience was on the young side, and their behavior childish. Its members killed time waiting for the Clash by continually knocking over the microphones. Once the Clash were onstage, they spent their time getting into fistfights and gobbing, which is what they were doing as the Clash played "Jimmy Jazz." (Gobbing was the act of the audience spitting at punk bands, which according to Joe began when the Damned's vocalist Dave Vanian spat at some unruly fans.) Gob rained on the stage during "Jimmy Jazz," and I could tell Joe was none too pleased. He was ad-libbing—almost scat singing—about how it was none too cool to be spat at. I don't remember his exact words, but I do remember thinking I was the only one in the audience listening—and I was the only one not gobbing.

"Jimmy Jazz" had gone his way before the police or mafia could grab him when Joe suddenly pointed and yelled, "You!" He then jerked his left forearm and caught a huge gob. It rested on his skin, glistening in the stage lighting. "No, you!" he declared, pointing at some other bloke in the audience before diving headfirst into the crowd and attacking whomever he either saw or thought had just spat at him. I was not five feet away from all this. Joe was swinging at this young guy whose mates were coming to his defense. Joe had to be fighting four guys! It was pure chaos as bouncers rushed forward; the other members of the Clash just stood there onstage motionlessly watching their singer. Joe brushed past me as bouncers' hands lifted him out of the audience and back onto the stage. El Clash Combo's singer strode to his mic. There was a welt under one of his eyes. Someone had landed at least one good blow. He grabbed the microphone and lifted the stand. Slammed it once, twice against the stage floor. "Rrrrrrrright! Next number!!!" With that, the Clash poured gasoline on the combustible situation by pounding out "London Calling."

(Kris Need's *Joe Strummer and the Legend of the Clash* briefly mentions Joe's fight with audience members in Coventry that night. He adds that Joe clobbered a skinhead with his guitar. That's not how I remember it. This was not Messelahh in Hamburg, where, on May 19, 1980, during another date on the same tour, Joe did clobber a skinhead over the head with his guitar and was arrested and spent a night in jail. As proof, I point to the fact that Joe jumped into the crowd just as "Jimmy Jazz" finished. This was a song on which Joe did not play guitar, so he did not have a guitar in his hands to clobber anyone with.)

Joe and Paul swapped instruments. It was unusual seeing the lanky bassist holding Joe's black 1966 Fender telecaster. The singer retreated to Paul's edge of the drum stand. Paul stood before Joe's microphone. He received a rousing reaction—perhaps the loudest all night. Paul scratched at the guitar strings. Joe contributed the seesawing bassline. Topper and Mick hopped onto the song's natural rhythm. And the unnatural singer "sang": "When they kick at your front door . . . How you gonna come?" Paul's

The bootleg recording of the Clash's infamous concert in Hamburg during the 16 Tons tour is one you have to hear to believe. *Author's collection*

not a singer, not by a long shot, but it worked for "The Guns of Brixton," his song about the rise of the underclass. His inarticulateness sold the song; either that or the resemblance to James Dean he was cultivating. He stood up there, center stage, a black lithe figure bathed in blue light, spitting out defiant lyrics. He abandoned his rhythm guitar and let the musicians in the band carry him to a noisy exit.

It was odd that Paul got to sing before Mick, but the band's founding member his took his turn with "Protex Blue" and later "Stay Free." The set consisted mostly of *London Calling* tracks, and one of my favorites that night was the first encore's first song: "Armagideon Time," a reggae cover and the B-side of the "London Calling" single. I had bought the 12-inch version since reaching Coventry, and this eight-minute version was a personal favorite. Still is. Anchored by Mickey Gallagher's organ and accompanied by Mikey

Dread toasts, it sounded to me like the "electric church music" Jimi Hendrix spoke of creating one day. It was a particularly spiritual moment.

Paul's droning, repetitive bassline locked in with Topper's hypnotic beat. Joe Strummer let out a shriek. Mick Jones contributed mournful guitar. "Alottapeople won'tgetno suppertonight." There was a lotta treatment on the vocals. Mick struck sharp chords as Joe cupped his left ear with his hand—a new mannerism. His eyes were closed. "Alottapeople use a calculator!" Spittle was flying, his body swaying to Topper's drum rim beat, left to right, while the drummer continued moving up and down behind him. Strummer inserted his left forefinger into his open mouth and wiggled the finger to moan for the masses. "Alottapeople."

Nearing what must've been the five-minute mark, Paul dropped his repetitive bassline for a walker . . . one that was nudged along by Topper's impatient tempo, and soon the band were playing "English Civil War," with its "When Johnny Comes Marching Home" melody. Even back then, it struck me as one of the most unnecessary Clash songs, but coupled to "Armagideon Time" it was most effective. It got everyone up front slam dancing again (the precursor to the mosh pits of today) and clamoring for another encore.

Two encores were the norm at Clash concerts, and that's what we got in Coventry. Unfortunately, I do not remember it, although I'm sure it was spectacular. (There was a lot of showmanship in Clash performances: the color-coordinated clothing, the occasional choreography. The Clash's front three were not only as mesmerizing as the Beatles or the Rolling Stones; they were far more energetic. With Mick's leaps, Joe's jittery left leg, and Paul's puppetry movements, there was always something to watch.) I do remember a policeman taunting me on my way out of Tiffany's and trying to provoke me into being his guest for a night in Coventry's jail. I walked home to my granny's instead, smoking a New Yorker's toothpick-sized joint, reveling in the performance I had been a witness to.

Stateside, Bournemouth, February 12, 1980

I saw the Clash again five nights later at the Stateside in Bournemouth, a seaside town on the south coast of England. As well as I recall the Coventry concert, I remember next to nothing of the Clash's performance in Bournemouth. The only reference I found in my old journals is this: "I have a feeling tonight's crowd won't be as punk-dominated as the crowd was in Coventry. I'll be glad if it isn't. That was quite an experience." I actually

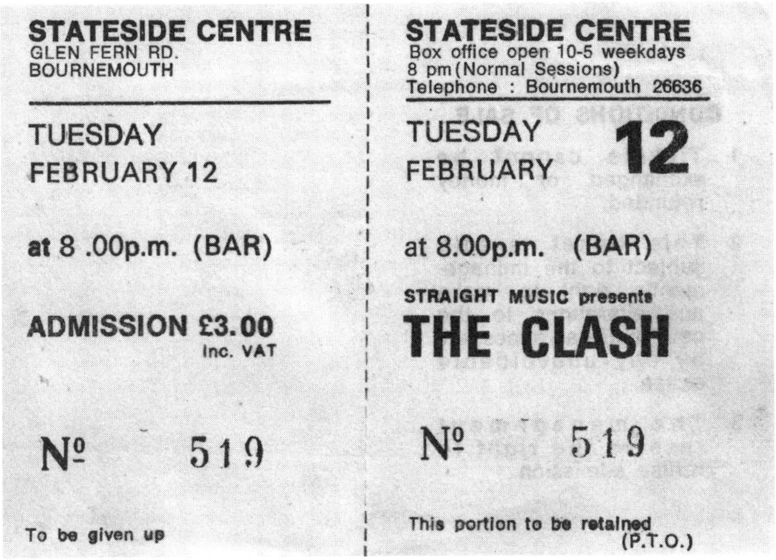
STATESIDE CENTRE
GLEN FERN RD.
BOURNEMOUTH
TUESDAY
FEBRUARY 12
at 8 .00p.m. (BAR)
ADMISSION £3.00
Inc. VAT
Nº 519
To be given up
STATESIDE CENTRE
Box office open 10-5 weekdays
8 pm (Normal Sessions)
Telephone : Bournemouth 26636
TUESDAY
FEBRUARY 12
at 8.00p.m. (BAR)
STRAIGHT MUSIC presents
THE CLASH
Nº 519
This portion to be retained
(P.T.O.)

A ticket for the Clash's performance at the Stateside Centre in Bournemouth on June 12, 1980. *Author's collection*

remember more about the wind that night and the B&B I stayed at. I do remember I watched the show from the back but not because I arrived late. Knowing me, I was probably the first person inside, but I stood at the back because I used to like to watch concert halls fill and swell with excitement and horniness and drunkenness. I also wanted to avoid having to contend with the slam-dancing and gobbing and sweat up front, as I had in Coventry. I'm sure the show was a good one. I saw the Clash twenty-five times, and only two shows stand out in my memory as being sub-par—and at one of those shows, in Derby, Mick Jones was so on fire that it didn't matter. He was such an underrated lead guitarist. That night in Derby, it was as if he was performing at a level the other members of the Clash could not match.

Another thing I remember about the Bournemouth show was the next day, getting the train back to my granny's "wee flat" on Stoney Stanton Road. I was elated at having seen the Clash in England but disappointed to note that they would be playing American dates in March, including one in New York City. Friends and lovers had already written me telling me they had gotten tickets to see the Clash at the Palladium on March 7 and/or the Capital Theatre in Passaic, New Jersey, the following night. Suddenly I felt as if I was stranded in England for another four months.

Then my luck took a freaky turn as I read in the *NME* a story about Topper tearing a ligament in one of his thumbs. (And it was a story: a complete fabrication to conceal the fact that Topper's hand had been stabbed with a pair of scissors in an altercation at one of the drug parties the drummer's flat was becoming known for. That's Joe's version anyway. Topper denies this but admits he doesn't know what did happen.) The damaged hand meant that the few remaining dates of the 16 Tons tour would have to be rescheduled, but not before late May or even June—just when I supposed to fly back to America. I'd surely be able to get me a ticket to at least one of those shows. Little did I know then that I would be at six of them, including two at the London venue the Clash had made famous with "(White Man) In Hammersmith Palais." Talk about seeing the Clash on home turf!

Great Hall, Derby, June 9, 1980

After whiling away the months seeing the likes of the Ramones, Stiff Little Fingers (twice), the Cramps (twice), Selecter, Elvis Costello and the Attractions (twice, including a marvelous instrumental rendition of "Moods for Moderns" in Leamington Spa, home of the enormously influential Swell Maps), Siouxsie and the Banshees, the Feelies, and the Undertones, I finally found myself sitting on Derby's cold pavement, my back leaning against the glass doors which would soon grant me access to the Great Hall, where the Clash were to perform the first of eight hastily rescheduled concert dates throughout England. I had tickets to six of the shows (plus a seventh to see the Specials in Bournemouth). The bell in the Derby Guildhall tower was ringing. The sun, which had eyed my train's arrival as it snuck into Derby a few minutes before 2:00 p.m., was sinking. Scattered throughout the city's central Market Place were concertgoers. You could say 75 percent were punks: colorful hair, black leather jackets, T-shirts, dirty denims, colorful socks, black footwear. Some were more extreme than others. Many wore zippered pants and chains. Most of the leathers declared an allegiance: Adam and the Ants or the Clash or Crass or PiL or Toyah or the UK Subs. Oddly, no SLF—maybe because they were Irish? A Newcastle punk rocker struck up a conversation with me. He asked if I had a ticket. I did. He didn't. As it turned out, all of those surrounding me were ticketless. Some were hoping to be admitted on the guest list. I killed time by seeing if I could get the Newcastle punk a ticket, which I did.

Once inside we parted as I raced for a spot up against the stage. The opening acts were a local band Anti Pasta (who released their successful debut album *The Last Call* the following year) and Peter Webber. When the Clash came out, Mick was wearing a red shirt and black pants, Joe was all in black, Paul in blue/black, and Topper's upper body was red. That was all

I could see of him from behind his Pearl drum kit with the mirror finish. Joe and Paul's heads were both seriously cropped.

It was not one of the Clash's best nights, but Mick was on fire so my eyes were fixed on him—one outstanding moment was his feedback laden lead on "Jimmy Jazz"—but because my eyes were on him, I could see the look of questioning fear on his face when a smoke bomb was ignited at the end of "Revolution Rock." It underlined the fact for me that the Clash's politics had to be taken seriously in their home country. Maybe because they were not on top of their game, the Clash's first encore was five songs long instead of the customary three.

Colston Hall, Bristol, June 10, 1980

For the first of two nights at Bristol's Colston Hall—which had assigned seating, unlike Derby's Great Hall—I found myself in the very last row of the orchestra. The opening acts had been Spartacus, and Holly and the Italians, (the latter act joining the Clash's 16 Tons tour for the remaining seven dates). The opening bands took longer to set up and perform than they had in Derby, and there was a reason for this: the Clash were late. Joe made light of this, saying, "Hello good afternoon, glad to see you could make it here," as the Clash finally took the stage. Then, turning to Mick, he said, "Monsieur Jones."

As Mick weakly struck the Who-ish chords of "Clash City Rockers," I was struck by something I first noticed in Derby, and which figures in my appraisal of every Clash concert: invariably Mick Jones or Joe Strummer emerges as the evening's dominant figure, the performer who gives the Clash concert we're experiencing its character. Tonight it was Joe who was in top form. From the greeting that preceded "Clash City Rockers" onward, he was in a talkative spirit. Introducing "Brand New Cadillac," he spoke of meeting Vince Taylor in front of a café; "It's nice to be home again," he said, perhaps alluding to neighboring Wales, where he went to art school; "Can't have another Cincinnati," an allusion to the eleven fans trampled at a Who concert six months earlier, when the fans started fainting up front.

The Clash rushed through their set and resorted to extending the pauses between encores just to prevent themselves from ending too early and cheating fans. It was 10:56 p.m. when Topper finally climbed to the top of his drum kit—I could see the time on an illuminated clock as bright as a full moon—and leaped down. Landing on the stage, he ended the show by throwing his drumsticks into the audience.

My hearing slowly recuperated from another night immersed in sound. My favorite song this night had been a stomping version of "Clampdown" and I couldn't get it out of my head. I was drinking a Coca-Cola and sitting on a black wooden bench on platform 3 at Bristol Temple Meads railway station waiting for the 01:10 to Sheffield—a long enough ride to allow me to sleep before making my way back to Bristol for the second show. My body was telling me how much I ached after two nights of following the Clash on the final leg of the 16 Tons tour. My ankles. My elbow. The backs of my calves. All of them ached. But I was not tired. To my right was another young man. He removed his biker jacket and unfolded his new 16 Tons tour Clash T-shirt to the accompaniment of a tapping locomotive and put it on over his shirt. Elbowing his way back into his jacket, he stretched himself across the bench to sleep. I empathized with his desire to stretch out. These Clash concerts were drainers.

Colston Hall, Bristol, June 11, 1980

How did performance three differ? Faster. Businesslike. A band on the run to the next city of the tour. It was the same set but without Joe's ad libs or Mick's fuming feedback:

1. "Clash City Rockers"
2. "Brand New Cadillac"
3. "Safe European Home"
4. "Jimmy Jazz"
5. "Revolution Rock"
6. "Guns of Brixton"
7. "Train in Vain"
8. "London Calling"
9. "Spanish Bombs"
10. "(White Man) In Hammersmith Palais"
11. "Somebody Got Murdered"
12. "Koka Kola"
13. "I Fought the Law"
14. "Jail Guitar Doors"
15. "Michael Row That Boat Ashore" / "Police and Thieves"
16. "The Prisoner"
17. "Clampdown"
18. "Stay Free"
19. "English Civil War"

20. "I'm So Bored with the USA"
21. "Complete Control"

Jamaican producer/DJ/toaster Mikey Dread then joined the Clash for a first: an all London Reggae encore:

22. "Armagideon Time"
23. "Rocker's Galore"
24. "Bankrobber"

And then it was return to punk era classics for the second encore:

25. "Janie Jones"
26. "Tommy Gun"
27. "Capital Radio"
28. "London's Burning"

The show ended at 10:25 p.m. After the show, it was the 01:10 to Sheffield again. This time, however, it's straight to Newcastle upon Tyne via Sheffield and Doncaster and York. The third town. The fourth show. Tomorrow night will be the first time in eighteen months that the Clash play Newcastle. I think the train has more passengers than yesternight's. I can hear the punks. I wonder if they're all going to Sheffield? Laughter.

Mayfair Ballroom, Newcastle upon Tyne, June 12, 1980

A Newcastle historian named Marshall Hall has described the now defunct Mayfair as being "a typical oblong-shaped Mecca ballroom, capacity 1,500, with the small stage built flush with one of the longer walls (instead of at one end of the room), a large oval-shaped wooden dance floor in front of this, and a large balcony right around the room (and above the stage)."

Local band Flesh opened, and were followed by Holly and the Italians. Then came a show that is woven into the folklore of Newcastle and considered among the best ever to have taken place in Chas Chandler's hometown. As I wrote immediately after while waiting for my train, "Straight to the point, this concert was the best: hot and tight." From the opening chord of "Clash City Rockers," the dance floor was completely hopping. I've said that invariably Mick or Joe dominates each performance. That wasn't the case in Newcastle. Tonight, the Clash dominated. It was a classic performance—maybe the finest I've ever seen them give. Each member of the band fit into the mold. There wasn't any spotlight-stealing. All four performers could be featured and then slip back and work at the rhythm and support the others. The crowd was explosive. Those up front were gobbing. During "Spanish

Bombs" a fistfight broke out near me. The Clash were forced to stop playing midway through to try and calm things down. The same thing happened during the opening moments of "Koka Kola." All totaled, there were four fistfights. Mick was noticeably agitated by the behavior of certain crowd members. He could be heard saying, "While you're all fighting the real fucker's laughing his bloody head off," under the opening drumroll of "I Fought the Law." He reiterated his anger a short while later: "My turn to be gobbed at, apologies, but I can't sing this song with conviction with all this gob going on my face, and I really mean it. This song is called 'Stay Free.'" It's a shame really. It was the best crowd, marred only by a few drunken hotheads. They had the Mikey Dread–accompanied reggae encore, like the second night in Bristol, except this time they followed "Bankrobber" with "Janie Jones," "Tommy Gun," and "London's Burning." The second encore featured "Capital Radio," "What's My Name," "Garageland," and "White Riot."

"White Riot" was special because members of the crowd jumped onstage to dance and sing, and the Clash even played a reprise for those on the stage to continue dancing to. It was an extraordinary ending. Just as I had read earlier in *NME* "Real rock is a combination of fabulous and frightening." I'd have to agree. I was often frightened and scared, and yet, of all the Clash concerts I ever saw them give, this was the finest.

Hammersmith Palais, London, June 16, 1980

This show was something of a letdown. Spartacus were back, as were Holly and the Italians. The concert could easily have been the best of the short tour, but the sound within the Palais sabotaged the Clash. For the first four songs there was a poor balance and Mick's guitar and Mickey Gallagher's organ weren't loud enough. (Yes, although I haven't mentioned him thus far, Mickey was still the fifth member of the Clash.) Things settled down, however. The Clash played the usual set, swapping only "Clampdown" for "Wrong 'Em Boyo." The former was saved for the opening number of the encore. Yes, that's right: the Clash only played one encore, maybe because they started having sound problems again during "Armagideon Time" (which closed the set), which continued to plague the encore. It was a good crowd: swaying and hopping and dancing. More details of this performance can be found in chapter 8. What touched me most that evening inside the Palais was that you could tell it was a hometown gig, and the Clash were striving to make it extra-special.

Hammersmith Palais, London, June 17, 1980

Sitting on the cold pavement outside the Hammersmith Palais, I was first in line for a number of reasons: I had to vacate my hotel room by twelve, I was practically penniless, and I was considering standing next to the stage. I couldn't make up my mind. It can be an ordeal: something you enjoy more afterwards than when it's taking place. You can congratulate yourself on having survived. During a concert there's always the possibility of fainting or being trampled or struck by stray gob. The balcony is a safer bet. But whenever I stood on the balcony at a concert, I felt detached. It's as if I wasn't even at the concert. It's more like watching a film. So I didn't know what I should do. Kids were fainting to the left and right of me last night. But who knew when I'd see the Clash again?

Around 4:30 p.m., members of the Clash's crew began arriving. Kosmo. The Baker. I realized I hadn't seen Johnny Green on this leg of the tour. Traffic snarled as it tried to go by on Shepherd's Bush Road. One by one, the crowd gathered. It was a wide assortment of fans: not only punks or

On June 16 and 17, 1980, the Clash made their only appearances at the Hammersmith Palais, the venue that inspired Joe Strummer's best song.
Author's collection

Londoners. Many tourists like me. "That's probably a product of *London Calling*," I thought. "You have about as much right to call the Clash a punk band as you do to still call the Who a mod band. The Clash have gone beyond punk. Post-punk. There's a lot of experimenting with reggae, reverb, and feedback." I wondered what the next album would sound like. I had read it was supposed to be produced by Mikey Dread. Remembering the London Reggae encore in Bristol, this made sense to me. With the rising popularity of bands like the Police and the Specials, and with the Clash experimenting with their own form of London Reggae, it felt like the direction they were taking.

June 17 was an unusual concert from my point of view. It was partly due to the number of views I had and a brief acquaintance I made with one "bloke," a Londoner, and two girls from Kent. I nearly spent the night in their company, which would've been preferable to spending the night in Euston Station. But we were separated during the course of the concert—very early on, really, during "Jimmy Jazz." Let me explain. I left my hotel shortly after eleven with a stolen British Rail ashtray in my pocket. (Still one of my prized possessions!) The rain followed me, so I ducked into various stores: W.H. Smith, Virgin Records, a fine bookstore. I then took the underground to Shepherd's Bush. It was still raining. I sheltered myself in a store, and when I emerged the sun was shining bright. I had fish and chips and Fanta orangeade and headed for Hammersmith Palais. It was a long wait.

Near 6:00 p.m., somebody asked me what time I thought the Palais might open. I said "near 8 p.m.," basing my opinion on the previous night's schedule. He asked me if I was from New York City, and we started talking about the USA. It seemed he'd spent some time there trailing the Clash via automobile—a nice way of seeing the country. Two girls next to us somehow entered the conversation, and we debated where we should stand. Unlike at other concerts, the band arrived informally and separately, or in pairs.

Mick.

Joe and Paul.

Topper and Mickey.

We were let in not too long afterward. In fact, the doors were opening just as Topper and Mickey were arriving. The four of us had to make a choice, and we shot up the balcony stairs. It was a clear view, but the Londoner felt detached as Spartacus played their set, so we decided to go back downstairs. By this time it was impossible to get near the stage, but we did move quite close, and we stayed there during Holly and the Italians' set, watching on while someone puked nearby.

The crush started as the road crew readied the stage for the Clash. Mick unleashed "Clash City Rockers'" opening chord and the mass of the crowd carried me back and forth, left and right. It was like an amusement park ride. Like a rollercoaster. There was risk. One of the girls, the quieter and cuter one, couldn't handle it. I couldn't light my joint. I almost lost my glasses. And so, half to help myself and half to help the girl, I forced myself out of the crowd and led her and her friend upstairs as the Clash provided a background score. I heard the opening chords to "Jimmy Jazz" and then, telling them I'd see them later, I ran back downstairs to look over bobbing heads at the distant Clash and dance a little.

Joe sported a cropped haircut when the Clash appeared in Los Angeles in April 1980. *Ann Summa/Getty Images*

The Clash never played the Hammersmith Palais again.

I was walking out at 11:20 p.m. It was a long walk to the Euston train station. That was okay with me. My train for Coventry wasn't scheduled to leave for over another six hours. I was happy to have seen the Clash play six concerts within nine days, but a little sorry I wouldn't have this opportunity again. How could I have known that, in less than a year, the Clash would be playing seventeen shows in my dirty old home town of New York City?

17

A Rudie Loot and a Rudie Shoot and a Rudie Come Up Then

Rude Boy

The Clash so vehemently objected to the release of *Rude Boy*, the 1980 film directed and produced by Jack Hazan and David Mingay, that they ordered and distributed badges from Better Badges stating, "I don't want *Rude Boy* Clash film." (They were designed as a parody of the band's "Complete Control" badge.) Why devote a chapter, then, to a film that the Clash not only distanced themselves from but tried to legally scuttle? Because *Rude Boy* captures the live fury of the Clash in concert better than any other video or documentary. The one superior visual document is their four-song performance in April 1980 on the ABC television program *Fridays*, of which only "The Guns of Brixton" is commercially available at the time of this writing.

The Making of *Rude Boy*

Filming of *Rude Boy* began with footage of the Queen's Jubilee in 1977, well before the Clash's involvement. The filmmakers had worked together previously on *Grant North*, a documentary featuring British nature painter Keith Grant, and *A Bigger Splash*, a project named after the large pop-art painting by David Hockney, which blended documentary footage of Hockney with staged scenes. This became the blueprint for their next project, which Hazan described in a bonus interview included on the various DVD and Blu-ray releases of *Rude Boy* as a "fictionalized story with real people."

They were intent on making a statement about the sorry state of British politics, although the means to this end was unclear. Since Hazan was a documentarian, for subject matter he latched on to the swelling ranks of the National Front by young men and began filming political demonstrations, including a confrontation between anti-fascist protesters and the National Front at general election meeting outside of Digbeth Town Hall in February 1978. A nearby line of police officers was filmed milling about and smiling until they found themselves caught in the middle of a clash of differing political sentiments. The resulting footage was very much like Rocco Macauley's image from the back cover of *The Clash.*

Around this same time period—possibly because of the Sex Pistols' performance on the Thames on the occasion of the jubilee—David Mingay became aware of punk rock and sensed a possibility. The young men attending the punk concerts were just as disaffected as those joining the National Front. "Punk was in the air," Hazan says in the DVD interview, "it was quite an advanced force. It was almost a political force." The filmmakers latched onto an idea of using a punk band as a central vehicle for a condemnation of how the British government had not met the needs of Britain's youth. Asking around, Mingay was told to film the Clash because, according to Hazan, "They were much more serious than the Sex Pistols."

Mingay knew Ray Gange, an employee in a record store specializing in soundtrack albums, and he mentioned his interest in filming the Clash for a movie. The film's future anti-hero surprised Mingay by saying he knew the band's singer, Joe Strummer; they'd met at a Wayne County show and were friendly. Gange offered to act as a go-between, but Mingay had another option.

"Our point of entry to the Clash was Bernie Rhodes," said Hazan, "and he'd heard of us, and that helped." Mingay had a friend who was an acquaintance from Rhodes's days designing clothing, and a meeting was arranged. The filmmakers didn't know it, but Malcolm McLaren had a Sex Pistols movie in the works, and Rhodes was eager to do the same with the Clash. The fact that two documentarians whose work he respected were interested in filming the band he was managing must've made it an easy decision. Mingay then met with the four members of the Clash individually to get their verbal buy-in. No contract was signed at this time.

Ray Gange told *Quietus* journalist A. P. Childs in 2010 that Mingay asked him a few weeks later "if I wanted to be in the film he was making. I'm like, 'Not really.' You know, I'm working in a soundtrack specialist shop in Soho, and this older guy is asking me if I wanted to be in a movie. Thought it was a bit suspect. Anyway, next time I saw Strummer I mentioned it to him and he confirmed that they were making a film and that I should be in it. So I said okay." Ray mistakenly thought he was only getting himself into a small role. He certainly didn't anticipate being the featured actor in *Rude Boy* posters and advertisements—or the target of film critics.

The Clash's active, if sporadic, participation on *Rude Boy* spanned approximately one year. The first performance filmed by Hazan was at the legendary Rock Against Racism/Anti-Nazi League carnival in Victoria Park in Hackney, London, on April 30, 1978, in front of a crowd estimated to number 80,000. "Police and Thieves" was filmed the following evening at Barbarella's, a small club in Birmingham, in a thrilling performance shot with one 35 mm Cameflex camera. Joe's voice is a little worse for wear than usual, but the visuals of him wearing his misspelt, red "Brigade Rosse" terrorist T-shirt, strumming passionately, the sweat pouring off his brow, is thrilling.

The filmmakers next filmed the Clash at three Scottish Out on Parole tour dates during the first week of July. In this, they were abetted by Clash road manager Johnny Green, who admitted in an interview included on the DVD release, "I thought this band was fucking magnificent and somebody should be fucking recording them . . . so I always told [the filmmakers] . . . where we would be . . . and so preparations were made for that. There was no keeping us waiting, and that's what makes [*Rude Boy*] vital. Not doing take after take after take. It's just us living our lives." Additional live footage was shot in London at the Music Machine on July 27 and the Lyceum (with a five-man film crew) on January 3, 1979.

The Clash also participated in few non-concert performances. Wearing old punk-era Letterist gear, they faked a rehearsal of "Garageland." The filmmakers were permitted access to the *Give 'Em Enough Rope* sessions at Island Records' Basing Street Studios in May 1978, where they captured Joe laying down vocals for "All the Young Punks" and Mick doing a sensitive take of "Stay Free." And finally, in April 1979, Joe did a solo scene with Ray Gange where he played a battered honky-tonk piano on two tunes: one original and one rock 'n' roll golden oldie.

Bernie Rhodes signed an agreement with the filmmakers, incorporated as Buzzy Enterprises, in October 1978, just as he was being dismissed as the Clash's manager. This probably accounts for why none of the Clash signed the contract, which guaranteed the band £4,000 and 10 percent of the net profits after the initial £25,000 earned, plus royalties.

When the Clash agreed to film "I Fought the Law" and "English Civil War" in the London Lyceum on January 3, 1979—two songs that fit in well with what was the filmmakers' perceived message of *Rude Boy*—they thought they were free and clear of the project, except possibly for some staged scenes. They were dismayed then when they learned that the sound of most of the concert recordings was unusable. The band would have to re-record their performances to match the concert footage. Back from their brief February tour of America, the Clash entered Wessex Studios on March 9, 1979, with recording engineer Bill Price, unpacked their gear, and got to work.

It was a painstaking process. Unlike most recording sessions, songs could not be completed in a few takes. The concert recordings had to be bounced down to one track of the twenty-four available at Wessex Studios. Sound then had to be manufactured to recapture the acoustics of the various venues, and each musician had to play along as they watched themselves on screen. They began with Topper, "the human drum machine" (see chapter 9), followed by Paul, Joe, and Mick. Vocals came next, and finally audience noise from the original film was added back in. Mixing was done in April at George Martin's AIR Studios, where Bill Price had worked previously. This doubled the film's already tight budget, but, except for a commitment to provide an original song for the movie, the Clash's daily schedule would no longer require them to devote any time to *Rude Boy*.

The Reviews Are In

Shortly after making the movie, the Clash were supportive of it in interviews. "It's about a 70 percent true story," Topper told *Creem*'s Stephen Demorest, in a May 1979 article. "There's film of actual gigs and incidents as they happened, like our court appearances, but rather than being a documentary it's a story of the group as seen through the eyes of this bloke named Ray who we hang around with. He's a young kid about twenty and he's a piss artist, y'know, he's alcoholic. He wanted to get a job with us and couldn't, and the whole story is about his hangin' around with the group."

Joe was even more enthusiastic, telling *NME*'s Charles Shaar Murray that it would be better than the just-released film based on the Who's rock opera *Quadrophenia*: "Wait'll you see our film. It's called *Rudi Can't Fail.* Ray Gant [sic] is the boy from nowhere." Clash members also compared the film favorably to Jimmy Cliff's *The Harder They Come.*

And then they saw the work in progress at an August 1979 pre-screening. They were not happy. As you can tell from Topper's comments above, they were not expecting any of the *cinéma vérité* footage of the very gray, politically stressed London that Buzzy Enterprises had weaved in. It has been repeatedly said by the actors, whose real names were used, that they never had an idea of the film's plot, and this is confirmed by Hazan: "We never asked them for advice as to what the film should be. It wasn't their film. It was our film."

The Clash demanded edits. Mick thought the film portrayed all white youth as fascists and all black youth as thieves. Some suspect he also was unhappy with his portrayal, and interviews with the filmmakers clearly indicate a preference for Joe. Many of Mick's flaws are on display: he turns up late for the "Garageland" rehearsal, and he runs his fingers through his hair with rock star egotism, but he also confronts Ray's racism directly, and his vocal performances on "The Prisoner" and "Stay Free" are highlights.

In September, the Clash's legal representatives, Compton Carr (a law firm specializing in entertainment contracts that had previously helped John Lydon take Malcolm McLaren to court), contacted Buzzy Entertainment in writing: "We believe that our clients have recently viewed the film and have expressed serious reservations about its content and its political overtones. They are very concerned that the film is not published until it has been edited to their satisfaction and terms have been agreed." The directors were incredulous at the Clash's objections to *Rude Boy*'s "political overtones," given the band's song lyrics, and refused to redirect the film's focus to the Clash in concert. The directors did cut approximately thirty-five minutes of footage, but the plot would remain the same.

Despite this legal wrangling, in November 1979 the Clash handed over "Rudie Can't Fail" (which Joe had written specifically for the film) and an instrumental version of "Revolution Rock" to be used as incidental music. Knowing Mick did not want *Rudie Can't Fail* used as the movie title, and uncertain if CBS Records would claim copyright infringement, Buzzy Enterprises decided to go with *Rude Boy*.

When the filmmakers kept refusing the Clash access to the film, Compton Carr again wrote to Buzzy Enterprises's legal representatives: "Your clients are not in possession of synchronization licenses in respect of the use of our clients' music in the film and for this reason your clients are not entitled to perform the music publicity or to sell or distribute the film incorporating our clients' music."

Having interacted with the band over an eighteen-month period, Buzzy Enterprises knew the Clash were perennially short on cash and probably did

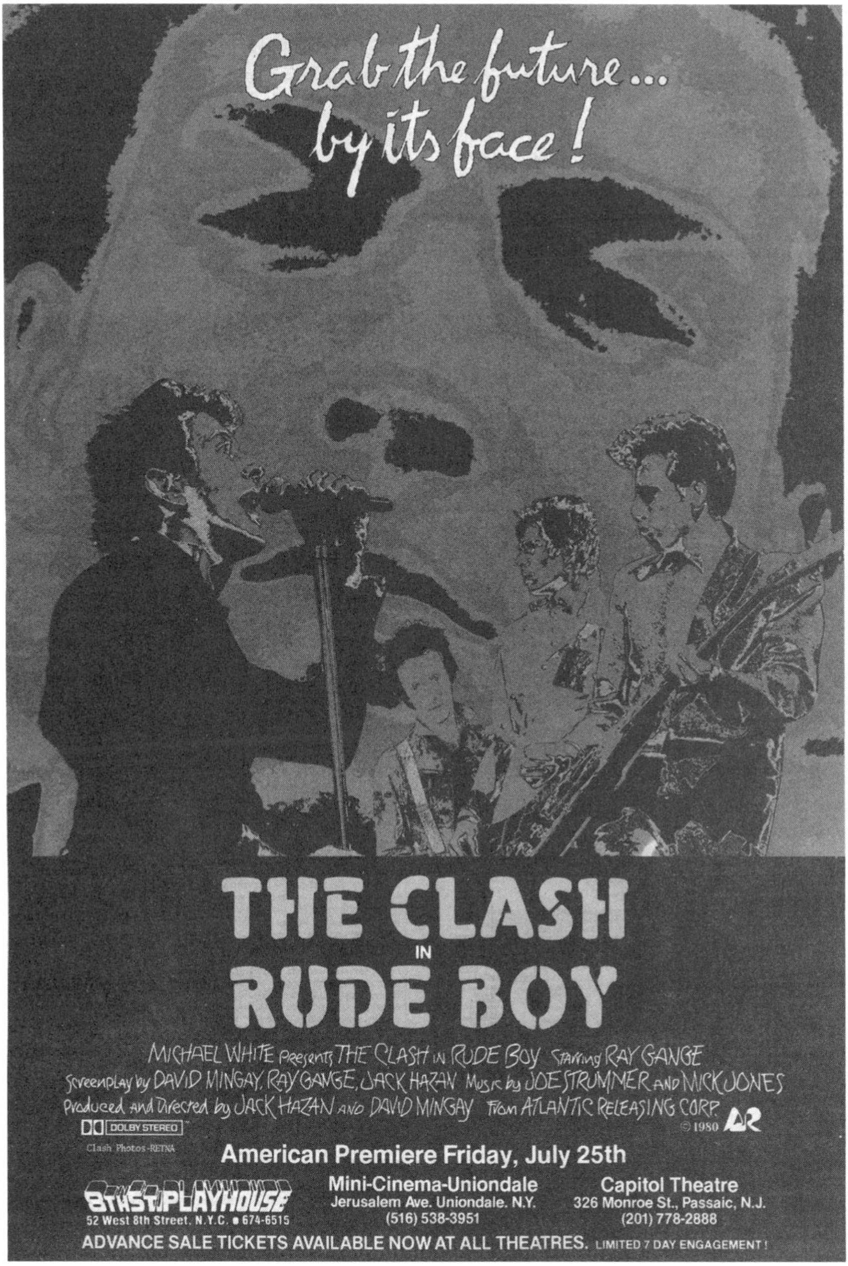

Rude Boy wasn't released in the US until July 25, 1980. *Author's collection*

not have the monies on hand for paying exorbitant legal fees, so they called the Clash's bluff: *Rude Boy* debuted at the thirtieth Berlin International Film Festival in February 1980, where it was nominated for the Golden Bear (best film award) and received an honorable mention.

Newspaper reviews were decidedly mixed, effusive either in praise or condemnation. Janet Maslin, writing for the *New York Times* in June 1980, said *Rude Boy* "is about as mixed-up as a movie can be, but the best parts are everything this British rock group's fans could hope for. The concert scenes capture the band, today's closest equivalent to the early Rolling Stones, in all its ragged glory. And the dramatic scenes, which amount to little more than transitional material, are mesmerizing as often as they're muddled."

Starring Ray Gange

If any actor's performance in the movie deserves re-evaluation, it is Ray Gange as the punk rocker who drifts away from the Clash's political message toward that of the National Front. It was without his knowledge that the character he was playing would share his real name *and* that he would be given partial credit for the screenplay. Many viewers thought Ray held the fascist and racist views he utters in the film, when in reality he was following a script written by others.

Ray did live in Brixton, but not in the tower block he's first seen in at the beginning of *Rude Boy*; he wasn't on the dole, he never supported the National Front, and he was never even a Clash roadie, although Bernie Rhodes did have him roadie for Subway Sect for "for two weeks, to get some experience before doing the film." The only true-to-life aspects of the character Ray Gange were his over-indulgence for Special Brew and his love of the Clash.

Ray moved to Paris and Los Angeles after filming *Rude Boy*, staying on friendly terms with the Clash and attending their shows, including Mick's with Big Audio Dynamite. "It's kind of weird now, because at the time of making the movie Mick was the person I had the most difficulty with, or the most conflict with," Ray says in his DVD interview. "But . . . these days we're very friendly." After returning to Brixton in 1992, Ray became a DJ and briefly started a record company. He also became a heroin addict in between, which led to a falling out with Joe. "Yeah, once you sort of crossed the line with him it was very difficult to get back on the good side of that line with him."

Still a DJ, Ray—like Mick and Terry Chimes—continues to offer his services to events sponsored by the Joe Strummer Foundation.

The Supporting Cast

Rude Boy captures the Clash during the transitional period when they were pivoting away from punk rock and via hardcore punk smelting themselves into a "middle-of-the-road punk" band, to use a phrase coined by Caroline Coon, who was a member of *Rude Boy*'s supporting cast along with the Clash's devoted road crew, Johnny Green and The Baker.

Caroline Coon

In *Rude Boy*, Caroline Coon is portrayed as Paul's older girlfriend from whose purse he steals money. In reality, she was also the Clash's acting manager, a position she accepted after becoming one of the band's earliest champions in articles, interviews, and reviews for *Melody Maker*. Born in London in 1945, Coon was a minor figure in Swinging London as a model, artist, interviewer, and founder of Release, an organization to help young people in legal difficulties over drugs.

Though she has made disputed claims that she was inspiration for Bob Dylan's "She Belongs to Me," it is undisputed that Soft Machine's Robert Wyatt was inspired by her to write "O Caroline." It is also undisputed that she started writing for *Melody Maker* in 1974. Clued in to the burgeoning punk rock scene by a Portobello Hotel barman, she was intrigued by the Sex Pistols' name and, after seeing a performance, Coon—unlike many others—saw a similarity between this new youth counterculture and the hippie movement she had been part of the previous decade. It was Coon who persuaded *Melody Maker*, after six months of badgering, to take punk rock seriously. Along with Vivien Goldman, she was one of the few women who contributed to rock 'n' roll journalism in the 1970s.

Coon published one of the first books on punk rock (*1988: The New Wave Punk Rock Explosion*) in 1977, and the following year she found herself managing the Clash through the Sort It Out and Pearl Harbour tours, although Joe would never own up to the Clash being managed by a woman. This macho sentiment was a determining factor in her dismissal in favor of Blackhill Enterprises, although the dissolution of her romance with Paul no doubt played a part.

A proud feminist, Coon has since pursued a career as a painter—often of controversial nudes—and remains politically active, fighting for human rights and drug legalization.

Johnny Green

Third billing for *Rude Boy* should've gone to the Clash's road manager, Johnny Green, but his name does not appear on film posters. He functions throughout the film as both the go-between for the Clash and Ray and as the band's conscience. It was a role that he fulfilled in real life, though, like most consciences, he was not often listened to.

A real character—in the best spirit of the word—Green graduated from Lancaster University with a degree in Arabic and Islamic Studies, married, had two children, divorced, and stumbled into his future position with the Clash. It was October 1977, and Green had already narrowly missed seeing the Clash in concert multiple times when he heard from a friend that the band's management had hired one of his trucks to move the band's equipment during a two-date foray to Ireland. Johnny asked if he could join him for the ride. He wanted to see the band in concert, which he finally did in Dublin, Ireland, although from behind the lights after being asked to help out. This led to a series of positions with the Clash over the course of three weeks: lighting crew, roadie, and finally driver of the band's minibus, with the Clash in the back. By Christmas, he was crashing on a mattress at Rehearsal Rehearsals and had become the Clash's road manager.

It was a position he was to hold for over two years until, at the end of the American wing of the 16 Tons tour, he turned in his notice and accepted a job as part of Joe Ely's crew. He told the Clash during a flight to Detroit for a benefit concert for ailing American soul singer Jackie Wilson. They wished him luck, adding there was always a job waiting for him back home should he change his mind.

Within a year, he had. The Tex-Mex Rockers weren't edgy enough for Johnny, and before long he was back in London. He re-enlisted with the Clash but asked out after a single day. He had strong feelings about the band's softening direction. He briefly remained in the music business as a road manager before succumbing to the heroin addiction that claimed the life of his second wife, Liddy. This traumatic event helped clean him up and, hoping his hard learned lessons might help others, he assumed the position of "Kent county education advisor on sex and drugs," according to the bio found in his memoir of his years with the Clash, the highly recommended *A Riot of Our Own: Night and Day with the Clash*, which he co-authored with Garry Barker. He has also written *Push Yourself Just a Little More: Backstage at the Tour de France*, a book on the premier cycling event circa 2003–04.

Barry "The Baker" Auguste

Barry Auguste's entrance into the Clash camp came via Subway Sect, Bernie's other punk band, whose members Barry had gone to school with. A skinhead, Barry was soon rechristened "The Baker" by Paul, who thought Barry looked like one. He switched allegiance to the Clash in the summer of 1976 and was along for most of the ride, leaving only when Mick was dismissed. He preferred Philly soul music to punk rock, which makes his role as a Clash insider all the more fascinating. His primary role was as the band's drum technician, but he used to drive the van with the gear, pick up meals, and even sat up with Joe in the hospital when the Clash's front man was recovering from hepatitis. In 1983 he moved to America where, after a short stint as a truck driver, he became a manager at the Strand Bookstore and its many miles of books in Lower Manhattan.

"With a Message on a Half-Baked Tape"

"My own view is [Hazan and Mingay] were trying to make a punk rock version of *A Hard Day's Night*, but without the comedy," Gange says in his DVD interview. "They were trying to be worthy. And everyone else found it really confusing."

So, "What's it all about?" as Joe asks in the Mescaleros track "Cool 'n' Out."

Director David Mingay thought the footage of black pickpockets being arrested and convicted that the Clash wanted edited out was vital, because it exposed a double standard in British society: "If you set out to be in an anarchic group who tried to overthrow the state . . . you would make a million, if you are white. If you are black, you would be arrested for stealing a pound and kept there for many years." The message of this subplot, however, is never explained in the film, although Mingay thought it was reflected in the Clash's lyrics.

The American version of *Rude Boy* is approximately six minutes shorter than the original cut, but even in this version you have wade through fifteen minutes of Ray Gange's poor acting and National Front *cinéma vérité* footage before the Clash appear. Had the film opened with Ray watching the Clash perform "Police and Thieves," followed with scenes of his empty, day-to-day existence working in a sex shop, collecting the dole, and getting arrested by the police, moviegoers might have had more patience when initially viewing *Rude Boy*. Topper's synopsis to *Creem* is all you need. Cut the riot footage, definitely remove the black pickpockets getting arrested subplot that's even more extraneous, and keep the plot simple: an on-the-dole punk rocker/Clash fan and National Front supporter named Ray Gange meets Joe Strummer in the Railway pub and, after a discussion about revolutionary politics over several pints, asks Joe for a job with the Clash. Joe rebuffs him, saying, "At the moment, how can I offer you a job? We gotta pay Johnny. We gotta pay Baker. And we ain't on the road at the moment. We're just rehearsing. How can I offer you a job? What are you going to do? See my point?" But when Ray stands up for the band at the Rock Against Racism rally in Victoria Park after their set is sabotaged by Tom Robinson Band roadies—a brave act on Ray's part that was not staged—Johnny Green hires Ray as a roadie on an upcoming Clash tour. Ray can't cut it as a roadie, however; he is more interested in drinking Special Brew and watching the concerts. So when he's not rehired for the next tour, he follows the band around from town to town, eventually becoming a target of the Clash's mischief and disapproval. In the end, he's seen not going to a Clash concert in London, symbolizing the way that many of the original UK punk rockers had drifted away from the band and toward the right-wing politics of the National Front. (Mingay and Hazen should've used the Clash's performance of "English Civil War" from the London Lyceum here instead of "I Fought the Law," because it musically stresses the movie's more cogent central theme.) Footage of Maggie Thatcher entering 10 Downing Street implies that all the friction between left wing and right wing protesters has resulted in is a Conservative government. End of story.

The poor acting by Ray Gange and various Clash members has been overstated by film critics. Once the viewer accepts some of the acting as being amateurish and tries to appreciate the historical validity of the *vérité* shots of late 1970s London, *Rude Boy* can be enjoyable. Here are the best things about Buzzy Enterprises's 1980 film.

Jack Hazan's Camerawork

What sets the Clash's concert footage apart from what is seen in most rock movies and videos is Jack Hazan's camera work. A minuscule budget forced Hazan to shoot the majority of the concert footage by himself on a single camera. This gives it a DIY punk feel. Hazan had previously filmed Jimi Hendrix and the Doors at the 1970 Isle of Wight Festival, which Joe had attended, and while working on the French rock program *Pop Deux*, he picked up a trick he applied to filming *Rude Boy*: "Never film a guitar from the front, don't ever film it face on, always along the neck or from the base to go toward the neck . . . and it worked. You were never sure what was going to happen."

So when Hazan shoots "Police and Thieves" inside Barbarella's from the perspective of a fan up against the lip of the stage—a few feet to Joe's left—the viewer is totally immersed in Joe's performance, never sure of what Joe will do next. Decades later, this is the closest that newborn Clash fans can get to standing in a Clash's audience. By contrast, *Rude Boy*'s final number, "I Fought the Law"—shot with five carefully placed cameras—is anticlimactic (the opposite of Hazan's intent). The Clash's performance is memorable, with Joe putting himself in Sid Vicious's boots and singing about how "I killed my babe," but having been carefully edited from five vantage points, the song's emotional power is undercut. It looks like a scene from any other rock movie.

Decades later, one senses a missed opportunity for both the Clash and Hazan that they never worked together on any other project. The only member of the Clash camp who spoke favorably of the film when it was first released was Johnny Green—he even squeezed in attending the Berlin premiere with The Baker between Clash performances in Europe—and, in his memoir, Green says he bluntly told the Clash that "[Mingay] knew how to film you lot."

The Clash's attempts to squelch *Rude Boy*'s release soured Hazan's relationship with the band, however, and not one member of the Clash could see beyond the film's politically incorrect message and acknowledge that, like photographer Pennie Smith and illustrator Ray Lowry, Hazan had visually captured the Clash's live tumult as few could. No attempt at rapprochement between the Clash and Hazan was ever made. The Clash instead left their video legacy in the hands of their friend Don Letts, with mixed results.

Rock Against Racism/Anti-Nazi League Carnival Performance

Shot from stage left and somewhat behind the Clash, this is an excellent example of Hazan turning a negative situation into a positive shoot. Because of where he was standing, he captured not only the Clash but also the bobbing crowd of 80,000 bodies going absolutely bonkers to "London's Burning." This was the largest crowd the Clash had performed to at this point, and Johnny Green has said that although he had tried to convey to the band the enormity of the crowd, they didn't get it until they stepped onstage and bashed out their opening number "Complete Control."

One of the limitations of Hazan's equipment was that he could not film more than a few songs so, although rumors persist that the Carnival promoters filmed the Clash's full concert for promotional purposes, only two songs are preserved from this legendary performance. "London's Burning" was the set's second song and the filmmakers' editing makes it seem that the plug was pulled on the Clash, but it actually happened after "Capital Radio," the set's penultimate number.

Johnny Green tells Joe why there's no power. The bootleg performance of the complete twelve-song set runs to forty-two minutes, so maybe the Clash were running over their allotted time. But Mick has said they never would have done so consciously since it was a benefit performance. Power is restored for one more number, with Sham 69 lead singer Jimmy Pursey joining the band for a performance of "White Riot" that Joe felt Pursey mugged more during than he should have.

It's a colorful performance nonetheless, with Joe in matching white pants and brothel creepers and his red "Brigade Rosse" T-shirt, which offended some of the rally organizers and music journalists. Mick, dressed all in black à la Jimmy Page from Zeppelin's 1976 tour, also offended them with the officer's cap he doffed. Too fascist, they thought. Only Paul, in a Day-Glo blue shirt, black pants, and white Converse sneakers, did not offend.

The Clash on the Out on Parole Tour

The year 1978 was a difficult one for the Clash. January began with the Sex Pistols disbanding in San Francisco. The exaggerated possibilities punk held for changing British society were evaporating—a disappointing turn of events for Joe Strummer, who had put his life on the line for the counterculture movement. The following month, Joe was hospitalized with hepatitis. Mick had his flat burglarized, his relationship with Viv Albertine was labored, he was abusing cocaine, and he was suffering from writer's block. The meticulous, drawn-out recording sessions for the band's second album were the antithesis of the first, which was recorded in three weekends. And Bernie was pouring his energies into other bands and a club he was opening. This left the band to their own devices.

For the first time since the band's formation, the individual personalities of the band were starting to be glimpsed. Paul reverted to being a skinhead, Joe's hair thickened and was combed back into a rockabilly quiff, and Mick's grew long and curly, making Keith Richards comparisons a staple of music articles during this period. All of Topper's personality was channeled through his drumming, so he retained the punk gear longer than the others, but eventually his love for Bruce Lee led him to dabbling in kung fu and asking Alex Michon to design comparable clothing, resulting in his wearing brightly colored jumpsuits in concert. This is the phase of the Clash captured by Hazan's camera in *Rude Boy*.

The one thing that bound all four together, however, was the live appearances. On the Out on Parole tour throughout July, the band members reclaimed their cohesion. Early B-side "1977" was retired as a memento from the previous year. The sets featured the best songs from *The Clash* (but not "Career Opportunities") plus 45 A-sides and B-sides, as well as the road testing of new material for *Give 'Em Enough Rope.* They also played an entertaining medley of two popular songs from 1976 forever associated with punk rock: "Police and Thieves" and the Ramones' "Blitzkrieg Bop."

Hazan filmed the Clash in Glasgow, Dunfermline, Aberdeen, and London during this tour. It has been said that only when captured on camera does an event happen. So while I saw Joe Strummer jump into a crowd in the Lacarno in Coventry and fight someone who had gobbed at him or participated in a small riot to force my way into Bond International Casino on opening night, those events are forgotten, unlike what Hazan filmed inside the Glasgow Apollo: Joe wading into the crowd and breaking up a fight; Mick yelling at the bouncers to leave the fans alone. It is these tense concert moments that decades later convey how Clash concerts were unlike any other. And there's the performances: a combative "(White Man) In Hammersmith Palais," a stirring "Tommy Gun," a psychotic "What's My Name" concluding with Joe on his back near the drum riser, legs wrapped around his microphone stand.

"Safe European Home"

Johnny Green has claimed that the Clash re-recorded every song in *Rude Boy*; the filmmakers insist they did so with only half of the performances. The truth lies somewhere in the middle. The *Rope* recording sessions and Joe's two numbers on the piano clearly did not require additional work, and "I Fought the Law" had been recorded on the 24-track Rolling Stones Mobile Truck, Buzzy Enterprises springing extra cash for what they intended on being the film's closing number.

Johnny enjoyed watching the Clash trying to replicate concert performances from over half a year earlier. "In their effort to be realistic," he wrote in his memoir, *A Riot of Our Own*, "they were alert to every detail of the film—re-enacting their stage movements, pulling mikes away from their

The Clash's entire concert at the London Lyceum on January 3, 1979, was professionally recorded and captured the Clash as they left punk rock behind. *Author's collection*

mouths in time with their image on screen, doing it so well that they became marionettes, with the celluloid Mick and Joe pulling the strings."

One "puppet show" they paid particular care to was "Safe European Home," possibly because they knew the final third of the song about how "nobody know what the rude boy know" tied in with the film's working title. Free of Sandy Pearlman's perfectionism and American corporate interference, Mick could record the song with Bill Price the way the Clash wanted it to sound. Joe's voice is shoved up front—it's buried in Pearlman's mix—and Mick and Paul's questioning, "Where'd ya go?" more insistent. Paul's bass is heavier with that reggae feel he was consistently searching for. Only the drums—almost the lead instrument in the studio version—are muddled.

The lyrics are re-arranged or altered, with Joe at one point singing, "They got the smoka!" as he feigns taking a toke of a spliff. Rather than sing about the safe European home he's relieved to back in, Mick starts singing, "I'll never forget you" over and over, while Joe ad-libs about the Rude Boy. Watching the live performance, Mick can get away with this substitution because you never see him, Hazan's single camera is focused on Joe, whose vocals are treated, rising and ominously echoing as the song suddenly stops. "Safe European Home" and not "I Fought the Law" is *Rude Boy*'s musical highpoint.

Joe Strummer's Scenes with Ray Gange

"I recreated some scenes with Ray Gange," Joe says, in the coffee-table book *The Clash*, "such as the one where he had actually come up to me in London and asked for a job as a roadie, and though some scenes were created for the film, most of it was true. Though he never was our roadie." These are best scenes in the movie, not including concert footage.

If you ever doubted that Joe sometimes perceived himself as a rock star, that first scene Joe refers to above will lay any doubt to rest. He is staring straight ahead, wearing a black leather jacket with badges and a white Clash T-shirt of the debut album's back over, exquisitely posing. His quiff is perfectly combed. His right forearm is upright but resting on the pub's countertop as his strumming hand holds a lit cigarette. He is Joe Strummer the punk rock star. He then engages Ray in his heartfelt, if half-baked ideas on left-wing versus right-wing politics. Ray is at his most likeable sharing the screen with Joe, perhaps because he is at his most relaxed.

Another great moment is the "pizza scene" when Ray visits Joe, who's washing his laundry in his hotel bathroom sink. Another discussion on revolutionary politics ensues, with Joe peering over his Brigade Rosse shirt, jokingly telling Ray it's the name of a pizzeria.

Then comes the *coup de grace*: the final scene between the two in the band's rehearsal space. Ray is still drinking his Special Brew while Joe has tea with honey. Joe sings an untitled song written specifically for this scene that some have speculated reflects Ray (the character) and his social position in Britain in the late '70s. It is incredible that the Clash never recorded this song officially because it's got one of Joe's best couplets: "Well the black man got the rhythm and the white man got the law / I know which one I'll be looking for." Those lines succinctly sum up Joe's worldview better than just

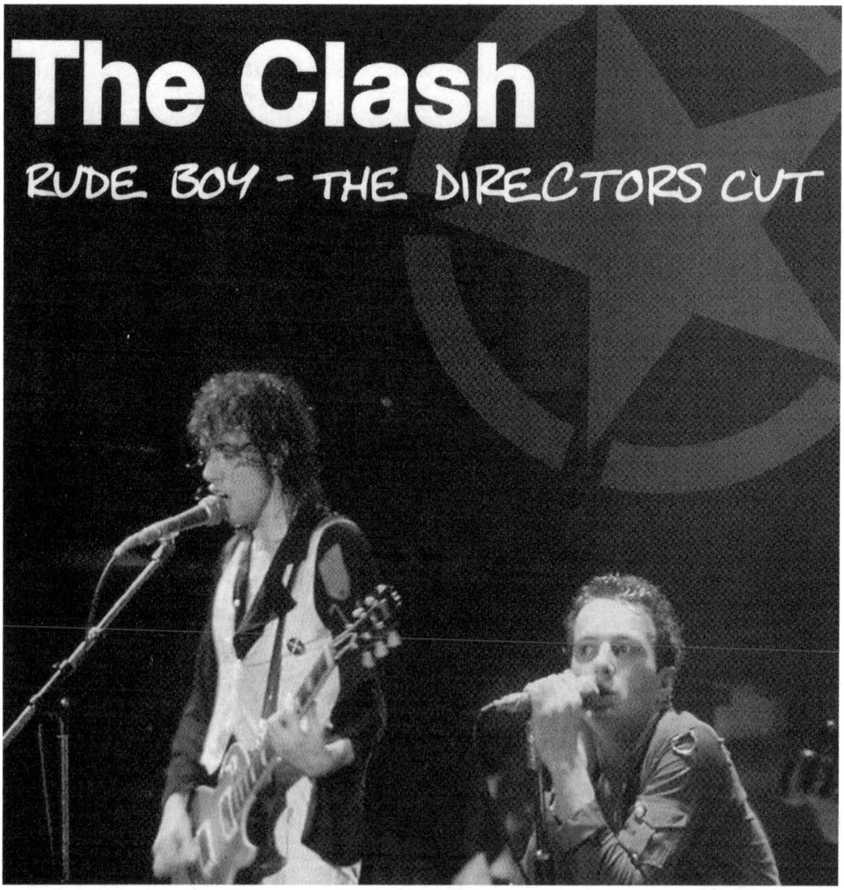

Rude Boy: The Directors Cut could have been sequenced better, but—since it mostly features re-recorded studio performances—it is one of the best Clash bootlegs available.
Author's collection

about anything else you'll find on a Clash recording. ("The Sound of the Sinners" from *Sandinista!* has been said to have its roots in this piano song.)

Ray then offers Joe the view of the fans drifting away from the band. The Clash are getting too political, says Ray. He doesn't like it when politics and music mix. And Joe—the Clash member with the strongest rockabilly roots—responds with a good-natured, minimalist version of Shirley and Lee's "Let the Good Times Roll," his smile lighting an otherwise gloomy movie as Ray "dances" and tosses his empty beer can into a corner.

Years later, Joe said of *Rude Boy*, "It all became messy in the end. But I think the film stands up well." It's thanks to scenes like these that it does.

Thought I'd Find a Rhythm in the Junkie Town

"Topper" Headon, "The Human Drum Machine"

Initially attracted to the kit by the Who's drummer, Topper Headon was an enrollee in the Keith Moon School of Drumming, but he picked up all the wrong lessons. As a drummer, Topper wasn't over the top of his kit. Nor had he abandoned the use of the hi-hat. Nor was he the chaotic whirling dervish of rhythm Moon was. No, by saying Topper was an enrollee in the Keith Moon School of Drumming, I mean he modeled himself after Moon's lifestyle of total abandon. It was Topper—not other members of the Clash—who was thrashing hotel rooms with roadies, whose life was one continuous party that saw his wife Wendy and girlfriend Dee come and go, and whose drug addiction left him without the band that made him famous.

"Make a Drum from a Garbage Can"

Nicholas Bowen "Topper" Headon was born in Bromley, a London suburb, on May 30, 1955. His parents Philip and Margaret were both schoolteachers. The family moved to Dover when Topper was thirteen years old after his father was named the headmaster of Dover Grammar School. Around this same time, Topper broke his leg playing football, and when it was set incorrectly, he was forced to wear a full-length cast for six months. This was a difficult adjustment for the hyperactive teenager, so his father bought him a drum kit.

"It was an Ajax kit, which had single-headed toms with a black mother of pearl finish," Topper told Steve Grantley of www.mikedtobear.com. The kit did not have a drum pedal, so the teenager went out and bought "a Premier pedal—the 250s," which he would continue using throughout his days with the Clash. He was largely self-taught; the only book on drumming instruction he bought was by the Shadows' Brian Bennett. From Bennett and his favorite jazz drummers, he learned the traditional grip, but by watching rock 'n' roll drummers on *Top of the Pops*, he discovered the matched grip.

Topper Headon in 1979, when he was one of the best drummers on the planet. *Virginia Turbett/Getty Images*

The traditional grip was good for "feel," but the matched grip was better for "power." Topper would put both grips to good use for the Clash.

"I wanted to be like Gene Krupa," Topper said—and he did later release a version of "Drum Boogie," the swing drummer's signature recording—"or Keith Moon . . . they certainly weren't at the back holding down the back beat. But by the time I'd got into drumming, I realized that's what a drummer had to do. Listening to Terry Williams from Man showed me how a drummer could hold the band together and power the band." Other drummers Topper cited to Grantley as influences were jazz drummers Billy Cobham, Steve Gadd, and Buddy Rich, as well as Keef Hartley from John Mayall's Bluesbreakers. As for rock drummers, in addition to Keith Moon and Terry Williams, Topper listed Led Zeppelin's John Bonham, Jethro Tull's Clive Bunker, and Deep Purple's Ian Paice. He wasn't impressed by many of his contemporaries, but he did acknowledge Budgie from Siouxsie and the Banshees and Blair Cunningham from Echo and the Bunnymen, and that "Stewart Copeland was a great drummer, I just didn't like his group."

The story that the Clash auditioned 206 drummers before finding Topper is not true, although the one about running several dozen aspiring Clash wannabe drummers through "London's Burning" is. Remembering London SS's lack of success, Topper did not take Mick's invitation to try out for the Clash seriously when they bumped into one another inside the Rainbow. But after seeing Mick beside Joe and Paul on the cover of *Melody Maker* the following week, Topper hurried over to Rehearsal Rehearsals for an audition. Once hired, he was immediately rechristened "Topper" by Paul because of his uncanny resemblance to Mickey the Monkey, the cover strip in the weekly *Topper* comic that ran for 1,074 issues. Terry Chimes kindly sat down with Topper, showed him his drumbeats, and left it to Topper—five-foot-six with brown hair and blue eyes—to redefine the drummer's role in the Clash.

Like Joe before him, Topper erased his past, his Year Zero occurring a year after Joe's; unlike Joe, Topper knew that playing with the Clash also meant remaking himself as a drummer. "I had all the jazz and funk styles," he said. "I could play all different styles of music but when I joined the Clash I readjusted my style so that I could play all these styles but—powerfully!" In order to be as flashy as his front men, he acquired a "mirror-finish kit." Accompanied by The Baker, his drum technician, he bought a silver Pearl Ambassador kit at Henrit's that he would use exclusively for all Clash performances and recordings. The only exception was *Combat Rock*, for which he used a Ludwig drum kit. The drum kit had Evans Hydraulic Heads, and Topper's preferred cymbals were Zildjian.

Topper with his right arm raised up at the Palladium on February 17, 1979.
Stephen Graziano

"This Here Music Cause a Sensation"

"We don't like to be called a new-wave band," Topper told *Creem*'s Stephen Demorest nearly two years after his hiring. "We're a punk band and proud of it—we ain't gonna change." But it was because of Topper's range that the band did change. The *Village Voice*'s John Piccarella noted that it was Topper who almost single-handedly extended the "one-punch knockout structure of [the Clash's] quintessential punk" by drawing on his apprenticeship playing with jazz outfits and soul revues to provide supple support for the "startling rhythmic shifts and harmonic extensions, countermelodies and keyboards and horn" the Clash began employing. Because of this, "the best English punk band became the best rock-and-roll band in the world."

It's Topper who gives "City of the Dead" its subtle yet powerful rhumba feel. Who can imagine "(White Man) In Hammersmith Palais" without his stuttering drumbeat right after Joe says, "Dress back jump back this is a blue beat attack"? It's impossible to imagine *Give 'Em Enough Rope* or *The Cost of Living EP* without Topper as "the engine room." Producer Sandy Pearlman called Topper "the human drum machine," and his performances were worthy of the three days spent miking his drum kit in Basing Street Studios. Topper pushed the tempo, helping usher in the genre of hardcore punk, although he receives little credit for this. He may have objected to "I Fought the Law" when Mick first played Bobby Fuller's hit for him on acoustic guitar, but it's Topper's opening drumroll on the toms—and the way it sounds like an outlaw's horse on the run—that makes the song the Clash's own.

With a running time of 1:46, "Koka Kola" is the Clash's final punk rock song, a vicious takedown of the corporate lifestyle. The first line is "Elevator going up!" and in concert, Topper really took the tempo up for "Koka Kola," charging through intricate time changes only to segue abruptly into the extended drumroll of "I Fought the Law" and leave audiences flattened. You can view this yourself on YouTube in footage from the Clash's March 1980 performance at the Capitol Theatre in Passaic, New Jersey.

When the Clash were ready to stretch out and attempt rhythm and blues or jazz rhythms, Topper already had the chops to get them there. Even reggae—something he had never played before—was easy for him: "I loved drumming, so I just thought, 'Right, I'm going to learn reggae now.' That's the way I was—I've got an addictive personality," he told journalist Mark Evans. "All I ever did was drum, drum, drum. Then I went on the road and discovered booze. All I did was drink, drink, drink. Then Mick turned me onto coke and all I did was coke."

In her book *The Clash: Before and After*, photographer Pennie Smith, compared the Clash to the Bash Street Kids (a British comic strip), a comparison more befitting Topper than the others. "I'd think we were getting out of it every night. One night Joe would come down and we'd get drunk, the next night Paul would be down and I'd get out of it with him and the next night it would be Mick. I'd be thinking, 'This is great, we're all partying.' I wouldn't realize that only I was there constantly." After some time it was just Topper and the roadies laying mayhem to hotels, but the Clash were left paying the bills because of their drummer's involvement. More worrisome was that Topper's out-of-control behavior was affecting their live performances, because by the time of the Impossible Mission tour in April and May 1981, Topper's drumbeats began most songs.

"A-Beatin' on the Final Drum"

Speaking of his Waterloo—the Lochem Festival in Amsterdam on May 20, 1982—Topper told Evans, "I don't know I'm being tested, do I? I don't know it's my last chance and I'm running round trying to score coke. They're all sitting in the dressing-room, combing their hair in the mirror against the wall and I run in and go: 'Can I use the mirror?'" According to Evans, Topper's bandmates "watched in silence as he placed the mirror on the floor and knelt beside it, chopping out generous lines of cocaine." The Clash's performance was a disaster. Some lay the blame on Mick's out-of-tune guitar, but it was Topper who took the fall.

As was typical with the Clash, misinformation was peddled about Topper's sacking, but in this case it was to spare their former drummer being tagged a drug addict. (It was common knowledge, though, that Topper had been arrested at Heathrow Airport the previous January for trying to sneak in heroin for his girlfriend, Dee. Fining him £500, the presiding judge had warned Topper, "Unless you accept treatment, you will be the best drummer in the graveyard.") So when *NME*'s Charles Shaar Murray asked Joe in May 1982 why Topper was let go, Joe said that it was Topper's own decision. "I think he felt . . . it's not too easy to be in the Clash. It's not as simple as being in a comfortable, we're-just-entertainers group, and he just wanted to do that, just play music. He's a brilliant multi-instrumentalist—what used to be called that—and it's a bit weird to be in the Clash at the moment. Well, it was. He has to sort of strike out in another direction, because I don't think he wants to come along with us." So Topper's abrupt departure was put down to *musical differences.*

"Joe went to his grave blaming himself for the Clash breaking up," Headon told *Uncut*'s Stephen Dalton in 2007. "But he had no choice. When you're an addict you lie all the time, I didn't give a fuck about anyone else. He didn't have a lot of choice."

After the Clash, Topper's name bobbed up occasionally in the music press as being part of new projects. There was the short-lived Top Risk Action Company with Mick Jones and the shorter-lived Samurai with former Pretenders bassist Pete Farndon, a project that ended when Farndon overdosed on heroin and drowned in his bathtub. Working with the Clash's former recording engineer Jeremy Green, Topper finally released *Waking Up* in 1986—an album mostly featuring his own compositions—and got married for the second time. Within half a year, Topper was serving a fifteen-month jail sentence for providing drugs to a friend who had overdosed.

Upon his release, Topper was reduced to busking on bongos for the £25 required to score each day. "Every hundred people who passed, there'd be one who'd stop and ask, 'Are you Topper Headon from the Clash?'" Topper told journalist Mark Lucas, "I'd have to say, 'Yeah, this is what I do now.' It was so humiliating."

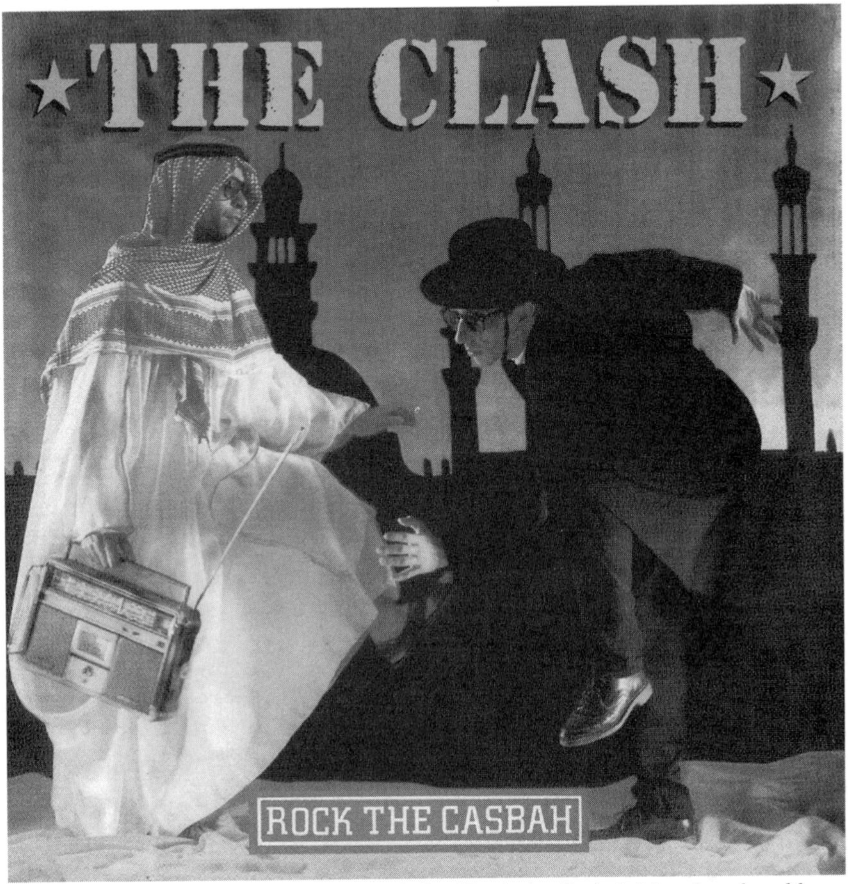

Topper Headon not only wrote the music for "Rock the Casbah," he also played bass, drums, and piano and laid down the basic track while waiting for other members of the Clash to turn up at the recording studio. By the time it was a Top Ten hit in the US, he had been out of the band for eight months. *Author's collection*

After Topper's second marriage ended, he spent nights at St. Mungo's hostel for the homeless, returned to Dover, was in and out of rehab over a dozen times, and contracted hepatitis C before forming a Narcotics Anonymous group in his hometown. Miraculously, he has survived all of this and now leads a quiet life as a cabbie in Dover. He has occasionally appeared onstage with Mick Jones and also works with the Strummerville Foundation.

In the second issue of the *Armagideon Times*, which was on sale at venues during the 16 Tons tour, Topper wrote that his ambition in 1980 was "to live through it all." He certainly did.

I Read It in the Paper—They're Crazy!

Sandinista!

"I can't stand bands who produce the same sound over and over because it's safe. We take risks a bit. We stick our necks out and one day we'll get our heads chopped off," Joe prophetically told London columnist Fiona Malcolm in April 1980. He was back in his hometown after wrapping up recording sessions for *Sandinista!* in New York City, which "has been a big influence, because in that city jazz and punk are meeting head [on]." Joe was talking of an album still in its formative stages, an album that would be "full of surprises and everyone will hate it." He clearly anticipated troubles ahead for *Sandinista!*, the album that would be the Clash's most controversial.

The American Recording Sessions

To paraphrase a T-shirt I once saw in Istanbul: you may call it chaos, I call it the Clash. A perfect illustration is the recording sessions resulting in *Sandinista!* The band's original intent was to follow up *London Calling* with a single disc of London Reggae produced by Mikey Dread at Channel One Studios in Kingston, Jamaica. Over the course of the 16 Tons tour, Willi Williams's "Armagideon Time" had morphed into a sonic gumbo with echo-drenched effects that almost always began an encore. "Bankrobber," the only song the band had recorded since *London Calling*, was receiving similar treatment. Originally played in the main set, it had since become an encore standard. Clearly, the natural direction in music for the Clash was the London Reggae that, frankly, no other British band had shown any aptitude for. The Clash were staking out their own musical turf.

And so, following an appearance on March 10 at the Motor City Roller Rink in Detroit, Michigan, the Clash, Mikey Dread, and others in the entourage set off for Bob Marley's home country. These sessions ended with only "Junco Partner" completed, however. Joe told *Uncut*'s Gavin Martin that he was sitting at the piano "fingering out chords" when Mikey Dread told him that they had to make a run for it because they hadn't paid off the "drugmen."

A few points should be made about this session. First, the Clash were joined by members of the Roots Radics, a local band Dread often worked with, for "Junco Partner." Second, it has been said that money was expected from the Clash in exchange for their guaranteed safety because the Rolling Stones had just been in town throwing money around. This is untrue. For the first half of 1980, Mick Jagger and Keith Richards were in New York City, mixing and bickering over what tracks should be included on *Emotional Rescue*, arguably their worst album ever. The closest a Rolling Stone got to Jamaica during this period was Ronnie Wood's bust in February for cocaine possession in St. Martin, another Caribbean island nation.

Finally, the Clash were winging it in Channel One Studios. "We came off [tour] full of go," Joe recalled, and the band was eager to bottle that "go" on record. The window of opportunity would be open for only a few weeks. Paul was due to fly to Vancouver at month's end to act in a movie project. The decision to go to Jamaica had been a sudden one, paid for by Paul's girlfriend's credit card. And as Joe confirmed in an article printed posthumously in 2012, "We had nothing written. You don't write on tour, it takes all your concentrating to make the gig—that's survival technique." So it was clear that the Clash were living by the seat of their collective pants in Jamaica. They'd do a few covers and hope inspiration struck. When they were forced to flee, they took this formula with them to New York City, where they booked some time at the Power Station. Unaware that CBS Records' refusal to release "Bankrobber" would mushroom, the plan was to record the next in the series of singles the Clash had planned for 1980. These sessions produced "Police on My Back" and an unfinished version of Prince Buster's "Madness."

London Calling may have been a commercial success, but the Clash's contract allowed their US parent label, Columbia, to hold back revenue due for six months. Stuck for cash, the Clash found themselves unable to afford the Power Station's fees, but still flush with the rush of their most successful tour, they negotiated a three-week block of time at Jimi Hendrix's Electric Lady Studios on 8th Street in Greenwich Village.

The Clash were in new creative waters. Their debut album had been the result of their earliest live performances; only "Police and Thieves" had been worked up in the studio. The material for *Give 'Em Enough Rope* was written on demand, but it too had been partially road-tested before the recording sessions. *The Vanilla Tapes*, released with the *25th Anniversary Legacy Edition* of *London Calling*, demonstrates that the songs for that album were largely complete before taping at Wessex Studios began. For their fourth studio album, however, the Clash had nothing but weeks of studio time at their disposal. They were undertaking a new approach in recording, and this accounts for *Sandinista!*'s experimental, forward-looking sprawl.

Topper went missing for days on end and was often in police custody when found due to his worsening drug addiction, but when the diminutive drummer did turn up, he was the first in the studio. He would lay down a bit of piano or jam with members of the Blockheads, who had flown over to assist, and when the others turned up at Electric Lady, they would then shape what was on tape into a song.

Joe constructed a novel bit of architecture called the SpliffBunker. Mick described it to *Uncut* in 2010 as "Joe's in-studio writing place, built out of flight cases. It had a little desk and a window you could see through." It was from within the SpliffBunker that Joe turned out an epic amount of lyrics.

As Joe recast American rhythm-and-blues idioms as rocksteady productions, Mick was discovering, via a Brooklyn record shop, hip hop, the sound of New York City's streets in 1980. But while Mick's growing interest resulted in the Clash's most successful recording from this period, it also laid the seeds for their eventual dissolution.

When the Clash returned to the road for shows in Europe and rescheduled performances in England in May and June 1980, the only *Sandinista!* track they added to the sets was Mick's vocal turn on "Somebody Got Murdered." This may have been because of Paul's absence at the New York City sessions and his unfamiliarity with the new material. They also played the *Sandinista!* outtake "Hit the Road Jack" on at least one occasion. The 16 Tons tour, which began in Aylesbury on January 5, 1980, finally ground to a halt on June 21 in the Laugardalshöll Sports Hall in Reykjavik, Iceland.

The Clash took a month off. CBS Records resolved the dispute over "Bankrobber" by releasing the single intended for spring in August. The band felt their point was made when it raced up the charts. Blinded by hubris, they booked themselves into Wessex Studios, where recording resumed. There was a torrent of new material: at least a third of *Sandinista!* was recorded at these sessions. The band—having assumed production duties—then proceeded, with the aid of Bill Price and Mikey Dread, to whip into shape recordings from five studios into their fourth album. During this time period at Wessex, they also participated in varying degrees on albums by Ellen Foley (credited) and Pearl Harbor (uncredited).

Sandinista!

While it is not explicitly stated, the title implies a musical revolution within the album jacket. Like *Sgt. Pepper's*, like *Bitches Brew*, like *Autobahn*, *Sandinista!* contained "new directions in music," as Miles Davis had characterized his music a decade earlier. *Sandinista!* was arguably the first global recording, a sonic landscape containing not only various strains of rock 'n' roll but also rocksteady, dub, jazz, rap, music hall, gospel, and even a Jamaican waltz. Mick's best tracks are examined in chapter 11, and the reggae numbers in

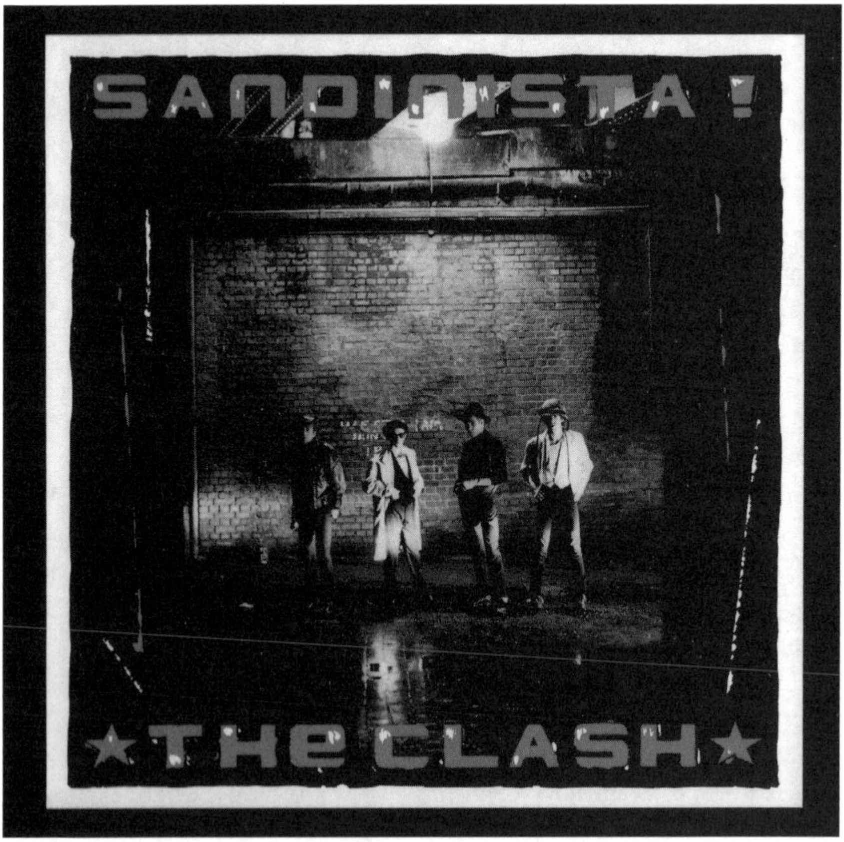

Reissues of *Sandinista!* restore the West Ham United Football Club graffiti in Pennie Smith's original photograph. It had been airbrushed out when the album was first released in December 1980. *Author's collection*

chapter 15. Here, however, are the best of the triple album's branches into musical idioms you never expected the Clash to tackle.

"The Magnificent Seven"

Much of *Sandinista!*'s difficult reception in 1980 can be attributed to Side 1's poor sequencing. This is somewhat incredible given that *London Calling*'s strongest suit was perhaps the running order of the album's nineteen tracks. *London Calling* began with the title track rocker, which sounded like a classic on first hearing, and the rockabilly romp of "Brand New Cadillac." Only when the rock fan was settled in and satisfied did the Clash introduce something a little different in "Jimmy Jazz."

Sandinista!, however, begins with something not only different but entirely unexpected: a rap song in an era when rap was considered to be nothing more than a passing fad, an illegitimate offspring of disco—a genre that most rock fans were glad to see fading from the charts. Nothing on the band's previous tour had prepared even the most die-hard of fans for "The Magnificent Seven." Credit the Clash then with prescience, if nothing else, because "The Magnificent Seven" foresees—and helps spur on—the dominant role hip hop would have over the latter fifth of the twentieth century.

When "The Magnificent Seven" is followed up with the Motown-driven "Hitsville UK" and a very reggae-fried "Junco Partner," however, the result is disorientation. Three songs in, three different musical idioms hailing from three different recording studios. In my view, *Sandinista!* is the Clash's best album, but Side 1 should've followed up "The Magnificent Seven" with "Ivan Meets G.I. Joe" and "The Leader," two medium-paced rockers that would've helped the rock fan come to grips with the opening track. Because "The Magnificent Seven" is nothing short of magnificent. The basic track (including vocals) was recorded in Electric Lady in a single day, and features Norman Watt-Roy's most memorable contribution to a Clash track. According to Topper, the Clash's crossover hit began as a jam between Gallagher, Watt-Roy, and himself while they were waiting for Joe and Mick to turn up. After Watt-Roy's ricocheting bassline was laid down and looped, the Clash built up the song from there, with Joe writing lyrics on the spot and playing electric piano; Mick adding guitars, backing vocals, and sound effects à la Mikey Dread; and Topper contributing drums as well as backing vocals.

The song's title works on three levels. To begin with, it immediately brings to mind the 1960 John Sturges film of the same name, an American remake of Akira Kurosawa's *Seven Samurai*. Seven gunslingers led by Yul Brynner and Steve McQueen are hired by Mexican villagers to defend their farming community from a gang of bandits who regularly raid the town of their crops and other supplies. The idea of seven men on the run, sacrificing themselves for simple farmers and their families would have appealed to the Clash's romantic notions and self-image. (Farming communities are also the subject of several *Sandinista!* songs such as "Corner Soul" and "The Equaliser.") On top of that, it was an inside joke, referring to those occasions when the band, joined by Johnny Green, The Baker, and DJ Barry Myers, skanked onstage during Mikey Dread's set. And, finally, it is an allusion to an alarm clock ringing at 7 a.m., the opening drumroll a rude awakening bringing a New York City workingman back to another day of drudgery.

Lyrically, "The Magnificent Seven" is among Joe Strummer's finest songs. Not only does it introduce a multitude of themes that would be explored on *Sandinista!*, it is Joe's fullest—and most humorous—exploration of the workingman's plight. The workingman gets up, gets the weather report, hears the news on the radio, and takes a bus to work, where he makes money for the pricey things his girl thinks are "nice." The morning hours go by slow, but then it's time for lunch and a "cheeseboiger!" and more news blasts and the afternoon hours. That evening, the workingman "hits the town, drinks his wages," and here Joe deftly brings in Karl Marx and Friedrich Engels, implying that in the hundred years since Marx published his theories on how capitalism exploits the workingman, nothing's changed. Consumerism has prevailed. In fact, other champions of the common man, such as Martin Luther King Jr. and Mahatma Gandhi, have only been "murdered by the other side"—the first of many sporting allusions to be found throughout *Sandinista!*

It was an unlikely subject for a hit song, but "The Magnificent Seven" was the third single from *Sandinista!* in the UK, released after the first two ("The Call Up" and "Hitsville UK") had struggled on the charts. Album designer Jules Balme credits this to Bernie Rhodes. "There were two lives to *Sandinista!*," Balme told *Uncut* in 2010, "pre-Bernie and post-Bernie. Once Bernie gets there, *Sandinista!* suddenly grows legs. The whole Mag 7 thing . . . that was obviously Bernie who got behind that."

"The Magnificent Seven" reached #34 on the charts. It was released on April 10, 1981, as was a 12-inch remix by Pepe Unidos created at Wessex in February 1981 called "The Magnificent Dance," which clocked in at 5:36. Pepe Unidos was a pseudonym for Joe, Paul, and Bernie Rhodes, and the first evidence of Bernie's ambition of replacing Mick in the recording hierarchy. (More on that in chapter 24.)

Over in America, a 12-inch EP containing this remix, a severe edit of "The Magnificent Seven" (only 2:16 long!), "The Call Up," and "The Cool Out" (another Pepe Unidos remix) was released to coincide with the band's Bond's residency. Picked up by New York City's black radio stations, "The Magnificent Seven" was a hit in America. This was not due to "The Magnificent Dance," which, frankly, is one of the Clash's most insipid recordings. Instead, WBLS—a black-owned FM station in New York City—created a version of "The Magnificent Dance" commonly known as the "Dirty Harry" mix. Incorporating dialogue from the movie *Dirty Harry* as well the voices of Warner Bros. cartoon characters such as Bugs Bunny ("the rabbit kicked the bucket!"), it's a real hoot. You can find the "Dirty Harry Remix" on the *Clash on Broadway 4: The Outtakes* bootleg.

"Something About England"

One of the album's most ambitious tracks on *Sandinista!* is the tale introduced by Mick of a British pensioner portrayed by Joe that closes Side 1. The comparisons back in the day of Strummer and Jones to Lennon and McCartney were always a stretch, but "Something About England" is Mick's most McCartney-esque stab at music hall. It's a song that traces the history of twentieth-century England from World War I through postwar depression and the Jarrow March of 1936 and World War II and well into the Atomic age, where "England never closed this gap" between the classes. Through bad times and good, England's class system is immovable. And so, while the music is very different, the subject matter is akin to what the Clash were railing about on their debut album.

Accompanied by a horn section comprised of Topper's friend Gary Barnacle, his father Bill, and David Yates, Mick reports on how he's heard National Front leaders blaming immigrants for society's ills. Topper taps four beats on his snare and, with Mick on piano, the narrator begins making his way home when he sees a homeless man. The London night is "snapped by sirens"—as it will be on the next side, during "The Crooked Beat"—and about a minute into the tune he asks the old man—portrayed by Joe—to explain how England has found itself in its current sorry state. The music up to this point has been more atmospheric than rhythmic, but picks up steam as Joe expresses the tale of a twentieth-century working class Englander. Despite the disparity in musical arrangement, this is Joe at his most Cashian. Finally, the man slinks off as a spectral chorus sings and the narrator notes that "England was all alone."

As was often the case with the songs on *Sandinista!*, consensus was in short supply among reviewers. Ira Robbins thought the Side 1 closer "as original an effort as [the Clash] have ever attempted," whereas Nick Kent condemned the same song for reminding him of Jethro Tull.

"Rebel Waltz"

"I slept and I dreamed of a time long ago," begins Joe, literally recalling a dream he had. The title "Rebel Waltz" and the musical idiom misled some reviewers into thinking Joe was singing of the American Civil War and Confederate rebels and their lost cause. It is highly unlikely Joe was ever going to sing from the perspective of rebels fighting to maintain the status quo of slavery, however, especially on a song recorded at Wessex when the Clash were trying to inject some more English subject matter into the album, lest *Sandinista!* be lambasted, like *London Calling*, for sounding too American.

The key lyrical reference is "five armies were coming," which alludes to the battle of the five armies in Yorkshire during the English Civil War of the 1640s, as well as to the Clash's song of the same title on *Give 'Em Enough Rope*. This is a song about rebellion in England, and one of their most daring: a waltz mixed with Jamaican studio techniques.

"Let's Go Crazy"

The Clash often draw on their now impressive back catalogue on *Sandinista!*, and "Let's Go Crazy" is a steel drum–driven piece of calypso conjuring up that August day at the Notting Hill Carnival in 1976 that inspired "White Riot." Radio voices are a feature of Side 3, with a WBAI DJ speaking before "Lightning Strikes (Not Once but Twice)" and reggae musician Ansell Collins expressing his hope for peaceful times at the festival, which are not to come at the beginning of "Let's Go Crazy."

"Let's Go Crazy" could have been named "Black Riot," because Joe describes a festival bubbling with repressed emotion. "The lawful force" is present, armed with the "SUS" law, as young black men wait for nightfall to "settle the debt." And, sure enough, the song ends with a riot.

Recorded at Wessex shortly after Joe attended the 1980 Notting Hill Carnival, this is one of his best vocals on the album, his voice sounding entirely comfortable with the percussive Calypso rhythms. One of Joe's strongest traits as a vocalist was his ability to immerse his voice in rhythm. It's one reason why he mastered rap so quickly. And with his rough, unpolished voice riding musical rhythms, he could convey a wide range of ideas.

"The Sound of the Sinners"

So good that Elvis Costello expressed interest in cutting his own version, "The Sound of the Sinners" is one of Joe's most humorous turns on *Sandinista!* as he tackles organized religion. A punk take on gospel music with a ragged (and much criticized) chorus, its drug-addicted narrator has turned to religion only because he is "looking for that great jazz note that destroyed the walls of Jericho." For this sinner, Valium has replaced Moses's tablets of stone, and he even thought he was Jesus. In this way, "The Sound of the Sinners" is a more flippant take on "Hateful."

"The Call Up"

President Jimmy Carter had issued a proclamation on July 2, 1980, requiring men born in 1960 and thereafter to register with the Selective Service System. This was a perfect song topic for the band that sang of how "they're gonna have to introduce conscription" in "Career Opportunities" years earlier. Though not much changed in America as a result of this move by the executive branch, it was a matter of importance to the Clash's young male fans in 1980, which is why the band felt compelled to write "The Call Up." The message of the song is antimilitaristic, advising the band's American fans not to "heed the call up." The record label for the 45 version proclaims "NO DRAFT" and features an image of a young, distraught soldier sitting on the ground.

Recorded at Electric Lady in April 1980, the song is fleshed out by Voidoid guitarist Ivan Julian, whom the Clash knew from 1977's Get Out of Control Tour. Alarms are ringing and marines are performing drills as the band settles into a camouflaged ska rhythm and Joe wonders what the ulterior motives might be behind the call for young men to sign up for the draft. Is war imminent? What is Washington, D.C. planning? Gone are the histrionics of yore, as if the band are aiming for a more reasonable debate on the issue. Some of the images are among Joe's best: city fathers watch their children march off to war with "tears in their eyes," but for each young man "there is a rose that I want to live for."

Sandinista! may have had thirty-six tracks but few were pop-chart material. "Police on My Back" was the most obvious choice, but it may have been passed over because the song did not reflect the overall mood of the triple album. (Mick's interest in playing guitar is at an all-time low throughout.) "The Call Up" was not an obvious choice for the UK market, given the subject matter, but it was nonetheless issued on November 28, 1980, as the first single from *Sandinista!* It reached as high as #40—their worst-performing single to date. The accompanying video by Don Letts of the Clash in military gear did not help matters, although it eerily foretold their 1982 stage gear.

"Washington Bullets"

This song was begun by Topper in the haphazard style that the *Sandinista!* sessions are now known for, with the other members of the Clash turning up at Wessex after Topper had laid down a rhythm track and adding to what was to become the album's centerpiece. "Washington Bullets" is about the CIA's nefarious role in overthrowing Central and South American governments. The title is a clever pun on the then-current name of D.C.'s professional basketball team (changed to the Washington Wizards in 1997).

The opening lines are about a murder Joe nearly witnessed in Kingston, Jamaica, during the recording of "Junco Partner"; from there he recounts the role of the CIA in propping up the Chilean government and trying to overthrow Fidel Castro in Cuba. Not just a diatribe against American power, "Washington Bullets" praises President Jimmy Carter for not supporting Somoza in Nicaragua and allowing the revolutionary Sandinistas to defeat a dictator America had previously supported. "Human rights in America!" Joe sings gleefully.

As in "Guns on the Roof," Joe points out that the communists are no better than the capitalists. He sings of abuse of power by the Russians and Chinese in Afghanistan and Tibet respectively. And neither is the British government innocent: they have been selling weapons and ammunition to mercenaries.

After the band recorded "Washington Bullets," it was Mick's idea—not Joe's—to name the album *Sandinista!*

"Broadway"

During the *Sandinista!* sessions, the Clash took several stabs at jazz, including an unreleased version of Roger Miller's crossover hit "King of the Road" and

Mose Alison's "Look Here," but neither match up to "Broadway." Another title for this Clash original could have been "Something About America," because the subject matter is similar to "Something About England," only from an American perspective. "Broadway" finds Joe talking to a down-on-his-luck American—a former boxer—with no money and another day to get by. "It ain't my fault it's six o'clock in the morning," he says, in another one of those insightful lines only Joe could write.

Unlike the British pensioner caught up in a stolid class system, Americans of all stripes have the American dream. And so this man, eyeing cars picking up people in the rain, starts telling Joe of his dream, of how he always "wanted one of those cars / Long black and shiny and pull up to the bars." The tempo of the song picks up, conveying the man's increased pulse as he recalls his lost dreams. The horns swing, and Broadway gleams again. This song would have fit nicely on *London Calling*.

Appropriately enough, "Broadway" first cropped up in Clash sets at Bond International Casino in Times Square on June 4, 1981. It was regularly featured throughout the year and even performed at the London Lyceum as the band's opening number. It was also performed during the Far East tour of 1982.

"Charlie Don't Surf"

Ray Lowry writes in his retrospective of the Clash's Take the Fifth tour of seeing *Apocalypse Now!* in a Philadelphia movie theater. He does not identify whoever it was he attended the movie with, but if any of the Clash joined him, they were more impressed than he was with Francis Ford Coppola's ruminative take on America's role in the Vietnam War. "[It] doesn't leave you, it's like a dream," Joe informed *Sounds* readers during a February 1980 interview. The film most definitely affected the Clash's subsequent work. Acting on Pablo Picasso's famous maxim, the Clash stole the film title's exclamation point for their next album's title and Lieutenant Colonel Bill Kilgore's famous line about how "Charlie don't surf" for a song title on Side 5.

As innovative as *Sandinista!* is, it also often ties the Clash back to their earlier recordings. Vietnam War veterans returning home with drug addictions were mentioned in "I'm So Bored with the USA," so it was no surprise when the Clash returned to the conflict and examined the limits of American imperialism. Mick played guitar synthesizer elsewhere on *Sandinista!* but used it to best effect on "Charlie Don't Surf." During the intro he mimics the same choppy sound of a helicopter landing that begins *Apocalypse Now!* And by doing so, he lands the listener back in Vietnam.

"Charlie Don't Surf" has a relaxed sway, like surfers lying in the sun, and shares a mood with "The Call Up." In an unusual move, Joe and Mick share the vocals. The chorus reflects the view of the Americans, whereas the verses provide the Vietcong perspective.

"Charlie Don't Surf" opened a new stylistic branch of music for the Clash that you could almost call the "Amerasian blues" that Joe later sang of in "Straight to Hell." In that song—as well as "Sean Flynn"—the Clash merged elements of American and Asian music and explored the Vietnam era and its after-effects on both societies. Unlike rap and funk, which Mick was more interested in pursuing, Amerasian Blues was a better fit for the Clash's musical talents and Mick's production.

Side 6

Side 6 is best heard as a single recording rather than six individual tracks. Based on contemporary reviews, it was probably a wise decision to ditch the idea of a roots rock rebel type of Jamaican album, because with a Mikey Dread toaster ("Living in Fame"), two of the Clash's best dubs ("Version Pardner" and "Silicone on Sapphire"), and an instrumental based on "Police and Thieves" from the "Bankrobber" sessions ("Shepherd's Delight"), Side 6 was the side closest in execution to the band's original intent for their follow-up to *London Calling*. It was also the side journalists took most joy in lambasting, generally only writing kind words about a poppy version of "Career Opportunities" featuring the signing talent of Mickey Gallagher's sons—the side's weakest track and the album's lamest joke. (Each boy was paid with a boom box.)

The criticism was undeserved and cruel. Ira Robbins of *Trouser Press* fame was generally sympathetic to the Clash, but—admitting his distaste for dub and believing it required "little skill"—he wondered in his *Sandinista!* review whether "American Clash fans (like those who were dragged in by 'Train in Vain') are ready for this aspect of reggae." It was not very open-minded, but sadly this was a common view among journalists whose role in society was supposedly to open ears and hearts to risk-taking bands like the Clash.

Side 6 is the most original and daring side in the Clash's discography and deserved platitudes not condemnation. Like many American Clash fans, I played Side 6 the most. Stitching the songs together with snatches of verse (the bit about how "I never went to Paris" sounds like a mockery of Ian Curtis and Joy Division) and jokes ("Have you ever wondered who holds the key that winds up Big Ben?") courtesy of Darts vocalist Dan Hegarty, the only comparison is to Side 2 of *Black Market Clash*, a similarly dub centric side; its relatively well-received success perhaps persuaded the Clash to see if lightning could strike twice.

Guest Musicians

If you consider the barking of Topper's dog Battersea on "Somebody Got Murdered" a performance, there are twenty-four contributors to *Sandinista!*, in addition to the Clash. And this doesn't include several unnamed members of Roots Radics, whose performances are heard on "Junco Partner" and "Version Pardner." More musicians guest on *Sandinista!* than on all the other Clash recordings combined.

Mikey Dread was the only holdover from the aborted Channel One Studio session. While Mick and Joe handled bass duties at the Power Station in Paul's absence, Mickey Gallagher's fellow Blockhead Norman Watt-Roy was brought over to help fill the gap during the Electric Lady sessions. Gallagher and Watt-Roy were joined by New Yorker Ivan Julian and Joe's busking mentor, Tymon Dogg. Even more players joined in the Wessex sessions, including three steel-drum percussionists and the various friends who contributed to the vocal choruses heard on "Something About England," "The Sound of the Sinners," and "The Call Up."

Norman Watt-Roy

When Paul returned from his acting gig, almost half of *Sandinista!*'s songs were already recorded. He overdubbed some of the basslines laid down by Mick, Joe, or Topper, but refrained from attempting those put down on tape by Watt-Roy, who was by far the more technically proficient bassist.

Norman Watt-Roy was born in Bombay, India, on February 15, 1951, and moved with his family to north London four years later. He began playing guitar at the age of eleven, and by the time he was sixteen he had already recorded a single for Phillips Records with his band the Living Daylights, his brother Garth by his side. Watt-Roy had moved over to the bass guitar by this time. The Watt-Roys' next band, the Greatest Band on Earth, recorded three albums before the brothers parted professionally.

Watt-Roy found commercial success in a roundabout way. While leading the Loving Awareness Band, he and his bandmates were asked to serve as backup musicians on an album vocalist Ian Dury was recording for the upstart record label Stiff. (Watt-Roy's trademark note-laden bassline for Dury's hit single "Hit Me with Your Rhythm Stick" would be a highlight of Dury's album *New Boots and Panties.*) Dury was more pub rock than punk, but he got lumped with the latter movement due to serendipitous timing. When Stiff Records released the first British punk record—the Damned's "New Rose"—other Stiff artists such as Nick Lowe, Elvis Costello, and Ian Dury were marketed as having punk stripes, and Stiff cashed in on the music's notoriety by staging the infamous Live Stiffs tour in late 1977. Once again, Dury needed a backup band, and suddenly Watt-Roy found himself a member of the Blockheads. His tenure with the band would extend beyond Dury's death from cancer in 2000.

When fellow Blockhead Mickey Gallagher arrived in New York City on Easter Monday (April 7, 1980) to participate in sessions for the Clash's next album, Watt-Roy accompanied him. They spent the next five days ensconced in Electric Lady. It was during this phase of recording that Watt-Roy laid down basslines for "Ivan Meets G.I. Joe," "Look Here," "The Call Up," "Hitsville UK," "Charlie Don't Surf," "Stop the World," and the two rap numbers "The Magnificent Seven" and "Lightning Strikes (Not Once but Twice)."

Although he was not credited for his songwriting contributions on *Sandinista!*, Watt-Roy willingly flew to Germany in 1984 at Bernie Rhodes's behest and laid down basslines for the *Cut the Crap* sessions. By then, Watt-Roy was in demand as a session bassist; he would go on to record and/or appear with Wilko Johnson, Nick Lowe, Rachel Sweet, Frankie Goes to Hollywood (he created the memorable bassline for their mega-hit "Relax"), and Nick Cave. His bass of choice is a Fender Jazz.

In 2013, Watt-Roy released his first solo album, *Faith & Grace*, which incorporates many of the famous basslines he could not copyright, including one the Clash made famous. As he told interviewer Pete Feenster, "I saw Mick Jones from the Clash a couple of weeks ago and told him I'd recorded 'The Magnificent Seven' riff on one of my songs on the album, and he said, 'Well, it's your riff!'"

Tymon Dogg

Of all the guest vocalists on *Sandinista!*, the most unexpected was Tymon Dogg leading off Side 5 with "Lose This Skin." The Electric Lady sessions occurred just as Transit Workers Union Local 100—all 34,000 of them—walked off the job on April 1, 1980, and for just the second time in its history crippled New York City. Joe mentions this when he begins the third verse of "Lightning Strikes (Not Once but Twice)" with "accidental hike in the transit strike." Accidental hike could also describe Mick walking home from a recording session because of the strike and bumping into Tymon Dogg, Joe's busking mentor. Invited to the Gramercy Park Hotel where Mick was staying, they later made their way uptown to the Iroquois Hotel on 44th Street. Joe and Topper had booked rooms there because an aspiring and penniless James Dean had lived there between 1951 and 1953. It is alleged that the members of the Clash did not know Dean's eighth-floor room number, so they switched rooms every few days to be sure that they had stayed in Dean's former room, which is now known to be room 803. When Dogg walked in and surprised his former bottler, they had not crossed paths since Joe's earliest days with the Clash.

Dogg was asked to attend the Electric Lady sessions where Joe, Mick, and Topper—accompanied by newly arrived Blockheads Mickey Gallagher and Norman Watt-Roy—supported him on "Lose This Skin," one of the best-received of the songs sang by non-Clash members on *Sandinista!*—including by director Martin Scorsese. The New York City–based director (who was to cast the Clash as extras in *The King of Comedy* and use music from *The Clash* on his soundtrack for *Bringing Out the Dead*) still remembers the first time he heard the song. "It was in New York," he is quoted as saying on www.tymondogg.com. "I had speakers the size of a wall . . . [the Clash] came into my apartment and shoved a tape into my machine. It was 'Lose This Skin' . . . suddenly thunder and lightning erupted . . . it was one of those great moments . . . all the forces came down into that room."

Dogg also played violin on "Lightning Strikes (Not Once but Twice)." That was the extent of Dogg's involvement during the Electric Lady sessions, but later that summer he resurfaced in London and overdubbed violin on "The Equaliser," "Mensforth Hill," and "Something About England," as well as playing keyboards on "The Sound of the Sinners."

Dogg returned and played piano on *Combat Rock*'s "Death Is a Star," and then, in 1983, flush with cash from his recent successes, Joe hired producer

Glyn Johns to man sessions for a Tymon Dogg solo album that was to be called *Hollowed Out.* The sessions were abandoned by Dogg, to Strummer's disappointment. Another fifteen years passed before Strummer and Dogg worked together again. After being reunited at a memorial service for 101'ers bassist "Mole" Chesterton in 1998, Dogg eventually joined Joe as one of the Mescaleros. Dogg was featured on *Global a Go-Go,* arguably Joe's finest album without the Clash. Though Dogg was inexplicably marginalized by the other surviving Mescaleros on *Streetcore,* his 2015 solo album *Made of Light* contains "A Pound of Grain," a song in the *Meat Is Murder* vein that Joe had planned to write lyrics for. It has also been rumored that Joe's *Hollowed Out* will one day be released.

"Lose This Skin" was never performed live by the Clash, but during his five-night residency at St. Anne's Warehouse in Brooklyn in early April 2002, Joe announced it was the anniversary of the recording of Dogg's composition, prompting Joe and the Mescaleros to perform a spirited version that is readily available on bootlegs.

Ellen Foley

To the general public, Ellen Foley is best known for her duet with Meat Loaf on "Paradise by the Dashboard Light," which despite only reaching #31 on the *Billboard* charts is part of the classic rock canon in America. To Clash fans, Ellen Foley is best known for her early-'80s relationship with Mick, which accounts for her appearance on *Sandinista!* In addition to singing on "Corner Soul" and the unreleased outtake "Blonde Rock and Roll," Foley is a featured vocalist on the Motown-influenced "Hitsville UK," the album's second single, which was not as commercially successful as "Paradise by the Dashboard Light."

Foley's notable vocal on the Meat Loaf hit led to her contract with Epic Records. Her debut 1979 album, *Night Out,* was produced by Mick's heroes Ian Hunter and Mick Ronson. Despite good reviews, however, it failed to chart. A year later, she became romantically involved with Mick, who produced her second album, *The Spirit of St. Louis* (named for the plane American aviator Charles Lindbergh flew on his legendary solo nonstop flight over the Atlantic Ocean, and also for the fact that Foley was born in St. Louis, Missouri).

The Spirit of St. Louis is essentially a Clash recording. Joe and Mick co-wrote half of the album's twelve songs, and the Clash are the only musicians on the album, with the exception of violinist Tymon Dogg, who also wrote

Ellen Foley's *Spirit of St. Louis* features six Strummer/Jones compositions, the last recording to do so until B.A.D.'s *No. 10, Upping Street.* *Author's collection*

three songs. Mick was the "boyfriend" cited as the producer, aided by the Clash's production team of Bill Price and Jeremy Green. Pennie Smith even took the cover photograph. Knowing all this, however, you'd be hard pressed to believe the backing band is the Clash, except for on "In the Killing Hour," the closing track.

Clocking in at 44:03, it is an uneven album marred by an attempt to make Foley sound like Kate Bush, but has its moments. Both "The Shuttered Palace" and "Theatre or Cruelty" hint at Joe's future work on the Spanish-themed *Walker.* "M.P.H." and "Phases of Travel" are solid mid-tempo rockers. The 1980 Dali exhibition in London must have been the impetus for "The Death of the Psychoanalyst of Salvador Dali," and the song would have fit nicely on *Sandinista!* The 2007 reissue contains three bonus tracks, including a French version of "The Shuttered Palace" and the racy "Black Boys," which unfortunately is only 1:15 in length. It's better than everything else on *The Spirit of St. Louis.*

Mick's relationship with New York City–based Foley meant he was spending more time apart from his Clash bandmates and accounts for his comprehension that the Clash's latest music was being well received, unlike Londoners Joe and Paul, who were in a defensive mode because of the weekly attacks they read in the British music press. This accounts for Mick's confidence in thinking that the Clash's eventual follow-up to *Sandinista!* could be a double album. Joe criticized Mick's sixty-five-minute mix as being "a home movie mix" and insisted it be trimmed to a single album. The issued version included Foley's backing vocal on "Car Jamming," her final contribution to the Clash's discography. It has also been speculated (without much evidence) that "Should I Stay or Should I Go" is about Mick's fraying relationship with Foley.

"They Said We'd Be Artistically Free"

Tallying up the tracks recorded over the course of 1980 and the Clash's dispute with CBS Records, it was Mick who first suggested *Sandinista!* be a triple album, even though triple albums of entirely original music are a rarity in the music industry. They are normally reserved for live recordings or greatest hits collections of well-established recording artists or labels. Only a few artists, such as George Harrison (*All Things Must Pass*) and Frank Sinatra (*Trilogy: Past Present Future*, which contains a version of Harrison's "Something"), had attempted this before the Clash. Harrison and Sinatra, however, had founded the record labels on which their triple albums were released (Apple and Reprise respectively), which makes the Clash's request even more audacious.

CBS was against the idea. As Joe explained in a 1994 interview with Chris Salewicz for *MOJO*, "They wanted to kill it off. It wasn't because of the subject matter. They were more worried that Bruce Springsteen had caught the same fever—he'd just released *The River.* They didn't want it to catch on, giving fans three LPs for the price of one. But [*Sandinista!*] was only meant as a fans' record. It was too weighty to be more than a fans' album. I think we knew that it would never sell huge quantities. We were just interested in the music. It just got out of hand when we were making it."

CBS suggested releasing the contents as three separate products over the course of a year, but the Clash rightly dug their heels in. Many of the thirty-six songs on *Sandinista!* only work as part of a whole. In the end, the Clash forfeited their record royalties on the first 180,000 or 200,000 (accounts vary) copies sold in the UK and agreed to let the album only count as one of the ten the Clash owed the label according to the terms of their contract. The battle won, *Sandinista!* sold for £5.00 in England and $9.98 in the United States.

"The People Must Have Something Good to Read on a Sunday"

Reviews in America were generally more favorable than in Britain, although Van Gosse in the *Village Voice* called Joe a "political peabrain" for romanticizing "the Nicaraguan guerrillas who overthrew A. Somoza."

Meanwhile on the other side of the Atlantic, *NME*'s Nick Kent dismayed the Clash camp by writing that "Strummer's singing on much of this new stuff is simply duff, because his fractured range is only truly effective when it's up front in the mix and allied to angry passions. When he's attempting to widen his powers of vocal interpretation, things sound perplexingly awry."

Still, the reaction of most music journalists to the Clash's triple album was baffling. The same critics who wrote rhapsodically about one day having hours and hours of Dylan's complete *Basement Tapes* to listen to or hearing the twenty or so unreleased songs from the Rolling Stones' *Some Girls* sessions were somehow offended by an album that was 144 minutes long. This wasn't the proper length of an album, they implied—it was the length of a movie. Just about every review cited this as a critical flaw. A few noted the generosity of releasing three long players at a reduced price, but they also suspected that Clash fans would never sit through all six sides.

They were wrong. Many fans did exactly that. There were two reasons for this. Firstly, when it was released on December 1980, *Sandinista!* provided consolation in the wake of John Lennon's unexpected murder for fans desperate to lose their depression in new music. Simon Firth wrote of this in *New York Rocker* in March 1981, adding that without Lennon, *Sandinista!* would not have been possible, because to Lennon "rock & roll was a form of expression in which anything could be said."

Secondly, as Mick says in *The Clash*, "You didn't have to listen to it in one go, you could dip in and out. Like a big book." (It has been compared to James Joyce's *Ulysses.*) Too often, music fans are considered by the industry to have short attention spans, but if you enjoyed the Clash's music, listening to 144 minutes and 29 seconds of music was a pleasant way to wait for their next release.

It must be noted that *Sandinista!* topped the *Village Voice*'s 1981 "Pazz & Jop Critics Poll" when, after being picked by 67 music critics, it totaled 862 points. X's *Wild Gift* and Elvis Costello and the Attractions' *Trust* placed second and third respectively with 790 and 784 points.

And in May 1981, as the Clash's Bond's residency was about to unfold, Debra Rae Cohen in the *New York Times* gave *Sandinista!* the type of summation it deserved: "The album's initially daunting two-hour sprawl turns out to be structured with both passion and purpose, skillfully paced to provide—like a live performance—breathing-spaces, humor, and moments for reflection, as well as high-energy barrages. While much of the music is a far cry from the Clash's original two-minute skirmishes, the record fulfills the promise of those early songs, extending their struggle by universalizing it."

Over the ensuing decades, as fan appreciation grew, so did the album's reputation. *Sandinista!* was ranked #407—even higher than Harrison's *All Things Must Pass*—in *Rolling Stone*'s "500 Greatest Albums of All Time." *Sandinista!* paved the way for a cross-pollination of global music and acceptance for subsequent musical endeavors such as Peter Gabriel's *So*, Paul Simon's *Graceland*, and Asian Dub Foundation's *Rafi's Revenge*.

Joe's opinion of *Sandinista!* would also shift over the years.

Interviewed by *Creem* in 1984, he said, "What's wrong with *Sandinista!* was that there was too much to give every track a good mix. It was brave to try, but unsatisfying in the end."

However, answering a question on conflict between art and commerce fifteen years later, he told *Punk*'s Judy McGuire, "Now you're talking to a man who forewent royalties on *Sandinista!* so . . . I took it in the neck for the sake of art and I wouldn't change a thing now."

Decades later, the only criticism of *Sandinista!* that stands up is that it has the Clash's worst album cover, a point that even photographer Pennie Smith supports. In 2010, she told *Uncut*, "I have to say no, I'm not happy with that shot. Tops had failed to bring the right clothes so they all just dressed him up—how he ended up in an artist's cap and smock, I don't know."

20

This Struggle Could Be Won

The Bond's Residency

You have to look no further than Epic Records' refusal to bankroll the 1980 tour of America the Clash proposed to get the picture: record company executives had concluded that *Sandinista!* floundering and not selling was in their best business interests. Triple albums left little margin for profit, and they did not want a successful Clash tour ramping up sales.

NME's Mick Farren originally reported the proposed length of the tour being thirty-two cities in thirty-four days, but subsequent biographies suggest that a sixty-date tour had been proposed. The former seems more likely. It's true the Clash at this point seemed determined to tour America and get themselves out of debt to CBS, their "company store" (as Tennessee Ernie Ford sings in "Sixteen Tons," the song played as the Clash took the stage on their 16 Tons tour) but sixty dates far exceeded the twenty or so shows (the exact number is unknown) they performed in North America in September and October 1979.

It has also been theorized that Epic Records objected to the reinstatement of Bernie Rhodes as the band's manager, and that this is why the label kiboshed the extended tour. If this is true, Epic's plan backfired, because, while Bernie did far more harm than good during his second tenure, it was his suggestion that the Clash play a "residency" in New York City: eight dates between May 28 and June 3, 1980, at Bond International Casino, a Times Square discotheque Bernie and Kosmo had scouted during a visit to the city in February. As Joe told New York City reporters at the first press conference before the shit hit the fans, "It's like the fans are going on tour instead of us, the mountain's coming to Mohammed."

May 28, 1980

In 1994, Chris Salewicz reported in a *Mojo* article that while the Clash played New York City for what would become two and a half weeks, "the temperature never dropped below 90 degrees" and "the temperature had risen again, to just over 100 degrees, on the Thursday night the Clash opened at Bond's." Salewicz is a fount of knowledge on everything Clash and wrote the best biography on Joe, but I wondered about this statement the first time I read it. If this was so, what was I doing wearing my leather jacket opening night? Memorial Day was the previous Monday, and I don't remember it being balmy, or what I used to call "Jones Beach weather." True, it was past 11:45 p.m. (a friend who worked at *New York Rocker* had assured me the word was the Clash were not going on before midnight) and raining lightly in deserted Times Square as I walked past hookers huddled in doorways, but if it had been 100 degrees, I would've been wearing just a Patti Smith T-shirt. (Cardinal rule: never wear the T-shirt of the band you're seeing in concert.) So I pored over old microfilm at the New York City Library, and the high for May 28 had been 77 degrees, with a mean temperature of 72. In fact, it was unseasonably cool for the Clash's entire run at Bond's; the temperature never exceeded the 85 degrees reached on four days and usually the mean temperature for the day was in the seventies.

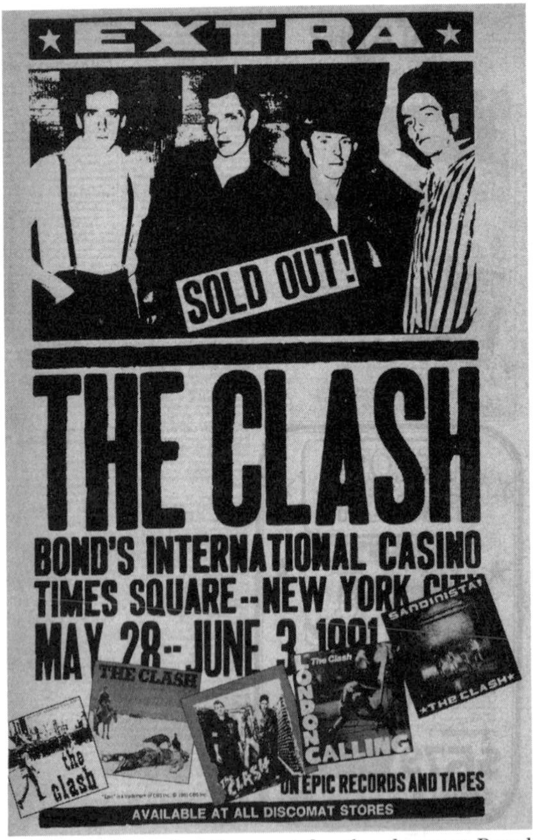

A *Village Voice* advertisement for the shows at Bond International Casino that ran the very week the Clash took Manhattan. *Author's collection*

Anyway, at 44th Street and Broadway, I passed some scalpers. "Clash tickets. Who needs Clash tickets?" I didn't, but imagine my surprise when I couldn't get in . . . even with a ticket that said "THE CLASH INVASION" (an obvious play on Adam Ant's

Ant Invasion of New York City the previous month). I was forced to get in line and wait . . . even if the Clash were soon to be taking the stage. I glanced around Times Square and a neon clock told me it was 12:04. After a few minutes the impatient line began chanting, "HEY HO! LET'S GO!" I remember thinking to myself, "That's the wrong chant." We weren't there to see the Ramones. We should've been chanting, "I WANNA RIOT! A RIOT OF OUR OWN!"

Rumor had it that we were being kept standing outside in the rain because the venue had oversold tickets and fire inspectors were inside, assessing whether or not the size of the crowd inside constituted a hazard. Rumor also had it that those standing at the head of the line had been waiting for over an hour. The rain began pouring and umbrellas sprouted like nocturnal flowers. I didn't have one, so I stood there dripping patiently, listening and watching as the line's impatience bloomed into anger. When the Bond's doors opened after hands continually banged on it amid a revival of the Ramones's chant, cries for the manager ensued, and someone shouted "I'm mad as hell and I'm not going to take it anymore!" to laughter. Some members of the crowd began demanding an explanation and cursing the tight-lipped, Mafioso-looking bouncers. It seemed like we'd never get in. Someone said it was 12:25. "The Clash have to be on already," I thought.

Suddenly—miraculously—the line, numbering no more than seventy wet fans, entered the ticket booth foyer where twenty-eight days earlier I had purchased tickets to all eight scheduled shows after spending the night on 45th Street. Our joy, however, was short-lived. We now came up against another row of doors. These were glass, not black metal, but they were doors nonetheless. Shoves and shouts filled the air as the frantic bouncers tried to get a grip on the glass doors so they could shut them. I was really worried that somehow those doors might get smashed and people cut and trampled. I was pissed off at the Bond's management, but they had made their first mistake: we were in, and now there was no stopping us.

I heard a megaphoned voice explaining how New York City Fire Department officials had closed Bond's down for the evening and no one further would be admitted: all tickets would either be refunded or good for another performance. That was the statement that broke the venue's back. It's never been written about, but a group of us fought our way in. It began when some punks pushed their way forward, cursed and argued with the bouncers, and then charged at them. They weren't getting through, and I thought the attempt would fail, but then I saw a couple of guys get in through an unguarded door to my left, not the one that was three feet away from me. "It's now or never," I thought. The chain of bouncers was weak. I pushed, as did others, and somehow I found myself inside.

I ran ten feet or so before I confronted a bouncer winding up a punch. I swerved and avoided most of his fist's impact, but it had been hard enough to send my glasses flying. Another frantic fan ran into him, causing some distraction and giving me time to find my glasses, gleaming faintly by a wall. They weren't damaged in any way. I started running up the stairs leading to the upstairs ballroom, where I could hear the Clash playing "Complete Control," when another bouncer yelled at me, "Where do you think you're going?"

"I've got a ticket," I said firmly, showing it to him briefly and not waiting for his response. I felt justified. I had stood all night in line to buy my ticket and I had every right to be inside Bond's, watching my favorite band. I ran faster, hurried up the curving staircase, jumped over and swerved between bodies in the upstairs foyer until I reached the ballroom. It was packed but I moved forward fairly easily. I sang along, danced, and lit a joint. I felt like I was being reunited with some of my best college friends.

I was surprised only the four of them were onstage. I was sure that Mickey Gallagher would be there, especially since the Clash were supposedly playing much of *Sandinista!* And they did. The next song was "Ivan Meets G.I. Joe," with Topper singing. The sound system inside Bond's was terrible, and the Clash seemed to be struggling as they played "The Leader" and "Charlie Don't Surf" to a slideshow backdrop. It was like watching a heavyweight champion having a bad fight—like Muhammad Ali boxing Ken Norton. The timing was off, the reflexes slow. Maybe it was the London Reggae that had seeped into their entire set. They were avoiding songs that dealt with British subjects, instead playing their American songs, like "The Call Up," "One More Time," and "I'm So Bored with the USA," which ended their second encore. They had played for two hours, but only when they played songs like "Career Opportunities" and "Janie Jones," their punk stuff, did they reaffirm themselves as the Greatest Rock 'n' Roll Band in the World.

As they played an apparently impromptu coda of "I'm So Bored with the USA," I stopped dancing and stared at the stage. Most of the crowd—myself included—had been teased and tricked by the false ending. Almost everybody was dancing, and my feet were moving again. The Clash never ran out of tricks, even on a night when two of them—Joe and Paul—were sleeveless. It was wild and weird, inspiring and puzzling, listening to the crowd sing along with the chorus. At the closing chords, Joe thanked New York City, and the Clash disappeared backstage.

Canceled Shows and the Riot in Times Square

According to the *Daily News* reporter Vincent Lee, "Deputy Fire Chief Elmer Chapman said he received a call early Thursday evening complaining about the crowding in the disco at 1526 Broadway." The question is: who made that phone call? Was it the police? Was it a concerned citizen? Or was it a rival rock-club owner worried about a week of low attendance at his club due to the Clash's residency? All signs pointed to the latter. Heat, Hurrah's, and the Rock Lounge had all recently closed and as the *Village Voice*'s Michael Hill reported, the Clash had "stepped into the guerilla warfare of the Manhattan club scene."

Bernie Rhodes later told the *Face's* Chris Salewicz, "It was definitely a set-up job. I've done a bit of research and I know who tipped off the Fire Department to visit the show. It was definitely down to club wars. People didn't want a specific club to have the Clash for a week and tie up the scene in this city. But so many of the clubs in New York are run by gangsters and the city's run by conservatives, and we've just been trying to operate in the middle area between the two."

Club manager Joel Heller appeared in court and apologized for the overcrowding, and the New York City Fire Department's order was rescinded for the second show on May 29, but only if maximum occupancy restrictions for the former men's department store were observed, and so admission was limited to the first 1,725 with Ticketron tickets. Then the City Department of Buildings got involved, and both shows scheduled for May 30 were canceled, resulting in the first riot in Times Square since over 30,000 bobbysoxers rioted outside a Frank Sinatra concert at the Paramount Theatre on Columbus Day, 1944.

Suddenly the Clash were on all of the local news programs and written up in the newspapers. Radio station WNEW-FM even sent a reporter down to Bond's to track the story. As Larry Sutton of the *Daily News* reported, "Armed with bullhorns, Bond employees told a crowd of about 1,000 waiting on line for yesterday's 2 p.m. show that the performance was postponed until June 13. That angered many, who chanted obscenities and stayed near the building until police dispersed them about twenty minutes later." Mounted police were called in and one woman was arrested.

According to the *New York Times*' Robert Palmer, writing on June 3, "After the club complied with building inspectors by installing fire-exit signs and making other minor alterations, [Bond's] was allowed to reopen—on the condition that audiences not exceed the legal limit." To ensure everyone who purchased a ticket got to see them, the Clash added nine further shows, for a total of seventeen. The originally scheduled shows would be limited to fans with Ticketron tickets, on the assumption they were bought by out-of-town fans whereas those with tickets bought at the Bond's ticket office were presumably tri-state area residents. Mick joked at the press conference announcing the rescheduled dates that "we hope that the hairdressers' union won't come in here tomorrow and shut us down."

"For those of you who had to wait on line for hours and days, well, you're here now . . . so let's get on with it," Joe said, as the band struck up "London Calling" and shows resumed on Sunday evening.

Bond International Casino

Ever wonder what the Bond International Casino looked like?

At the southeast corner of 45th Street and Broadway was the Xanadu clothing store. Next door were the four black metal doors of Bond's (when it was not gated), then the Criterion Center (a six-screen Cineplex where films such as *Outland* and *This Is Elvis* were playing while the Clash were in town), and then an assortment of cheap clothing and electronic stores. Above Xanadu and the Bond's entrance was "BOND," a large orange neon sign, the only holdover from Bond Clothing Store that had been a staple of Times Square between the late 1940s until 1977. In the center of the letter "O" was a neon clock. Before it became a clothing store, the site had been occupied by an international casino in the 1930s, hence the discotheque's name, which nobody ever used. New Yorkers called it "Bond's," and the Clash shows there came to be known as the Bond's residency.

The price of admission to Bond's for the Clash shows was $10. Doors opened at 8:00 p.m. After passing through one of four black, narrow metal doors—each with "BOND" in gold lettering above them—and the box-office foyer, you found yourself in the lobby, where there was a T-shirt stall and the Committee in Solidarity with the People of El Salvador stall distributing leftist leaflets warning young Americans about Ronald Reagan's planned invasion. More notable was a wide, curving musical staircase, and each white step emitted the sound of the black musical note painted on it. At the top of the staircase there was a bar, some seating, and beer and burger

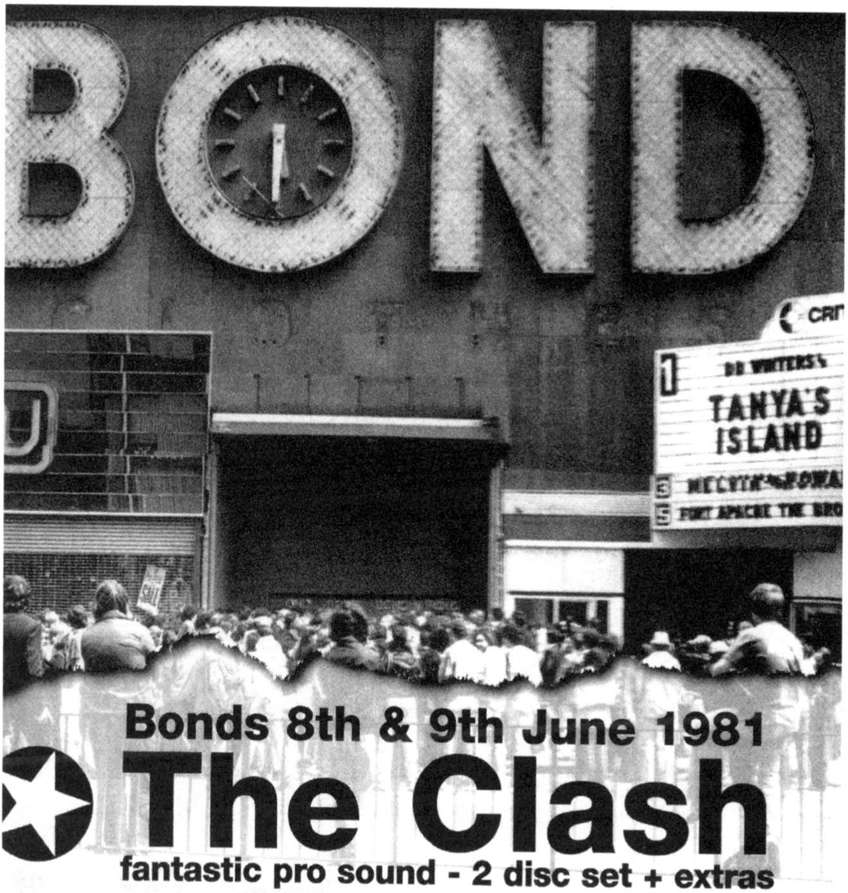

BOND
TANYA'S
ISLAND
Bonds 8th & 9th June 1981
The Clash
fantastic pro sound - 2 disc set + extras

All seventeen shows at Bond International Casino were recorded and bootlegged. This bootleg cover shows the crowd outside Bond's on May 30 when the matinee show was canceled.
Author's collection

stands. The beer was served in plastic cups—a precaution prompted by all the beer bottles thrown and broken when fans rioted at PiL's Ritz concert a few weeks earlier.

Slightly to the right at the top of the staircase were four side-by-side double doorways leading to the disco's futuristic ballroom. When the disco first opened, it had Liberace's fountains from the set of his television show, but they had since been replaced by a concert stage. Paul's girlfriend, Pearl Harbor, was spinning records. She was the DJ for all seventeen shows, and she mostly played rockabilly. I remember hearing Bobby Fuller, Chuck Berry, the Jackson Five, the Cramps, and Elvis Presley. (Pearl Harbor has said she played reggae, but I don't recall that.) This was much to the chagrin of the club's owners, who blamed her song selection for fans not lingering and dancing and running up bar tabs after the Clash performed. The venue's regular DJs also resented her doing their job and allegedly spiked her drink with LSD one night, resulting in a visit to Bellevue Hospital.

The Opening Acts

Clash concerts always had two opening acts. The idea was to give fans more show for the money, and also to help other new acts get noticed. This is why the first act was usually a band local to whatever city they were in. During the first two tours of America, they made sure the band that went on just before them was an R&B hero they admired, such as Bo Diddley, Lee Dorsey, or Screamin' Jay Hawkins. They did this while still insisting ticket prices be kept affordable. (The list of significant bands that the Clash aided over the years included the Jam, Buzzcocks, the Slits, the Cramps, the Undertones, the Specials, and the Pogues.)

The Clash stuck to this format during the Bond's residency. The first act went on at 10:00 p.m. and the second at 11:00. The plan for every show to highlight an American act and an English or Jamaican act went awry when several British bands couldn't get visas to enter the USA. Instead, on the first night (May 28, 1980), two American acts—Grandmaster Flash and the Furious Five and the Sirens—were the support. According to the *Village Voice*'s Michael Hill, "Grandmaster Flash opened his set with a live rendering of 'The Adventures of Grandmaster Flash on the Wheels of Steel,' mixing brief breaks from Chic's 'Good Times,' Blondie's 'Rapture,' and Queen's 'Another One Bites the Dust' into jagged rhythm cut-ups . . . at first the audience seemed bewildered by this single black man using nothing but two record players." When the Furious Five joined the Grandmaster and started rapping, they were pelted with empty plastic cups and coins. They left the stage after fifteen minutes, saying, "We've played a lot of places to a lot of faces, but we've never seen shit like this." Other acts such as ESG and Lee "Scratch" Perry received similarly disrespectful treatment.

"It's disgusting, it's so fucking narrow-minded. I mean, it's an insult to us when you look at it," Mick complained to *NME*'s Mick Farren. "We picked the bands that opened for us, so, supposedly we liked them and we wanted to turn the crowd onto something."

The brave opening acts for the first week of shows were:

- May 29, 1981: ESG; Grandmaster Flash and the Furious Five
- May 31, 1981: Funkapolitan; the Slits

- June 1, 1981: (unknown)
- June 2, 1981: Bad Brains; the Slits
- June 3, 1981: the Senders; the Treacherous Three
- June 4, 1981: the Bloods; the Bush Tetras
- June 5, 1981: Unidentified foursome (four young women singing *a capella*); Lee "Scratch" Perry
- June 6, 1981 (matinee): the Brattles; Funkapolitan

Little is known of who appeared at the evening performance on June 6 or the shows that followed. The Fall were definitely the second act on June 9. Bassist Steve Hanley speaks about this performance at some length in *The Big Midweek*, his memoir of life in the Fall. I remember walking in as their set was beginning. They were remarkable, sounding very similar to the live performances released in 1982 on Cottage Records' *A Part of America Therein, 1981.*

On June 13, the Rockats and the Dead Kennedys played the matinee. Elsewhere, the Dead Kennedys have been mentioned as being an opening band for the evening show, but this is not possible as I was present, knew the DKs quite well, and certainly did not see them that evening. I do remember the Rockats, a rockabilly band, playing one of the evening shows, possibly on June 13.

Though the dates of their performances are lost to time, other confirmed opening acts were, in alphabetical order: the Blades, Joe Ely, KRAUT (in fact, this was the hardcore punk band's debut performance, as they had only formed weeks earlier), Miller Miller Miller & Sloan (who according to Jonathan Lethem played "Aretha Franklin covers and disco-y funk"), the Nitecaps, those rapping innovators the Sugarhill Gang, and the Waitresses.

The Bond's Gear

For each show, the Clash walked onstage to Ennio Morricone's "Sixty Seconds to What?," the title theme to Sergio Leone's *For a Few Dollars More*, the spaghetti western starring Clint Eastwood. The stage would be bathed in a dark red light with a black curtain backdrop, which suggested that they were walking onto the *Sandinista!* album cover. The first thing you noticed if you had been up front at previous Clash concerts was that Joe had had his teeth fixed and capped.

The Clash were wearing new clothing designed for the Bond's residency. Joe wore an unbuttoned sleeveless vest (in red, white, or turquoise) that revealed a Clash T-shirt resembling the type of emblem found on

One week later, this advertisement ran in the *Village Voice*, indicating nine hastily added shows. *Author's collection*

US Air Force planes. It was a large white star against a red circle and red-and-white stripes with the Clash in black lettering over the white star. T-shirt seller Ned Flood has commented in an online post that he personally gave the shirt to Joe and watched as the Clash front man "cut the sleeves off with a switch blade." This marked the beginning of Joe wearing Clash T-shirts in concert. He also wore the "'CLASH' IN TIMES SQUARE" T-shirt that replicated a bogus "EXTRA" edition of the *New York Post*. Joe usually wore red or white pants.

Paul was typically all in black. His shirt was also sleeveless (and often unbuttoned) and his pants leather. On occasion his pants were white. Mick sometimes wore suits but more often than not he retained his look from the time of the 16 Tons tour. Topper often performed without a shirt. His drum riser had rows of black and yellow diagonal lines.

The Standard Bond's Set

It wasn't until the seventh show that the standard nineteen-song set in Bond's hardened:

1. "London Calling"
2. "Safe European Home"
3. "The Leader"
4. "Train in Vain"
5. "(White Man) In Hammersmith Palais"

6. "This Is Radio Clash"
7. "Spanish Bombs"
8. "The Guns of Brixton"
9. "The Call Up"
10. "Bankrobber"
11. "Complete Control"
12. "Lightning Strikes (Not Once but Twice)"
13. "Ivan Meets G.I. Joe"
14. "Charlie Don't Surf"
15. "The Magnificent Seven"
16. "Broadway"
17. "Somebody Got Murdered"
18. "Police and Thieves"
19. "Clampdown"

It was nearly a year since the end of the 16 Tons tour, and the set list had been completely revamped. "London Calling" had finally risen to its rightful spot as the set opener. Thirteen of the songs were from *London Calling* and *Sandinista!*, with only one song each from the debut and sophomore albums, plus four non-album singles, although "This Is Radio Clash" would not be released until almost six months later in the UK. American fans were flabbergasted to hear the Clash play a new, unreleased song. We were unaware of the April recording session for the next single. A new song, when they had just released thirty-six of them on *Sandinista!*, was a true surprise.

The earliest sets at Bond's switched "Train in Vain" and "Somebody Got Murdered"; "Junco Partner" was dropped for "Corner Soul," which in turn was dropped for "Spanish Bombs"; "Wrong 'Em Boyo" was dropped in favor of "Broadway"; and "Career Opportunities" was replaced by "Police and Thieves" as the penultimate song in the set.

There was also a slideshow, which the *Village Voice* found fault with. The slides of "a rioting crowd during 'Guns of Brixton,' lurid newspaper headlines during 'The Leader,' familiar scenes of Vietnam during 'Charlie Don't Surf'—have all the impact of a *Combat* rerun."

The Clash also had—as Joe explained at their June 9 show, which was broadcast on FM radio—"a new toy by the kit here." It was a pair of computerized drums that Mick enjoyed striking with a drumstick during performances of "This Is Radio Clash," "The Call Up," and "The Magnificent Seven." Mick was the most acrobatic onstage, whereas Paul stayed put to Joe's left, except when singing "The Guns of Brixton." Flashes of his old energy were only on display during the punk classics. Despite his deepening drug addiction, Topper was still very ably manning the engine room. Mike Farren summed the Clash up well at this juncture, writing, "[The Clash] have matured and they've acquired a definite authority. Where once they were enthusiastic but ragged and all over the place, they are now tight, tough, and confident."

Typically, there were two encores of varying lengths. Usually, the first encore consisted of:

20. "One More Time"
21. "Brand New Cadillac"
22. "Washington Bullets"
23. "Janie Jones"

The second encore often began with "Armagideon Time," but on a few occasions it was "The Street Parade." It would consist of between two and four songs. "Armagideon Time" would be followed by a surprise number, such as "Jimmy Jazz," "Spanish Bombs," or "Junco Partner." The closing number at first was "I'm So Bored with the USA," but this was soon replaced with "London's Burning," and even that morphed on a few evenings into "New York's Burning."

Several shows ran longer. On June 1, they played nine songs over two (maybe three encores) for a total of twenty-eight songs. On June 10, Allen Ginsberg joined the Clash for his "song" "Capitol Air," so the show included twenty-seven songs. And at the final show on June 13, the Clash played only one encore, but it was eleven songs long (for a total of thirty). It included "Pressure Drop" and ended with "White Riot," marking only the second time they played their debut single inside Bond's.

After hours, the Clash would gather at a bar on 49th Street and Broadway and drink and play pool before heading downtown to the Gramercy Park Hotel, where they were staying. (U2, who made their NYC debut at the Palladium on May 29, were staying at the same hotel.) The Clash would also hang out at a reggae club downtown.

Even before the Bond's brouhaha, Don Letts was on hand to film the Clash's performances for a film tentatively titled *Clash on Broadway*. What he caught on celluloid was far more important. It is not an exaggeration to say that he was filming the band's transformation from punk heroes to rock stars. The impact of the canceled concerts, mini-riots, unexpected and extended press and television coverage (including an appearance on Tom Snyder's nationally syndicated talk show, *The Tomorrow Show*), the decision to play nine additional shows and not let down fans who had bought tickets,

Joe Strummer onstage at Bond's. That's The Baker, the Clash's drum technician, in the lower right-hand corner.

Ebet Roberts/Getty Images

and blistering two-plus-hour performances elevated the Clash to the front ranks of rock bands in America.

It is a shame then that this precious footage was allowed to be destroyed. Topper's legal representatives put an injunction on the reels of film when he was fired from the band the following year. Stories vary as to what happened to them. According to biographer Pat Gilbert, the processing laboratory that had the film destroyed it in the mid-1980s; Chris Salewicz was later told by Joe that the film was tossed in the garbage when Bernie Rhodes failed to pay the rental fees at the place where the film was stored in Manhattan.

Luckily, Letts found a leftover reel in the 1990s that was edited to create a short documentary named *Clash on Broadway*. It is available as an extra on the *Westway to the World* and *The Essential Clash* DVDs.

What a loss. If the film was saved, I'm sure it would have included Joe kicking over the television set on Mick's side of the stage that was broadcasting the Clash's *Tomorrow Show* appearance on June 5. Or the kids invading the stage and dancing wildly to "London's Burning" at the end of the underage matinee on June 13, as Mick, Joe, and Paul stood and played their instruments side by side by side. I was a late arrival, and from where I was standing at the back of the ballroom, there were so many kids on the stage that I couldn't see the Clash when the song ended. I remember watching Mick's black Les Paul seemingly float above the heads of the stage crashers as he held it aloft and walked offstage.

But best of all were the final seconds of the June 17 concert. The Clash have just finished "White Riot." I am standing at Joe's feet. Next to me, a young woman hands him a red rose. I watch as Joe Strummer walks over and places the rose on Topper's drum kit.

The Bond's residency was over.

Selling Is What Selling Sells

Combat Rock

Though the Clash continued to be victimized by the press in their home country, the USA was decidedly not bored with them. The 1981 Reader's Poll in the March 1982 issue of *Creem*—"America's Only Rock 'n' Roll Magazine"—revealed the Clash's skyrocketing popularity among American rock 'n' rollers. *Creem* readers deemed the Clash to be the second best group and eighth best live group; Strummer and Jones the third best songwriters (disregarding the fact that all songs on their previous album had been credited to all four members); and *Sandinista!* was the fourth best album of the year. Mick, Paul, and Topper were all ranked in the top five for their respective instruments. Joe Strummer was voted eighth best male vocalist and came in fourth in the "Punk of the Year" category.

These are amazing results for a band whose American tour in 1981 had been confined to seventeen concerts in one city, and who throughout their entire career had appeared on a *Creem* cover only once. What no one realized was that while the band may have played a series of sold-out seven-day residencies (as in "The Magnificent Seven") on three continents in New York City, Paris, London, Tokyo, and Sydney, the band was engaged in an intense internal power scuffle over its direction in music.

"This Struggle Could Be Won!"

Let me set the backdrop. The Clash and Blackhill Management mutually dissolved their managerial relationship with the release of *Sandinista!* After a year, Blackhill felt the Clash's socialistic impulses were counterproductive to being a profitable enterprise. The final straw for Blackhill appears to have been the cheaply priced triple album *Sandinista!* while members of the Clash felt Blackhill's involvement in day-to-day operations had zapped some of the creative spark spurred by their previous chaotic existence. For a short period, the Clash tried self-management as a collective enterprise, with Kosmo Vinyl as their publicist and spokesperson, but in February 1980, Joe issued an ultimatum to the other members of the Clash: either Bernie Rhodes was reinstated as manager or Joe would quit.

Despite previous run-ins and contractual disputes and frozen monies, Bernie had always lurked in the Clash's background since his firing in November 1978 with mere weeks remaining on his management contract. He was rumored to have been seen in Joe's hotel rooms at various times in 1979 and 1980, while in a December 1980 interview with *Melody Maker*'s Paolo Hewitt, Joe had even said that if straightening out the band's financial situation meant more legal maneuvers, then "I don't want to sue Bernie . . . I think Bernie's great."

Mick resisted Joe's ultimatum. He had not forgotten how, in the summer of 1978, ex–Sex Pistols guitarist Steve Jones had turned up at several Clash concerts, guitar in hand, and joined the band during encores. It was suspected at the time that Bernie was scheming an overthrow of the Clash's founding member because of the guitarist's excessive cocaine abuse and lengthening hair.

Clash decisions, however, were still something that the band arrived at democratically. Paul's relationship with Mick had deteriorated; they were barely on speaking terms. Paul sided with Joe, as somewhat quizzically did Topper. Bernie was reinstated, but on different contractual terms: he would be compensated from the band's net profits, not advances, as had been the case previously. Mick put a smiley face on things, telling Paolo Hewitt in June, "Now Bernie's here. It does connect. It all fits. It takes some looking at, this punk group in 1981."

Recording sessions for the Clash's fifth album were underway. In early spring, at the Vanilla rehearsal space, the band had begun working on new numbers, avoiding the critically lambasted and financially foolish process of working up songs in the recording studio. Mickey Gallagher was on hand for these rehearsals, too, despite his hard feelings about not having received songwriting credit on *Sandinista!* (and despite having once said, as Joe recalled to Paolo Hewitt, that *Sandinista!*'s "got one good album, and two thrown in as a Christmas present"). When he broke his arm during one of the football games the Clash played while taking breaks, however, Gallagher was replaced by saxophonist Gary Barnacle.

Lost among the various recording sessions, endless remixes, and series of recording engineers, are the extensive contributions Barnacle made to the Clash's music during this period. He supplemented the Clash at the first formal recording sessions for what would result a year later in *Combat Rock*. These April recording sessions were held at Marcus Music in Kensington Gardens. With Mick reasserting himself as producer—a role Joe could not assume—the Clash laid down the basic tracks for "Car Jamming," "Sean Flynn," and "This Is Radio Clash," a song they would unveil during the upcoming Impossible Mission tour of Europe. Mick remixed "This Is Radio Clash" with tape operator Jeremy Green at AIR Studios in London in August 1981. As if in retaliation for the insipid remixes of "The Magnificent Seven" that Bernie, Joe, and Paul had made, Mick created three alternate, inventive remixes that were very much in the New York City hip-hop vein he thought the Clash should be exploring.

It was, however, this inability to bridge the gap between Mick's all-consuming, musically forward-looking interest in hip-hop with Joe and Paul's growing retro, almost punk desire to revisit rockabilly that was causing friction within the band. (It should be said, though, that it is with much irony that Mick's rocker "Should I Stay or Should I Go" was the closest thing to rockabilly on the final recording.) Conquering New York City had not resolved the band's internal differences. It was Mick versus Joe and Paul, while Topper was nowhere to be found. Topper may have told The Baker, as related in Johnny Green's memoir, that he could handle his drug addiction, but he was increasingly absent. When he did turn up, however, Topper sided with fellow muso Mick. The Clash had irreversibly split into two warring camps.

In September, with residencies in Paris and London looming, the Clash turned up at Ear Studios in People's Hall on Freston Road with the Rolling Stones Mobile Unit and recorded basic tracks for eight more songs:

1. "Midnight to Stevens"
2. "Should I Stay or Should I Go"*
3. "Long Time Jerk"
4. "First Night Back in London"
5. "Overpowered by Funk"
6. "Know Your Rights"*
7. "Inoculated City"*
8. "Ghetto Defendant"*

Those songs marked with an asterisk above would be played in London and Paris, as well as at sporadic shows staged elsewhere in England and Scotland. Once the contracted shows had been played, the Clash returned to the task of finishing their fifth studio album. Mick, however, insisted that these sessions would have to take place at Electric Lady in New York City if the Clash expected his participation. He later claimed that this was just a joke, but it's more likely he was serious and wanted to be near his current flame Ellen Foley.

The Electric Lady sessions were held in December 1981 and January 1982. In addition to complying with Mick's desire of the re-recording of songs committed to tape at Ear Studios, the Clash recorded eight new songs:

1. "Cool Confusion"
2. "Red Angel Dragnet"
3. "Atom Tan"
4. "Kill Time"
5. "The Beautiful People Are Ugly Too"
6. "Straight to Hell"
7. "Rock the Casbah"
8. "Death Is a Star"

The outcome of this was Mick's decision that the Clash's fifth album would be double length. He produced a fifteen-track, sixty-five-minute mix titled *Rat Patrol from Fort Bragg* that contained all the Clash's new material with the exception of "Long Time Jerk," "Midnight to Stevens," and "Overpowered by Funk." To Mick's dismay, he was the only band member who approved of his mix. Joe was especially vocal about releasing a single album that could compete commercially in the rock 'n' roll market.

CBS Records was demanding that the tapes for the album be delivered in time for an April release, but the Clash were contractually committed to a tour of Japan, Australia, New Zealand, Hong Kong, and Thailand—profitable territory the band had never visited. Hopes of remixing the tapes while on tour were quickly dashed; it was an impossible task when the Clash's ears were still ringing after long concerts that often included thirty songs. CBS Records would have to wait until March, when the Clash were back home in London.

With Joe in charge, Mick marginalized, and Paul and Topper's opinions not being heard, producer/recording engineer Glyn Johns was brought in at Bernie's suggestion as an outsider who could salvage the band's unreleased recordings. Most closely associated with the Rolling Stones, Johns had done this previously with two other major rock acts. Many believe his *Get Back* production of the *Let It Be* sessions that the Beatles rejected is superior to the Phil Spector result the public wound up with. He also took the tapes for Pete Townshend's aborted second rock opera, *Lifehouse*, and delivered the Who's classic album *Who's Next.*

Reliving the interminable angst of the *Give 'Em Enough Rope* sessions, it appears that only Joe and Mick participated at the remixing and overdubbing sessions at Johns's home recording studio in West Sussex. By then, much of Paul's bass work had been re-recorded by Mick, Topper, and even Electric Lady tape operator Eddie Garcia. Advised by Johns that remixing would begin promptly at 11:00 a.m., Mick turned up characteristically late the first day and was told that three songs were already in the can. Mick objected but eventually gave in to Joe's ultimatum that it was time to finally complete masters for the Clash's fifth album so that it could be handed in to CBS Records. Joe redid his vocals for "Know Your Rights," as did Mick for "Should I Stay or Should I Go"; conga intros, extended codas, and saxophone jams were excised; and the final product—now named *Combat Rock* by Joe—was done, a year after the initial rehearsals at Vanilla.

"This Is Radio Clash"

Television and then cinema would play a great role in the Clash's music. On *The Clash* alone, 1970s television characters New York City police detective lieutenant Theo Kojak and Starsky (of Starsky and Hutch) are named in the closing seconds of "I'm So Bored with the USA"; *Dr. Who*'s Daleks are mentioned in "Remote Control"; and "Career Opportunities" alludes to *Opportunity Knocks*, a BBC TV talent show.

Film comes into the picture with *London Calling*. Actor Montgomery Clift is the star of "The Right Profile," and the Brixton rebel in "The Guns of Brixton" is compared to Ivan from *The Harder They Come*. Clift is not the last screen star to be named in a Clash song. There's Errol Flynn in "If Music Could Talk," Lauren Bacall in "Car Jamming," and even Rin Tin Tin in "The Magnificent Seven."

Then the music itself begins to reference movie soundtracks. Both "Charlie Don't Surf" and "Sean Flynn" use tricks from the *Apocalypse Now!* soundtrack, and you don't get more musically cinematic than the "dan-daan-daaan-dan-daaaaaah" notes at the beginning of "This Is Radio Clash" (spelling stolen from Richard Archer's liner notes from *The Clash: The Singles* boxed set).

When Mick remixed "This Is Radio Clash" in August 1981 at AIR Studios, he created three alternate versions. "Radio Clash" retained the villainous intro but then it is the same basic track as "This Is Radio Clash," except with different lyrics and an emphasis on instrumentation. Whereas "This Is Radio Clash" has Barnacle's sax snaking under the thumping bass and echoing snare and handclaps, "Radio Clash" pushes the sax and Mick's funky guitar to the forefront. "Radio Clash" is the better version of the two.

"Outside Broadcast" and "Radio Five" are dub versions. Clocking in at 7:33, "Outside Broadcast" features Joe speaking Spanish and spouting silly verses amid the sounds of airplanes, car horns, typewriters rat-a-tat-tating like tommy guns, and a chorus of female vocalists reminding us, "This is Radio Clash!" Like "The Magnificent Dance," this version found its way onto the playlists of black radio stations in metropolitan areas.

"Radio Five" is the most experimental version, with conga lines and backward tapes swooshing and the female chorus thrown into a chaotic, ineffective dub. This is the only version that fades out.

"This is Radio Clash," with its three alternate versions, was released as a 12-inch EP in the US on March 26, 1981. In retrospect, it was one of the band's best EPs.

"I Like the First Side of *Combat Rock*"

So said Joe to Jim Shelley in the late '80s, when asked what he thought were the Clash's best recordings. He also cited *The Clash* and *London Calling*, but he's on the money with *Combat Rock*. It's half of a great album. Side 2 is admittedly the weakest side of their recording career. The lead track, "Overpowered by Funk," is undermined by graffiti artist Futura 2000's lame rap, and the rest of the side never recovers. (It was also a missed opportunity. Grandmaster Flash and the Furious Five, as well as the Treacherous Three, had both opened for the Clash at Bond's. Both acts were New York City–based, so could easily have turned up at the doors of Jimi's studio and turned in raps full of swashbuckling wordplay to help lift Joe's game.) "Atom Tan" is underrated, but the truncated "Sean Flynn" never lives up its promise and—like "Hitsville UK" on the previous album—"Inoculated City" would have been best relegated to a B-side. The closing track, "Death Is a Star," is the type of drivel UK punk rockers rebelled against in 1976.

Side 1, however, ranks up there with the Clash's best album sides. Four songs are arguably among their twenty-five finest. "Know Your Rights" opens with polished punk blast; "Rock the Casbah" and "Should I Stay or Should I Go" are the band's only two songs to make the Top 20 in the US; and "Straight to Hell" wraps up the side with the Clash's most soulful tune. Even "Car Jamming" was to become the vehicle for introducing Terry Chimes to American audiences when he replaced Topper during the Casbah Club tour in May and June 1982.

"Radio Clash" was recorded during the *Combat Rock* recording sessions. *Author's collection*

Every album by the Clash opens strongly, but what "Know Your Rights" establishes quickly is that *Combat Rock* is going to be a rock record. (This, though, is somewhat of a canard; the commercial success of *Combat Rock* camouflaged the record's debt to *Sandinista!* Except for the dub production techniques, it is for all extensive purposes stylistically the same.) But it's not until the fifth track "Red Angel Dragnet"—with what Mick once described as Paul's Marlene Dietrich–ish vocals—that *Combat Rock* returns to this musical alley, and by then rock fans have heard four songs full of satisfaction.

Apocalypse Hotel

During the photo shoot for the *Combat Rock* cover in Thailand, Pennie Smith photographed the Clash in front of an establishment named the Apocalypse

Hotel. Given the content, *Apocalypse Hotel* would have been a more apt title than what was chosen—not that it was ever considered. *Apocalypse Hotel* as a title reflects the lyrical content within. Thematically, the Clash's fifth album is the American equivalent of *The Clash.* It too depicts a malfunctioning society, but now the focus is on America, with its tossed-aside Vietnam War veterans, a government subservient to war contractors, and citizens who have taken the law into their own hands. The same government that can send you off to distant lands to fight or crush your rights cannot keep you safe.

Lyrically, *Combat Rock* was the result of Joe's obsession with Vietnam War–related movies such as *Taxi Driver* and *Apocalypse Now!*, as well as *Dispatches*, a 1977 collection of *Esquire* war correspondent Michael Herr's notes on the war. (Herr had also significantly shaped Colonel Willard's narration of *Apocalypse Now!*) And so, in "Car Jamming," we have disabled vet whose "boots [were] blown off in a '60s war"; in "Red Angel Dragnet" we have the voice of *Taxi Driver*'s Vietnam vet Travis Bickle, who will clean up the American streets as he did Vietnam; in "Straight to Hell" we have American bastard children left behind; and "Sean Flynn" tells the story of an actor's son who like so many others lost their future in Vietnam, Sean literally and others figuratively.

The world's a mess. America is threatening war in El Salvador ("Should I Stay or Should I Go") and the Middle East ("Rock the Casbah") and demanding you love its Western ways ("Overpowered by Funk") even if Western society is crumbling in "Red Angel Dragnet," "Atom Tan," and "Ghetto Defendant." In the final track, "Death Is a Star," Joe reveals he was "gripped by that deadly phantom / I followed him through jungles" only to discover that America's violence is its *raison d'être.*

"Know Your Rights"

"It's the sarcastic Bill of Rights," Joe says of the lead track, in a fascinating bit of footage of the Electric Lady mixing session with recording engineer Joe Blaney found at www.electricladystudios.com. (Although Joe, Mick, and Kosmo Vinyl were all in attendance, this version did not make the finished product, as we shall see.) There's nothing sarcastic, however, about this recording. First you hear Mick's guitar brimming with reverb—an instrument that was in short supply on *Sandinista!*—before Joe speaks in an increasingly passionate voice: "This is a public service announcement . . . with guitar!!!"

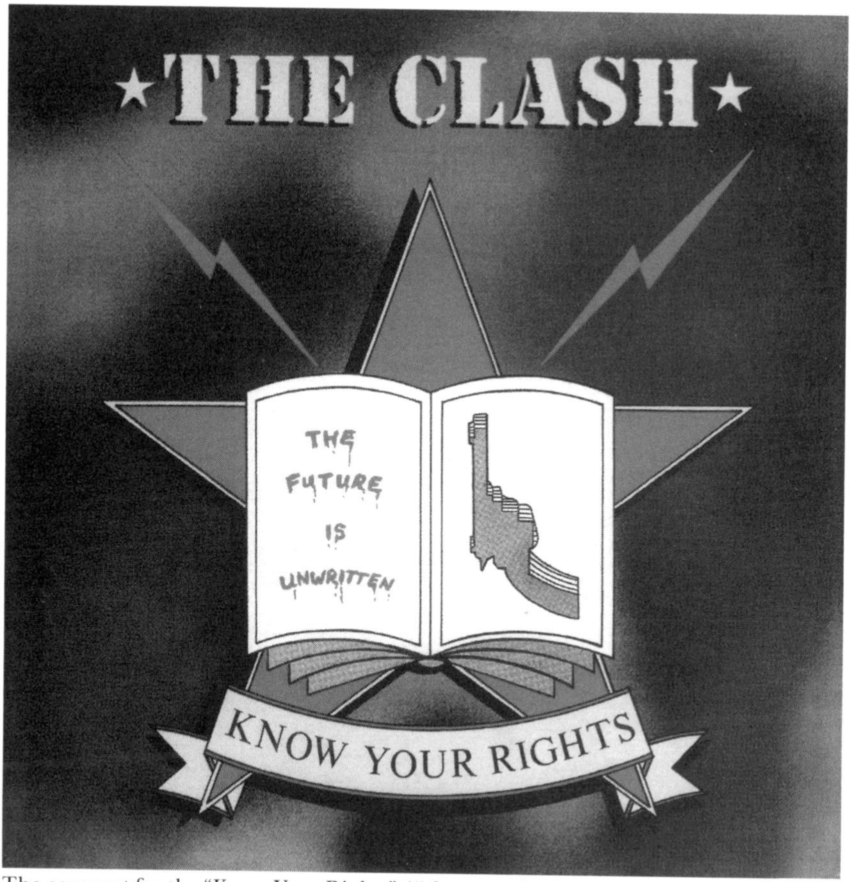

The cover art for the "Know Your Rights" 45 features the Clash's optimistic observation that "The Future Is Unwritten." *Author's collection*

Sadly, the song's lyrics continue to ring true today. Topper's drumbeats swing like truncheons crashing down on the heads of citizens who falsely believe they have rights. Three are specified in this spectacularly rhyme-free song: the right not to be killed, the right to food money, and the right to free speech. Tell that to black men, the impoverished, and illegal immigrants in America today. Mick's lead is eerily stirring, evoking the theme song to *The Scarecrow of Romney Marsh*, a three-part 1963 Walt Disney production for *The Wonderful World of Disney*, starring Englishman Patrick McGoohan, that was reedited and distributed as a successful movie in England, which Mick may have seen as a young lad. (McGoohan's ITV television series *The Prisoner* was an influence on the Clash's song of the same name.)

Over the course of various remixing sessions, "Know Your Rights" lost nearly one and a half minutes, as well as some lyrics that can still be found on the album's lyric sheet. Two alternate, listener-worthy recordings are available on bootleg. *The Clash on Broadway 4* features a raspy-voiced Joe sounding like a man who has tried to use his three rights only to have been smashed by the legal system. This version does not fade out but instead draws to a close as a smattering of hands clap, as if you've just heard a performance in a small club, like on Jimi Hendrix's "Voodoo Chile." The version on *Rat Patrol from Fort Bragg* is missing the bravado opening but is more similar to the final mix. A feature of this version is a triple splice where the rhythm stutters and Joe says menacingly, "Know your rights . . . know your rights . . . know your rights." This edit is also on the version from *The Clash on Broadway 4*, but it is only heard twice on the *Rat Patrol from Fort Bragg* version.

"Rock the Casbah"

"And now a song by Topper Headon," is how Joe would occasionally introduce his greatest Clash hit when performing with the Mescaleros in 1999. He was being honest. The song had its musical origins in a piano riff Topper had been toying with for several months. One day he turned up before anyone else at Electric Lady and, feeling restless, asked the recording engineer to roll the tapes. With the song's signature piano committed to tape, he then added drums and bass. When Joe turned up at the studio, what he heard fit perfectly with some new lyrics he had written. When Topper protested that what he'd recorded was too short for a song, the tape was simply looped, and the backing tracks were in place. Mick was not a fan of the song, however, and had to be persuaded by Joe to add his guitar track.

"Rock the Casbah" hit #8 on the *Billboard* Hot 100 on January 22, 1983, which accounts for song placing at #52 on its Top 100 Songs of 1983. By then, Topper had been out of the band for eight months, and the Clash with Mick in the lineup only had eight performances left in them.

"Straight to Hell"

If *Combat Rock* had to be the Clash's final album, at least it had the saving grace of including "Straight to Hell" as their swan song. It touchingly describes the fault lines of the British class system before traveling across the Atlantic to fully encapsulate the far-ranging consequences of America's misbegotten war in Vietnam. Typed with a deft, sensitive touch Joe was not known for having, these were a highpoint of his latter-period lyrics and almost Dylan-esque.

What prevents "Straight to Hell" from being Dylan-esque, though, is a musical arrangement crafted out of Mick's Amerasian guitar lines and Topper's bossa nova beat. The merging of two musical styles creates a universal mood that befits Joe's lyrics, which in the final verse depicts an underclass that plutocrats have neglected and which turns to drugs to subsist. This is almost the Clash's "Armagideon Time." Sadly prescient, sadly timeless.

Guest Appearances

The number of guest performers was scaled back from *Sandinista!* proportions. As band insiders, Gary Barnacle, Tymon Dogg, and Ellen Foley all returned, but keyboardist Poly Mandell (real name Tommy Mandel), who added keyboard to "Overpowered by Funk" during the Electric Lady sessions, was the only musician new to Clash recording sessions. All the other newcomers' participation was limited to vocal overdubs made in New York City. These include Tex-Mex musician Joe Ely, graffiti artist Futura 2000 (who added his rap at the same sessions Mandell attended), beatnik poet Allen Ginsberg, and Clash spokesperson Kosmo Vinyl as the voice of Travis Bickle on "Red Angel Dragnet."

With the decision to have the Clash produce the album themselves, *Combat Rock* was the first recording without Bill Price's participation since 1979's *The Cost of Living EP.* His tape operator Jeremy Green, however, repeated this role for Mick at Ear Studios and then again in January at Electric Lady. Recording engineer Joe Blaney and tape operator Eddie Garcia, both of whom were employees at Electric Lady, worked here on their first Clash recordings, as did legendary recording engineer/producer Glyn Johns.

Joe Ely

Joe Ely and Joe Strummer not only shared first names; there was a physical resemblance between them, too, especially when Joe Strummer wore a Stetson. You could at times swear they were brothers, if not twins.

Our Joe apparently heard Ely's name for the first time when the Clash made a personal appearance in Tower Records' San Francisco store in

February 1979. Joe objected to management playing *Give 'Em Enough Rope* over the store's sound system and ordered Johnny Green to make sure something else was played. According to his memoir, the band's road manager recommended Joe Ely, then a little known country-and-western recording artist. When asked by Joe if Ely was any good, Johnny assured the Clash's front man that he was.

Fast forward seven months and the Clash are back in the San Francisco area and happy to find that Ely is sharing the bill at the Tribal Stomp Festival in Monterey, California—an attempt to rekindle the spirit of Janis and Jimi, even if they were hippies. The show was poorly attended, but a bond was formed, and Ely even joined the Clash during their encore for "Fingernails," a rockabilly-flavored tune of Ely's, which he sang. With Jones playing "some classic Chuck Berry guitar," according to *NME*'s Michael Goldberg, "the song seemed symbolic of the link between the Clash's modern rock vision and their acknowledged roots in the classic rock of Presley, Berry, and Jerry Lee [Lewis]." Ely and his band were invited as the support act for the Clash's shows in Texas the following month.

Ely next linked up with the Clash at shows in London in February 1980, again joining the Clash for an encore of "Fingernails." Unfortunately, what was supposed to be a showcase in England for Ely was curtailed when Topper was stabbed in his hand during an altercation over drugs at Topper's flat, the result being that the final six dates of the British leg of the 16 Tons tour were postponed and rescheduled for June.

The Clash and Joe Ely did not cross paths again for several years. The possibility of Joe and Mick participating in Ely recording sessions in New York City in March 1980 fell through, and it wasn't until January 1982 that the two Joes bumped into one another again. The location was New York City. Joe was not happy about the subject matter of Mick's next musical vehicle, "Should I Stay or Should I Go," until it was suggested that the two Joes add a Spanish counterpoint vocal to Mick's vocals. With the help of Puerto Rican tape operator Eddie Garcia, the lyrics were translated, and the two had a blast in the studio. Unintentionally, the Spanish vocals politicized the song, as some reviewers now interpreted Mick's lyrics to be a *double entendre* about a possible US invasion of El Salvador.

Allen Ginsberg

You only need to hear the 6:13 early mix of "Ghetto Defendant" now available on *Sound System* to fully appreciate how good *Combat Rock* could have been. Like the snipping of Samson's hair, shortening the song to 4:44 zaps its strength. Contrasting the words of the beatnik poet as "the Voice of God" with that of a punk poet as "the frustrated citizen" was a masterstroke. It was a long, long way from the stripped down lyrics of *The Clash*, but not far from where Joe's lyrical interests originally lay. If anything, the released version of "Ghetto Defendant" is the song that lays bare Joe's insecurities. In interviews, he downplayed the role Ginsberg played in the "Ghetto Defendant," saying he had asked the author of "Howl" for a word once. It's another example of a journalist getting under Joe's skin. By my count, "Ghetto Defendant" was the 134th song the Clash released. Surely by this point Joe had proven his ability to write lyrics without anyone's aid?

Still, you never expected to hear about French symbolist poet Arthur Rimbaud dying in Marseilles in a Clash song. Among the punk generation, this was Patti Smith and Tom Verlaine's neck of the woods; how was it that beatnik poet Allen Ginsberg wound up on a Clash recording in any shape or form anyway? Previous guest performances on Clash recordings had been restricted to friends, lovers, pets, and contemporary musicians. But Ginsberg had appeared with the Clash once during their Bond's residency the previous summer.

It was June 10, 1980, when the first encore began with Joe in a talkative mood: "Something never before seen and never likely to again. May I welcome President . . . President Ginsberg. Allen Ginsberg." Beat poet laureate Allen Ginsberg, friend of Burroughs and Kerouac, then walked onto the stage. Balding, dressed in a button-down shirt with sleeves rolled up the forearms, Ginsberg looked more like a college professor than a beat poet. "I don't like the government where I live," began Ginsberg, at the start of six-minute litany of things he didn't like to the band's 4/4 rhythm. "I don't like dictatorship of the rich . . . I don't like communist censorship of my books . . . I don't like capitalists selling me gasoline coke."

"Yeah, what are we going to call that?" asked Strummer at the conclusion. Joe honestly may not have known the title, but it was "Capitol Air," a piece Ginsberg had written in 1980 after a tour of Eastern European countries, where he noticed a frightening similarity to police tactics in America. On the Ginsberg Project blog, he is quoted as saying, "[In 1981] I was listening to a lot of punk, and I'd heard about the Clash . . . I went backstage once . . . at [the] Bond's club . . . and Joe Strummer said, 'We've had somebody say a few words about Nicaragua . . . but the kids are throwing eggs and tomatoes . . . Would you like to try?' I said, 'I don't know about making a speech, but I've got a punk song about that.' Simple chords, we rehearsed it five minutes and got it together . . . it's punk in ethos . . . but elegant in the sense of having specific political details."

Ginsberg had hoped one day to formally record "Capitol Air" with the Clash (it was finally released in 1993 on *Holy Soul Jelly Roll: Poems and Songs 1949–1993*), so it's no surprise that when he was invited to Electric Lady in January 1982 to co-author a song of Joe's, he accepted. By all accounts, Ginsberg offered Joe more than a single word. According to his recollection, Ginsberg was in the studio with the Clash for seven days and wrote his spoken counterpoint to Joe, who told Ginsberg the names of some punk dances, such as "the worm," which Ginsberg wanted to reference. Ginsberg also recites the "Heart Sutra," a Buddhist mantra during the song's fadeout.

With Ginsberg's sonorous voice sounding more like that of the government than God and Mick's tuneful turn on the harmonica brought to the fore, the early mix of this track about how state-sponsored drug addiction keeps a populace complacent is more arty and earthy, as contradictory as that sounds, on the album version. The tune played on the harmonica recalls rural blues, but it is modernized with Paul's reggae bassline.

The Reviews Are In

In his capsule review, Robert Christgau gave *Combat Rock* a B+, while *Rolling Stone*'s David Fricke gave out four stars and called the Clash's fifth album "a snarling, enraged, yet still musically ambitious collection." That *Combat Rock* was a hit in America was not a surprise, but despite the absence of references to unmerry olde England, it was also a success back home. It reached #2 on the UK charts and was ranked #387 on *NME*'s "500 Greatest Albums of All Time."

Rat Patrol from Fort Bragg

Engaged in what was to prove a losing battle with consumers with how its product is enjoyed, the music industry began issuing "legacy editions" of previous mega-hit or culturally important albums containing a supplemental disc or two in addition to the remastered original recording. These releases would contain session outtakes, alternate and/or live versions, promo footage, expanded liner notes, alternate artwork, and so on. And after the release of *25th Anniversary Edition* of *London Calling* was released in 2004, Clash fans eagerly awaited the announcement for a similar edition of *Combat Rock* in 2007.

The assumption was that there wasn't any leftover alternate mixes or outtakes from *Sandinista!*, an album the Clash had struggled to stretch to a sixth side, but the difficult labor of *Combat Rock* was well known. (By the way, Sony did announce a 30th Anniversary Japanese edition of *Sandinista!* in 2010; not even a list of the contents, however, ever came to fruition.) Despite their enormous differences in personality, one habit both Mick and Joe shared is that they were hoarders. Surely, if Mick could locate the decades lost *Vanilla Tapes*, his sixty-five-minute "home mix" of *Rat Patrol from Fort Bragg* would be easier to find. Despite high hopes, however, an anniversary of *Combat Rock* was never to be released.

One explanation for this is the emergence of a two-disc bootleg recording of *Rat Patrol from Fort Bragg* in 2004. This and other Clash bootlegs were the result of "a gentleman living in northern Italy who goes by the nom du

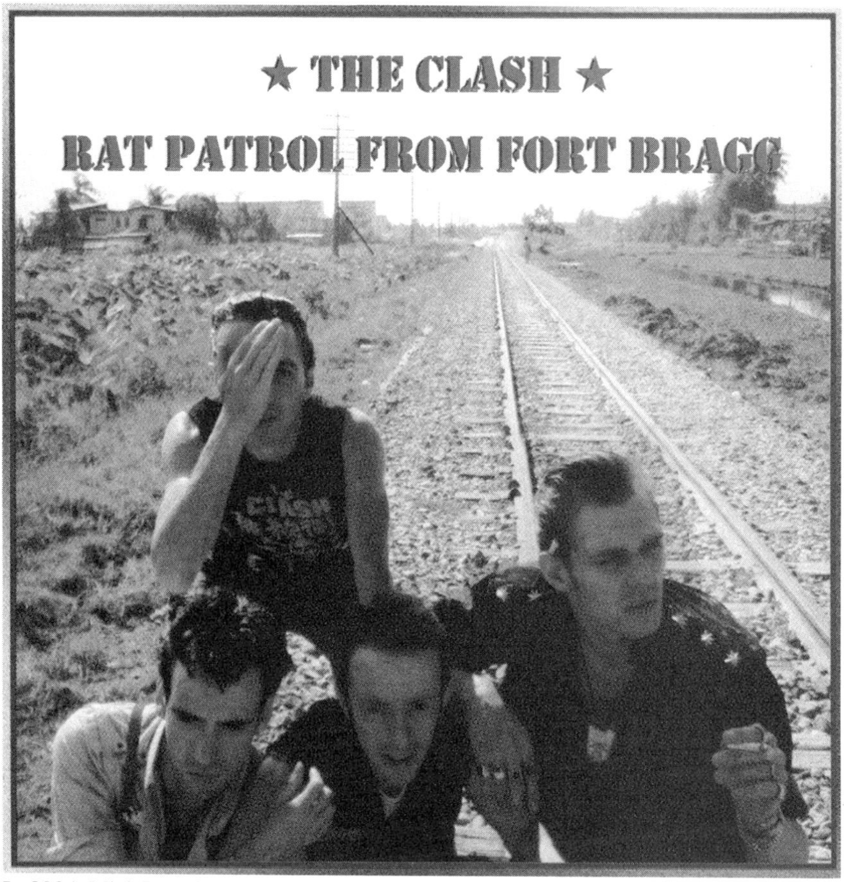

In 2004, Mick Jones's original mixes for *Rat Patrol from Fort Bragg* were bootlegged with the *Combat Rock* cover art. *Author's collection*

rock 'Arnold Finney,'" as *Harp*'s Fred Mills reported in November 2004. In this brief interview, "Finney" says that "with *Rat Patrol* the idea was to nail those demos for good as soon as a great sounding tape appeared." Finney's bootleg editions such as *Clash on Broadway 4* and *Rude Boy—The Directors Cut* are among the best Clash bootlegs. Not only is production top notch, the artwork and inserts are of high integrity—comparable to CBS's own liner notes—and reasonably priced. As "Finney" rightly says, "Music was recorded to be shared and listened to, not put in boxes in the loft." Especially the music of a band that sang the praises of pirate radio.

The foldout insert of the liner notes to *Rat Patrol from Fort Bragg*—complete with Futura 2000's handwritten lyrics and more Pennie Smith snapshots than are found in *Combat Rock*—state that the music contained within was "recovered from an RCA office and contains Mick's early mixes." It is not, as some have reported, Mick's double album "home mix" that was rejected by Joe in favor of a trimmed down single disc. Clearly the seven-minute piano-drum jam of the band's musos, Mick and Topper; the demo of "Overpowered by Funk"; and two versions of "Inoculated City" would not have been on the "home mix." (It's also doubtful that Mick heard the salsa driven "The Beautiful People Are Ugly Too," "Walk Evil Talk," and the funky "Kill Time" as opening tracks. They would have, however, worked well alongside "Overpowered by Funk" on a Side 3 featuring inner-city rhythms in a manner similar to *Exile On Main St.*'s gospel side.) But what this bootleg *does* contain is superior versions of more than half a dozen of the songs on *Combat Rock*, most importantly every song on Side 2 except for "Atom Tan."

With its inclusion on *Sound System*, you can judge for yourself now whether or not the seven-plus-minute "Cinemascope Mix" of "Sean Flynn" is superior to the truncated version on *Combat Rock*, but the early and less poppy mix of "Inoculated City" makes clear this song was an improved upon and catchier version of "The Call Up," and "Death Is a Star" with Joe's spoken lyrics and Mick's sung chorus nicely sums up the ideas contained on what is the Clash's most fully realized concept album.

You Really Thir About It Too

The Breakup of the Clash

The year 1982 began on a high note for the Clash.

They were in New York City, trying to wrap up their fifth studio album. On New Year's Eve, 1981, the Clash had spent the evening in Electric Lady Studios, where Joe committed to tape the vocals for "Straight to Hell," the song that would prove to be the centerpiece of *Combat Rock.* They had laid down the backing track the previous day, with Topper playing a variation on a bossa nova drumbeat alongside Mick's synth guitar work and Joe hitting the bass drum with a glass lemonade bottle wrapped in a towel.

"We took the E train from the village up to Times Square, because the Iroquois was off Times Square," Joe remembered, when helping compile the *Clash on Broadway* boxed set. "I'll never forget coming out of the Times Square subway exit, just before midnight, into a hundred billion people, and I knew we had just done something really great."

The year 1982 should have been spent building on the successes of 1981. Despite criticism, *Sandinista!* had outsold *London Calling.* After the Mission Impossible tour of Europe, the band was financially solvent for the first time ever. The Bond's residency had elevated them to the front rank of rock bands in America and re-bonded the band, and now new material for the next album came easily. During the weeklong residency at Theatre Mogador in Paris, a short swing through Great Britain, and another weeklong residency at the Lyceum Ballroom in London in September and October, they unveiled five new songs that would wind up on *Combat Rock.* Even more satisfying was that the shows in London were a triumphant return that quashed all the criticisms British music press had been heaping on the band

The vocals for "Straight to Hell" were recorded on New Year's Eve, 1981, at Electric Lady Studios. *Author's collection*

for several years. The Clash had a fan base in Great Britain matched that of the critical favorites the Jam.

So 1982 should've been the year the year the Clash coalesced all their strengths and emerged triumphant. And, on the surface, 1982 was a banner year for the band. Their shows worldwide—in the Far East, Great Britain, and the USA—sold out consistently. *Combat Rock* was a hit album, and several singles from it reasserted the fact that the Clash was that rare rock band that could make serious music and still succeed on the pop charts. And the reviews of their concerts and recordings were glowing. But this success camouflaged fault lines that were exposed and giving way throughout 1982 and 1983, and which resulted in the dissolution of the Clash.

The Marginalization of Mick Jones

Because of the songwriting partnership that propelled the Clash over the course of three albums and multiple singles, Joe and Mick were often compared to John Lennon and Paul McCartney. Joe, like John, wrote the better lyrics; Mick, like Paul, had a gift for melody. As with John and Paul, Mick was a better musician than Joe—something even Joe would not deny. And as with John and Paul, there was an ongoing struggle between them over who should set the band's course. At first they worked in tandem for the common goal of getting the band known and recorded. But then, as Joe suffered with Hepatitis B and bouts of depression, Mick took charge—only to relinquish authority to Joe when his relationship with Slits guitarist Viv Albertine soured and he went through a prolonged period of songwriter's block. And so it went, back and forth, until early 1981, when Joe foisted Bernie Rhodes back on Mick and insisted Bernie be reinstated as manager—which was similar to what John had done when he wanted Allen Klein to manage the Beatles.

Outvoted, Mick went along with the decision but countered by reasserting his authority as the Clash's musical mastermind. He was determined for the fifth Clash album to have his stamp of approval. Joe was forced to go along and agreed to recording at Electric Lady. By January, however, work on the fifth album was in its tenth month. CBS was badgering the band for the next album. Mick and Paul were not on speaking terms, forcing Joe to act as the go-between, which was difficult because Mick and Joe were not on good terms either. They did their overdubs separately, and worked with different recording engineers, Joe having flown over Jeremy Green to work exclusively on his vocal tracks. And then they were forced to attempt final mixing during a tour of the Far East—an exercise that produced dismal results because mixing tapes was impossible when their ears were still ringing from the concert they had just given.

Back in London, Mick unveiled his double-album-length version of the Clash's fifth LP. The Clash, led by Joe, rejected this version, as described on chapter 22 and, as John Lennon had done with the *Get Back* tapes, Joe handed the reels to an industry respected engineer (Glyn Johns) for trimming. For all intents and purposes, Joe was removing Mick from a position he had held over all previous Clash recordings, with the exception of the remixes for "The Magnificent Seven" and "The Call Up."

Joe was determined that the Clash's fifth album be a single album. If it was, he was confident from the reaction the band had received in the

Far East that the Clash could triumph on the charts over the likes of REO Speedwagon, who had had the #1-selling album in America when the Bond's residency began. Mick reluctantly participated in the overdubs demanded by Glyn Johns (such as changing the original bawdy line in "Should I Stay or Should I Go" about going "around your front or on your back"), but was not present for the final mixing—an act of silent protest against *Combat Rock*.

The Disappearance of Joe Strummer

The Clash had a habit of getting new years off to a good start by touring, and 1982 was no different. On January 24, the Clash appeared at Shibuya Kokaido, a theater that had been built for the 1964 Olympics Weightlifting Competition. The first show in Tokyo, Japan, opened with "Should I Stay or Should I Go"—for the only time in the band's career! It was the commencement of a triumphant five-week tour through the Far East. By all accounts, Joe was the dominant voice during the tour, commandeering press interviews and establishing himself as the Clash's spokesman. This would be true for the remainder of the Clash's existence but, as is often the case, his bluster was masking his growing confusion about the level of celebrity and income he was willing to accept if the Clash were to compete with the likes of the Rolling Stones and the Who.

Because Joe Strummer in early 1981 clearly made a conscious decision about the Clash finally putting their financial house in order. During 1980, Joe was declined a mortgage. Here was a man whose face moved music tabloids, who sold out concerts worldwide, but he could not get approval on a bank loan. Joe may have lived a squatter's existence and encouraged his band to adhere to socialist tendencies, but he was also the middle-class son of a man who had been awarded an MBE by her majesty's government. Part of him must have felt he had little to show for almost five years of constant work (and longer, if you added in the two years with the 101'ers). He might have told *Musician* journalist Vic Garbarini that he'd gotten "into music because . . . it was the thing that had the least laws and restrictions about it," but the business he was in was not known for its longevity. The Clash could be over in a flash, and there'd be nothing to show for it.

This accounts for his insistence that Bernie replace Blackhill, although some of the attraction must have been the fact that Bernie was a fount of novel ideas. And in the spring of 1982, with tickets for an upcoming tour of Great Britain moving slowly, Bernie came up with his most novel idea yet: Joe Strummer must disappear.

The manager told Joe to visit Joe Ely in Texas, then sold the story that Joe had vanished because he was questioning the relevancy of the Clash in a world where the pop charts were more pap than pop. How this would spur ticket sales never made sense: why buy tickets to see a band whose lead singer might not turn up by the night of the show? I remember discussing this with other fans when lining up to buy Clash tickets for their Asbury Park concerts over Memorial Weekend, when Joe was still missing.

And really missing. Perhaps to demonstrate to Bernie that he still had the upper hand in steering the Clash's course, Joe and his girlfriend Gaby Salter fled to a Montmartre flat in Paris on April 21 without informing Bernie or Kosmo Vinyl. While they whiled away the days visiting museums and running the Paris Marathon (according to photographer Richard Schroeder, Joe finished all 26.2 miles but Gaby did not), the Clash were forced to cancel the tour of Great Britain, which threatened the band's newfound solvency. When Mick, Paul, and Topper learned this stunt was Bernie's idea, they were not pleased. They'd be even deeper in the red if the upcoming twenty-six-date tour of America was also canceled.

Joe had been missing for over three weeks when the now-bearded vocalist was found in a bar by Kosmo who—after some detective work—turned up Joe's location in France. Kosmo has said that rather than having to cajole Joe, they had sat around drinking and banging out Bob Dylan songs on the "pianner" until the Clash's front man persuaded himself that he'd proven his point by disappearing: the Clash could not carry on without Joe Strummer.

But another underlying cause of Joe's disappearance remained unsettled even after Joe agreed to return. Topper's drug intake had escalated to the point where he was ineffective as a drummer. Joe shared a trait of many other notable leaders, however: he couldn't fire anybody. The interim period between the end of the Australasian tour and the delivery of the Clash's fifth album to CBS Records had put off a pressing question confronting the Clash: what do we do about Topper?

Joe knew Bernie had been advocating the drummer's termination since the tour, on which the drummer's ability to perform without drugs had proven impossible. Kosmo had replaced Mickey Foote at Bernie's ear, and he too was advocating Topper's dismissal. For Joe, this was a confrontation he had wanted to avoid. For Bernie, this was a baby step in wresting control of the Clash from Mick and ultimately Joe. The Clash had broken down into two camps. Joe labeled Mick and Topper the "musicians" while he and Paul were the "entertainers." (This was a blatant denial of Mick's palpable star qualities, especially in America.) If Bernie could rid the Clash of Topper, Mick—the one member still bristling over Bernie's return—would be further sidelined. Unfortunately, Topper was unwittingly aiding Bernie's plans.

Joe returned with Kosmo in time for the Clash's next appearance at the Lochem Festival in Amsterdam on May 20—and for what became a turning point in the Clash's existence.

The "Suspension" of Topper Headon

The Clash were one of the few bands whose lyrics never glorified drug use. From the Vietnam vet shooting "some skag" on the debut album's "I'm So Bored with the USA" to the "addicts of metropolis" in "Ghetto Defendant," drugs are never presented as a good recreational option. There's the police playing their games in "Julie's Been Workin' for the Drug Squad" and "Drug-Stabbin' Time" and busting musicians in "Jail Guitar Doors." "Hateful" is about a drug addict whose only friend left is his dealer. Actor Montgomery Clift is looking for "another roll of pills ("The Right Profile"); the singer's so "pilled up that [he] rattle[s]" ("Revolution Rock"); the believer's taken so many drugs he thinks he's Jesus ("The Sound of the Sinners"). And, once you know the story of the Clash, it's impossible to listen to "Junkie Slip" without thinking it's about Topper's drug addiction.

It has been said the Clash ran on Red Stripe, a pale lager brewed in Jamaica, and spliffs, which are cigarettes laced with marijuana. Usage of stronger drugs within the Clash had been frowned upon, but their own habits made this condemnation hypocritical. Keith Levene used both speed and heroin during his months in the Clash, and this was probably a factor in his dismissal. During the Clash's first year, Joe was regularly mixing amphetamines with beer, which accounts for his sometimes-frightening persona as punk took off. As Joe stopped taking pills, Mick started doing cocaine and continued to do so throughout the remainder of his days in the Clash. He saw it as part of his due as a rock star. But this also meant he self-created the sense of isolation he felt within the band he had founded. Topper has said it was Mick who turned the drummer onto cocaine. And Joe was also known to snort a line or two himself, so who was he to object to Topper's recreational use?

But the drummer, whom many credit with having the innate drum skills that fostered the Clash's growth from punk rock to world music, was increasingly unreliable. A drug bust at Heathrow Airport the previous December and a stern warning from the presiding magistrate had not led to soul searching. He was a drug addict with a junkie girlfriend who did not socialize with his other bandmates, who were now subject to endless Customs searches for drug contraband as they flew into Japan, New Zealand, Australia, and so on because of Topper's bust. More worrisome was that Topper could no longer be relied upon to maintain the engine room. There were concerns over whether he was physically able for the sure-to-be-grueling American tour.

Upon arriving back in London on May 18, Joe convinced Paul that the Lochem Festival appearance should be a test of Topper's reliability; if the drummer didn't pass, he'd have to be suspended. Mick was noncommittal. But a festival near Amsterdam—the city with world's most lax drug laws in 1982—was certainly not the fairest place for such a test, and, even worse, no one had told Topper he was being judged. So he hung out with Joe, Mick, and Paul, smoking hash and marijuana, not knowing his future with the group hung in the balance.

The Clash were headlining a bill that included Bow Wow Wow, Carlene Carter, Normaal (a Netherlands-based rock band), and Saxon. The festival had not sold out, partly due to Joe's disappearance, and those who attended had to contend with thunderstorms throughout the day. The Clash's slot was set for 4:30 p.m.—a rare daylight performance. Fans scuffled with bouncers, to Joe's dismay, so he welcomed them onto the stage.

By 1982, the Clash's fervent fan base was taping almost every live appearance, and the fifteen-song, fifty-seven-minute set at Lochem was no exception. From this sonic evidence we can deduce Topper was not fired because of his performance. It was not exceptional, but it was better than that of raspy-voiced Joe and out-of-tune Mick. (For the record, the recording contains the only live performance of "Ghetto Defendant" with Topper.) What probably toppled Topper from his drum riser was his nodding out during breakfast at Heathrow Airport on the flight out and then later rudely grabbing a mirror Joe was using so he could line up rows of cocaine in the dressing room. This was nothing new for Topper. He was reliant now on snorting a line of coke every two or three songs to keep his energy level up.

Back in London, Topper was told there was a mandatory meeting at Paul's flat. Joe quickly informed the drummer that he was being suspended and—in Topper's recollection—Terry Chimes would be returning for the American dates. In the interim, he had to go cold turkey and kick his heroin habit. Joe had meant it when he told Topper in the Far East that the drummer's drug addiction was compromising the Clash's anti-drug stance. Both Mick (who had been outvoted again) and Topper were crying.

The drummer desperately begged to be brought along for the tour and promised he'd live the straight-and-narrow lifestyle, and if he didn't, then Terry could take his place on the stage. Joe later said he too was wavering, but he never admitted as much, and Topper's suggestion was rejected.

In a case of déjà vu all over again, Topper's absence for the upcoming American tour was attributed in *NME* to "political differences," which had been the same explanation for Terry's departure five years earlier. "Topper's main interest is the music," it was reported, "and the rest of the band is concerned that they don't lose sight of their determination *not* to become part of the 'rock industry.'"

That Topper was not fired is also explicit in the press release and other press clippings. He is described as having "left" the Clash of his own choice, which certainly implies he could return if he changed his mind. After his bust at Heathrow Airport and industry rumors, journalists must have sensed the true unsaid reason, and one got Joe to admit as much over drinks. Topper—who told drummer and author Spike Webb in a 2014 interview the "the one place in the world where I was 100 percent confident" was when he was sitting on his drum stool—was trying to kick his habit and return to the Clash when he read the interview where Joe revealed that the Clash's former drummer was a junkie, which undermined Topper's confidence. By now he was shooting up heroin. It was the beginning of a serious drug addiction that spanned twenty-two years and ruined his career, destroyed his second marriage, and included a ten-month incarceration in the late 1980s for supplying heroin to an acquaintance who overdosed.

The Reenlistment and Resignation of Terry Chimes

Like one of *The Magnificent Seven*'s hired guns, Terry Chimes warily agreed when asked to rejoin the Clash for the Casbah Club tour of the USA. Bernie initially approached Terry, but the drummer only "signed on" after speaking with the Clash's founding member. He wanted certainty that Bernie's invitation wasn't another one of the manager's underhanded moves. It was only upon rehearsing with Joe and Mick (Paul had flown ahead to America to buy some artwork) and then as the tour started that Terry realized that Joe had the upper hand in the ongoing power struggle for control of the Clash.

"The Year of the Body" was in full swing. It had begun with the tour through Japan, where drugs were impossible to obtain. Unable to smoke marijuana, Joe had embraced a lifestyle of exercise, multivitamins, and Rémy Martin, the spirit of choice for both Joe and Paul. This had been another factor in the dismissal of Topper, who had only survived the shows in Japan by taking hits of oxygen between songs. Topper's abuse of his body with drugs was not viewed favorably by Joe. Once the band arrived in New Zealand, Mick had resumed his cocaine habit and wanted nothing to do with "The Year of the Body." For Mick, this was "The Year of the Clash," and only the band's success helped him endure communication breakdowns with Joe and Paul as the band now played larger venues throughout the southern and western states of the USA.

The Clash songbook had significantly expanded since they recorded their first nineteen songs, but Terry got down-to-business and quickly adapted. Terry's drum style gave the songs a heavier backbeat, which worked well with American audiences, many of whom were seeing the Clash for the first time. Reviews from this tour remark on the band's sonic wallop, and some of the credit has to go to Terry's Zeppelin-ish drumming. Truman Capote once compared reading Proust's *A la recherche du temps perdu* to diving into a tidal wave; the same could be said of the Clash's performances in 1982.

While it is true that Joe created a new set for every show on this tour, it was basically the same songs, just reshuffled. Thirty songs were in the rotation. The only constant was opening with "London Calling" (except for the Houston show, which began with "Jimmy Jazz"). The average set comprised eighteen songs followed by two three-song encores, for a total of twenty-four. "The Magnificent Seven" was almost always played seventh and, as the tour wound down, the second encore always ended with "Garageland." Most of the material came from *London Calling* and *Combat Rock*. Neither "(White Man) In Hammersmith Palais" nor "White Riot" appear to have been played. All of which is my longwinded way of saying a standard set list for the Casbah USA tour does not exist.

With Topper's deepening drug addiction, Terry remained onboard for the rescheduled British dates, a return to America, and then a series of dates opening for the Who. During this time period, Terry said the band was very busy touring and heard very little of Joe and Paul plotting about Mick's dismissal, but he did tell me that "Paul was more irritated than Joe, so no one was arguing the other side." My questions about Mick's firing the following year did trigger this memory for Terry: "I will say—never thought about it for forty years—but there was a guitar roadie who said,

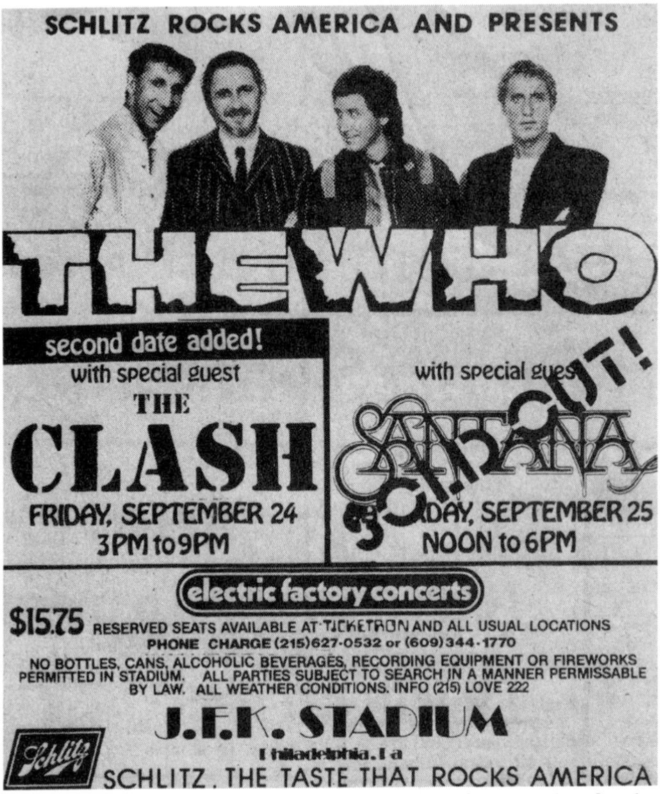

The Clash never recovered their equilibrium after opening for the Who in September and October 1982. *Author's collection*

'You're not criticizing "the golden boy," are you?' Because he knew what Mick brought to the band was gold."

The final show of the year, at the Bob Marley Centre in Kingston, Jamaica, on November 27, 1982, turned out to be Terry's swan song performance with the Clash. Band members took off for the holidays with plans of touring America in January, where "Rock the Casbah" was racing up the charts. This tour never happened, however, because Joe was still trying to get the mortgage on a home to move into with Gaby. Further delays occurred when Paul's father and stepmother were injured in a car accident in France, an accident Paul's stepmother did not survive. With no income due him from the royalties the others were reaping from the success of *Combat Rock*, Terry Chimes found work with Billy Idol and left the Clash camp for the final time.

Shea Stadium, New York City, October 13, 1982

Unbeknown to anyone at the time, when the Clash arrived in New York City on October 7, 1982, it was for what were to be their final shows in their American "hometown." They had played a typical-length set (twenty-four songs) at Southeastern Massachusetts University (SMU) in North Dartmouth, Massachusetts the previous night. On October 9, they made their only appearance on *Saturday Night Live*, playing "Straight to Hell" and "Should I Stay or Should I Go." Three nights later, they opened for the Who, in the first show of two shows scheduled at Shea Stadium, home of the New York Mets baseball team in Flushing, Queens.

I lived in Flushing, so the following night, October 13, I walked through Flushing Meadow Park to Shea, best known to rock fans for the Beatles' concerts in 1965 and 1966. Maybe this is why "Revolution 9" was the first song that came over the PA that evening? I doubt it, but it sounded wonderful hearing "number nine, number nine, number nine" while sitting in the upper level where I had watched seventeen Mets games in the championship year of 1969. It was even windier than usual, and a threat of rain hung in the air. I had dilly-dallied about buying a ticket because I felt that in 1982 it should have been the Who opening for the Clash, not the other way around. But eventually I admitted to myself that I couldn't pass up seeing the Clash, even if I had seen them three times six weeks earlier at the Pier. Who knew when they'd be back? How could I know it was the last time I'd be seeing Mick Jones with the Clash? Nor was I the sole attendee whose attraction was the Clash. "There were as many Clash fans . . . as Who fans," reported the *New York Post* decades later—an exaggeration, but still, I was not alone.

The stage was set up in centerfield, where Tommy Agee once roamed, and there was festival seating on the field itself. Former New York Dolls front man David Johansen was the first act. As he performed, I noticed ushers were not preventing fans from accessing the field via the field-level seats, so I raced down Shea Stadium's winding ramps and soon found myself approximately a hundred feet from the stage. The concert I was at is preserved on *Live at Shea Stadium*. As that 2008 recording indicates, the Clash's opening sets for the Who were comprised mostly of tracks they had previously released as singles. It was a "greatest hits" set list, designed to win over legions of new fans, and I must admit Who fans were more respectful of the Clash than Clash fans were of opening bands at Clash shows. The highlight for me that evening was the unexpected "The Magnificent Seven" / "Armagideon Time" medley, but even if it was otherwise all the hits, it was still enjoyable. As a longtime fan, I couldn't fault the Clash's victory lap. Little did I know that opening for the Who was unnerving Joe. The band's camaraderie was coming apart.

Remember that not-so-new Cadillac the Clash are seen riding over the 59th Street Bridge on their way to Shea Stadium at the beginning of the "Should I Stay or Should I Go" video? As Joe told Jim Shelley in the late 1980s, "We thought we needed something to make us feel better [than the Who], so we used to hire Rent-a-Wrecks, some '50s Cadillac convertibles . . . [and the driver] looks at us in the rear-view mirror, and says, 'Great disguises guys!' We weren't in disguise. Mick was all hip-hopped up; he was sincere. I looked at him, and us, and thought, 'What have we come to?' After that, it used to be, 'Why are you wearing those stupid glasses?' We were falling apart then. We couldn't even agree what was cool anymore."

This is odd, because in Julien Temple's earliest footage of the Clash, the glasses Mick is wearing are similar to the ones he sports in Don Letts's video. They are like aviator's goggles. But a much-quoted statement of Mick's from *Westway to the World* is, "I was so gone with [hip hop] the others used to call me 'Whack Attack.'" The source of this nickname was probably graffiti artist Futura 2000's awful rap about civilization during "Overpowered by Funk" ("It's environmentally wack / So presenting my attack").

Also unnerving Joe was the band's direction. Having now played in front of crowds as large as 90,000, he worried that this was the band's fate. The Clash were easily positioned to fill the American arenas and stadiums vacated by the retiring Who and the Rolling Stones, whose 1982 European tour would be their last for seven years. The greatest irony is that Joe had seized the reins, melted Mick's version of *Combat Rock* down to a single release, toured and sold it and competed with Boston and REO Speedwagon, but this triumph had left Joe in a state of depression. "Make sure that you're in a position to be able to *say* what you want," Joe had told *NME*'s Charles Shaar Murray in May 1982. The Clash had achieved that. Even Mick eventually agreed that Joe's single album version of *Combat Rock* had achieved a commercial success his mix would not have managed.

Interestingly, Joe had also said the following to Murray: "You have to be independent enough to remember what you were there to do in the first place, or you're fucked." By the end of 1982, the Clash were "independent enough," but Joe thought they were "fucked," and their hard-won, new-found success was a millstone around the Clash's neck that would prevent them from "what [they] were there to do in the first place." Ever since the critical lambasting of *Sandinista!*, Joe had been spending more time with former members of the 101'ers, even approving the release of *Elgin Avenue Breakdown*, a compilation of 101'ers recordings. He was playing with them sporadically, and anonymously, as the Soul Vendors. Joe wanted to retrench and go even further back than punk's roots. He saw the Clash's future in rockabilly, and so did Paul. Despite "Should I Stay or Should I Go's" own rockabilly roots, "Whack Attack" Mick saw the Clash's future in NYC hip hop. They were at an impasse.

Hell W10

Finding themselves directionless and drummer-less in early 1983, Joe hit upon the idea of making a movie as a way of lifting the spirits of the Clash camp. He would finance and direct the project, and everyone in the entourage—roadies, girlfriends, relatives of girlfriends—would play a role, even if for some, like The Baker, it was behind the scenes. The Baker has turned down all interview requests from Clash biographers, so stumbling upon his blog is akin to Egyptian farmers foraging for manure and finding the Gnostic Gospels in December 1945. His retelling of the filming of *Hell W10* offers a fascinating look at the Clash's deterioration, especially since The Baker left the Clash's employ following Mick's sacking in September.

"Digging down to the subliminal messages contained within the film," The Baker writes, "there are also clear indications of what was really happening consciously and subconsciously back then with the Clash."

Describing the roles of the Clash's lead guitarist and bassist, the Baker writes, "Mick's role as the bad guy and Paul's role as the hero correctly [portrayed] the tensions of the period. At the time, Mick was seen as the villain in all things by most of those around, and certainly in Joe and Paul's eyes." Further on, he adds, "Kosmo proved presciently typecast considering his role in the group's real-life drama that unfolded later that year, as one of the motivating forces ousting Mick from the Clash."

Kosmo Vinyl unintentionally played a key role in the "disintegration" of the Clash—"disintegration" being the word often used by members of the Clash's inner circle. Kosmo had first met Joe and Mick when he honored their request to not sell "Remote Control" at his outdoor stall in Brixton. He entered the Clash's circle as part of Blackhill Enterprises and was in charge of publicity. He survived Blackhill's termination and ingratiated himself with Bernie Rhodes to emerge in the music press as the Clash's official spokesman. When it came time for *Combat Rock*'s promotion, he threw his whole being into the project and played a significant role in its success. (It helped that he was promised a percentage of the profits, which he never received.) Unfortunately, success and its attendant fame was not something Joe was comfortable with, and this fueled the perplexing decisions that led to the group's "disintegration."

Joe later dismissed *Hell W10* as "shit," but The Baker remembers the making of the film as the last happy period of the Clash. Bernie had dismissed the project as being frivolous, and so was not involved, which was no doubt a pleasing development to Mick. (*Hell W10* is only available on the *Essential Clash* DVD.)

US Festival Tour

Soon after the editing of their heavily *Taxi Driver*–influenced movie, the Clash accepted an offer to headline New Wave Day at the second annual US Festival, approximately nine months after the first, for a reported $500,000. The justification for accepting such a large paycheck was later given as being that the Clash needed monies to finance the Lucky Seven, the new name for the rock club they had promised to open as far back as their earliest interviews.

The need to find a replacement for Terry Chimes was also suddenly urgent. Bernie Rhodes and Kosmo Vinyl placed an ad in *Melody Maker* in late April. As the band's drum tech, sorting through approximately 200 applications became The Baker's duty. In this he was aided by Mick's guitar tech, Digby Cleaver. Ten British drummers were selected to play along to prerecorded Clash tracks and finally four had thirty-minute auditions with the Clash. By May 18, Pete Howard—a drummer from Bath—was behind the kit, playing as a member of the Clash in Amarillo, Texas. (The new drummer was paid on the same sliding pay scale as the roadies: £100 if not working, £200 if rehearsing, and £300 when touring.) The Clash swung through Texas, Nebraska, and Arizona, playing some unusual songs such as "Lost in the Supermarket" and "Sound of the Sinners" as they fine-tuned their act for their festival appearance. Set lengths were similar to those from the previous year.

US Festival, San Bernardino, California, May 28, 1983

"All right then," Joe says as he inserts his jack into his black Fender Telecaster. "All right, here we are in the capital of the decadent US of A." The crowd cheers in approval as Joe stamps his mic stand twice and then once more. "This here set of music is now dedicated to making sure that those people in the crowd with children have something left here for them in the centuries." And with that, Joe—dressed in a white outfit reminiscent of his Bond's attire and a black Clash T-shirt—turns to his new drummer, who counts off the intro to "London Calling" and Mick's final concert with the band he founded. (Topper, incidentally, was nearby, in the Californian rehabilitation hospital he had been checked into by Pete Townshend.)

Behind the scenes, it had already been a combustible evening. Two hours had passed between the end of the preceding set by Australian new-wave act Men at Work and the Clash's entrance. The reason for the hold-up was the Clash staging a press conference and demanding the festival's organizers donate $100,000 to a local summer camp for disadvantaged children. This was aimed mostly at Steve Wozniak who, having developed the Apple Computer I, was hoping, according to Wikipedia, "to encourage the 1980s to be more community-oriented and combine technology with rock music."

This is why, before "Rock the Casbah," Joe unleashed the following tirade: "I know the human race is supposed to get down on its knees in front of all this new technology and kiss the micro-chip circuits. It's never impressed me all that much. You ain't nothing but a you buy . . . "You make, you buy, you die!" that's the motto of America. You get born to buy it." Joe went on to talk about the impoverished living in East Los Angeles, but his comments were aimed at Wozniak, who had put up $18 million to stage the festival. In a 1984 *Record* article, Kosmo Vinyl said Wozniak finally coughed up $32,000 for the summer camp.

A red banner with "THE CLASH NOT FOR SALE" in white lettering had been unfurled as the Clash took the stage, evidence that someone in the Clash's management had planned the press conference ahead to stir up some faux outrage and generate press coverage for the band. It was an attempt to recreate the Bond's brouhaha on the West Coast, except the overselling of tickets to the concerts at Bond's was not caused by the Clash, so the press was favorably disposed to the band, especially when they added nine shows to ensure all fans received their money's worth. It is said that Bernie had wound up Joe for what would be one of his most embarrassing moments with the Clash, which unfortunately was about to become the norm.

At the second and final US Festival, the Clash played a set of twenty songs, two more than was normal, but there were to be no encores. Festival organizers had ordered the DJ to play prerecorded music as soon as the Clash left the stage. Kosmo saw this as a move to prevent an encore—let alone the Clash's customary two—and attacked the DJ. Festival security intervened, and then Mick jumped in to help Kosmo. Joe and Paul soon joined the fray. The Baker and Digby Cleaver dismantled the Clash's equipment as the scuffling parties were broken up.

It had been a terrible concert. Only drummer Pete Howard had impressed. But the Clash's frontline was reinvigorated, and when they reconvened in London, they rehearsed new material in the hope of jump-starting their dormant sixth studio album. It was not to be.

The Perfidy of Paul Simonon

In an echo of *Apocalypse Now!*, the decision was made to terminate with extreme prejudice Mick's command of the Clash. In this, Bernie and Kosmo were co-conspirators, working on Joe to convince him that Mick had lost sight of the original mission of the Clash. In reality, they were looking after their own self-interests. With Topper gone, Mick may have been marginalized, but he still had a full vote, and he had yet to support any of Bernie's initiatives. In addition, Mick had infuriated Bernie by refusing to sign a management contract until his lawyers had vetted the language within. This too Bernie twisted and used as evidence of Mick looking after his own interests and not those of the Clash.

In fact, this was what Joe cited as the deciding factor, when talking with *NME*'s Richard Cook in February of the following year: "The final straw was when he went on about his lawyer. When we started out there was no lawyers in the room with us! Back in the summer he eventually said, I don't mind what the Clash does—as long as you check it with my lawyer first. I sat back and thought, hang on . . . and I said go and write songs with your lawyer. Piss off."

Despite all Bernie's whispering in Joe's ears, though, it was Paul who terminated Mick. This would not have surprised Topper, who had also been summarily dispatched without emotion by his partner in the Clash's rhythm section. As Topper later told Kris Needs, in *Joe Strummer and the Legend of the Clash*, of his own sacking, "[Paul] took the easy option." Robin Banks told Needs that while Topper held no grudge against Joe or Mick, he did hold one against Paul for a long time.

In 1981, the black lettering on Joe's white Fender Telecaster proclaimed "I MAY TAKE A HOLIDAY," but when Mick expressed a desire to do so and not tour in 1983 he was met with the response that a proletariat band like the Clash did not take holidays. Rock stardom—a cardinal sin in clash dogma—was blinding Mick to the original mission. And so the deciding factor may have been Mick's desire to take a holiday. According to Paul, in *The Rise and Fall of the Clash*, "We had a tour set up and just about to start the tour, Mick's off on holiday, so obviously we didn't do the tour, which is a bit of a pain in the neck."

On the fateful day in question in late August 1983, Mick had turned up first at the Clash's rehearsal studio, which was extremely unusual for him. Finding that no one else was around, he went to a nearby bookshop. When he returned, Paul swung the ax. As Paul recounts in *The Rise and Fall of the Clash*, "Mick did get a bit out of hand in a very—in an Elizabeth Taylor way with his moods and whatever. At the time that's what we felt. We felt we've had enough, let's kick him out and that's what we decided on and to hell with the consequences."

Leave it to the women to have more common sense. As former Slits guitarist Viv Albertine says in the same documentary, "Firing Mick from his own band is absolutely insane. You know, they had no right to fire Mick, you know it's either: do you want the Clash to disband or do you want whatever, but you don't fire Mick from his own band, he was the Clash, you know? Whatever Bernie thinks and whatever Joe thought, Mick was the Clash."

"I was totally shocked about the breakup with Mick," Joe's common-law wife Gaby says in *I Need a Dodge*, a 2015 documentary about Joe Strummer. "I thought that was stupid. At times I would express my opinion and at times I would keep quiet. And I thought if I'd keep quiet, they'll find a way . . . out of the shit. But I totally didn't believe in the second Clash. And that whole time, I just thought it was ridiculous."

In the September 10 issue of *NME*, the Clash's official "terse statement" announcing Mick's dismissal was reprinted in full: "Joe Strummer and Paul Simonon have decided that Mick Jones should leave the group. It is felt that Jones has drifted apart from the original idea of the Clash. In future, it will allow Joe and Paul to get on with the job the Clash set out to do from the beginning."

The same *NME* article also included Mick's reply, in which he was clearly parroting and mocking the Clash office's statement: "I would like to state that the official press statement is untrue. I would like to make it clear there was no discussion with Strummer and Simonon prior to being sacked. I certainly do not feel that I have drifted from the original idea of the Clash and in future, I'll be carrying on in the same direction as in the beginning."

Neither succeeded.

The Local Guitar Picker

"Rock 'n' Roll Mick" Jones

Michael Geoffrey "Mick" Jones was born on June 26, 1955, at the South London Hospital for Women in Clapham, in the borough of Lambeth. His parents were a taxi driver named Thomas Gilmour Jones and a jeweler named Renee Zagonsky. Mick's infancy was spent in Clapham, but with the onset of his toddler years, his parents relocated to Brixton, the London district (also in the Lambeth) that he would help put on the musical map of the world. His parents' marriage was not a happy one, and by the 1960s his mother had abandoned Mick and his father for the American dream and emigrated to Ironwood, Michigan, where she married her second husband.

Thereafter, Mick was raised by Renee's mother Stella, a legendary figure in Clash lore, and her sisters and sister-in-law, in an upbringing that seems like the British version of Truman Capote's childhood. Unlike many future British rock 'n' rollers, Mick's overriding interest was music. Sure, he proved himself adept at football, and his autograph book contained the signatures of famous players, but he also joined the Kinks and Animals fan clubs and listened to the pirate radio stations playing the rock 'n' roll music that the BBC would not play. (This was the impetus for Clash's later imaginings of being a pirate radio station for their fans.) By 1967, he had a paper route and scrounged up enough money for Cream's *Disraeli Gears.* He must have been drawn to power trios, because in spring of 1968 he purchased the Jimi Hendrix Experience's stopgap release *Smash Hits*, compiled mostly of 1967 single recordings omitted from the UK version of *Are You Experienced.*

Later that summer, on July 27, 1968, Mick found himself attending his first concert: a free concert featuring Traffic, the Nice, and the Pretty Things in Hyde Park. Almost one year later, on July 5, 1969, Mick was in attendance for the Rolling Stones' free memorial concert for the Master

Musician of Cheltenham, Brian Jones, their founding member, who had died three days earlier. In the interim, Mick had also seen Led Zeppelin, but it was the Rolling Stones' music that held him in thrall. While Joe, his future partner in rhyme, preferred the Berry and Bo era of the Stones, Jones followed assiduously the Keef period, also known as the Jimmy Miller period, when the producer helmed their greatest albums.

By the time of the free Stones concert, Mick was about to start his fourth year at the Strand School, an all-boys grammar school. Spurred by classmates, he became interested in the Faces (before Rod Stewart's fame over took them) and Mott the Hoople, developing a personal relationship with the band's road manager—who let him and his school friends in for free—and the band members as Mick and his friends traveled around England by train to see Mott in concert. One of these friends, Kelvin Blacklock, even managed to worm his way onstage and sing with Ian Hunter several times. Who could blame these boys, then, for returning to London and forming a band called Schoolgirl? Mick was younger than his friends and didn't play an instrument but offered his services as their roadie—the first step taken by many future rock 'n' rollers.

The Delinquents

As Schoolgirl's roadie, Mick found opportunities to try his hands at drumming. Keeping a beat came naturally to him, but he felt drumming was too far removed from the stage action. Mick wanted to be a guitarist near the front, and over the next several years he acquired a Hofner and then a Fender Telecaster. Schoolgirl disbanded after the boys graduated from the Strand School, but Mick was still in touch with bassist John Brown, who was agreeable to Mick's suggestion of forming a band. They agreed it would be called the Delinquents. It was May 1974.

Guitarist Paul Layman, another former Strand School classmate, and drummer Mike Dowling, scrounged up via an advertisement in *Melody Maker*, soon rounded out the foursome. The Delinquents were an active band for approximately nine months. They performed little but rehearsed often. Mick began writing his own songs for the band, and in the purchase of a reel-to-reel tape recorder took his first steps in acquiring the skills he would later put to good use as the Clash's producer. They also had photos taken and recorded two demos, but their attempts at finding management came to naught and Dowling and Layman left around January 1975.

Little Queenie

The remaining Delinquents placed another ad for a drummer in *Melody Maker.* The next band that had wowed Mick after Mott the Hoople was the New York Dolls, an American glam-rock band, so he was impressed when Geir Waade, former drummer in the Hollywood Brats, the Dolls' British equivalent, responded. Mick had readily adopted the glam look. Waade was in, and soon after so too was the Brats' former lead guitarist, Eunan Brady. This move relegated Mick to rhythm guitar, but as the band's songwriter he felt he held a secure position.

Schoolgirl vocalist Kelvin Blacklock was recruited, too, and soon after they auditioned for manager Tony Gordon. He liked what the band had to offer but not their name and agreed to manage the rock 'n' roll outfit only if they renamed themselves after Chuck Berry's "Little Queenie." Waade at this juncture was replaced by former Schoolgirl drummer Jim Hyatt.

Gordon had connections with Pye Records, and a demo session was arranged at their studios for Little Queenie. Blacklock was unhappy with the results and took it upon himself to look up former Mott manager and producer Guy Stevens, whose career was spiraling downward due to alcoholism. It's doubtful the young rock 'n' rollers knew this, and three members of Little Queenie were thrilled to be discussing their future with the man who had guided Mott the Hoople to stardom. It's easy to understand why they left Gordon's management for Stevens.

After one rehearsal, Stevens thought Little Queenie needed a keyboard player, not a rhythm guitarist, and John Brown was coaxed by the thought of a contract with Warner Bros. into replacing Mick. The young man was devastated. While Mick could be extremely vain, he was also extremely loyal, and he was shocked at this turn of events, especially since it was Stevens, a hero of his, who had orchestrated his dismissal. Suffering is, as many philosophers and writers have pointed out, necessary for personal growth, and Mick's suffering led him to "practice daily in his room," as he later wrote in "Stay Free." His take on his ouster was that he had to be a better guitarist to escape reliving his fate with Little Queenie. As documented in chapter 1, Mick moved on, formed London SS, and finally, in January 1976, using his art-school grant money, Mick purchased the same type of guitar that Johnny Thunders of the New York Dolls played: a Les Paul Junior with a P-90 pickup. It was the guitar he would become associated with in the Clash from 1976 and into the beginning of 1978.

"With My Good Eye on the Beat"

As a leading punk rocker in the UK, Mick soon found himself in a quandary. Punk dogma led him and Joe in their earliest interviews to misrepresent their pre-punk days. Joe cut his age by a few years, tried erasing the 101'ers, tried to sound more street. Mick played up being from Brixton and living in the Westway tower blocks, made it sound like his future was either punk rock or a life of petty crime, and tried his best at looking tough.

This was easy for Paul. He was the real punk deal: a twenty-one-year old youth from a poor part of London whose musical apprenticeship as a bassist was with the Clash. It was easy for Terry, too, because although he never participated in interviews (since he had already told the band he was quitting) he was also an honest, forthright "bloke" who wasn't lying about his past.

(Joe's economy with the truth led to an embarrassing moment at the Roundhouse on November 5, 1976—an embarrassing moment that is preserved for eternity on a bootleg recording known as *5 Go Mad in the Roundhouse*. It was the band's fifth show, and Keith Levene's last, and they were one of the opening acts. Joe has determined that interaction between the front man and the crowd is important, but he's nervous and not good at banter. The Clash are about to perform "Mark Me Absent," and Joe is battling hecklers who are there to see either Crazy Cavan 'n' the Rhythm Rockers or the headliners, the Kursaal Flyers. Asked if he was in the 101'ers, Joe insists, "Never heard of them." Eager to change the subject, he asks, "How many of you are in your normal consciousness?" A voice in the impatient crowd tells Joe to "Shut up, smart-arse, get on with it," to which Joe answers, "You big twit, so what if you've got five A-levels, what do I care, that's just a dirty trick." Then someone gives Joe a verbal twist to the gut: "Your drummer's got them!" The reference to Terry's education leaves Joe momentarily speechless. Situations such as these may account for Joe later developing an indirect means of interaction with the audience. After this, he would either recite the opening lines of the next song as a means of introduction or make a cryptic statement.)

Mick realized earlier on than Joe that these attempts at conforming to a punk stereotype were going to come back to haunt. He may not have seen the roots of these accusations of mythmaking, but he knew that it would eventually come out that while he did live on the eighteenth floor of a tower block, he was living with his grandmother! Not exactly ideal for the punk image. With no criminal record, the worst thing in Mick's future was probably an office job. When things got out of hand at Clash concerts, it was Joe and occasionally Paul wading into crowd and sorting things out.

When called out on this, Mick would retort that someone in the band's got to stay in tune, haven't they?

The Clash never supported left- or right-wing political organizations but were still seen as rebels, and "White Riot" as their clarion call-up for revolution. This is what Paul Rambali, in the January 5, 1980, issue of *NME*, called, "The myth of the Clash as urban guerillas with guitars for guns and brilliantine for berets." Mick contributed to this impression by telling *Sniffin' Glue*'s Steve Walsh that "rock 'n' roll is about rebellion," but he foresaw the grief the Clash would catch when riots erupted in England in May 1981 and the Clash were off in America playing their extended residency at Bond International Casino. There were fans and even some journalists who expected the Clash to cancel the concerts and come lead the revolution. Mick knew the day would come when the Clash would have to answer for "White Riot." Rambali confronted Mick on this in an October 1981 issue of *NME*, noting, "A lot of people asked where you were this summer . . . implying that you had some sort of obligation to be there because of [the rioting] going on."

"I don't even know if I agree with them," Mick replied. "Destroying your own places. Especially if the government ain't going to give you another one—it seems really double dumb. I do my thing and it's a creative thing—that's how I feel I contribute to that. And if my absence is conspicuous on

Always in motion in concert, Mick Jones flies across the Clash's stage.

Peter Noble/Getty Images

these occasions then I say don't look to me in the first place. I'm not the street fighting man."

Joe later apologized to *NME*'s Gavin Martin, in the issue dated July 26, 1986: "The rebel chic, the Belfast photos, H-Block T-shirts, and Baader-Meinhof shirts; they were all my fault. When you're gung ho, you're gung ho, and I was certainly gung ho. I'm sorry that's the vibe that was given off, I was only writing the shit that I felt."

"You're My Guitar Hero!"

Joe's exclamation of "You're my guitar hero!" during Mick's guitar solo in "Complete Control" was something Mick had to downplay during his years with the Clash for fear of being labeled not a true punk rocker but a "muso" in disguise. What this meant is that the trajectory of Mick's development as a guitarist was overlooked and largely undocumented.

When Keith Levene's departure left a gaping hole in the Clash's sound, Mick welcomed the opportunity to become the band's lead guitarist. There was a reason Joe was called Joe Strummer; as he told Caroline Coon in 1977, "I can jam out some chords but I can't do no lead guitar fiddley [sic] bits." Within a short time, Mick was punk's equivalent of George Harrison, his short, tuneful leads hidden beneath the band's musical snarl.

The startling growth and reach of the Clash can be attributed to Mick's journey as an inventive, restless guitarist. He really strove to emulate the guitar hero on *Give 'Em Enough Rope* where, with Joe's help, he overdubbed myriad layers of guitars. As noted previously, Pearlman deserves credit for having Epic Records acquire better equipment for the Clash, and it was at this time that Mick acquired the Gibson Les Paul he is known for. Writing for *Premier Guitar* in May 2010, Wallace Marx Jr. itemized the guitars and amplifiers used by Mick with the Clash from 1978 onward: "A sunburst '58 Standard, a wine-red '70s Custom, a white '70s Custom, and a sunburst '70s Custom. On the road in America in 1979, he picked up a rare all-white Gibson ES-295 that he used for a short period. In the studio, Jones frequently played a late-'70s all-black Fender Strat with a maple fretboard."

Seeing as how Sandy Pearlman was responsible for the band's equipment, it's no surprise to learn that the *Rope* producer turned Mick on to "quality tube amplifiers—specifically Mesa/Boogies." According to Marx Jr., Mick had fallen for "the 100-watt Mark I in combo form. He unloaded the speaker and used . . . a single Marshall 4 x 12 . . . but by the end of 1979 he had added a blond 100-watt Mark II to drive one of the cabinets."

Mick started experimenting with foot pedals, chiefly an MXR Phase 100 (also used by Keith Richards for the *Some Girls* sessions), an MXR Flanger, and the Roland RE-201 Space Echo. These effects allowed him to whip up a cauldron of sound during live performances. He was forever testing out new leads and rhythms that made no two Clash concerts alike.

Then came Mick's Roland guitar synthesizer.

Following the Clash's rather embarrassing appearance headlining the Saturday bill at the US Festival in San Bernardino, California, the band regrouped in London at Ear Studios in June 1983 and began working up songs for the follow-up to *Combat Rock*. Despite the album's success, Mick still believed that hip hop and studio technology, not rockabilly and distorted guitars, was the future direction for the Clash. His habit of turning up late had worsened, and when he did arrive at Ear Studios he was armed with a Roland guitar synthesizer that didn't mesh with how Joe and Paul heard guitars sounding on future Clash recordings. It didn't help that they believed Mick hadn't mastered his new instrument yet. The rehearsals hardly lasted a week. For Joe and Paul, they were not fruitful, but some of the material the Clash were working would form the basis of songs on Big Audio Dynamite's debut album. (For example, a song called "Trans Cash Free Pay One" was an early incarnation of "The Bottom Line.")

Mick was handed his severance check around the time of the 1983 Notting Hill Carnival, and later that year Joe had this to say to music journalist and *New York Post* columnist Lisa Robinson about the role the Roland guitar synthesizer had in Mick's dismissal: "He'd plug the guitar into the synth, but what he ended up liking to do best was holding a note on the guitar and then . . . twiddling knobs to make it . . . sound like a Volkswagen or a symphony . . . but after he had his fun, I wanted him to play the guitar . . . so why didn't he play the guitar? No, it was too passé, it was non-artistic, geniuses like him didn't have to stoop so low as to play a punky chord full of roaring distortion, which is my favorite guitar sound."

If Mick was going to take the electric guitar to the next level, it'd have to be with a new band.

"You Could See the Bad Go Down Again"

Unfortunately, Mick could be temperamental, and he had many selfish habits that over the course of the Clash's eight-plus years of existence began getting under everyone's skin. Some originated from being a pampered grandson, while others were simple excesses of rock 'n' roll stardom that—over time—Mick began to see as his due as the member of a very successful band. It is what he dreamed of growing up and reading the American rock 'n' roll magazines his mother mailed him from overseas.

In the early days of the Clash, Johnny Green or The Baker were expected to drive over to Mick's and pick him up and deliver him for rehearsals or recording sessions, for which he was characteristically late, as depicted in the "Garageland" sequence of *Rude Boy*.

Mick could also be a difficult person to tour with. He was peevish and insisted on staying at finer hotels as the band's success grew. Stories abound of difficult days on the road with Mick, such as the time he refused to board a tour bus in Spain unless he was served the English breakfast he had a hankering for. On another occasion, in Canada, he held up the bus until drugs were secured for the journey.

It was an in-joke around the Clash that everyone who entered their circle was subject to having their hair cut. So it wasn't taken kindly by Joe or Paul when, in the latter half of 1977, Mick—tiring of punk orthodoxy—began growing his hair long (deliberating stressing his resemblance to Keef). During this same time period, his cocaine consumption escalated—another symbol of rock 'n' roll excess that punk rock allegedly abhorred. Journalists who policed punk bands for infractions had a field day with this.

The bonding of the destitute band members over the summer of 1979 was shattered by Joe punching Mick backstage on January 27 in Sheffield a month into the 16 Tons tour. They tried to brush it under the tour bus, but it was a defining moment. While Joe, Mick, and Topper began working on the band's fourth album, a schism began forming when Mick found hip hop in a Brooklyn record shop. For Joe, it was something worth experimenting with, but Mick saw it as a new direction. *Sandinista!* actually outsold *London Calling*, but criticisms of the record stirred up Joe's insecurities, and he strongly felt that the Clash had to retrench. Mick, who was now living in New York City for long stretches, hearing positive things about the Clash's recent work and being feted like a rock star strongly believed the Clash needed to go deeper down the hip-hop rabbit hole.

Kosmo Vinyl, the Clash's "Minister of Disinformation," says in *Westway to the World* that the breakup of the Clash could be attributed to three men having drifted as they grew up and found themselves in demanding romantic relationships, but this is a simplification. Joe and Paul and their significant others socialized together. Mick had his own circle of friends. So it was only natural that Paul would find himself in agreement with Joe's dissatisfaction with Mick after the band conquered the world in 1982 with a hit album, hit singles, and sold-out performances on several continents. With Mick turning up late at rehearsals, no progress was being made on new material. Finally it was Paul, not Joe, who made the decision: Mick was ousted from the band he founded.

Jones at the Controls

As the Clash's principal arranger, Mick would hole up in hotel rooms with the lights out, thinking about how best to present the Clash's material. It was Mick who blended punk rock and reggae and created "the sound of the Westway." He studied the work of contemporaries to enrich the Clash's records; trying, for example, to determine how Bruce Springsteen got a certain drum sound. When Sandy Pearlman and Corky Stasiak were roped in to produce and engineer the second album, it was Mick who was at their mixing elbows, picking up the tricks of their trade, educating himself well enough that he oversaw the overdub sessions for *London Calling*, and although it was credited to the Clash, *Sandinista!* was largely produced by Mick.

In 1981, Mick received the co-producer's credit with Mick Ronson on an album by his childhood hero Ian Hunter (*Short Back N' Sides*), and sole credit on albums by his girlfriend Ellen Foley (*Spirit of St. Louis*) and Theatre of Hate (*Do You Believe in the Westworld*). But the writing was on the wall when Mick's next production effort was the rejected mix for *Rat Patrol from Fort Bragg*, the Clash's work-in-progress fifth studio album. "That was the time when we found out . . . I didn't know how to mix records anymore," Mick says sarcastically, in *The Rise and Fall of the Clash*. Within eighteen months he would be out of the band.

General Public

When the English Beat opened for the Clash at their shows in California in 1982, their lead singer, Ranking Roger, would join the headliners for versions of "Rock the Casbah" and "Armagideon Time," but by 1983 the English Beat had disbanded, and Ranking Roger and guitarist Dave Wakeling were, like Mick, band-less. The three formed General Public along with members of the Specials and Dexy's Midnight Runners. They even appeared once together in concert, at the Crompton Arms in Birmingham. But midway during the recording of their debut album (*All the Rage*), Mick dropped out of the project. He can be heard playing guitar on at least seven of the album's ten tracks.

During a 2009 interview, Wakeling recalled the recording sessions: "I had to control Ranking Roger a bit, though, because . . . Mick Jones would be starting to play something, and Roger would be on the intercom straight away, 'Uh, Mick, could you try something like . . . .' And I could see Mick Jones start to get frustrated, y'know? . . . and I said, 'Here's an idea, Roger: why don't you let the best guitarist in the world play what he wants? And if, at the end of the night, you still don't think you've got what you need, then come up with a suggestion.'" A recording session like the one described by Wakeling sounds a little like what Mick experienced with the Clash in June 1983, so it is not surprising that he left soon after. He wasn't about to listen any longer to a lead singer telling him how to play guitar. In his next band, he would be the lead singer.

Top Risk Action Company

Mick threatened at one point to carry on with the Clash's name—it was, after all, his band, even if Joe was the figurehead—and to form an alternative band that would compete with Joe and Paul's rebellious punkabilly revival. He strengthened his position by pairing with Topper. Each Clash outfit now had two former members. According to Vince White's memoir, *The Last Days of the Clash*, Joe saw this as a true threat. It was a race to see who could get an album out first and lay claim to the name, but Mick's lawsuit against Joe, Paul, and Bernie also undermined both camps by freezing the assets garnered from the successes of 1982. The Clash, Round Two hit the road to raise cash, but Mick soon dropped both the lawsuit and his threat to continue recording under the Clash moniker.

Bassist Leo "E-Zee Kill" Williams of Basement 5 and saxophonist John "Boy" Leonard (who had played on the Theatre of Hate album Mick had produced) came onboard and the Top Risk Action Company (T.R.A.C.) was formed. The foursome recorded demos, but this musical enterprise fell through due to Topper's unreliability—a situation that was exacerbated after the drummer received £200,000 in previously frozen songwriting royalty money for *Combat Rock*. This was a windfall that could be spent—*and would be spent*—on an eighteen-month drug binge. If Mick was going to succeed, it would have to be without any former members of the Clash onstage with him.

Big Audio Dynamite

Mick jettisoned John Boy but kept Leo for his next project—the one that would give Mick the post-Clash commercial success that eluded everyone else. In a stroke of DIY audacity, legendary punk DJ and documentarian Don Letts, who couldn't play an instrument, was also asked to join. Mick liked the way Leo and Don looked together and thought the three of them looked like a band. He was running on instinct. When Letts countered that he couldn't play an instrument, Mick reminded him Paul had been in a similar position when the Clash began. (Ironically, Letts would provide the new band with its most innovative component.) Drummer Greg Roberts answered an ad in *Melody Maker* and replaced Topper.

Recalling the recording of the first album twenty-five years later, Roberts told www.slicingupeyeballs.com, "Mick sort of thrust the drum machine—it was a Linn 1, really, which was one of the first ever drum machines—and said, 'Work that out. See what you can do with that.' I don't think he was really sure what we wanted to do, whether we wanted to have all drum machines or live. The mix was both, especially when we played live. When I first started playing, I thought I'd have to play sort of in and out of the beat, sort of fills over the top. But it soon became apparent that you just sort of locked in with the groove. It sounds like two drummers."

Finally, at a photo shoot (arranged by Paul's future wife Tricia Ronane), the photographer Dan Donovan let it be known that he played keyboards when asked if he knew anyone who did. He hadn't studied piano in seven years, but he soon found himself in the Big Audio Dynamite lineup.

This Is Big Audio Dynamite

The sound of Big Audio Dynamite was described by Don Letts in the liner notes for the Legacy Edition of *This Is Big Audio Dynamite* as "a blend of New York beats, Jamaican basslines, English rock 'n' roll guitar and . . . sampled dialogue and movie stuff." In other words, the sound Mick had been advocating the Clash pursue, minus the "sampled dialogue and movie stuff." *London Calling*'s sound may have been compared to a sonic cinemascope, but with his first "solo" album, Mick was going to go even further. With Don Letts's deep knowledge of film, Big Audio Dynamite were way ahead of the curve and would feature film dialogue as an integral part of their music. Identifying the samples was part of the fun of listening to *This Is Big Audio Dynamite* when it was first released. Like the Beastie Boys' *Paul's Boutique*, it was the samples that made the recording so revolutionary.

On the liner notes, Letts is credited with "F.X. Voc.," which I interpret to be film effects voices, though he did sing in concert. He has since written that during the recording sessions at Basing Street Studios (where the Clash had recorded basic tracks for *Give 'Em Enough Rope*), the members of Big Audio Dynamite would "have mini-film festivals in the 'green room' with the intent of using bits of dialogue" for the songs they were recording. Possibly because of the success of WBLS's "Dirty Harry Mix" of "The Magnificent Seven," the album's lead track "Medicine Show" only included dialogue from Clint Eastwood films. Likewise, "$E=MC^2$" only contains dialogue from films directed by Nicholas Roeg, including some choice lines from *Performance*, starring Mick Jagger and James Fox.

The most interesting sample to Clash fans on *This Is Big Audio Dynamite*, however, is on "Sony," a critique of the Japanese conglomerate. Heard throughout is Joe's nuclearized seagull cry from "London Calling," aka the call of the wildebeest. It is ironic that Sony eventually acquired CBS Records, the label Big Audio Dynamite (and Joe Strummer) were signed to.

This Is Big Audio Dynamite is a fine album. Mick set out to remake his musical image as completely as Paul McCartney did with Wings after the breakup of the Beatles. He was abetted greatly by Paul "Groucho" Smykle, a London producer of Jamaican descent who had produced Gregory Isaacs, Aswad, and Black Uhuru, and who got his start doing album cover design. A devotee of King Tubby, he was well known for his dub mixes.

The album's title is obviously indebted to "This Is Radio Clash" and as a rebuke to "We Are the Clash." All the songs on Side 1 hold up, but as "A Party," the opening track on Side 2, implies, this is an album to party to. With the beat boxes, large drums, synthesizers, and clean guitars, it may be dated, but that's because it sounds like so many other albums from 1985. "The Magnificent Seven" sounds timeless because the basic track was recorded in April 1980 and released that December, before hip-hop rhythms were being used by every other band on the planet. Mick's ideas for using beat boxes for the Clash were innovative in 1981 and 1982, when he first wanted to use them. By 1985, he was no longer ahead of the curve.

And while the lyrics retain the Clash's social consciousness and address apartheid and AIDs and other issues of the day, this too has dated the album. The genius of Joe Strummer's political lyrics is that, unlike the Dead Kennedys or Crass or Big Audio Dynamite, he did not invoke current events. He'd sing of the Spanish Civil War in the 1930s or the *coup d'état* in Chile in 1973, tapping into a timeless sentiment for social justice.

Still, when it was originally released, two months after the Clash's *Cut the Crap*, Mick's effort was deemed superior to that of Joe's. In an age when record companies sought to get as many hit singles from one album as it could, *This Is Big Audio Dynamite* had three singles that cracked the UK Top 30. "E=MC²" even got as high as #11.

The 2010 Legacy Edition includes a second disc with 12-inch remixes, dubs, B-sides, and even a "vocoder version" of "BAD." There are alternate versions of every song on the original LP in the same playing order for the ultimate party version of *This Is Big Audio Dynamite.*

This is the Big Audio Dynamite album preferred by fans whose favorite Clash member was Mick.

This Is Big Audio Dynamite was B.A.D.'s most commercially successful recording.
Author's collection

No. 10, Upping Street

Picture this: it is mid-summer 1985, Mick has completed mixing *This Is Big Audio Dynamite* and is vacationing in Nassau, the capital city of the Commonwealth of the Bahamas with his girlfriend Daisy Lawrence and their one-year-old daughter Lauren Estelle. He is also working with Talking Heads bassist Tina Weymouth. Who should turn up but Joe, on a moped with an ounce of marijuana, intent on patching things up and resurrecting the Clash. Mick plays the unreleased *This Is Big Audio Dynamite* for Joe, who is not impressed and tells Mick that what Mick's new music is missing is Joe Strummer. Understandably, Mick turns down Joe's offer to reform the Clash. Almost two years have passed since Mick's dismissal and his next musical project is wrapped up and in the can. It's time to move on.

But they did work together again the following year. First, after some resistance, Joe agreed to provide the title song for director Alex Cox's work-in-progress *Love Kills*, a film about Sid Vicious and Nancy Spungen's relationship, his downfall, and her murder. Mick generously turned up and played guitar on "Love Kills" and "Dum Dum Club" for the soundtrack, but his contributions were mixed out by producer Eric "E. T." Thorngrun. Cox's film was eventually released as *Sid and Nancy*, starring Gary Oldman as Sid Vicious. No longer tied to the film's title, "Love Kills" deservedly received little attention, because it was an uninspired track. "Dum Dum Club," however, was one of the few good songs Joe recorded in the second half of the 1980s.

Emotionally battered by the deaths of his mother and Gaby Salter's brother, Big Audio Dynamite's success, and writer's block, Joe was at an emotional low, drinking heavily. Then, in June 1986, he turned up in Studio 1 at Trident Studios in Soho with Don Letts. Thus began the last sustained project Joe and Mick were to work on together: Big Audio Dynamite's second album, *No. 10, Upping Street*, its title conceived by Joe as a pun on the British prime minister's address in London.

The drummer gets equal time with the beat box, the guitar regains it's rock 'n' roll growl, the film dialogue subsides. Joe gets a co-writing credit on seven of the twelve tracks. The opening track, "C'mon Every Beatbox," is not one of them, but it is a wonderful merging of hip-hop production with rockabilly song structure. The song's title even acknowledges the fact that it is based on Eddie Cochran's "C'mon Everybody." This was to be the closest we'd ever get to hearing what the Clash might have sounded like if they had mashed up Mick's ideas with Joe's in 1983.

Still, contrary to press reports, things had not been perfect in the studio while producing *No. 10, Upping Street.* In a late 1980s Q&A with Jim Shelley, Joe admitted that there was a lot of arguing throughout the sessions, with Joe advocating a "crunchy drum sound" and manning the day sessions while Mick did the night. Since Big Audio Dynamite was not Joe's band, he felt he had little say in the final result.

You can hear why this is the Big Audio Dynamite album preferred by fans whose favorite Clash member was Joe. It must be noted, though, that *No. 10, Upping Street* was remixed by Mick for its CD release, so to hear the Joe Strummer–approved mixes, you have to play the original vinyl.

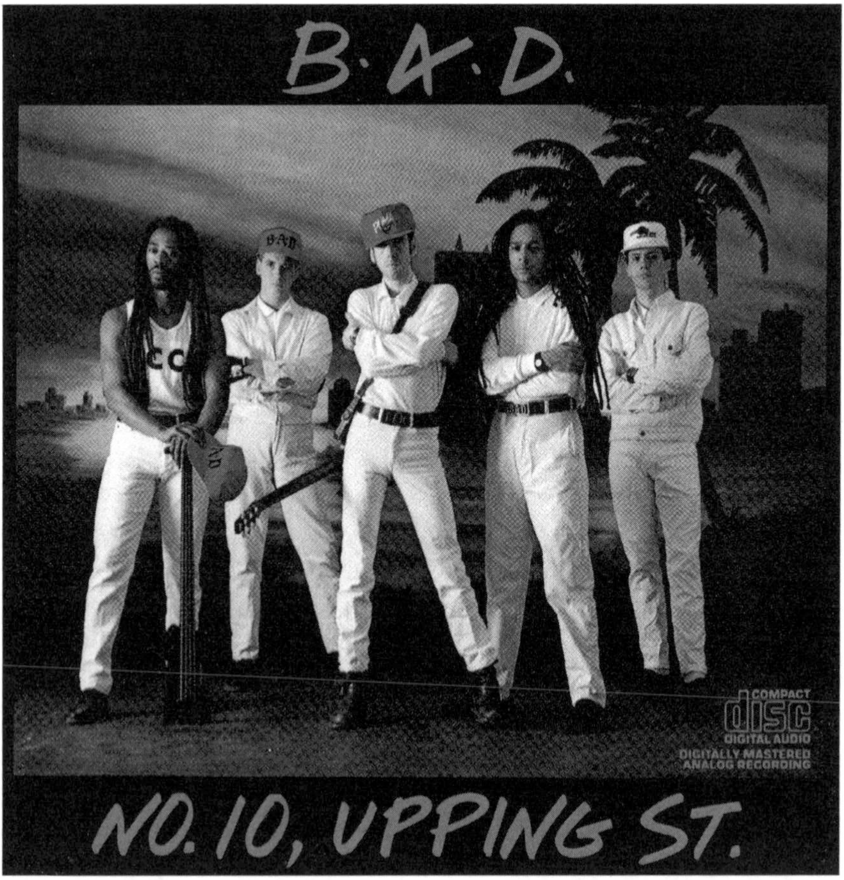

No. 10, Upping Street reunited Mick and Joe as recording partners. It was the last time they worked together professionally. *Author's collection*

The Globe

In 1988, Big Audio Dynamite's third album, *Tighten Up Vol. '88* (inspired by similarly titled reggae albums), had just come out to poor reviews when Mick caught chicken pox of the mouth, throat, and lungs from his daughter, which then escalated to pneumonia. For ten days he lay near death, paralyzed and in a coma, at St. Mary's Hospital in Paddington. Months of rehabilitation followed, as did, in 1989, Big Audio Dynamite's fourth album, *Megatop Phoenix.*

Soon after, the original members of Big Audio Dynamite abandoned Mick and formed Screaming Target, a short-lived band who released only one album, *Hometown Hi-Fi.* Drummer Greg Roberts then formed Dreadzone in 1993 with musician and sound engineer Tim Bran. His ex-bandmates in Big Audio Dynamite, Leo Williams and Dan Donovan, were subsequently added to the lineup. Dreadzone have released nine studio albums and a series of singles over the years, a few of which charted in the UK. At the time of this writing, the rhythm section of Williams and Roberts that was first formed for Big Audio Dynamite was still touring and going strong after thirty years.

Mick regrouped, literally, with B.A.D. II: a new name for a new lineup. The key member was bassist Gary Stonadge, who emerged as Mick's songwriting partner. Surprisingly for a musician who was once critical of the similarity in Ramones' recordings and adamant that he would never do the same, Mick had stuck to a winning formula with Big Audio Dynamite's original lineup. With Letts gone, the film dialogue samples were replaced with samples of music by the Who, Deep Purple, and even the Clash, but the overall formula of pop melodies atop hip-hop beats remained. (The use of the Who's "Baba O'Riley" was almost a natural extension for a songwriter who once pilfered "I Can't Explain.") "The Globe" samples the opening notes of "Should I Stay or Should I Go," and Mick had his greatest success with the song in the US as the song reached #3 on *Billboard*'s Modern Rock Tracks chart in 1991.

Big Audio Dynamite—regardless of the lineup—were always popular with MTV and college crowds, so this was not a surprise. In fact, by the early '90s, Mick was more famous in the US for Big Audio Dynamite than the Clash, who were viewed as a cult favorite band—a one-hit wonder—he had once played in. But although *The Globe* was a hit recording, you have to wonder what the frat boys thought of the album bought for the hit single. Sure, there are rock tracks ("Can't Wait/Live" and "Green Grass") and even a power ballad ("Innocent Child"), but most of the tracks abruptly change direction or have weird edits. For example, "Innocent Child" concludes with a funky fadeout. And then there's the professorial voice expounding on rhythm theory in "Rush" and "I Don't Know." *The Globe* is a rewarding listen, but it's very experimental: there are unexpected between-song interludes of classical music and Beatles-esque arpeggios and even guest vocalists. *The Globe* is a sonic collage and Mick's most daring recording—even more so than *Sandinista!*

This may explain why fans pulled the plug out on Big Audio Dynamite. *Higher Power* from 1994 was the length of a double album but lacked hits and failed to chart. The band then signed to Radioactive Records, and *F-Punk* was released less than a year afterward. It too failed to chart. Radioactive refused to release Big Audio Dynamite's next album, so *Entering a New Ride* was made available as a free download. It was the last stop in the studio for Big Audio Dynamite.

Producing the Libertines and Babyshambles

It is fair to say that the most consequential music Mick has played a role in since the Clash is his production of the Libertines, one of the better neo-punk bands to emerge, and their Babyshambles offshoot. He was hired to produce their debut album, *Up the Bracket*, which was recorded at RAK Studios in St. John's Wood. It proved tremendously successful, but Mick was only brought back to produce the second album after sessions with Bernard Butler were unfruitful. Friction between the Libertines front men Carl Barât and Pete Doherty was front-page news in Great Britain at the time, and yet Mick managed to successfully produce their eponymously named second album, which ended up being superior to the debut. Soon after, Doherty split from the Libertines and formed Babyshambles. Amid his deepening drug addiction and numerous arrests, Babyshambles released the grossly underrated *Down in Albion* in 2005, with Jones again at the controls.

Carbon/Silicon

Being the Clash's musical mastermind, it's no surprise that Mick has been the most musically active of the band's former members. And in the aughts he finally undertook a project with his old friend Tony James that actually came to fruition. While Mick was busy producing records for the Libertines, they began sharing mp3 files via the Internet. According to their website, they saw "the Internet as the savior of creativity—not its downfall." Within sixteen months, they had enough material for two promising albums that were regrettably unusable because the files were heavily indebted to sampling.

In February 2004, the "punk rock duo" (as Wikipedia describes them) decided to play live. With both Mick and James playing guitar, they rounded up two friends to play bass and drums. They named themselves Carbon/Silicon after "a magazine piece by Susan Greenfield about the future of human intelligence enhanced by use of silicon computer implants" and explained that it was perfect for them because it represents the sound of the band: Mick's "soul" (Carbon) combined with James's "computers" (Silicon).

By May they were touring the UK, playing only new material (no Clash! no Sigue Sigue Sputnik!), creating a fan base, and impressing reviewers. Playing live allowed Carbon/Silicone to move away from sample-based compositions. A year after they first played in clubs, Patti Smith asked them to play the Meltdown Festival, which she curated in 2005, and by winter they were formally recording. Initially, the first album, *A.T.O.M.*, was issued as a free download, as were tracks from the follow-up, *Second Front*. A third mini-album (*The Crackup Suite*) was issued on their website in March 2007. That's two-and-a-half albums worth of music released within thirteen months!

Finally, in June 2007, Carbon/Silicon released an EP, *The News*, on CD. Another EP, *The Magic Suitcase*, followed in September, and then a full-length CD (*The Last Post*) arrived in October. Clash alumnus Bill Price mixed the album and received a co-production credit with Mick. *The Last Post* consists of material from the previous releases. Former B.A.D. bassist Leo "E-Zee Kill" Williams is on the recording along with drummer Dominic Greensmith, but don't let that fool you: Carbon/Silicon sound nothing like B.A.D.

The twelve tracks are endlessly catchy, address political and social issues, and demonstrate Mick's newfound love for the guitar. It's a very upbeat experience. Several songs are built from old rock 'n' roll chassis: you can hear the Kinks' "You Really Got Me" under "The Whole Truth" and Blondie in "Really the Blues," and "What the Fuck" it is so undergirded by the Clash's "Guns on the Roof" that you keep waiting for Topper's dynamic drumrolls to come cascading down during the outro.

Of interest to Clash fans is "Ignore Alien Orders," a track from *The News* EP that is named after the iconic sticker on Joe's 1966 Fender Telecaster.

Carbon/Silicon released *Carbon Casino*, a live recording, in 2009, but have been inactive since 2013's "Big Surprise."

The B.A.D. Reunion Tour

Partaking in what the Fall's Mark E. Smith sardonically called the "Reformation TLC" trend circa 2010, Big Audio Dynamite, like so many other 1970s and 1980s acts, reformed and cashed in on reunion tours. By then, though, Big Audio Dynamite's star had burned out, and the Clash's shined more brightly than ever. The reunion show at Roseland in New York City on April 19, 2011, might have been sold out, but as www.according2g.com reported, when the original Big Audio Dynamite took the stage, "immediately the crowd went bonkers as it seemed to hit everyone all at once that Mick Jones from the Clash was performing for us!"

This underscores the point I think Joe was trying to make when he hunted Mick down in Nassau in the Bahamas in late summer 1985 and told him, after hearing the unreleased but completed *This Is Big Audio Dynamite,* "I don't like it. There aren't any songs. You need me." Chris Salewicz agreed with Mick that it wasn't the most diplomatic statement. But, in hindsight, what Joe was saying was that Mick would probably continue to be commercially successful with his dance music with political undertones, but the music he was making would no longer be as artistically vital as his work the Clash has proven to be.

24

This Is Joe Public Speaking

The Clash, Round Two

The second incarnation of the Clash was never formally referred to or advertised as being anything other than the Clash, a decision Joe justified to *Creem*'s Bill Holdship thus: "Even if Vince [White] and Nick [Sheppard] weren't in the Clash before, they were buying the records and standing in the front row. The fact that they learned to play is great because we can use them now. But we are the Clash because it certainly ain't U2, and it certainly ain't the Alarm, and it certainly ain't the make-up brigade, and it certainly ain't the heavy metal thing, and it certainly ain't Mick Jones. *We are the Clash* and I'd hope that if I started to act funny that I would be fired, and the Clash would continue to roll on without me."

But we do need a way to differentiate between two very different incarnations of the Clash.

In February 1984, Joe told Richard Cook, a clearly skeptical *NME* journo, that "This is like Round Two," and that is how I will refer to Joe and Paul and three young men who were poorly repaid for putting their talents and reputations on the line for "getting on with the job": Pete Howard, Nick Sheppard, and Gregory "Vince" White.

Movers and Shakers

In 2007, guitarist Vince White penned his recount of the Clash's last days so he could pay off his bar tab, as he says in the book's Intro. The Joe Strummer plummeting in White's memoir differs dramatically from the Joe Strummer ascending in Johnny Green's memoir depicting the events of five years earlier. In Green's book, as the Clash are leaving Tower Records after an in-store promotional appearance for *Give 'Em Enough Rope*, Joe tells his road manager, "We ain't ever doing that again." But in 1984—with Green long gone and White now a member of the Clash, Round Two—Joe is back in California being interviewed on radio shows, drumming up ticket sales, raving about "Rebel Rock!" That says all you need to know about the state of the Clash after Mick's termination. In 1984, Joe—pushed by Bernie and with shows on college campuses not selling out—feels he's got to move product; in 1979, the product moved itself.

"[Joe] believed passionately in everything he did. Right or wrong," Topper told *Uncut*'s Stephen Dalton in 2007. How else to describe Joe's actions with the Clash after Mick's firing, then? Or, as Nick Sheppard puts it in *I Need a Dodge,* when discussing the disastrous *Cut the Crap* sessions, "I met Joe over the road for a coffee and I said, 'I'm fucking losing it here . . . I'm really losing my shit.' And he said, 'Don't say that. Don't go there. I've got to believe this is going to work.'"

This partially explains the rush to get the Clash, Round Two on the road as soon as possible with the Out of Control tour. There were also legal threats from Mick's attorneys (later joined by Topper) over the rights to the band's name, and this too has been put forth as a reason for touring. It would further establish their rights to the band's name. It may also have just been Joe and Paul's sincere belief that the Clash had a responsibility to perform.

Never ones to shy away from controversy, the Clash and their management decided to resume touring in California in January 1984, where memories of the US Festival debacle eight months earlier were still fresh. Saying he is quoting Joe, Clash spokesman Kosmo Vinyl explained the return to the *Record*'s John Mendelsohn by postulating that "rock 'n' roll is best when it's fought on enemy territory." It has also been speculated that the Clash, Round Two were road-tested in California because it was far away from the caustic eyes of the British press.

In interviews from the American tours of 1984—there were two—Joe also stressed the importance of road testing the Clash, Round Two's new songs before stepping into a studio. He compared this to what the Clash had done throughout 1976, telling Lisa Robinson—never the Clash's biggest fan—that it will be "like we road tested the first album. And we're hopefully going to end up with a solid, straight ahead album with no nonsense."

"I go back to our first record and I like the writing style on that record," Joe stressed to Cook. "It's lean. Trim! Makes a point, then another song starts. Imagine in your mind an ELP number. Then imagine punk rock like a blowtorch sweeping across it. That to me is what punk rock did, and that's what's got to happen again." And, remarkably, for the first six months

The Clash, Round Two. Left to right: Nick Shepherd, Gregory "Vince" White, Joe Strummer, Pete Howard, and Paul Simonon. *Brian Brainerd/Getty Images*

through tours of the USA, Europe, and the UK, the Clash, Round Two did exactly that. Joe and Paul had stripped the sound down, with Mick's guitar effects no longer whipping around like sonic hurricanes. The two new hired hands, Nick Sheppard and Vince White, were each given Gibson Les Paul guitars, so that the Clash, Round Two would sound more like the Sex Pistols in concert; they were told to play unvarying leads at each show. By late May, the band was firing on all cylinders, the dedication of the musicians listed below inspiring of the young men in the audiences to go on to form the likes of the Dropkick Murphys and 311.

Pete Howard

Pete Howard, a holdover from the final "tour" with Mick Jones, had a drum style that fused Terry's Bonham-isms with Topper's deft touches and that ably carried the Clash, Round Two into the new era. This is important because the Clash, Round Two was not a complete retrenchment to 1977 and 1978. Songs such as "This Is Radio Clash," "Broadway," and "One More Time" are as far removed from *The Clash* as a back-to-basics band can possibly get, but the Clash, Round Two did eventually play down stripped-down versions that Howard propelled with intense magnificence. Further testament to the drummer's talent is that Mick later said he would've recruited Howard for Big Audio Dynamite if Joe hadn't already reached out to him.

Following the US Festival, Howard was kept in the dark as to any further involvement with the Clash. He has said in interviews that four months passed before hearing anything from the Clash camp—and that he eventually did only after Mick's termination (which indicates that he had not been invited to the unproductive June 1983 rehearsals). In 2005, he recalled a phone call from Joe to Clash, Round Two champion Chris Knowles, describing Joe as "an extreme velocity kind of guy. 'I fuckin' sacked the fuckin' stoned cunt! Whose side are you on, mine or his?' And I was like, 'Uh . . . uh . . . uh . . . yours, Joe, yours!'" It was, as it turned out, a decision Howard would come to regret. He wasn't even allowed to drum on *Cut the Crap*, the album he's credited with appearing on, but we'll get around to that below.

Nick Sheppard

When he originally turned up at Camden's Electric Ballroom in October 1983, twenty-four-year-old guitarist Nick Sheppard knew exactly what band he was auditioning for because he was seeing a girl who worked in Bernie's office. Eight years earlier, the Bristol lad had been one of the many British teens who formed a punk rock band. Named the Cortinas after the car that "Janie Jones"'s bored office worker drives, they released two singles on Step Forward Records ("Fascist Dictator" and "Defiant Pose") and one album (*True Romance*). None of the other bands he had played in after the Cortinas, such as the Viceroys or the Spics, enjoyed similar marginal success, but

An advertisement for the Clash's 1984 Out of Control tour. *Author's collection*

Sheppard was confident he had the pedigree to replace Mick Jones. (Once in the lineup, Nick sang lead vocals for the two Jones holdovers in the set lists: "Should I Stay or Should I Go" and "Police on My Back." He also sang lead vocal on "North and South," the one Clash, Round Two song that Joe did not sing.) After he was selected and began rehearsing with Joe, Paul, and Pete, however, Sheppard was dismayed to learn that Joe planned on limiting his role in the Clash, Round Two to that of vocalist (as originally projected way back in 1976, when Levene and Jones were to be the Clash's guitarists). Shepherd would be partnered with a novice guitarist selected from a new round of auditions.

Gregory "Vince" White

Gregory Stuart Lee White was born on March 31, 1960, in Marylebone, an affluent neighborhood in central London. He graduated with a degree in astronomy and physics from University College London before auditioning for the Clash in late 1983 and getting the second guitarist position more on attitude and looks than skill. He was quickly renamed Vince White after British rock 'n' roller Vince Taylor (best known for penning and recording the original version of "Brand New Cadillac") by Paul Simonon, who didn't believe "Gregory" sounded rock 'n' roll enough.

Despite his middle-class upbringing and university education, White turned out to be a live cannon—a man brimming with true punk spirit and Rotten wit—so it is not surprising that when Paul asked the obstinate young man to, in Nick Sheppard's words, "Name me one cool guy called Greg," White retorted with that of Gregory Isaacs, a Jamaican reggae musician and vocalist best known for *Cool Ruler*. It was a cool rebuff. And with Paul's love of reggae, he perhaps should have let Gregory be "Greg," but instead the university graduate was still renamed Vince.

Dictator

Remember that it was Joe who, over Mick's objections, restored Bernie in the manager's chair. Soon after, the Clash were for the first time a profitable enterprise. Some credit is due to Bernie for organizing the Impossible Mission tour and conceptualizing the "residencies," but a large part of the newfound financial success came from *Sandinista!*'s strong sales in America, where the Clash were receiving full songwriting royalties. Still, Joe saw this as vindication of his belief that only Bernie could successfully manage the

Clash and began siding with Bernie's opinions over those of Mick when it came to the band's business decisions.

Three Card Trick

Joe would have seen the "three card trick"—also known as the "three-card Monte"—in Times Square during the Bond's residency if he had not seen it previously. It's a street con game dating back to the fifteenth century in which, as described by Wiki, a player "or mark, is tricked into betting a sum of money, on the assumption that they can find the 'money card' among three face-down playing cards." The cards are usually marked with bent corners so that the dealer, abetted by one or more shills, can outfox the mark before indicating that he has spotted the police as a means of making his getaway.

It's not a stretch then to see the Clash, Round Two as an elaborate three-card trick in which Bernie Rhodes (the Dealer) outfoxed Joe (the Mark). (In this version, Kosmo Vinyl acts as the shill, although Vinyl is admittedly something of a victim as well.) Joe is like a mark being taken in. As he places his bet, Bernie is moving the cards around.

Mick's sacking is due in part to the impasse over musical direction, as well as his desire for holidays (true but hard to imagine, because of all the members of the Clash, he seemed to relish the concert stage more than the others) and chronic tardiness, but Bernie also stirs up the paranoia and resentment that Joe and Mick are already feeling toward one another. With Mick ousted, two new musicians are brought onboard that Bernie and Kosmo can easily manipulate. The concerts are going well enough, with more favorable reviews than negative ones from fans, if not the press. It's a return to basics that fans love, but the press has a difficult time seeing how the "return to basics" Clash meshes with Frankie Goes to Hollywood or Culture Club or Cyndi Lauper, the new acts dominating the airwaves. This is what Joe meant when he said, "Imagine punk rock like a blowtorch sweeping across it. That to me is what punk rock did, and that's what's got to happen again." The Clash, Round Two were out to obliterate Frankie Goes to Hollywood and Culture Club and Cyndi Lauper.

Then Joe's father suddenly dies in on February 29, while the Clash, Round Two are touring Europe, having just played two concerts in Milan, Italy. No mention of this is made to the new members, and the March 1 concert in Paris is performed as scheduled. Even on the day of the funeral (March 3), Joe flies up to Edinburgh, Scotland, in time to perform. The death triggers an emotional tailspin, but one that is camouflaged by the band playing mostly in London and Ireland before flying to America for what would be their final American tour.

On April 14, I crossed paths with the Clash at Hofstra University in Hempstead, New York. It was the twenty-fifth and final time that I saw them. I was near the stage but not up against the lip. It was very crowded, probably oversold. I have read that the local fire department expressed concerns over safety. When Joe and the others came out, I was hopeful at first but quickly disappointed. I was (and am) more of a Joe fan than a Mick fan, but knew I was watching damaged goods. I actually felt bad for many of those around me who were seeing the Clash for the first time. They were having a good time hearing "Rock the Casbah" but not knowing what they were missing due to Mick's absence. The tempos were too fast and the finesse gone. The only song I truly remember is "Armagideon Time," with Joe strapping on his Fender Telecaster and turning and facing Pete Howard, strumming in an effort to anchor the correct "riddim." Only then did Joe begin singing.

After the second American tour, the Clash, Round Two rarely performed in concert again.

I Need a Dodge! Joe Strummer on the Run

London Calling's "Spanish Bombs," with its lyrical politics delivered melodically, has often been likened to the Beatles. And, with some imagination, you can hear John Lennon singing about the Spanish Civil War and Paul McCartney and George Harrison throwing in "oh ma côrazon" during the chorus. The song is a paean to "freedom fighters" such as the poet Federico Lorca who "died upon the hill," fighting for the democratically elected government that ultimately lost to the pro-Fascist Nationalists. As such, it fits in neatly with the Clash's politics, but what made the song an easier sell for Joe was his heartfelt attachment to Spain, a country he first visited in 1975 with Paloma Romera—his girlfriend at the time, several years away from her role as Palmolive, the drummer in the Slits—whose parents lived in Málaga, a seaside city in Andalusia. With this trip, Joe's lifelong affinity with Spain—and in particular the cities of Granada and Madrid—was kindled. (This affinity is now acknowledged by Granada government officials who, in 2013, after a Facebook campaign, renamed a small square as Placeta Joe Strummer.)

In October 1984, Joe turned up in Granada on a quest for Lorca's unmarked grave but instead found 091, a local rock group named for

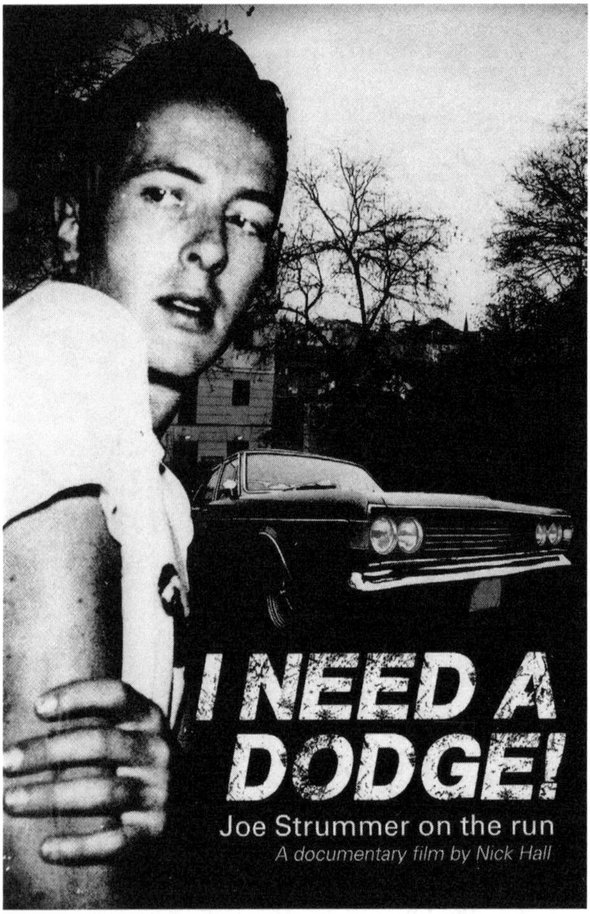

Nick Hall's 2016 documentary explores Joe Strummer's days in Spain before and after quitting the Clash. *Author's collection*

the Spanish emergency services phone number. Joe would have been struck by its similarity to the 999 he dials in "London's Burning." Nothing came of this at the time—Joe returned home to the participate in recording sessions in Germany and a busking tour—but in June the following year, he returned and offered his services as 091's producer.

Joe was a cultural freedom fighter on the run. His mother had just died, he was questioning Bernie's motives, and he no longer had faith in his decisions. He likely was undergoing an emotional breakdown. The recording sessions began in earnest in late summer, but while the band were thrilled Joe Strummer was producing them, their record label was not. The label was looking at the bottom line: production costs were rising because this rock star posing as a producer had unorthodox ideas and believed endless recording sessions would result in important music. In other words, he was producing much the way Mick Jones had produced *Sandinista!* and *Rat Patrol from Fort Bragg*. According to Chris Salewicz's liner notes for the documentary *I Need a Dodge!*, Joe asked the brother of one of the musicians in 091 to explain, "I just want them to put into music the ideas I'm having. Guy Stevens did the same with the Clash and it worked. The first time we met Guy Stevens we thought he was crazy. And look what happened. I feel like the poor Guy Stevens of 091."

But 091 were a struggling band without the dedicated following or publicity that the Clash had in their favor during bleak times, and as soon as Joe returned to England to be with Gaby Salter for the birth of their second daughter, the tapes were remixed and scrubbed clean of Joe's unusual production quirks. The band's second album was released as *Más de cien lobos* (*More Than a Hundred Wolves*) on Zafiro Records in 1986.

Cut the Crap Recording Sessions

In the wake of the band's poorly reviewed shows at London's Brixton Academy in December 1984, Joe began reshaping the Clash's new material with Pete Howard on drums, Mickey Gallagher on keyboards, and Norman Watt-Roy from the Blockheads on bass. The result is said to have sounded like pub rock, and Bernie quickly quashed this lineup. Watt-Roy would be invited to the recording sessions, but Gallagher and Bernie had had an argument that nixed the former's rumored involvement in the finished product.

Hurting for cash due to legal shenanigans, the Clash's sixth studio album was recorded on the cheap in Munich, Germany, in January and February 1984, by Joe, Bernie, Norman, and Michael Fayne, an engineer enlisted for his so-called expertise in electronic drum programming. Only when the basic tracks were completed was Nick Sheppard called in to lay down "punk rock" guitar. Vince White had even less involvement, but still more than Pete Howard, who wasn't even allowed to drum along with the programmed drum tracks. The chanted choruses were added toward the end of the production.

The decision to replace Mick Jones's backing vocals with chanted choruses rather than go with Nick Sheppard says a lot about the state of the Clash, Round Two, but then you could study the Clash's approach to vocal interplay and see how it revealed the inner dynamics of the Clash. The barked backing vocals of Mick and Paul during choruses that are such a strong point of "Deny" and "White Riot" or the "Where'd cha go?" responses during the verses of "Safe European Home" were a distinctive trait of the Clash's punk period but a thing of the past by the end of 1978. Paul and Mick's strained relationship over production ideas and Mick's habitually tardy behavior also dates back to 1978. Could the reason they scrapped these types of choruses stem from their strained relationship?

There's evidence of the growing distance in the relationship between Mick and Joe in their vocals as well. A strong feature of songs such as

"Remote Control" and "Hate and War" is the interplay of the two men as they take alternate lines or verses. Mick has said a reason Joe and he were such an effective guitar team is because they mixed the "sweet" (Mick's lyrical leads) with the "sour" (Joe's frantic strumming). The same could be said of the interplay between Joe's gruff, man-of-the-street vocals ("sour") and Mick's choirboy vocals ("sweet"). Sure, this can be found as late as "Atom Tan" on *Combat Rock*, but by 1982 it was more of a rarity than the norm. And this was because Joe and Mick were barely on speaking terms.

Chants had been used effectively while Mick Jones was in the Clash. The best examples are the choruses of "The Magnificent Seven" and "The Call Up" from *Sandinista!* But those work—as does the chant in "This Is England"—because the subject matter of the songs suggests the collective voice of nine-to-five workers or marching Marines or forgotten citizens. On *Cut the Crap*, the chants are there primarily because the Clash, Round two did not have an answer for Mick Jones's missing background vocals.

Life Is Wild: The Busking Tour of May 1985

Still in Munich and disheartened by the recording sessions, Kosmo suggested to Joe and Sheppard that they do something outlandish and put the experience behind them. Various ideas were bandied about, and it's easy to imagine Joe saying to Sheppard something about having only really enjoying playing music when he was busking with his ukulele in the London Underground, and then getting excited and saying the next Clash tour should be a busking tour. Paul, Pete, and Vince were in agreement, and the plan was made to leave their flats with only £10 and their instruments and turn up near the rail station in Nottingham, England, on May 3, 1985.

Thus began the busking tour that then headed north to Glasgow via Leeds, York, Sunderland, Newcastle upon Tyne, and Edinburgh. Several impromptu concerts were held in each city outside and inside pubs, near underpasses and universities, next to monuments, and in public parks. Typically they'd draw a small crowd and then more as word spread that Joe Strummer was in town. Most of these "concerts" were broken up by local police. The Clash, Round Two were known to play songs associated with classic rockabilly acts, the Cramps, and the Clash. The last known performance was at Glasgow's Fixx Pub on May 18. The band members had bonded and things were going well, but Joe had lost his voice. Nick Sheppard was walking around with a credit card tucked in his sock, and he paid the train fare for everyone to get back to London—and, unfortunately, Bernie. Whatever high spirits the busking tour had generated quickly dissipated.

The *This Is England* EP

The Clash, Round Two got off to a good start on vinyl when the *This Is England* EP was released on September 30, 1985, with the songwriting credit given as "Strummer & Co." Opening with programmed drums and swirling synths, this seemed to be Joe's way of showing Mick that he could keep up with the new trends, and lyrically "This Is England" was a fitting condemnation of Maggie Thatcher's Britain. Everything worked: the football crowd choruses, the churning electric guitars, Joe's impassioned vocals. It even had a classic Clash line: "I got my motorcycle jacket / But I'm walking all the time." The EP reached #24 on the UK charts, and for a month or so it felt as if Joe might just pull it off. Maybe the Clash would go on.

The 12-inch B-side tracks "Do It Now"(originally titled "Out of Control") and "Sex Mad Roar" were a bit disappointing, but B-sides often are. Today,

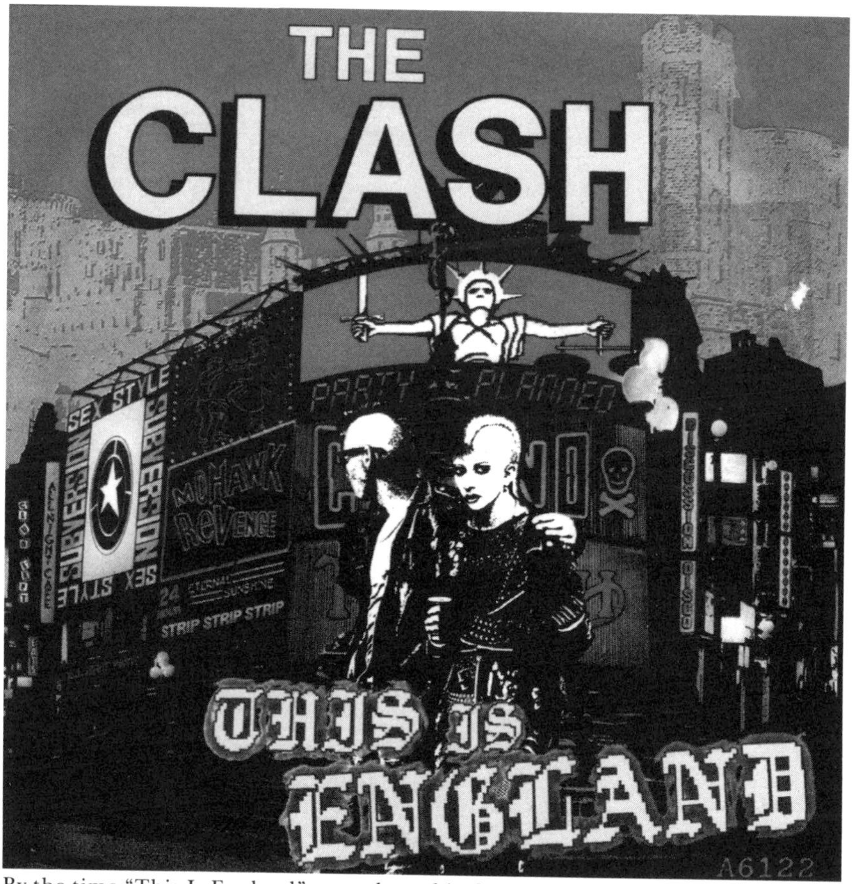

By the time "This Is England" was released in September 1984, Joe Strummer had already played his last gig as a member of the Clash. *Author's collection*

both tracks are recommended because they are the only two recordings made by all members of the Clash, Round Two.

Most recordings attributed to the Clash, Round Two, have been eradicated from the Clash songbook. None appear on the *Sound System* boxed set. "This Is England," however, was included in *The Essential Clash*, a double-CD greatest hits package originally issued by Sony to cash in on the Clash's Rock and Roll Hall of Fame induction. With Joe's unexpected death, this forty-song compilation became a homage to the man's work, and so the inclusion of his last great song castigating Thatcher's England was satisfying. All three tracks on the 12-inch EP were also included in the *Singles Box* issued on October 30, 2006.

Cut the Crap

The effect of cinema on the Clash's worldview did not end with Mick's departure. As *Apocalypse Now!* and *Taxi Driver* permeated *Sandinista!* and *Combat Rock*, so *Cut the Crap*'s worldview is derived from Australian director George Miller's *Mad Max 2*, which is better known in America as *The Road Warrior.* This is fitting, since the world of Mad Max is post-apocalyptic. The title of the Clash, Round Two's only album is derived from a scene where Pappagallo (Michael Preston), the leader of the settlers, is confronted by an injured Mad Max (Mel Gibson), who insists on driving the oil tanker that everyone's future depends upon:

> Mad Max: "If it's all the same to you, I'll drive that tanker."
>
> Pappagallo: "The offer is closed. Too late for deals."
>
> Mad Max: "No deals. I wanna drive that truck."
>
> Pappagallo: "Why? Why the big change of heart?"
>
> Mad Max: "Believe me, I haven't got a choice."
>
> Pappagallo: "And how do you think you'll do it? I mean, look at you. You couldn't even drive a wheelchair. You should look at yourself, Max. You're a mess."
>
> Mad Max: "Come on, *cut the crap*. I'm the best chance you've got."
>
> Pappagallo: "Right, let's get moving."

This explains the album's awful title. Mad Max's worldview was applied to what Joe Strummer (and Bernie Rhodes) saw as their mid-'80s mission: the back-to-basics Clash, Round Two—like the initial band of UK punk rockers—were going to eradicate the meaningless New Romantic bands dominating the British pop world. They were "the best chance [the world's] got."

Except, in 1984, did the world really care? For the majority, it was morning again in Reagan's America and—by extension—Thatcher's Great Britain. Someone, probably Bernie, was getting cold feet about what would sell. One of the opening acts during the Clash, Round Two's swing through California was former Sex Pistols manager Malcolm McLaren, who eventually had two Top 10 hits in Britain ("Buffalo Gals" and "Double Dutch") merging American and African musical genres. It has been speculated that—in another instance of Bernie trying to prove himself the equal of McLaren—Bernie wanted to prove he too could produce a commercially successful record. In this, Bernie was ignoring McLaren's natural panache for showmanship; Bernie worked better in the shadows.

"We're touring without a record, without anything to sell, 'cos we're not going to make a record until we know we can do one that'll last ten years," Joe had told Richard Cook. No one can doubt Joe's sincerity, but by November 1985, when *Cut the Crap* was released, it was a record that wouldn't last ten days, let alone ten years. The trouble was evident from the songwriting credits. Whereas the single version of "This Is England" was credited to "Strummer & Co.," on *Cut the Crap* the song was attributed to "J. Strummer / B. Rhodes." So, too, were the other eleven tracks. It was an ominous sign, especially for a band that once ridiculed Stiff Little Fingers for letting their manager Gordon Ogilvie write lyrics. On top of this, it was Bernie who oversaw the final mixing of the tracks at Mayfair Studios in London, with Joe noticeably absent.

Cut the Crap was a record produced by a manager with musical ambitions who lacked any discernable musical talent, and the end result was an alienating amalgam of humorless lyrics, stifled punk rock guitars, funky basslines, clumsy drum machines and "oi" chants ("oi" being the British equivalent of hardcore punk in America—that is, an offspring of the original punk bands—but while both are lyrically political, appealed to skinheads, and created underground communities, the defining characteristic of oi was not the breakneck tempos of hardcore but chanted choruses similar to those sung by football fans in the UK). It certainly wasn't the back-to-basics record

Joe had been boasting the Clash's next album was going to be throughout 1984.

"Dictator" was the poorest possible choice for the opening track. Hyperactive drum machines are quickly joined by synthesizers, the voice of a Spanish dictator, Joe's singing, and buried guitars. It's a cacophonous melee, and there is nothing catchy for the listener's ears to latch onto. The second track, "Dirty Punk," at least has raring guitars to nod your head to, before the programmed drums and Joe pile on top. This is the back-to-basics rebel rock Joe had been promising.

Today, of course, you can reprogram the album's twelve tracks to reveal a more satisfying recording. "This Is England" should have opened the album, and would have made total marketing sense. By reprogramming the songs, you can resuscitate tracks that would sound good on any Clash

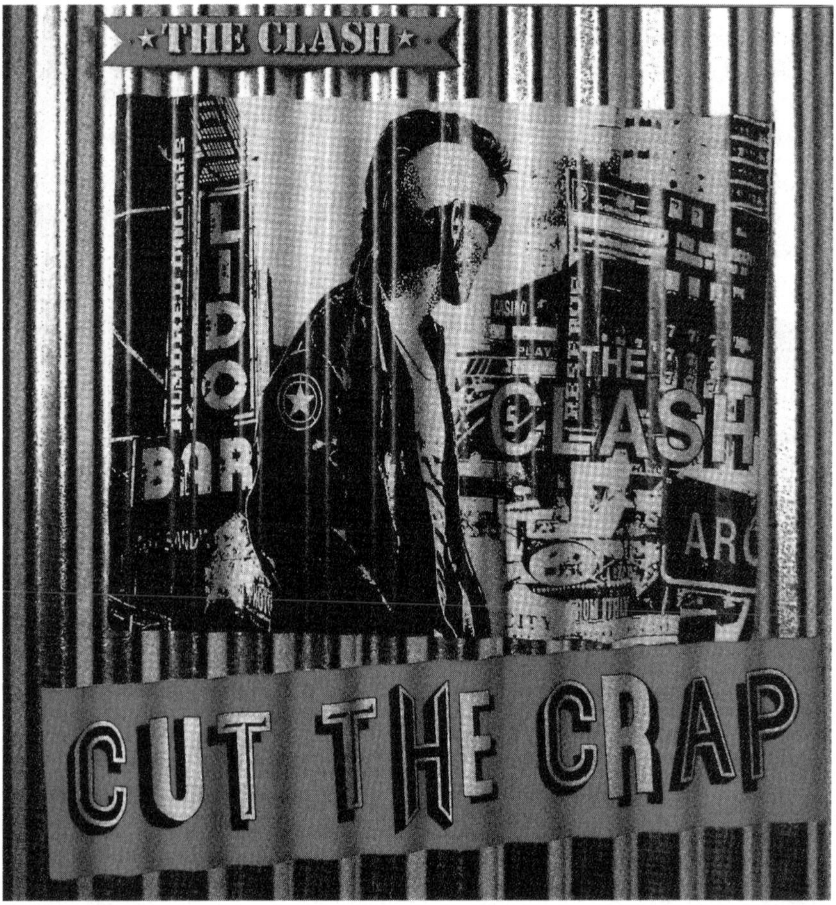

The title for *Cut the Crap* came from *Mad Max*. *Author's collection*

album. By this I mean "Three Card Trick" and "North and South." These tracks reveal that by the mid-'80s, Strummer was more adept at writing mid-tempo songs. "Three Card Trick" even revives the cry of the wildebeest, while on "North and South" Nick Sheppard proves he could have been just as satisfactory a vocal foil for Joe as Mick had been.

The biggest flaw in *Cut the Crap* was not allowing the Clash, Round Two to record their album and take their chances with their public and their critics. Instead we have an album recorded by the following:

- Michael Fayne—drum machine programmer, vocals on "Play to Win"
- Bernie Rhodes—drum machines
- Nick Sheppard—guitar, vocals on "North and South"
- Joe Strummer—lead vocals
- Norman Watt-Roy—bass
- Herman Weindorf—keyboards and synthesizers
- Vince White—guitar

Neither bassist Paul Simonon nor drummer Pete Howard is on the finished product.

And neither is "In the Pouring, Pouring Rain" or "Ammunition" (aka "Jericho"), two of the Clash, Round Two's best songs. It has never been explained why they were not recorded when bunk such as "We Are the Clash" and "Play to Win" was. But the blame falls largely on Bernie Rhodes's shoulders because—as was to become clear over time—in order to be effective, Joe Strummer needed a collaborator when making an album. Bernie could manage rock bands but he couldn't make rock songs. Paul Simonon had strong musical convictions but no compositional talent. The reason Joe's first solo album, "Earthquake Weather," stank was not because of the raw material but because Joe chose to collaborate with former Circle Jerks guitarist Zander Schloss, another capable musician without creative vision. Joe's artistic revival with the Mescaleros toward the end of his life stemmed not from his sudden improvement as an arranger but from his decision to work with Pulp's Antony Genn and Martin Slattery.

Running away to Spain does not absolve Joe of his role in this debacle, however. It does appear that Bernie entertained the idea of finding a new singer and running the Clash like a football team. This was unheard of in the mid-'80s, but it is exactly what Mark E. Smith has done profitably with the Fall. And this begs the question: could the Clash have carried on in 1986 with a new lineup? If Mark E. Smith could reconfigure musicians for subsequent lineups of the Fall, couldn't Joe and Paul have done the same with the Clash? We'll never know, because as David Fricke presciently wrote in his Rolling Stone review, "With *Cut the Crap*, one might well wonder if Joe Strummer's at the end of the road." He was.

"We Have Parted as Friends"

The end was clearly written in between the song titles on the Clash's 1985 set lists. Whereas a year earlier, sets could contain anywhere from seven to ten new titles, by 1985 only "Three Card Trick" was still being performed.

"We have parted as friends," read Joe's press statement, regretfully announcing "the departure of Nick Sheppard, Vince White, and Pete Howard. The decision is mutual . . . me and Paul would like to thank them for the dedication and enthusiasm." Also severed was the band's relationship with Rhodes and longtime publicist Kosmo Vinyl.

Strummer immediately took off for Spain, where "me and Paul are going into the studio to record our next tune, called 'Shouting Street.'" It was to be the first in a series of forthcoming Strummer projects that never saw light of day beyond a press release.

Interestingly, both Nick Sheppard and Vince White have since cited the Clash's final concert in Athens, Greece, as one of their best, possibly because they too knew it was the end.

As Joe told Richard Cromelin of the *Los Angeles Times* in an interview that appeared on January 31, 1988, "I was trying to prove that I was the Clash and it wasn't Mick [Jones]. I learned that that was kind of dumb. I learned that it wasn't anybody, except maybe a great chemistry between us four, and I really learned it was over the day we sacked Topper . . . because it's between humans. Bernie Rhodes and Cosmo [sic] Vinyl I think perhaps didn't understand that. You couldn't just jigsaw-puzzle it, take out a piece and put in another piece. That it was something weird between four humans that when they played it sounded OK, you know. And that's fairly rare, that's all."

Pete Howard's Post-Clash Career

Pete Howard was the first to sense the ship was sinking, and when offered £10,000 in severance pay, said he'd take it. That turned out to be just another management mind game; he never got anything more than the £1,000 Joe handed him at the Clash, Round Two's final meeting. He went on to play and record with swamp rockers Eat, a short-lived rock act named

Vent 414, and Queenadreena, an alternative rock group who formed in 1999 but who Howard joined in 2002 and played with into late 2008.

Nick Sheppard's Post-Clash Career

Joe's statement to Bill Holdship that he'd "hope that if I started to act funny that I would be fired, and the Clash would continue to roll on without me" almost became true, because Nick Sheppard has confirmed in interviews that *auditions were held for a vocalist to replace* Joe in the Clash, though no mention is made of the attendance of other members, including Paul. Nothing came of these auditions, which Sheppard says he only participated in hopes of hooking up with prospective collaborators for his own next musical project. He did form Head with guitarist/keyboardist Gareth Sager, who had been a member of Bristol's most successful band of the time, the Pop Group, and released three albums that although they did not have much chart success would prove influential on the UK's trip-hop electronic music scene in the 1990s. Sheppard then played in Shot with vocalist/guitarist Koozie Johns, but they never released any recordings, despite signing to IRS Records.

In 1993, Sheppard relocated to Perth, Australia, where he continued pursuing a musical career by forming and playing guitar with first Heavy Smoker and then the New Egyptian Kings. It was in Australia in 2001 that Sheppard had an opportunity to meet Joe again and make peace with the past. As Chris Knowles quotes him saying in "The Last Crusade," a 2005 article for *Classic Rock* magazine, "We did speak about my time in the band; Joe apologized for what happened. He was upset at how things turned out for everyone. I told him I didn't regret a moment of the time I had spent in the band. I know we were never the 'classic' Clash, and that circumstances prevented us from reaching our potential. " Like everyone else, Sheppard was shocked by Joe's passing the following year.

Since then, Sheppard has soldiered on, forming the DomNicks, a retro-sounding garage rock band, with vocalist/guitarist Dom Mariani. They released an EP, *Hey Rock 'n' Roller*, in 2009, and an album named *Super Real* in 2013.

Vince White's Post-Clash Career and *The Last Days of the Clash*

A shared disdain for Vince White from Pete Howard and Nick Sheppard has survived the ensuing decades and—like the original Clash members before Joe's death—they are never interviewed together. Whereas Sheppard made peace with Joe and Howard came to terms with his unsatisfying Clash experiences, White has remained bitter, at least in his interviews and his memoir, *The Last Days of the Clash.*

At first it's an unrelenting read: the negativity . . . the discontent . . . the mind games. And then the humor shines a little light as White documents two-plus years in the Clash from his perspective. To him and the other hired hands, it's never the Clash, Round Two. *The Last Days of the Clash* is hard to find but an essential read—even with all the typos, which were retained apparently at the author's insistence, and probably historical inaccuracies, too.

You hear stories of Bernie's manipulation, the exhilaration and drudgery of touring, the sapping of Joe's ego. White makes it clear that the Clash, Round Two were never the Clash; they weren't even the Clash, Round Two except on the busking tour. "It leant some credibility to a band that didn't have much left," he writes. He doesn't know what to make of Paul but admires his ability to go with the flow. When White tells Paul he thinks the band is at the end of the line, Paul responds, "Ever since this band began it's been on the cards. There hasn't been a single day where it might end at any moment." And Paul means back in 1976. Paul "just takes each day as it comes"; he doesn't even care that he's not playing bass on the album. By then, Joe's already revealed to Vince that Paul's bass is mixed down in concert because Paul can't play.

In time, White finds himself agreeing with the absent Mick Jones: Bernie's played every member of the Clash against one another so well that Joe can't see it. There's a sad moment when Joe speaks of Mick divulging his disappointment that the success he dreamed of for the Clash wasn't to be, and a sadder moment of Joe depressed and complaining of the pressure. The Clash, Round Two's album was to be called *Out of Control*, and the band really was spinning beyond his grasp. There are a few festival appearances. You expect there to have been a tremendous row at the Athens concert—*the* final Clash concert—but no, according to White, it's one of band's better performances. By then Joe has confided in him that "we may not be able to carry on this way" and turned up unannounced at White's flat, so it's no surprise when, after the release of "This Is England," Howard calls him and tells him Joe doesn't want to work with Bernie anymore. Is it over? He's informed of the name of the Clash album he's on: *Cut the Crap.* He can't believe it. It really is over.

There are video shoots for the single, band meetings, final meetings with Joe, broken promises, and an unflattering opinion of Joe that one assumes is the author's summation of the Clash's front man. There's a confrontation with Bernie, and then *The Last Days of the Clash* peters out, as most memoirs do, with the author allegedly finding himself. I'm not sure about that, but it is a worthwhile read.

Best Bootleg of the Clash, Round Two

What is interesting is that the Clash, Round Two are at their best in surviving bootleg recordings from their first half year on the road. This is because the sets lists from this era include a fair portion of new material, with arrangements that sound like "rebel rock" and not the weird fusion of oi and German techno re-arrangements that made it onto *Cut the Crap*. It is as Chris Knowles writes in *Clash City Showdown* (essential reading for the Clash fan): "Skip the album, get the bootlegs." The best of these bootlegs is one derived from 1988's *Give 'Em Enough Dope* CD. The original CD contains seven tracks from the Clash in Sun Plaza Hall in 1982, but a later version compiles three four-song batches, each culled from a different 1984 appearance, of the Clash, Round Two. These are professionally recorded performances, probably soundboard recordings. No one has owned up to bringing these recordings to market, but it has been speculated that it is Nick Shepherd or Kosmo Vinyl we need to thank. This bootleg includes "In the Pouring, Pouring Rain" and superior versions of "Are You Red-y for War" and "Sex Mad Roar," as well as the Clashics.

I Guess My Race Is Run

Joeseph Strummer

The final album released during Joe's lifetime starts off with "Johnny Appleseed," a song about men such as John Chapman and Martin Luther King Jr. who spread the word about conservation and freedom. And it is apt that Joe Strummer sings of Chapman, a conservationist and missionary better known as the folk legend Johnny Appleseed, because Joe in 1996 helped start Future Forests, an organization dedicated to environmental issues. (In 2003 the organization created the Joe Strummer Forest on Scotland's Isle of Skye in his memory.) It is fitting that Joe should sing of the legendary Johnny Appleseed, who shortly after America ratified its constitution was said to spread apple seeds throughout the young countryside. According to www.bestapples.com, "To the men and women [Appleseed] was a news carrier; to the children he was a friend. He was also very religious and preached to people along the way." It is not too far of a stretch of the imagination to see Joe Strummer as a modern-day Johnny Appleseed, a news carrier, touring the world and sowing creativity as well as left-wing ideology to fans, the "children" to whom Joe "was a friend."

John Mellor

John Graham Mellor was born in Ankara, Turkey, on August 21, 1952, the younger son of Ron Mellor, a Foreign Office clerical officer, and his wife Anna, a nurse. His father had been born in India and was of British and Armenian descent, while his mother had been born in Scotland. John Mellor was eight years old when he first set foot in England. By then, he had already lived in Turkey, Egypt, Mexico, and Germany: the perfect childhood for a nomadic musician with a socialistic viewpoint that his father had imparted to his son.

John lived in southeast London with his parents and older brother David for two years before both boys were enrolled in the City of London Freemen's School, formerly an orphanage but now a boarding school. A year later, when John's parents were reassigned by the Foreign Office to Tehran in the Middle East, their sons remained behind in the boarding school. During the four years their parents were in Tehran, the boys spent their summer holidays in the Iranian city, and, when possible, John's mother returned to England and visited with them.

In 1963, John discovered rock 'n' roll via the Beatles and the Rolling Stones, but it was a greatest-hits record by the Beach Boys that most impressed the young man. Then in 1965, while vacationing in Tehran, he bought the Chuck Berry EP that hooked him on American rhythm and blues. It was to prove a lifelong addiction.

After serving three years in the east African country of Malawi, John's parents returned to London. Both children had graduated from the City of London Freemen's School, but rather than this being a time for bonding, the family splintered. Already something of a loner, the elder son, David, moved out. He began studying to be a chiropodist and was attracted to the radical National Front. Then, in late July 1970, his body was found on a Regent's Park bench. He had committed suicide by swallowing a huge amount of aspirin. With the stiff upper lip that the British are known for, the Mellors buried David, stayed calm, and carried on. John's brother was rarely mentioned thereafter.

Woody Mellor

John had lost interest in the Beatles by the year they delved in psychedelia, and had discovered the blues via John Mayall's Bluesbreakers. When Mayall's lead guitarist, Eric Clapton, branched out to form Cream, John followed; he was soon buying everything by Cream and Clapton's main competitor, an American bluesman named Jimi Hendrix.

"In 1968, the whole world was exploding," Joe says, in *The Future Is Unwritten*. "There was Paris, Vietnam, Grosvenor Square, the counterculture. I think that gave me an edge to put into punk. It was a great year to come of age."

Around this time, John also discovered the underground rock scene, with Captain Beefheart and His Magic Band making a lasting impression on the young man—including being the source of his first change of name. Beefheart's band had all followed their leader in adopting pseudonyms, and

John Mellor changed his name to Woolly Census—an example of his offbeat sense of humor—which soon morphed into Woody Mellor.

After leaving the City of London Freemen's School, Woody received a grant to attend the Central School of Art and Design in the hope of one day becoming a cartoonist. His warm personality endeared him to many fellow students, but he felt his talent was not appreciated by his teachers, and his interest in art dissipated. But even if he owned an acoustic guitar said to have once been strummed by Who mastermind Pete Townshend, he exhibited little evidence that he'd one day "be the leader of a big old band," to quote Woody's hero, Chuck Berry.

Woody moved into a flat on Ash Grove with Deborah Kartun, a fellow art student who was also his love interest. It was, however, Tymon Dogg, a visitor turned resident, who would have greater impact on Woody's future. Dogg was a musician who had briefly been on Apple Records roster of artists and was making ends meet by busking, an activity that Woody soon had a role in, serving as Dogg's bottler, which meant he was responsible for collecting money from the passersby that Dogg had entertained. Woody soon purchased himself a ukulele for £2.99, learned "Johnny B. Goode," and started busking in on the London Underground.

After living at Ash Grove, Woody moved to a flat on Ridley Road but was soon evicted when he upset the landlady by taking in a homeless black man. This is where Joe Strummer's future campaign against the police began to take root, because during the course of forcibly evicting the young man from the premises, a police officer smashed Woody's record collection, including the Chuck Berry EP he had bought many years earlier in Tehran. When Woody filed a complaint, he found the law was not on his side.

When Debbie Kartun departed for the Cardiff School of Art and Design, Woody soon followed her, but he was unsuccessful in rekindling their relationship. Intending on hitching back to London, he wound up in Newport in South Wales, where he found work as a gravedigger. He also enrolled in a local art college and made friends at whose flat he was soon crashing. One of these friends was Mickey Foote, future producer of *The Clash*. Woody then moved into a flat with Allan Jones, another art student. Jones played bass guitar in a rock band that was splintering and was desperate for musicians to play with. Woody had acquired a drum kit in Cardiff, and he offered the kit to Jones on the condition that Woody be the new singer of Jones's band, the Vultures. And that is how Woody found himself fronting a rock 'n' roll band for the very first time.

Joe Strummer in concert in 1978. *Gus Stewart/Getty Images*

The 101'ers

"I got into music because . . . it was the thing that had the least laws and restrictions about it," the Clash's front man told *Musician* journalist Vic Garbarini in 1981. And by living a lifestyle that was "outside of society" (as Patti Smith might describe it), he was telling the truth.

Seeing little future in either playing with the Vultures or working as a gravedigger (an occupation that Woody was so bad at that he was reassigned to the cemetery's sanitation duties), he returned to London, where he temporarily moved in with Tymon Dogg, his former musical mentor, and then into a squat at 101 Waterton Road, where some friends of Dogg were staying. Squatting entails living in an abandoned building, and would provide his primary means of residence for the next five years. Though condemned, 101 Waterton Road still had electricity, which meant that when Woody decided to start a rock 'n' roll band a few months later, they could rehearse in the basement. Jamming with other primitive musicians, they were soon joined by a Chilean tenor saxophonist named Álvaro Peña-Rojas, who had had several hits in his native country, which he had fled following a military coup in 1973. An active member of the dissident Chilean community living in London, he enlisted Woody's band as his support act at a benefit concert. They would be listed as El Huaso and the 101 All Stars on a bill headlined by Matumbi, a British reggae band, on September 14, 1974.

In the months that followed, musicians came and went, many often using the arsenal of guitars Joe had acquired. The 101 All Stars learned cover tunes, but not well enough for hiring. The solution was to form their own club at a Chippenham public house named the Charlie Pigdog Club after the dog that squatted with the others at 101 Waterton Road. Around this same time, the band's name was shortened to the 101'ers, and the lineup solidified. The lead guitar slot was filled by Clive Timperley, and Richard Dudanski settled in behind the kit. The 101'ers would have two bassists over the course of their eighteen months as an active unit. First, the bottom was handled by Marwood "Mole" Chesterton, and then, after October 1975, by Dan Kelleher. Simon "Big John" Cassell joined Peña-Rojas on sax. Both Timperly and Kelleher also sang.

It 1974, Woody had had an epiphany when he saw Wilko Johnson, the guitarist frantically playing a Fender Telecaster for the pub-rock band Dr. Feelgood. Years of practice had taught him that he would never be an accomplished guitarist, so it wasn't *how* Johnson played guitar that affected Woody so much as the *way* he played guitar. Johnson was a marvel to watch, and Woody began mimicking Johnson's moves as a means of camouflaging his limited guitar technique. He would strum frantically as his left leg moved faster than a jackhammer, and not only was his classic onstage stance born, but so too was the stage name that would stick.

Just as Captain Beefheart had given stage names to all members of his band, Woody did the same to the 101'ers, including himself. At first, he tried out Johnny Caramello, and then Joe Strummer, a pun on his musical inability. In *The Future Is Unwritten*, Joe says, "I can still only play all six strings or none. Not all the fiddly bits, which is why I call myself Joe Strummer."

Pete Silverton, writing for the *Observer* in 1991, had a good take on the stage name John Mellor was known by in his obituary: "grease-monkey Christian name teamed with adjectival surname, the simplicity and directness of which reached back to when all surnames were job descriptions: all Bakers baked, all Smiths smithed and, I suppose, all Strummers strummed."

Around this time, Joe was offered £100 to marry a South African woman named Pamela Jill Moolman so that she could legally stay in England. He accepted, and with the money he bought his legendary Fender Telecaster, although the color was sunburst—he painted it black in Year Zero. As 101'ers guitarist Clive Timperley told biographer Marcus Gray, "Basically Strummer married his Fender."

In late February 1975, the 101'ers played a Brixton venue and—like the Butthole Surfers would one day also do—bought a hearse to transport their equipment from gig to gig. Álvaro Peña-Rojas left in March, apparently unhappy that the 101'ers were being led by Strummer despite the fact that Peña-Rojas had more professional experience. The band got tighter, rocked mightily in concert, staged wild shows, and started selling out the Charlie Pigdog Club, which the public house's proprietor closed down after one visit too many by the police.

The closing of their club forced the 101'ers in May to find venues to play. Flashing a *Melody Maker* press clipping penned by Allan Jones, Joe's former sidekick in the Vultures, they secured a one-night stand at the Elgin, parlaying that performance into a weekly gig that ran throughout the rest of 1975. "Big John" the saxophonist left soon after the first Elgin gig, and the 101'ers' sound shifted to something more like that of Chess Records rhythm-and-blues artists like Chuck Berry and Bo Diddley, who were now known as rock 'n' rollers.

Pub rock dominated London's local scene in 1975, and Dr. Feelgood and the 101'ers were precursors of the punk rock bands that gained popularity the following year. As documented on recordings released after Joe joined the Clash (1981's *Elgin Avenue Breakdown*, 1993's *Five Star Rock 'n' Roll*, and 2005's *Elgin Avenue Breakdown Revisited*), the 101'ers played high-octane rock music with titles like "Letsgetabitarockin" and "Motor Boys Motor" derived from the covers of songs by Them, Bo Diddley, and the Beatles that they had started out playing. Their spirited performances featuring a lead singer in a brown zoot suit strumming madly—and whose left leg was so hyperactive that its source was attributed by concertgoers to amphetamines and not total passionate abandon—caught the attention of Chiswick Records president Ted Carroll. He arranged for their first recording session at Pathway Studios, with Roger Armstrong producing. "Keys to Your Heart" was deemed single-worthy, and Chiswick, which had only released two other records to date, contracted the 101'ers for the sale of their first 45.

It turned out to be their last 45 as well, though, because a few weeks later, on April 3, 1976, Malcolm McLaren, Johnny Rotten, Steve Jones, and the Sex Pistols entourage walked into the Nashville Rooms and forever altered the trajectory of Joe Strummer's life.

Year Zero Joe

Joe Strummer embraced the Clash and punk rock with the passion of a religious zealot. He cropped his bushy hair, hung up his zoot suit, left the 101'ers with only his sunburst colored Telecaster. He dropped a few years from his age in press releases and started wearing a "CHUCK BERRY IS DEAD" T-shirt. For Joe Strummer it was now Year Zero, and nothing that had happened to John Mellor or Woody Mellor had happened to him.

One thing Joe couldn't leave behind was his assortment of rotting, jagged teeth, which reminded one of a bomb scene. As a result of both neglect and a punch to the mouth, he had a mouth worthy of *The Amazing Colossal Man*, the 1950s B-movie horror flick, and it was the image of Joe's bombed-out mouth spitting lyrics that convinced American fans of the Clash that Joe Strummer was a true blue punk rocker, a man of the streets. We had so little information at first other than photos in *Rock Scene*, and it was clear from those photos that Johnny's rotten teeth had nothing on Joe's. We couldn't wait to hear what that mouth had to say.

Year Zero Joe was mesmerizing. Here are some sightings: *NME*'s Paul Morley described him in December 1976 as "play[ing] a crushing consistent rhythm guitar"; in a Caroline Coon article he "grabs the mike"; *ZigZag*'s Kris Needs wrote of a performance where "Joe's bent double at the front, tearing his throat apart." Needs is especially memorable when writing of Joe. Here's another: "Joe jerking across the stage like an electrocuted piranha fish." According to *Sounds*' Vivien Goldman, Joe "spits out the lyrics like poison darts."

And Year Zero Joe was also nothing short of terrifying. He seemed so certain of himself in interviews. *NME*'s Miles described Joe as lunging at a remark during an interview where he has been flicking a jackknife. *Sounds*' Giovanni Dadomo began an article about the White Riot tour with, "Joe Strummer says he'll smash my face in if I so much as print a syllable of what's said in the dressing room of the Aberdeen Students Union hall in the first few minutes of last Saturday morning, so I won't." Hyped up on amphetamines, pumped up from performances, abusing alcohol, Year Zero Joe was an intimidating character, but one that he would have to give up, like David Bowie gave up Ziggy Stardust, if he was to move forward.

Joe Hepatitis

When Joe became ill with Hepatitis B in late 1977/early 1978, it could be seen as a metaphor for his emotional state as the UK punk scene petered out. Yes, the fashion was influential enough that it would be the subject of museum exhibits decades later, and the music birthed several sub-genres including oi, no wave, hardcore, post-punk, and even grunge, but it had failed to improve British politics. The racist National Front flourished, and Maggie Thatcher and her Conservative Party would sweep the Labour Party out of office. If the whites of Joe's eyes were turning yellow from Hepatitis B, so too was his soul from punk rock's ineffectiveness.

As 1977 drew to a close, Joe was increasingly ill. As *ZigZag*'s Kris Needs wrote at the end of the year, "Joe Strummer will take the stage for a punishing hour-long set a few hours after a doctor has told him he must rest for three weeks to get rid of the glandular fever which has kept him in pain for days." Joe's condition was attributed to the sorry state of his teeth, but it soon became clear that it was more serious. Still, the tour must go on, so instead of checking in to the hospital, he spent his time between shows in his hotel, conserving his energy for the evening's concert.

On January 27, 1978, the day after the Clash concluded a three-date tour arranged so that they could showcase their wares for American producer Sandy Pearlman, Joe was admitted to St. Stephens Hospital on Fulham Road, suffering from Hepatitis B. As Joe told Pete Silverton, Rocco McCauley, a Spaniard who was the Clash's in-house photographer during their earliest days, had said to him, "'Ey, my friend, you looks a lettle yellow.' And he turned round with this floodlight and my eyeballs were bright yellow and my face was all yellow, and I took off my shirt and my body was all yellow.'"

Joe recuperated in the hospital for two weeks. The oft-repeated cause of Joe's hepatitis was swallowed gob during a concert performance. However, in *Redemption Song: The Ballad of Joe Strummer*, biographer Chris Salewicz finally puts this myth to rest. As we have seen, over the course of the Clash's recordings, Joe increasingly preached an anti-drug message. He even admonished Topper Headon in early 1982 that the drummer's heroin abuse was undermining this message. In *The Rise and Fall of the Clash*, however,

Tymon Dogg suggests that the source of Joe's anti-heroin ran deeper: "It was more than the fear of a dependent drug getting into the band than what it was actually doing to Topper. It was more of a mental thing that particularly Joe had, that if heroin came in, it would be destructive." This ties in with Salewicz's conclusion that Joe's hepatitis was not the result of swallowed gob, but that it came from a dirty needle Joe shared with Keith Levene and Keith's friends during the band's early punk days. (This may even have been a cause of Keith's abrupt eviction from the Clash.)

"It Was the Sweet and the Sour"

An integral aspect of the Clash that is often seriously overlooked is the manner in which Mick and Joe's guitar styles complemented one another. In this way, they were a tandem pulling the Clash along. "With my playing and Joe's playing, it was the sweet and the sour," Mick told *Backstage*. "See, Joe was a left-handed player but he played right-handedly, so his most dexterous hand was the opposite. That contributed considerably to his strumming style. That's why it is so specific to him."

Joe's contribution to the Clash as the band's rhythm guitarist is another thing he has in common with John Lennon. You always hear about Paul McCartney's bass work or George's succinct and tuneful leads, but not John's rhythm. Same with the Clash. Praise is bandied about for Mick's inventive guitar lines and Topper's range, but Joe's ferocious strumming is presented as evidence of his punk purity. This is unfair.

"Joe's more of an intuitive guitar player," recording engineer Bill Price told www.mixonline.com's Chris Michie. "He used to bash the living daylights out of his guitar when the song demanded it. He also had a sort of unconscious way of damping the chord with his right hand, which used to produce this incredibly urgent, clanging and clashing sound, which I've never heard any other guitarist ever produce."

The "sweet and sour" was also a result of Mick's sweet-sounding Gibson guitars clashing with Joe's moody Fender. During the height of his Clash days, Joe played two Fender Telecasters—one white and one painted black—that dated from 1963–64 and 1966. He also had a 1952 Esquire. He plugged his guitar directly into his amp and did not use any pedals. His amp of choice since 1979 was a Music Man HD-212, 150W. As he told *Musician*'s Vic Garbarini, "I don't have time to search for those old Fender tube amps. The Music Man is the closest thing to that sound I've found."

Che Strummer

During his time in the Clash, Joe was at his most lost, lyrically, in 1978. Bernie was no longer baiting him, the London punk scene had vanished, and he was recovering from illness. Although still coming across as sure of himself in interviews, he was anything but. He was flailing for lyrical fodder and resorted to using newspaper articles to feed his creativity. This resulted in the revolutionary part of the Clash canon, which was later derisively termed "terrorist chic." Even his clothing was targeted. Much was written about the red and white Brigade Rosse T-shirt he first wore at the Anti-Nazi Carnival on April 30, 1978, and continued to wear throughout the year. How could the Clash's front man wear a shirt supporting the Red Brigades of Italy, a left-wing terrorist organization bent on destabilizing the country through violent means, including the assassination of Christian Democrat politician Aldo Moro?

Joe Vanilla

Despite the humor in his lyrics, Joe was not a happy man. This has been confirmed by his biographer, Chris Salewicz, as well as by Mick and many others who have said Joe was prone to bouts of depression because he was too aware of reality. However, he was probably at his happiest during the period following the Clash's ouster from Rehearsal Rehearsals up until Nick Kent's savage *NME* review of *Sandinista!*

At the beginning of the summer of 1979, the Clash were in a desperate position. They didn't have a manager, Joe was paranoid about CBS Records canceling their contract because domestic sales paled compared to those of other new wave acts, and as far as the music weeklies were concerned they were yesterday's news. Their mindset as they went about finding rehearsal space and recording their third album is clear from said album's working title: *The Last Testament.*

But all the chances the band took during this period—hiring Guy Stevens to produce them, tricking CBS Records into including a second disc, recruiting Mikey Dread—paid off handsomely. The Clash were too busy to bicker as they buttressed their position within the rock 'n' roll industry. They were the best live act around, bar none. U2's Bono would say later that the Clash was the one band he never wanted to follow onto a stage. The labors were bearing fruit. And Joe was in the first year of his relationship with Gaby Salter, the attractive blonde teenager whom he would be with for the next fourteen years, and who would become the mother of his two daughters, Jazz Domino and Lola Maybelline.

In the second issue of the *Armagideon Times*, which was on sale at venues during the 16 Tons tour, each band member and key crew personnel completed a fact sheet. Asked his name, Joe cleverly answered "Joeseph Strummer," which always encapsulated for me his full name during this period. He also described himself as being five-foot-eight with brown hair and eyes.

Joe Clash

In concert and in interviews, Joe came across as a man confident in the Clash's direction and worldview, when in reality he was constantly wrestling with doubt and depression. And so it was no surprise that he panicked when *Sandinista!* was widely panned by British journalists whose weekly writings carried extraordinary weight in shaping his view of the Clash's position in the music industry. Having once been championed by these writers, he was anxious to be in their good graces again.

And so Blackhill Enterprises—with its mature advice and well-run tours—was ousted (without £40,000 it was owed, which led to its bankruptcy) and the Bernie Rhodes redux began, despite the objections of Mick and Topper. But by asserting himself and assuming leadership of the band behind the scenes, as well as in the spotlight, Joe sowed an irrevocable clash within the band's ranks.

In the second verse of "Jail Guitar Doors," when Mick sang, "I'll tell you 'bout Pete, didn't want no fame / Gave all his money away" about Fleetwood Mac founder and guitarist Peter Green, he did not know he was eerily describing his songwriting partner's own aversion to fame. While he certainly did not give "his money away" or was not "certified insane," Joe was palpably uncomfortable with fame, and when he found his plans to compete with the big boys had panned out and he now had worldwide fame, he did everything he could to sabotage it.

First, on their biggest stage—the headlining spot at the US Festival—he engaged in disputes with the festival organizers, disparaged other acts, kept the audience waiting two hours, and acted like a complete asshole. It was akin to Lou Reed releasing *Metal Machine Music* after *Sally Can't Dance* made the Top 10 and brought fans to Lou's concerts that he didn't care for. Joe was actively doing anything he could to avoid having success on the level of the

Rolling Stones or the Who, despite the seven years of hard work, grueling tours, and penniless existence that had led to this point.

Mick inarguably contributed to the deepening clash between the two, but it was Joe with Bernie who orchestrated Mick's dismissal—even if it was Paul who wielded the ax. Then he formed the Clash, Round Two, an idealistic endeavor that was run like a Stalinist regime. By December 1984, reduced to tears by Johnny Green telling him "Your band's shit" after a concert at the Brixton Academy, he knew he needed a reconciliation with Mick, but waited another nine months, and by then any possibility of the Clash reforming was non-existent.

"Those five years, from 1977 to 1982, were very intense," Joe later said. "Yak-yak-yak, non-stop yak. I didn't have any more to say because we'd done eight slabs of long-playing vinyl inside a five-year period. I think I was exhausted—mentally, physically, every which way."

Joe DeNiro

It's not surprising that Mick would smoke a peace spliff with Joe in the Bahamas but rebuff his former co-writer's suggestion that they revive the Clash; any peace offering that might have resuscitated the Clash needed to have been made in 1983 or 1984.

This left Joe with no options in 1986 but to "start all over again," as he sang in "Wrong 'Em Boyo." Where he turned for artistic salvation was a bit of a surprise, however: filmmaking. When he agreed to write "Love Kills," the title track for director Alex Cox's work-in-progress project about Sid Vicious and Nancy Spungen, Joe entered a five-year phase of contributing to soundtracks and/or appearing in films as an actor. He did not appear in *Sid and Nancy*, but did contribute two songs. He also wrote the complete instrumental score for *Walker* (1987), which was well received. "It's all acoustic," Joe said of his score for Cox's bio of William Walker, an American who invaded Mexico and declared himself Nicaragua's president. "I thought, let's be 1850. Nothing's plugged in." The 2005 reissue includes three vocal tracks.

The last film he made a significant musical contribution to was 1997's *Grosse Point Blank*. While the only song of Joe's to appear on either of the two soundtracks issued is "War Cry," Joe did contribute all of the incidental music, and he was disappointed with the film producers' disregard of the music he recorded. Watching the film is the only way to hear some of Joe's best music written for the screen.

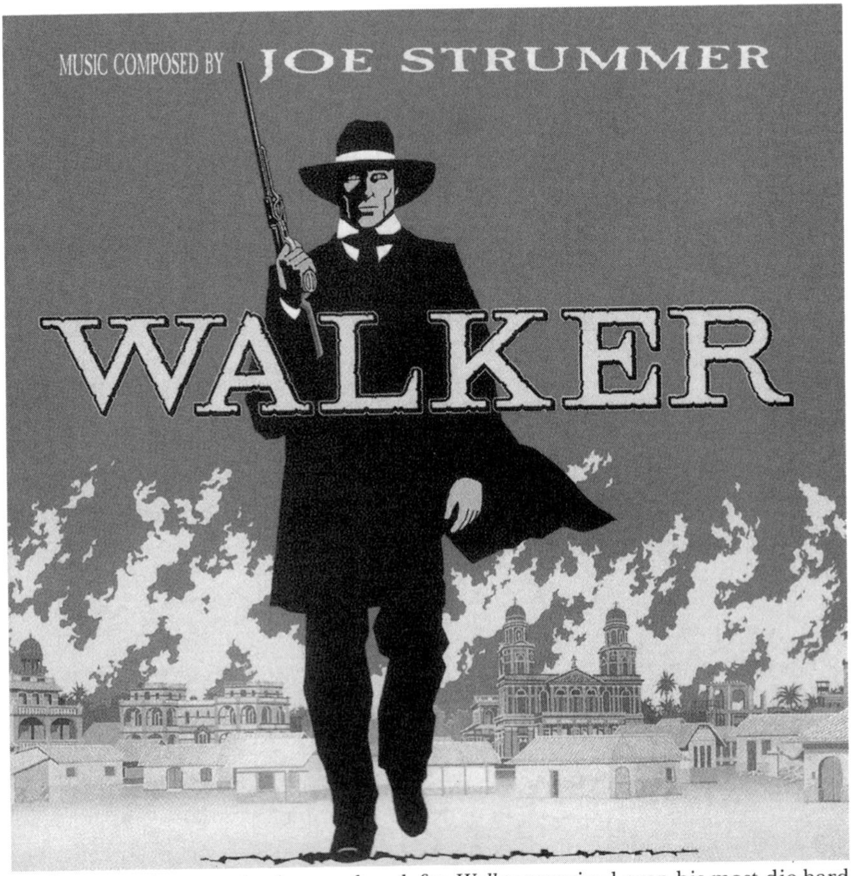

Joe Strummer's atmospheric soundtrack for *Walker* surprised even his most die-hard fans. *Author's collection*

Joe did turn up onscreen as well in both *Straight to Hell* and *Walker*, but it is his performance in Jim Jarmusch's *Mystery Train* that is essential viewing. The film is comprised of three vignettes depicting the exploits of foreigners in Memphis, Tennessee, on the same evening. The third vignette is titled "Lost in Space" and stars Joe as an Englishman named Johnny who is out of work, has been dumped by his girlfriend, and is stranded with two men who insist on calling him Elvis.

Joe Latino

The less said about Joe's late 1980s band the Latino Rockabilly War, the better. I'd like to omit the outfit entirely, but it was a wobbly stepping-stone. In 1988, Joe had contributed to the soundtrack to *Permanent Record*, a drama about suicide. The five tracks that made it onto the soundtrack are all top-notch, especially "Trash City" and "Nothin' 'Bout Nothin'," and so Joe felt the musicians he had worked with would be ideal for his next recording outfit. In November 1988, he booked time at a Hollywood recording studio for his first solo album, the self-produced *Earthquake Weather*. Lightning did not strike twice. All Joe got out of *Earthquake Weather* was his foundation's logo.

The problem lay in Joe's inability to produce others. He'd leave the song structures for the band to record, and while *Earthquake Weather* does include the participation of Jack Irons, the Red Hot Chili Peppers' original drummer, on six tracks, it was also weakened by the song arrangements by guitarist Zander Schloss, whose previous claim to fame was as bassist in the

"Trash City" was a catchy single that should have revived Joe Strummer's flagging career.
Author's collection

Circle Jerks, arguably the worst hardcore punk band to crawl out of Los Angeles. Schloss quickly proved he was not Mick's equal as an arranger.

Earthquake Weather is a worse album than *Cut the Crap*, but it was the impetus for a good tour. The man still had the goods in concert. Set lists reveal a pattern Joe was to follow with the Mescaleros: he would begin with new material, and only after he had won over the crowd would he trot out Clash classics—often songs that Mick sang originally, such as "Police on My Back."

Joe was dispirited, though, when while in New York City for a concert at the Palladium, he visited Tower Records and discovered that the store had no stock of his new album. Sensing that his label, Columbia, was not 100 percent behind him, Joe came to the conclusion he would have to wait out the remainder of his twenty-year contract before seriously venturing on a solo recording career.

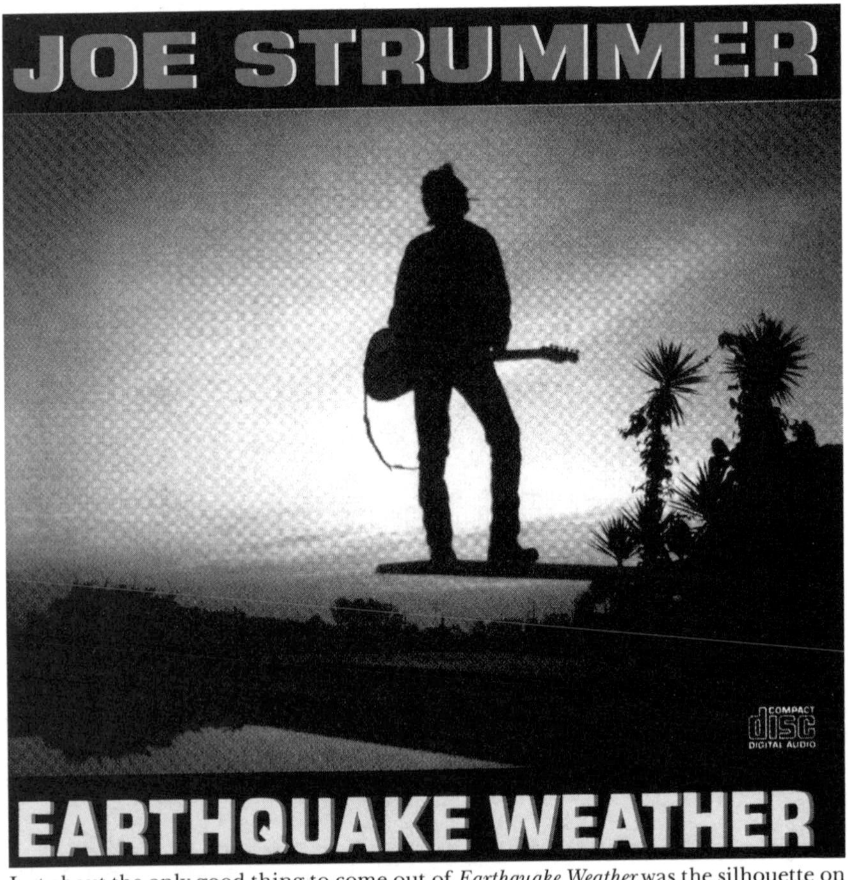

Just about the only good thing to come out of *Earthquake Weather* was the silhouette on the cover that would become Joe's logo. *Author's collection*

Joe Mahone

When the Pogues played Atlanta's Tabernacle on March 9, 2009, their sets were immediately preceded by an airing of the Clash's "Straight to Hell." This author took it as the band's hat tip in memory of the unexpected role Joe had played between 1987 and 1991 with the best makers of Irish music.

Shane McGowan, the legendary vocalist, songwriter, and front man of the Pogues, was a familiar face at Clash concerts in London in 1976 and 1977. You can see him in early concert footage and photographs, and he was even the young man mentioned in reviews of the Clash's concert at the Institute of Contemporary Arts on October 23, 1976, after a punkette named Jane had bitten his earlobe bloody.

Fast-forward eight years, and Shane was now on the stage as part of the Pogues as they opened shows for the Clash, Round Two. Joe would increasingly intersect with the Pogues over the next few years. Both contributed songs for Alex Cox's *Sid and Nancy* soundtrack in 1986 and then appeared in *Straight to Hell* in 1987. That same year, when Pogues rhythm guitarist Philip Chevron was unable to tour America because of a stomach ulcer, Joe stepped in. The Pogues were already rocking a little harder, but Joe's no-frills approach to rhythm led them to step it up a gear, and the Pogues graciously featured Joe on lead vocals for accordion-driven versions of "London Calling" and "I Fought the Law" during encores. The sound of both Joe and Shane shrieking like nuclearized seagulls on "London Calling" is sublime. Live versions were later released and can be found on *Just Look Them Straight in the Eye & Say Poguemahone!*, a 111-track boxed set that also includes Joe singing "Turkish Song of the Damned" and two studio versions of "Afro-Cuban Be-Bop," a song Joe recorded for the *I Hired a Contract Killer* soundtrack on which the Pogues acted as session musicians.

In 1990, Joe was persuaded to produce *Hell's Ditch*, the Pogues' fifth and final studio album with Shane at the helm. Joe was brought in specifically because it was thought he was one of the few musicians around who Shane might behave around, because between dropping LSD and drinking, Shane's behavior had been out of control for several years. The Pogues had been drifting away from playing unadulterated Irish music, albeit with a punk kick (several members had been in a punk band called the Nips) toward rock 'n' roll, and Shane, having just returned from Thailand, wanted to continue in this vein.

Joe was very much in the producer's chair and encouraged the new music to be more rock than reel. Accordionist Jem Finer's descriptions of Joe's antics during the recording sessions—including smashing objects—indicate that his approach to production was more Guy Stevens than Sandy Pearlman. The Pogues during these sessions were an eight-man outfit, and the resultant album is uneven due to Joe having to weigh so many competing points-of-view. Still, Joe did an admirable job, and some of the songs are classic Pogues; others, such as "Sayonara" and "Summer in Siam," have that Amerasian blues feel Joe showed mastery of in "Straight to Hell" and "Sean Flynn."

Internal differences and Shane's increasing drug abuse and alcoholism led to his dismissal in 1991. Unfortunately, contracts were already signed for concerts by a band now without a lead singer. Reluctant but willing to help some friends out, Joe agreed to join the Pogues as their front man from September 1991 through March 1992. Joe knew it was a ridiculous situation, and was quoted by Chris Salewicz as saying, "What's life for but to make reckless decisions?" Luckily, this one turned out better than the ouster of Mick Jones.

In addition to resurrecting "I Fought the Law" and "London Calling," the Pogues played "Brand New Cadillac" and a stirring version of "Straight to Hell" during Joe's third phase with the band. Luckily for us, we have an officially released document of a Pogues concert featuring Joe. For Record Store Day in 2015, *The Pogues with Joe Strummer—Live in London* was finally released on vinyl as a double album. Previously, this 1991 concert was only available as the eighth disc of *30 Years*, a Pogues boxed set issued in 2013.

With its twenty-two tracks, it is a full performance, and it fully demonstrates that the "with" in the album title is true. Joe may be filling in for Shane, but he has not replaced the Pogues' singer. Rather, he is helping out. He sings occasionally, but others, including Terry Woods, Philip Chevron, and Spider Stacy, get their turns at the microphone. There are several instrumentals as well. There is some justification for the view that the Pogues didn't mold their material to showcase Joe, though, so while it was a riveting concert—and I can say that from having seen Joe with the Pogues several times—on record something is lost in the transference.

Joe Mescalero

Although accordionist and songwriter Jem Finer had broached the subject of a musical collaboration while Joe was "with" the Pogues, midway during the tour Joe wrote to Finer that he had to find his true musical direction on his own. I'm sure he did not foresee this taking the eight years it did; years that are known as his wilderness years. But when Joe did hit the road with the Mescaleros on June 5, 1999, it was the beginning of a fitting cap to an important artist's body of work.

The seeds were sown innocently enough in the late summer of 1995, when Joe began working on an album with Richard Norris, a computer programmer who played with the Grid (a techno dance band) and percussionist Pablo Cook. Joe had married Lucinda Tait on May 31 and was ready to begin a new chapter in his life.

Joe had warmed up to "dance music" and "raves" and admitted that he finally saw where Mick was trying to go with the Clash in 1982. Although Joe and Norris would have a falling out, many of the songs on the Mescaleros' debut album were first recorded at these sessions. Norris would also work with Joe and Black Grape on 1996's "England's Irie," a football anthem. It was at this session that Joe made the acquaintance not only of percussionists Pablo Cook and Ged Lynch but also of Martin Slattery, a natural musician who could play any instrument he touched, and a future significant Mescalero.

But it was meeting not Slattery but Antony Genn that sparked Joe's final creative outburst. Genn, who played in Pulp and toured with Elastica, had met Joe a few times before 1999, but it was during a drunken conversation at the Pharmacy, a bar owned by their mutual friend (and artist) Damien Hirst that, as Genn told Anthony Davie, author of *Vision of a Homeland*, the best book to date on Joe Strummer and the Mescaleros, "Me and Joe got in a very deep conversation about music. I just said to him, 'You should be making a record, you're fuckin' Joe Strummer, for fuck's sake.' He kinda called my bluff on it and said, 'OK, I'm gonna call you tomorrow, me and you are going to go in the studio.'" The result was the first of three fine albums Joe would record with a shifting cast of musicians.

Rock Art and the X-Ray Style

Damien Hirst's caveman-like drawings on the cover hint at Joe's hieroglyphic, Beefheartian lyrics within, and the otherwise pink cover—a color associated with the Clash—is a clue that Joe's true musical direction required a U-turn. He may have described the music as "hip-hopabilly" to *Mojo*'s Pat Gilbert, but in truth, now that he was at peace with *Sandinista!* and *Combat Rock* and understood those albums contained music that only Joe Strummer could create, that is where he returned to jumpstart the final legs of his recording career.

The sax driven "Tony Adams," the combat-rocking "Techno D-Day," the anti-communist China rant "Forbidden City," and the acid-jazz groove of "Willesden to Cricklewood"—which would be played at Joe's funeral—could all fit comfortably on *Sandinista!* On an album with only one weak track ("Sandpaper Blues"), the highlight lyrically is the Dread-worthy "Yalla Yalla." Talking of "liberty," Joe mournfully observes that she "didn't show, not in my time," but, ever the optimist, he adds, "But in our sons' and daughters' time, when you get a feeling, call." For a man who should be beat down after all that creative wandering, he could still inspire.

Rock Art and the X-Ray Style was the height of the Strummer/Genn collaboration. While Cook, Slattery, and bassist Scott Shields would play significant roles in the sophomore Mescaleros album, Genn would depart mid-summer 2000, due to a deepening heroin addiction.

Global a Go-Go

Not only the best album Joe recorded with the Mescaleros, not only one of the best albums of 2001, but one of the best albums of the decade, *Global a Go-Go* is a musical *tour de force* brimming with global rhythms. The music is impossible to categorize, as if Joe was deliberately taunting the critics who are only satisfied when they can classify. Joe was well aware of the musical melting pot he was stirring, even making a joke out of it during "Bhindi Bhagee," the album's fourth track, which describes a chance meeting with a New Zealander looking for "mushy peas," where all Joe can direct him to are restaurants serving foreign cuisine. When the New Zealander learns that Joe is in a band and asks what is it like, Joe hems and haws and then finally gushes, "Ragga, bhangra, two-step tanga, mini-cab radio, music on the go! Umm, surf beat, backbeat, frontbeat, backseat, there's a bunch of players and they're really letting go!"—hence the song's title and a fine piece of cultural observation by Joe.

With Genn's departure, Slattery moved into the principal arranger's seat, but it was the addition of another musician that fueled *Global a Go-Go* and the Mescaleros' growth: Tymon Dogg. Joe and Pablo Cook were playing at a poetry benefit when the two former buskers bumped into each other and Dogg accepted Joe's invitation to join him and the percussionist onstage. A few days later, Dogg turned up at the recording studio where Joe was developing "Gamma Ray," *Global a Go-Go*'s eventual fifth track, and soon after, Tymon Dogg and Joe were in their first band together.

As if knowing he had assembled a band that could jam, Joe limited his participation during the six-month-long *Global a Go-Go* recording sessions to vocals, songwriting, and production. Slattery was a multi-instrumentalist who played guitar, saxophone, flute, and all manner of keyboards; he's even credited with a "bedroom fuzzbox" solo on "Bhindi Bhagee." Cook is just as talented on percussion instruments (he is credited with playing Ayanuesca percussion, bodhrán, wavedrum, guiros, go-go bells and shakers, and "weird bank noises" in the liner notes), as is Dogg on stringed instruments (violin, mandolin, Spanish guitar) and Scott Shields on bass, drums, guitars, and so on. Heck, this is a multi-instrumentalist band.

Giving the fans their money's worth, *Global a Go-Go* concludes with a mostly instrumental, 17:49 version of the Irish patriotic song "Minstrel Boy." A version with lyrics can be found on the *Blackhawk Down* soundtrack.

Let's Rock Again!

With product to move, Joe Strummer and the Mescaleros hit the road in Sheffield on June 5, 1999. Joe was a little puffier from drinking bottles of wine during the wilderness years, and the band a little ragged, but Joe was still a natural front man, and after a few shows the band's talents caught up with him. Joe Strummer and the Mescaleros were one of the best bands on the road between the middle of 1999 and the end of 2002.

Set lists would include between eighteen and twenty-two songs, including encores, and could run as long as two hours. Although Clash sets occasionally began with a slow number, such as "Jimmy Jazz" or "Broadway," they far more commonly kicked off with three explosive numbers that would wham-bam-slam the fans. With the Mescaleros, Joe took a different tactic and invariably opened with a slow number. In 2001 and 2002 this was usually the traditional, violin-led "Minstrel Boy" or "Shakhtar Donetsk," a mournful dirge about a Macedonian trying to make his way to a better life in England, only to die in the back of a lorry.

After several musicians outwore their welcomes—including Antony Genn, Ged Lynch, and Pablo Cook (unavailability) and drummer Steve "Smiley" Barnard (inability)—by July 2002 the touring band consisted of Joe (vocals/guitar), Slattery (keys/guitar/saxophone/backing vocals), Shields (guitar/backing vocals), Dogg (violin/Spanish guitar), Luke Bullen (drums), and Simon Stafford (bass/trombone).

This lineup is featured in Dick Rude's *Let's Rock Again!*, a documentary filmed over the last eighteen months of Joe's touring career. Dick and Joe

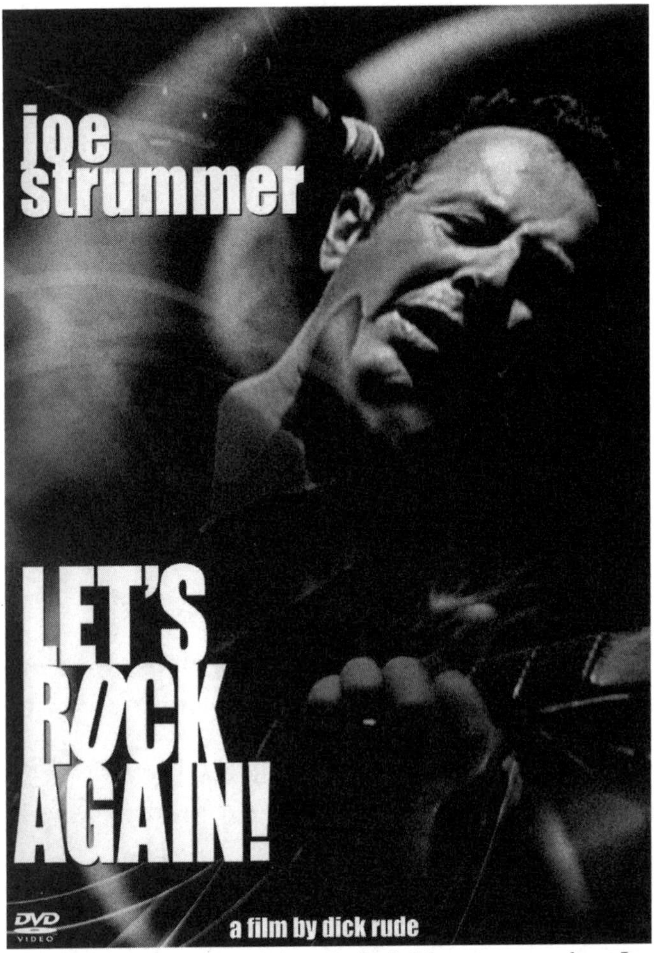

Dick Rude's *Let's Rock Again* is a wonderful documentary about Joe Strummer and the Mescaleros touring America and Japan in 2000.
Author's collection

had bonded while collaborating on Alex Cox's film projects. Shot during tours of the US and Japan, it is the only film focused on Joe Strummer and the Mescaleros. Well filmed, it has a touch of pathos, too, as Joe strives to get his new music heard by an uninterested public. It also features five songs performed in their entirety, including versions of Jimmy Cliff's "The Harder They Come," Lone Ranger's "A Quarter Pound of Ishen," and the Clash's "Rudie Can't Fail." "A Quarter Pound of Ishen" is Joe's best cover tune from the Mescaleros years but is only available on *Let's Rock Again!* and bootleg footage and recordings.

Joe Hall

Joe Strummer was on what would be his final tour with the Mescaleros when it was announced that the Clash would be inducted into the Rock and Roll Hall of Fame in March 2003. Nine inductees were announced, including Elvis Costello and the Attractions, and the Police, whom the Clash disdained. The response of former Clash members ran the gamut of emotions from Paul's visceral disinterest to Joe's determination to not only accept the award but perform at the ceremony.

While Joe and Mick had long made peace with one another—their daughters even played together—the induction truly laid the past to rest. When Joe and his Mescaleros turned up at Acton Town Hall in West London on November 15, 2002, to play a benefit concert and raise money for striking firefighters, Mick was in the audience with his girlfriend, Miranda. After the second number, Joe informed the audience that Mick was not only present but also celebrating the birth of his daughter, Stella, named for Mick's grandmother. Joe then dedicated a rousing version of "Rudie Can't Fail" to Mick.

That alone would have made the concert memorable, but then, following the thirteen-song set, which included new numbers such as "Get Down Moses" and "Coma Girl," Mick joined Joe onstage for the first time in nineteen years as the Mescaleros played "Bankrobber," "White Riot," and "London's Burning." (A recording of this concert was released by Hellcat Records in 2012.) It surely appeared that Mick was amenable to a Clash reunion at the induction ceremony. Topper was willing to do so as well. The only holdout was Paul, who was adamant that he would not perform in front of the music industry executives he felt had not properly supported the Clash during their years together. Joe was determined to go on without him and threatened to have Blur's bassist Alex James perform in his stead. He was still trying to persuade Paul to reconsider, and in fact was having trouble faxing him about the issue the morning of December 22, 2002, before stopping to take his three dogs for a walk.

Death Is a Star

December was almost always a splendid month for Clash fans: the band tended to release albums in time to be presents under Christmas trees or play concerts in London during the holiday season. But the morning of December 22, 2002, was dreadful as we woke to news that Joe Strummer had unexpectedly passed away at his house in Broomfield in Somerset. He was only fifty years old.

As George Binette writes in *The Last Night London Burned*, "News of Joe Strummer dead after walking the dogs was all but unbelievable: no car crash, no plane crash, no last Byronesque gesture, no overdose—only a doctor's discovery of an extremely rare congenital heart defect."

The tributes flowed from rock musicians and film directors. Bono admitted, "The Clash was the greatest rock band. They wrote the rule book

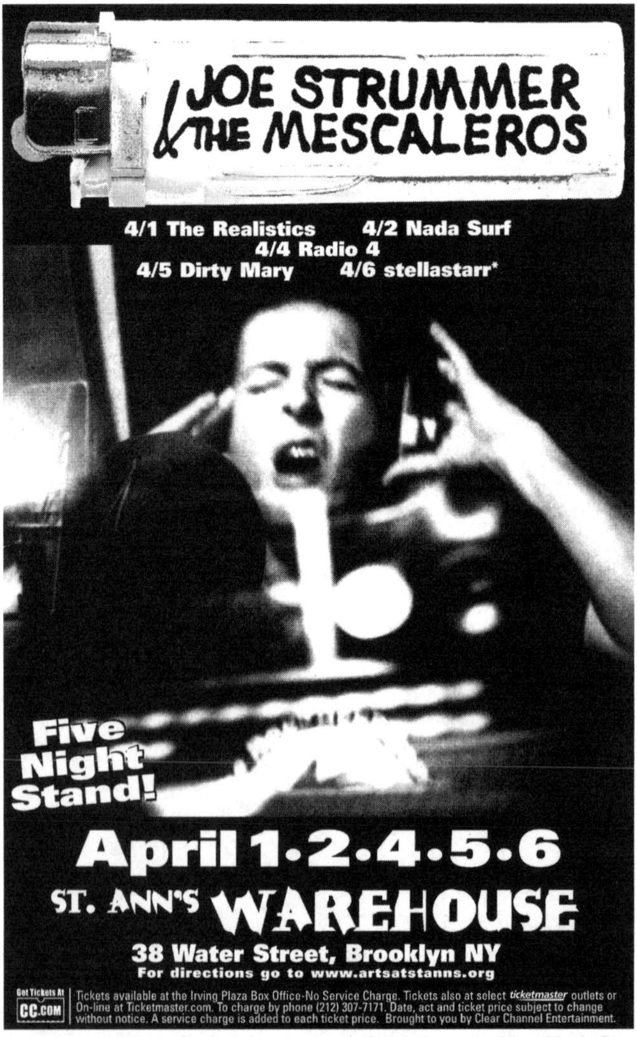

An advertisement for Joe Strummer's final shows in New York City in early April 2002. *Author's collection*

for U2." Billy Bragg said, "I have a great admiration for the man. His most recent records are as political and edgy as anything he did with the Clash. His take on multicultural Britain in the twenty-first century is far ahead of anybody else."

Joe's funeral was held in Kensal Green on December 30. In addition to family members, his fellow musicians in the Clash and Mescaleros were present, as were old faces from the Clash's inner circle (Johnny Green, Pennie Smith, Kosmo Vinyl) and various rockers, including Chrissie Hynde, Glen Matlock, and Rat Scabies. The procession went past the Elgin pub, where Joe had performed with the 101'ers and dipped into during the 1976 Notting Hill Carnival riot that inspired "White Riot." Joe's simple coffin had stickers on it stating that "Vinyl Rules" and reminding one to "Question Authority." A Stetson rested atop the coffin. His remains were cremated in the West London Crematorium.

Streetcore

Mick, fresh from recent successes with the Libertines' *Up the Bracket*, offered to produce Joe's posthumous album, but his widow, Luce, entrusted the project to Martin Slattery and Scott Shields, two of Joe's Mescaleros. The result was 2003's *Streetcore*, one of the best posthumous releases ever—up there with Janis Joplin's *Pearl* and Jimi Hendrix's *Rainbow Bridge*, suitable company for a man who finally admitted in the 1990s that "I am a hippy."

Streetcore is credited to Joe Strummer and the Mescaleros, but it contains three songs from sessions with Rick Rubin and Danny Saber. Slattery and Shields masterfully sequenced the album, which includes rockers, jams, and folk songs. Joe plays his Fender Telecaster one last time on the opening track "Coma Girl," but otherwise he only contributed vocals to the album's ten songs. There are at least six classic Joe Strummer tracks, including "Get Down Moses," "Ramshackle Day Parade" (about 9/11) and "Arms Aloft," the most Clashical song Joe recorded without the Clash.

"Long Shadow" was a song Joe wrote for Johnny Cash to sing. The Man in Black declined (as he had "The Road to Rock and Roll" years earlier) but Rubin, the producer of Cash's final series of albums, arranged for Johnny and Joe to record a duet. The result was a moving version of Bob Marley's "Redemption Song." Upon Joe's death, Rubin sent the tapes to Joe's widow for possible inclusion on the posthumous album. The version on *Streetcore* does not include Cash's vocals. That version was released as part of Cash's

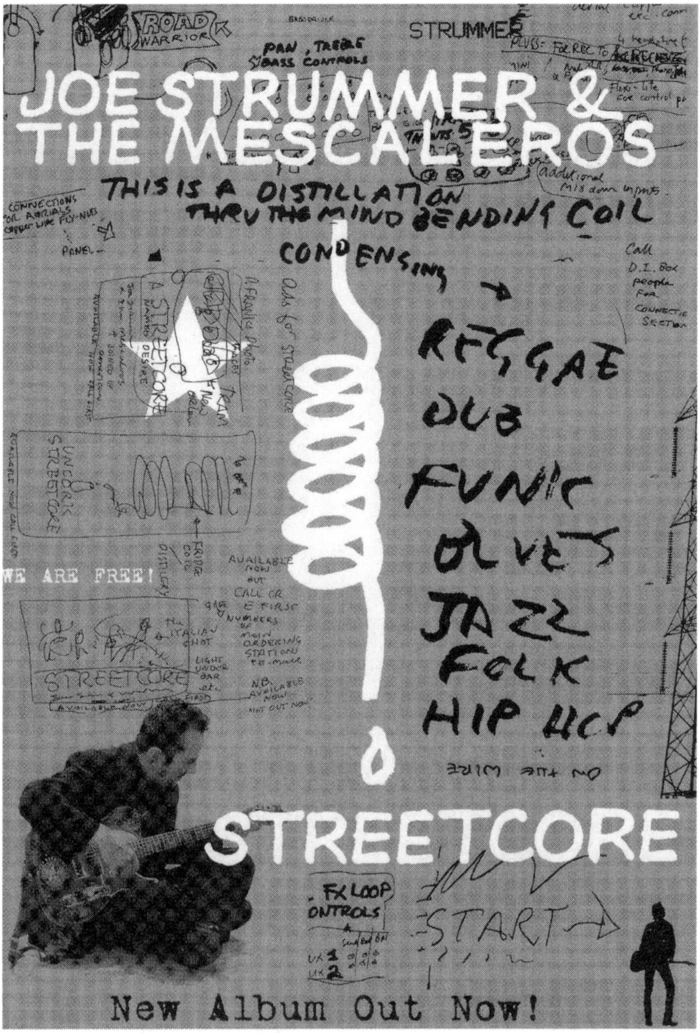

A postcard advertisement for *Streetcore*, Joe Strummer's final album with the Mescaleros. *Author's collection*

posthumous boxed set *Unearthed.* Johnny and Joe's version was nominated for a Grammy award.

Streetcore concludes poignantly with "Silver and Gold," a version of Bobby Charles's "Before I Grow Too Old." It is an old New Orleans number—a region of music Joe had a special fondness for, and a fitting way to end an album by a man who died far too young. The lyrics truly reflect Joe's lifestyle of "fancying every night" (he often brought up the dawn) and why he had to "hurry up before I grow too old." It's as if he knew he would not be with us too long.

The Future Is Unwritten

Joe's death finally brought him the recognition he deserved. He is up there with John Lennon and Bob Marley as a man whose work reflected his times and was an inspiration to fans to strive and realize their potential. No one has to look further than *The Future Is Unwritten*, director Julien Temple's 2006 documentary film about Joe, which includes testaments from Bono, Steven Buscemi, Johnny Depp, Martin Scorsese, Flea, and many others. In the mid-1990s, Joe began attending festivals and camping out and starting bonfires around which friends and family and strangers would talk and sing. Temple does the same here. He gathers groups of Joe's family, friends, and fellow musicians, and as they reminisce, Joe's life story unfolds via home movies, animations of Joe's artwork, his BBC radio broadcasts, film performances, and concert footage. All former members of the Clash except Paul Simonon offer their memories of the "punk rock warlord," as Joe once characterized himself. My only criticism is the absence of any Mescaleros, other than Antony Genn and Tymon Dogg.

The Future Is Unwritten is vastly superior to *Westway to the World*, and since Temple was perhaps the first filmmaker to shoot the Clash, he had reels of priceless footage to draw from, including early rehearsals. It is a truly "warts and all" presentation of Joe and his philosophies about how we need to question authority and be creative in the moment, and that "without people, you're nothing." As he says in the film, "I don't have any message other than, don't forget you're alive!"

Or, as Johnny Green put it best, in a 2012 interview with *Quietus*: "[Joe's] legacy is that he showed people that you can have a bash at whatever you try: don't feel intimidated by it, give it your best shot, whatever your dream is."

He Said Go Out and Get Me My Old Movie Stills

The Clash on Film

Like the Rolling Stones, the Clash were best experienced in concert. They were so visual, with Joe's pumping left leg, Mick's leaps, and Paul's good looks, that it is no wonder they attracted the attention of filmmakers early in their career. Luckily, they attracted filmmakers who were up to the task.

The Clash: New Year's Day 1977

Some of the oldest footage is the newest as fans in Great Britain welcomed in the New Year of 2015 viewing a BBC TV broadcast of a seventy-five-minute special featuring the Clash's concert at the Roxy in Covent Garden, thirty-eight years earlier to the day. Discovering that this footage existed is akin to what the feeling would be if Don Letts's lost Bond's reels suddenly turned up.

The Clash: New Year's Day 1977 is a film by Julien Temple, so you know it's going to be good. Not only has he shot music videos for David Bowie, Janet Jackson, the Rolling Stones and Neil Young, and directed two documentaries on the Sex Pistols (*The Great Rock 'n' Roll Swindle* and *The Filth and the Fury*), he also directed *Joe Strummer: The Future Is Unwritten* and some of the Clash's earliest videos. Few fans knew Temple had filmed the Clash at the Roxy, a legendary punk club that was staging shows for approximately one hundred days. When asked by Vincent Dowd, an arts reporter with BBC News, where the film had been stored, Temple answered, "Rotting away in my shed!"

Now you must put this into context. Yes, the Clash had been on the Sex Pistols' controversial Anarchy in the UK tour the previous month, but they were unknown except to a few hundred British punk rockers. This was approximately their thirtieth show. Terry Chimes steadfastly refused to play the two scheduled gigs, so interim drummer Rob Harper provided the backbeats. They hadn't even signed to CBS Records yet, let alone released any recordings. Footage of the Clash in concert at this point in their career is priceless. It's like seeing their debut album cover come to life.

Temple cleverly edits in images of New Year's Eve revelers ushering in 1977 while Culture play "When Sevens Clash" and recreates a time when it appeared that Jamaican gadfly Marcus Garvey's prediction of chaos on July 7, 1977, might come true. Dire views of British life circa 1976–77 follow as a television studio audience is asked for opinions on the country's future; politicians present their views, punk rockers in the UK cavort, and the Clash are interviewed, rehearse, and perform. It is, as Joe says, "the first time I've ever been filmed."

So we get glimpses of the Clash's life at Rehearsal Rehearsals, posing for photo shoots, auditioning a drummer, even having their clothing spray-painted in the auto-repair shop Bernie owned. The black-and-white footage reminds the viewer that the director was as down and out and punk as the band he was filming. A favorite moment is the Clash laughing while watching a playback of themselves doing their punk poses on a "telly."

There's also some background on Covent Garden, the district where a former gay club Shaggy Ramas was now reopening as the Roxy. We are told it is the "epicenter of Cockney London" and "the heart of libertine London where high and low culture have always famously collided." Like other parts of London, it is down on its luck, especially since the closing of the market place in 1974.

Inside the Roxy we see the Clash go through a soundcheck and find their PA system is on the blink. There's nothing to do but "get on with it"—a favorite expression of Joe's. Onstage footage from both sets is interspersed as the Clash play their classics "London's Burning," "I'm So Bored with the USA" (the first performance with Joe's new lyrics for an old tune of Mick's), "Career Opportunities," "Janie Jones," and "White Riot." Joe's playing his Gretsch White Falcon, the Roxy stage is tiny, there's tuning up between songs, but the punk energy is palpable.

Unfortunately, none of the songs are presented as full performances, but they all get commentary from one of the Clash, usually Joe, explaining the song's genesis. Finally, the second set concludes as the Clash bash out "1977." "Happy new fuckin' year," Joe says, before walking off the stage.

The Essential Clash

From memory, "not essential" was an accurate critique of the DVD counterpart to a similarly titled CD collection released in 2003 and tied to the Clash's induction into the Rock and Roll Hall of Fame, until pressing the "PLAY ALL" feature wiped away that perspective.

Shortly after Joe Strummer's death, *The Essential Clash* DVD was released. It contains all of the band's promo videos and Joe's movie *Hell W10*.
Author's collection

The Essential Clash contains the Clash's eleven official promo films, plus a trailer for *The Clash on Broadway* and other extras. The music for over half the promo films is from live recordings—a good source for latter-day Clash fans seeking a glimpse of what the band must've been like in concert. There's a combustible "White Riot" from the dawn of the punk era; "Workin' for the Clampdown" and "Train in Vain" (with Joe's dismissive introduction that "We'd like to take the Soul Train from Platform 1. Be leaving for three minutes. If you don't want to come, there's always the toilets.") from the Lewisham Odeon in south London on February 18, 1980, featuring all band members in Johnny Cash black, including temporary fifth member, keyboardist Mickey Gallagher; and the spirited Shea Stadium performances of "Should I Stay or Should I Go" and "Career Opportunities," with Terry Chimes back behind the kit. They should have relegated the *Clash on Broadway* trailer to the "Extras" section and not started the collection with Don Letts's leftover footage from the Bond's residency. Starting with "White Riot" and wrapping up with "Career Opportunities" would have provided a more satisfying symmetry. The fact that promo films were never made for "Clash City Rockers" and "(White Man) In Hammersmith Palais" lends credence to the band's contention that their label never provided adequate marketing support.

Admittedly, the mimed videos are a mixed bag. "Bankrobber" (session footage interspersed with roadies Johnny Green and The Baker playing bank robbers) and "The Call Up" (with the Clash in combat gear) are awful, but "Tommy Gun's" rat-a-tat-tat editing befits the song; "London Calling," filmed in the pelting night rain on the Thames is gripping; and "Rock the Casbah," shot on a Texan oil field outside Austin, is as much of a hoot as it was when first viewed on MTV in 1982.

The extras include 1977 promo footage shot by Lindsey Clennell interposed between snippets of a Tony Parsons interview, "I Fought the Law" from *Rude Boy*, and an interview on the *London Weekend Show*, but of the most historical interest is *Hell W10*, a never-before-released, Joe Strummer–directed silent movie about London mobsters made in the summer of 1983 that was considered lost until a fan found a copy at a car boot sale. With Strummer now deceased, the film was not edited, but music from *London Calling*, *Sandinista!*, and *Combat Rock* was added. The music is the main reason to play *Hell W10*, especially since the majority of the *Combat Rock* tracks are allegedly Mick's original instrumental mixes for *Rat Patrol from Camp Bragg*.

It's kinda fun to see how many people from the Clash inner circle you can identify. There's Kosmo Vinyl, Ray Jordan (security), The Baker (in an Elvis Presley wig), Pearl Harbor, and Gaby Salter, Joe's common-law wife. Paul plays a Jimmy Cliff–type Londoner caught up in a drug kingpin's ventures when he steals porn-film canisters containing heroin. (The fake porno titles are funny: *Bum Chums at Cambridge, Cath O' Licks, Nuns on Heat.*) Joe gives a credible performance as a corrupt policeman, and Mick is cast as the villain (with some resemblance to Michael Corleone), perhaps reflecting Joe's feelings about the band member he would dismiss when the summer of 1983 was gone.

All of the promo videos and Letts footage are also available on the *Sound System* boxed set. *Hell W10* is not.

Rude Boy

The Clash's best cinematographer was Jack Hazan. Regrettably, he was one of the co-directors of *Rude Boy*, the 1980 movie that the Clash collectively took a hard stance against, so Hazan was never allowed to film the band after 1979. Not that he wanted to. He was as fed up with the Clash as the Clash were with *Rude Boy*. Everybody's loss. So, although Hazan's footage has been used for countless Clash documentaries and videos, the only place to view his full body of work on the Clash is *Rude Boy*, an uneven movie with a muddled political message but some of the best Clash performances captured for posterity. Essential doesn't begin to describe it. If you can only see one film with the Clash, see *Rude Boy*. The DVD even comes with a feature that allows you to watch only the Clash's performances. (See chapter 18 for a deeper dive into the filming and recording of *Rude Boy*.)

Capital Radio (Bootleg)

The Clash were at their performance peak throughout the various legs of 1980's 16 Tons, even if Johnny Green thought "the lads were getting soft." True, they are not as visually exciting as in the punk performances shot by Julien Temple and Lindsey Clennell, or even the 1978 performances preserved in *Rude Boy*, but this was a mature band at the height of their powers, comparable to the Rolling Stones in 1972. They were pacing themselves, only exploding during the punk classics, because their concerts had doubled in length from a year earlier.

Stray concert footage from 1980 can be found on YouTube of the Clash in Edinburgh and Boston, but the lengthier performances are of the band in Paris, France (February 27 at Le Palace); Passaic, New Jersey (March 8 at the Capitol Theatre); and Torino, Italy (June 3 at Parco Ruffini). The Capitol Theatre show is the one to see, but the shows in Paris and Torino are in color and were professionally shot for television, and they too have their strengths, including shots of Topper, who in New Jersey is reduced visually to being a frame for Joe.

The Le Palace performance is the most ragged of the three, but there's Mick singing "Protex Blue"; Paul in a white tank top undershirt, thumping his left leg and punishing his bass with his right hip; and Joe talking in pigeon French, doing his modified duck walk, and pantomiming the throwing of dice during "Wrong 'Em Boyo." My favorite moment is when Joe and Mick are at Joe's microphone, singing "I don't give a flying fuck where the rich are going" in unison during "Garageland."

The footage of the Torino performance is a little dark but worth hearing for Mick's performance. He truly was a guitar hero this evening. You can tell from the closing distress signals of "London Calling," which hang ominously in the air after Joe's stopped singing. It's June, and the band's been busy touring or recording what will be *Sandinista!*, and by now Mick's perfected his lead for "The Guns of Brixton." It's still Paul's vehicle, but if you're listening, Mick's stealing the show. Joe plays his white "I may take a holiday" Fender Telecaster throughout, and he even sings a verse of "Jail Guitar Doors."

Video of the show at the Capitol Theatre has circulated for decades. The drawbacks are that it is in black-and-white and shot on videotape, but it is the complete show, with both encores, and the excitement in the theater is tangible. Tennessee Ernie Ford's "Sixteen Tons" is playing as the Clash come onstage. Mick, dressed in white—almost Pete Townshend-ish—shields his eyes with his right hand and gazes out at the audience. Joe steps up to his center-stage microphone: "Good evening. I'm not sure, but I think it's Saturday night in New Jersey." He raises both arms. You can tell it's gonna be a great night.

The Clash blast through "Clash City Rockers," Brand New Cadillac," and "Safe European Home." There is a majesty to the live version of "Safe European Home" as the bass undertones rumble and the song pivots to the outro about the rude boy. Joe introduces Mickey Gallagher, who contributes tasteful organ licks to the next number, "Jimmy Jazz." Gallagher's organ is a wonderful addition on the reggae numbers, but when he plays electric piano on the punk rockers it can be cloying.

We are now into the *London Calling* portion of the set: six of the next eight songs are from the band's third album. The highlights are a tight "Train in Vain," with Joe not disappearing into the shadows (as was his wont during Mick's hit), and the "Koko Kola" / "I Fought the Law" medley, featuring Topper's precise drumming. Another Topper highlight is his drum intro to "Police and Thieves."

By now, the movements of the men on the front line have changed. They are no longer flying around the stage: Mick is forever swaying while Joe seems to be going up and down; even as he moves across the stage, the thrust of his strumming hand gives the impression of moving up and down. Paul's developed a cool shimmy as he moves back and forth. It's as if they are saving their energies for the wham-bam-thank-you-slam ending of "Janie Jones" and "Complete Control."

As the stage is fixed for the encores, there are glimpses of The Baker and Johnny Green, who was soon to leave the Clash's employ. Mikey Dread joins the Clash for the first song of each encore, a highlight being a medley of the then unreleased "Bankrobber" and "Rocker's Galore." As the Clash shoot their way into the final song, "Tommy Gun," you realize their alleged dislike of *Give 'Em Enough Rope* has been overstated. They've played half of their second album.

The film ends with a shot of the Clash's stage backdrop of smoking power plants, as alluded to in "Clampdown."

Live in Tokyo, Japan 1982

You can find this performance on YouTube, but don't be misled by the text indicating it is of the full concert. It is not. Running to 54:45, this footage for Japan's *Young Music Show* was culled from the Clash's two-and-a-half-hour performance at the Sun Plaza on February 1, 1982. They were one week into their Far East tour and well oiled. It's an excellent view of the Clash during their final period with Topper manning the engine room—the culmination of his five years as the band's drummer.

Live in Tokyo, Japan 1982 begins with Ennio Morricone's intro music as the Clash assemble on the stage to an uproarious welcome. Joe is wearing a red bandana with Japanese lettering with matching red pants (no lettering) and black shirtless vest. He plays his black 1966 Telecaster throughout. Paul and Mick are dressed in black. Mick plays a white Les Paul and is still flying around the stage. Topper wears a white bandana and, after a few songs, ditches his shirt. There's good footage of the drummer throughout.

The concert was well filmed; you can watch Joe play the riff to "Brand New Cadillac" and his spit flying as he sings "Safe European Home." He drags his mic over to Mick to share vocals and can later be seen banging the body of his guitar against his forehead as the song ends. Many songs are rearranged and extended with vocal ad libs, guitar noises, London Reggae dropouts. It's a lesson in how a band not able to jam still jams.

Other highlights include Joe substituting train sounds for Mick's guitar solo on "(White Man) In Hammersmith Palais," Mick's solo on "Charlie Don't Surf" (very similar to his work on "Sean Flynn"), and "Clampdown" segueing into "This Is Radio Clash"—a song that was always a powerhouse in concert.

The final encore is presented in its entirety, with the Clash supporting Pearl Harbor on a very Cramps-ish arrangement of "Fujiyama Mama," "Police on My Back" (Mick's only lead vocal), and a rowdy "White Riot." The only complaint with *Live in Tokyo, Japan 1982* is that it isn't the full concert.

The US Festival (San Bernardino, California, May 30, 1983)

Even if the Clash did have the rights to this performance—Mick's final appearance with the band he founded—they wouldn't release it. Alas, is it easily accessible on YouTube. The only point of comparison is with the Beatles' film *Let It Be,* which stars a bickering band and as of this writing has still not been officially re-released. The Clash's performance at the US Festival captures Joe Strummer giving way to his worst instincts and the stress of success and sounding like a deranged spokesman for his generation.

Still, it is a good place to see what new drummer Pete Howard might have brought to future Clash recordings, and the set list indicates where the Clash's mindset and worldview was when their "rock 'n' roller coaster" came to a halt:

1. "London Calling"
2. "This Is Radio Clash"
3. "Somebody Got Murdered"
4. "Rock the Casbah"
5. "The Guns of Brixton"
6. "Know Your Rights"
7. "Koka Kola"

8. “Hate and War”
9. “Armagideon Time”
10. “The Sound of the Sinners”
11. “Safe European Home”
12. “Police on My Back”
13. “Brand New Cadillac”
14. “I Fought the Law”
15. “I’m So Bored with the USA”
16. “Train in Vain”
17. “The Magnificent Seven”
18. “Straight to Hell”
19. “Should I Stay or Should I Go”
20. “Clampdown”

Interestingly, Mick sang five of the set’s twenty songs (or 25 percent). This was unheard of. Perhaps he was demanding more mic time, which may have played a role in his eventual termination.

Westway to the World

Westway to the World gives you the story of the Clash directly from the four horsemen’s mouths. The 2000 documentary was directed by Don Letts, the reggae-spinning DJ at the Roxy Club—the first club that catered to punk—who had the foresight to film the London punk scene before anyone else. He would go on to direct almost all of the Clash’s promo videos, and it is mostly this footage, along with clips from *Rude Boy* and archival news clippings, that illustrates the memories of the talking heads. (The oddest clip is of a dance troupe known as Pan’s People performing to “Bankrobber” on *Top of the Pops.*) Other witnesses pop up, including drummer Terry Chimes, road manager Johnny Green, photographer Pennie Smith, and recording engineer Bill Price, but this documentary—clocking in at 1:19:52—is mostly just the Clash talking. There are no full videos or concert performances.

This was the only time the Clash told their story, which we all know had one of the most ludicrous breakups in the annals of rock ’n’ roll. The feelings about the breakup were still raw enough, fifteen years after the fact, that each member gives his testament alone. “We all wanted to do the documentary,” Joe told the *Guardian*’s Caroline Sullivan in 1999,” but we couldn’t do it in the same room. It’s still too heavy.” There’s not even a shot of the four members together at the end. So it’s appropriate that after an opening quote from Joe, *Westway to the World* begins with images from the Bond’s residency scored to the intro to "Charlie Don't Surf," the Clash's homage to *Apocalypse Now!*, because we are entering the Clash's collective heart of darkness. The Clash are soon seen playing "London Calling" on the Bond's stage, and then Joe, Mick, and Paul begin talking about their childhoods. Joe's parents were serving in the Foreign Office and distant, and both Mick and Paul's parents had divorced so it was music that was a solace when they were young.

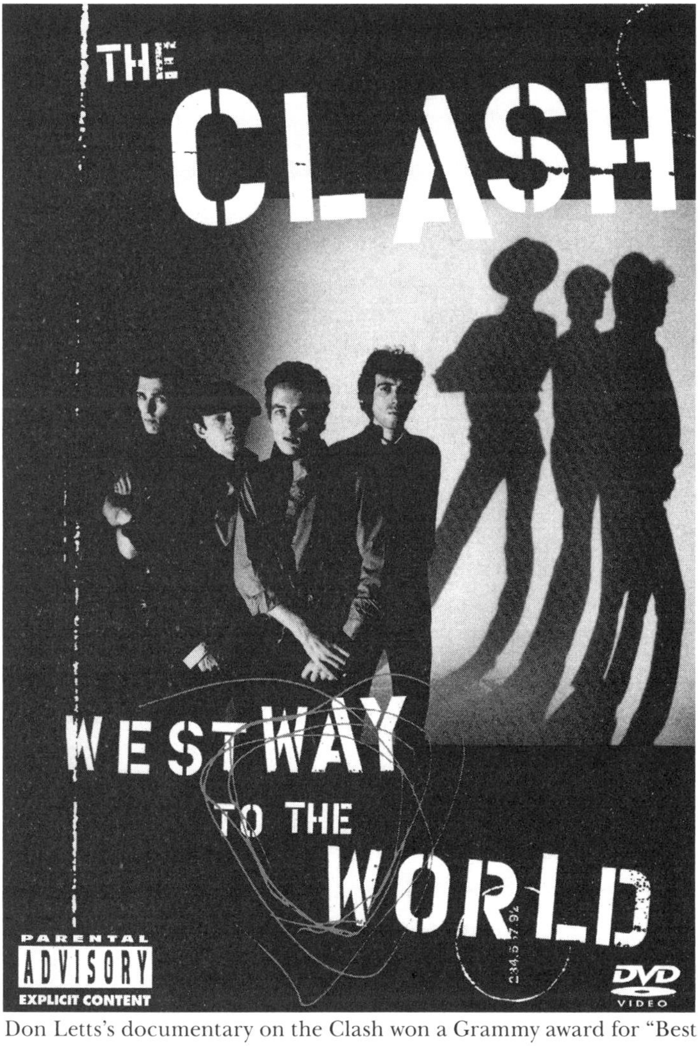

Don Letts's documentary on the Clash won a Grammy award for "Best Long Form Music Video" in 2003. *Author's collection*

The personalities that shone onstage shine through on film, too. Joe is forthright with glimpses of his humor. Paul is rakish; Mick a gentleman. Most dismaying is Topper's appearance. Characterizing him as thin when his interview was filmed just does not cut it: he looks shrunken and like a character out of the reception-room scenes in *Beetlejuice*. It is said that the audience gasped when he appeared onscreen at the documentary's premiere.

This impression is reinforced by the white shirt he is wearing. It is too large for him. Apparently, Topper turned up for his interview in a T-shirt dotted with cigarette burns, so Mick lent him a clean one. But Mick is taller than most fans realize, and his white shirt seems intent on swallowing Topper.

The other members were glad to hear their drummer finally apologize for the drug addiction that probably propelled the band's eventual breakup—"for going off the rails"—but Topper also admits, "I think that if it happened again, I'd probably do the same thing. I'm just that sort of person, you know?"

The central flaw of Letts's documentary is that the band members only gingerly discuss the breakup. They tiptoe around the subject. Joe, Mick, and Paul are not as honest in explaining their differences as Topper is about his drug addiction. Mick's insufferable, rock *prima donna* behavior is given as the primary cause, but there's no mention of manager Bernie Rhodes's orchestration of Mick's ouster or his manipulation of Joe's naivety. The lawsuits that followed—and the Clash, Round Two—are not even mentioned. This documentary makes it sound like Mick was fired and the Clash disbanded the next day.

Westway to the World may have been awarded a Grammy for "Best Long Form Music Video" in 2003, but it's not worth owning. Catch it on YouTube and then watch *The Rise and Fall of the Clash* to better understand the breakup.

The Rise and Fall of the Clash

Winner of "Best Documentary Feature" at the Coney Island Film Festival in 2012, first-time director Danny Garcia's film focuses on *the fall* and fills in a gap smoothed over in *Westway to the World*. The ninety-plus-minute film is essential viewing for the Clash fan, but because the images draw on archival footage—including Letts's various Clash projects and Buzzy Enterprises's *Rude Boy*—it is not worth owning.

The majority of the interviews were shot specifically for the documentary, however, and are informative. You get hear from all of the major Clash and/or Strummer biographers, old flames (Slits guitarist Viv Albertine and Pearl Harbor), sidekicks (Tymon Dogg and Blockheads Mickey Gallagher and Norman Watt-Roy), and the three new members of the Clash, Round Two (drummer Pete Howard and guitarists Nick Sheppard and Vince White). Of the five members of the Clash, Joe and Topper occasionally have their say via archival interviews, and Paul's view is absent entirely, but Terry and Mick do contribute new insights to the events of 1982 through 1986.

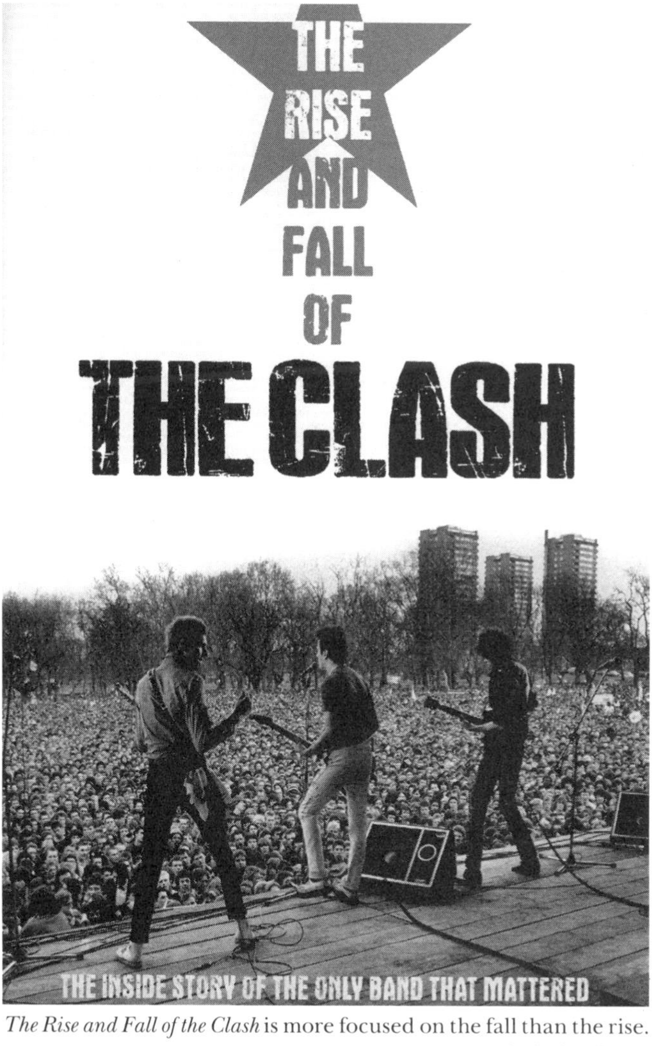

The Rise and Fall of the Clash is more focused on the fall than the rise.
Author's collection

An interview with Mick is a major coup and good reason to watch *The Rise and Fall of the Clash.* He is known to be a reticent interviewee, so it's a surprise he sat down and made himself available for a lengthy interview until you see the credits and learn that the interviewer is Robin Banks, Mick's childhood friend who was the subject of "Stay Free" and close enough to him to have been mentioned during Mick's Rock and Roll Hall of Fame induction speech. Banks also shares co-writing credit with Garcia.

It's also nice to have the observations of two members of the Clash, Round Two on the demise of the Clash, especially since they do not get their say in *Westway to the World.* As discussed in detail in chapter 24, we learn how they auditioned, toured, busked, had scant involvement in the recording of *Cut the Crap,* and then were abruptly informed their services were no longer required and paid off with £1,000 each. Joe lamented their treatment in later interviews, but what is even more reprehensible is that so many fans believe *Cut the Crap* reflects the Clash, Round Two sound. It does not. Take a listen to "In the Pouring, Pouring Rain" on the soundtrack to *The Future Is Unwritten.* A Clash, Round Two highlight puzzlingly omitted from *Cut the Crap,* this song truly reflects their sound. It's flawed, yes, but not a band without its moments. There's no telling what the Clash, Round Two might have achieved if Joe Strummer—his ego shattered from the death of his father, his mother's illness, and a growing awareness that he had been manipulated—had stayed calm, cast Bernie Rhodes aside, and carried on with true British fortitude.

But while the future may be unwritten, the Clash's race has clearly been run, and it is founding member Mick Jones—who's shown enormous maturity (and dare I say chivalry?) in the wake of his songwriting partner's passing—who sums it up best in the documentary: "So we did something good, obviously, and that's why we should leave it at that."

Bibliography

Books

Bangs, Lester. *Psychotic Reactions and Carburetor Dung.* Vintage Books, 1987.

Buskin, Richard. *Inside Tracks: A First-Hand History of Popular Music from the World's Greatest Record Producers and Engineers.* Avon Books, 1999.

Chimes, Terry. *The Strange Case of Dr. Terry and Mr. Chimes.* Crux Publishing, 2014.

D'Ambrosio, Antonino, ed. *Let Fury Have the Hour: The Punk Politics of Joe Strummer.* Nation Books, 2004.

Davie, Anthony. *Vision of a Homeland.* Effective Publishing, 2004.

Doane, Randal. *Stealing All Transmissions: A Secret History of the Clash.* PM Press, 2014.

Fletcher, Tony. *The Clash: The Complete Guide to Their Music.* Omnibus Press, 2005.

Gilbert, Pat. *Passion Is a Fashion.* Da Capo Press, 2005.

Gray, Marcus. *Last Gang in Town.* Henry Holt and Company, 1995.

Gray, Marcus. *Return of the Last Gang in Town.* Hal Leonard, 2001.

Gray, Marcus. *Route 19 Revisited.* Vintage 1998, 2009.

Green, Johnny and Barker, Garry. *A Riot of Our Own.* Faber and Faber, 1999.

Hanley, Steve; and Piekarski, Olivia. *The Big Midweek: Life Inside the Fall.* Route, 2014.

Headon, Nicky; Jones, Mick; Simonon, Paul; and Strummer, Joe. *The Clash.* Grand Central Publishing, 2008.

Hemes, Will. *Love Goes to Buildings on Fire.* Fabre and Faber, 2011.

Heylin, Clinton, ed. *The Penguin Book of Rock & Roll Writing.* Viking, 1992.

Kent, Nick. *Apathy for the Devil.* Da Capo Press, 2010.

Kent, Nick. *The Dark Stuff: Selected Writings on Rock Music.* Da Capo Press, 1995.

Knowles, Chris. *Clash City Showdown: The Music, the Meaning, and the Legacy of the Clash.* PageFree Publishing, 2003

Levene, Keith and DiTondo, Kathy. *I WaS a TeeN GuiTariST 4 the CLaSH!* Self-published e-book, 2014.

Levene, Keith and DiTondo, Kathy. *Meeting Joe: Joe Strummer, the Clash and Me!* Self-published e-book, 2014.
Lowry, Ray and Myers, Ben. *The Clash Rock Perspectives.* Angry Penguin Publishing, 2007.
Lydon, John. *Anger Is an Energy.* Dey Street Books, 2015.
Needs, Kris. *Joe Strummer and the Legend of the Clash.* Plexus Publishing, 2005.
Payress, Mark. *Break It Up: Patti Smith's Horses and the Remaking of Rock 'n' Roll.* Portrait, 2006.
Quantick, David. *The Clash.* Thunder's Mouth Press, 2000.
Robb, John. *Punk Rock: An Oral History.* PM Press, 2012.
Salewicz, Chris. *Redemption Song.* Faber and Faber, 2006
Savage, Jon. *England's Dreaming.* St. Martin's Griffin, 2001.
Smith, Patti. *Just Kids.* Ecco, 2010.
Thompson, Dave. *Dancing Barefoot: The Patti Smith Story.* Chicago Review Press, 2011.
Topping, Keith. *The Complete Clash.* Reynolds & Hearn, 2003.
White,Vince. *The Last Days of the Clash.* Moving Target, 2007.

Websites

daltonkosshq.wordpress.com
dl.dropboxusercontent.com/77994754/blackmarketclash
streetsyoucrossed.blogspot.com
www.3ammagazine.com
www.according2g.com
www.allmusic.com
www.amplex.com
www.art-for-a-change.com
www.bestapples.com
www.billboard.com
www.carbonsilicon.com
www.cartoon.ac.uk
www.clashmusic.com
www.classicbands.com
www.dailymail.com
www.discogs.com
www.dreadzone.com
www.downbeat.com
www.electricladystudios.com

www.getreadytorock.me.uk
www.globalbass.com
www.guitar.com
www.guitarplayer.com
www.guitarworld.com
www.huffingtonpost.com
www.jimshelley.com
www.joestrummer.org
www.ijamming.net
www.independent.co.uk
www.mikedtobear.com
www.mikeydread.com
www.mixonline.com
www.musicradar.com
www.nme.com
www.npr.org
www.paster.com
www.popmatters.com
www.premierguitar.com
www.repeatfanznie.co.uk
www.robertchristgau.com
www.rocksbackpages.com
www.rollingstone.com
www.sharoma.com
www.slate.com
www.songfacts.com
www.soundonsound.com
www.strummerguitar.com
www.tennessean.com
www.theclash.org.uk
www.theclashblog.org
www.theguardian.com
www.thequiteus.com
www.trouserpress.com
www.tymondogg.com
www.ultimateclassicrock.com
www.wikipedia.org
www.youtube.com

Index

THE FAQ SERIES

AC/DC FAQ
by Susan Masino
Backbeat Books
9781480394506 .... $24.99

Armageddon Films FAQ
by Dale Sherman
Applause Books
9781617131196 .... $24.99

Lucille Ball FAQ
by James Sheridan and Barry Monush
Applause Books
9781617740824 .... $19.99

Baseball FAQ
by Tom DeMichael
Backbeat Books
9781617136061 .... $24.99

The Beach Boys FAQ
by Jon Stebbins
Backbeat Books
9780879309879 .... $22.99

The Beat Generation FAQ
by Rich Weidman
Backbeat Books
9781617136016 .... $19.99

Black Sabbath FAQ
by Martin Popoff
Backbeat Books
9780879309572 .... $19.99

Johnny Cash FAQ
by C. Eric Banister
Backbeat Books
9781480385405 .... $24.99

A Chorus Line FAQ
by Tom Rowan
Applause Books
9781480367548 .... $19.99

Eric Clapton FAQ
by David Bowling
Backbeat Books
9781617134548 .... $22.99

Doctor Who FAQ
by Dave Thompson
Applause Books
9781557838544 .... $22.99

The Doors FAQ
by Rich Weidman
Backbeat Books
978161713017-5 .... $24.99

Dracula FAQ
by Bruce Scivally
Backbeat Books
9781617136009 .... $19.99

The Eagles FAQ
by Andrew Vaughan
Backbeat Books
9781480385412 .... $24.99

Fab Four FAQ
by Stuart Shea and Robert Rodriguez
Hal Leonard Books
9781423421382 .... $19.99

Fab Four FAQ 2.0
by Robert Rodriguez
Backbeat Books
9780879309688 .... $19.99

Film Noir FAQ
by David J. Hogan
Applause Books
9781557838551 .... $22.99

Football FAQ
by Dave Thompson
Backbeat Books
9781495007484 .... $24.99

The Grateful Dead FAQ
by Tony Sclafani
Backbeat Books
9781617130861 .... $24.99

Haunted America FAQ
by Dave Thompson
Backbeat Books
9781480392625 .... $19.99

Jimi Hendrix FAQ
by Gary J. Jucha
Backbeat Books
9781617130953 .... $22.99

Horror Films FAQ
by John Kenneth Muir
Applause Books
9781557839503 .... $22.99

Michael Jackson FAQ
by Kit O'Toole
Backbeat Books
9781480371064 .... $19.99

James Bond FAQ
by Tom DeMichael
Applause Books
9781557838568 .... $22.99

Stephen King Films FAQ
by Scott Von Doviak
Applause Books
9781480355514 .... $24.99

KISS FAQ
by Dale Sherman
Backbeat Books
9781617130915 .... $24.99

Led Zeppelin FAQ
by George Case
Backbeat Books
9781617130250 .... $22.99

M.A.S.H. FAQ
by Dale Sherman
Applause Books
9781480355897 .... $19.99

Modern Sci-Fi Films FAQ
by Tom DeMichael
Applause Books
9781480350618 .... $24.99

Morrissey FAQ
by D. McKinney
Backbeat Books
9781480394483 .... $24.99

Prices, contents, and availability subject to change without notice.

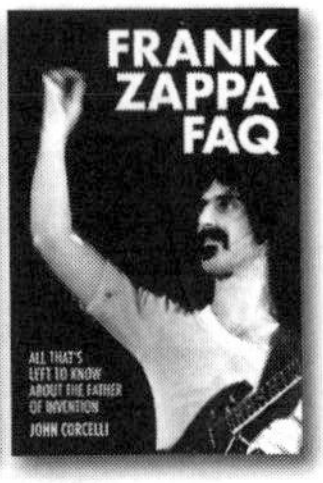

Nirvana FAQ
by John D. Luerssen
Backbeat Books
9781617134500 .... $24.99

Pink Floyd FAQ
by Stuart Shea
Backbeat Books
9780879309503 .... $19.99

Elvis Films FAQ
by Paul Simpson
Applause Books
9781557838582 .... $24.99

Elvis Music FAQ
by Mike Eder
Backbeat Books
9781617130496 .... $24.99

Pearl Jam FAQ
by Bernard M. Corbett and Thomas Edward Harkins
Backbeat Books
9781617136122 .... $19.99

Prog Rock FAQ
by Will Romano
Backbeat Books
9781617135873 .... $24.99

Pro Wrestling FAQ
by Brian Solomon
Backbeat Books
9781617135996 .... $29.99

The Rocky Horror Picture Show FAQ
by Dave Thompson
Applause Books
9781495007477 .... $19.99

Rush FAQ
by Max Mobley
Backbeat Books
9781617134517 .... $19.99

Saturday Night Live FAQ
by Stephen Tropiano
Applause Books
9781557839510 .... $24.99

Seinfeld FAQ
by Nicholas Nigro
Applause Books
9781557838575 .... $24.99

Sherlock Holmes FAQ
by Dave Thompson
Applause Books
9781480331495 .... $24.99

The Smiths FAQ
by John D. Luerssen
Backbeat Books
9781480394490 .... $24.99

Soccer FAQ
by Dave Thompson
Backbeat Books
9781617135989 .... $24.99

The Sound of Music FAQ
by Barry Monush
Applause Books
9781480360433 .... $27.99

South Park FAQ
by Dave Thompson
Applause Books
9781480350649 .... $24.99

Bruce Springsteen FAQ
by John D. Luerssen
Backbeat Books
9781617130939 .... $22.99

Star Trek FAQ (Unofficial and Unauthorized)
by Mark Clark
Applause Books
9781557837929 .... $19.99

Star Trek FAQ 2.0 (Unofficial and Unauthorized)
by Mark Clark
Applause Books
9781557837936 .... $22.99

Star Wars FAQ
by Mark Clark
Applause Books
978480360181 .... $24.99

Quentin Tarantino FAQ
by Dale Sherman
Applause Books
9781480355880 .... $24.99

Three Stooges FAQ
by David J. Hogan
Applause Books
9781557837882 .... $22.99

TV Finales FAQ
by Stephen Tropiano and Holly Van Buren
Applause Books
9781480391444 .... $19.99

The Twilight Zone FAQ
by Dave Thompson
Applause Books
9781480396180 .... $19.99

Twin Peaks FAQ
by David Bushman and Arthur Smith
Applause Books
9781495015861 .... $19.99

The Who FAQ
by Mike Segretto
Backbeat Books
9781480361034 .... $24.99

The Wizard of Oz FAQ
by David J. Hogan
Applause Books
9781480350625 .... $24.99

The X-Files FAQ
by John Kenneth Muir
Applause Books
9781480369740 .... $24.99

Neil Young FAQ
by Glen Boyd
Backbeat Books
9781617130373 .... $19.99

Frank Zappa FAQ
by John Corcelli
Backbeat Books
9781617136030 .... $19.99

HAL•LEONARD®
PERFORMING ARTS PUBLISHING GROUP

FAQ.halleonardbooks.com

Prices, contents, and availability subject to change without notice.

0316